Children Bound to Labor

Children Bound to Labor

The Pauper Apprentice System in Early America

Edited by
RUTH WALLIS HERNDON AND JOHN E. MURRAY

CORNELL UNIVERSITY PRESS
ITHACA AND LONDON

Copyright © 2009 by Cornell University
All rights reserved. Except for brief quotations in a review, this book, or parts thereof, must not be reproduced in any form without permission in writing from the publisher. For information, address Cornell University Press, Sage House, 512 East State Street, Ithaca, New York 14850.
First published 2009 by Cornell University Press
First printing, Cornell Paperbacks, 2009

Printed in the United States of America

Library of Congress Cataloging-in-Publication Data

Children bound to labor : the pauper apprentice system in early America / edited by Ruth Wallis Herndon and John E. Murray.
    p. cm.
  Includes bibliographical references and index.
  ISBN 978-0-8014-4624-5 (cloth : alk. paper)
  ISBN 978-0-8014-7559-7
  1. Apprenticeship programs—United States—History—18th century. 2. Apprenticeship programs—United States—History—19th century. 3. Indentured servants—United States—History—18th century. 4. Indentured servants—United States—History—19th century. 5. Poor children—United States—History—18th century. 6. Poor children—United States—History—19th century. 7. United States—Social conditions—18th century. 8. United States—Social conditions—19th century. 9. Child labor—United States—History—18th century. 10. Child labor—United States—History—19th century. I. Herndon, Ruth Wallis. II. Murray, John E., 1959– III. Title.

   HD6250.U3C453   2009
   331.3′1097309034—dc22   2008038925

Cornell University Press strives to use environmentally responsible suppliers and materials to the fullest extent possible in the publishing of its books. Such materials include vegetable-based, low-VOC inks and acid-free papers that are recycled, totally chlorine-free, or partly composed of nonwood fibers. For further information, visit our website at www.cornellpress.cornell.edu.

Cloth printing   10 9 8 7 6 5 4 3 2 1
Paperback printing   10 9 8 7 6 5 4 3 2 1

To Jack—RWH

To Rose and Sarah—JEM

Contents

Acknowledgments ix

Part I: Overviews 1

1. "A Proper and Instructive Education": Raising Children in Pauper Apprenticeship 3
   RUTH WALLIS HERNDON AND JOHN E. MURRAY

2. Recreating Proper Families in England and North America: Pauper Apprenticeship in Transatlantic Context 19
   STEVE HINDLE AND RUTH WALLIS HERNDON

Part II: Binding Out as a Master/Servant Relation 37

3. "Proper" Magistrates and Masters: Binding Out Poor Children in Southern New England, 1720–1820 39
   RUTH WALLIS HERNDON

4. Orphans in City and Countryside in Nineteenth-Century Maryland 52
   T. STEPHEN WHITMAN

5. Bound Out from the Almshouse: Community Networks in Chester County, Pennsylvania, 1800–1860 71
   MONIQUE BOURQUE

Part III: Binding Out as a Parent/Child Relation 85

6. Preparing Children for Adulthood in New Netherland 87
   ADRIANA E. VAN ZWIETEN

7. Mothers and Children in and out of the Charleston Orphan House   102
JOHN E. MURRAY

8. The Extent and Limits of Indentured Children's Literacy
in New Orleans, 1809–1843   119
PAUL LACHANCE

9. "To Train Them to Habits of Industry and Usefulness":
Molding the Poor Children of Antebellum Savannah   133
TIMOTHY J. LOCKLEY

Part IV: Binding Out as a Family/State Relation   149

10. Responsive Justices: Court Treatment of Orphans and Illegitimate
Children in Colonial Maryland   151
JEAN B. RUSSO AND J. ELLIOTT RUSSO

11. The Stateless and the Orphaned among Montreal's
Apprentices, 1791–1842   166
GILLIAN HAMILTON

12. Apprenticeship Policy in Virginia: From Patriarchal to
Republican Policies of Social Welfare   183
HOLLY BREWER

Conclusion: Reflections on the Demand and Supply
of Child Labor in Early America   199
GLORIA L. MAIN

Notes   213

Bibliography   255

Contributors   259

Index   261

Acknowledgments

This project began in 1998 with our first discussion of the fate of illegitimate children in colonial America. Over the intervening decade, the project has acquired many friends and many debts, rich evidence that it takes a community to produce a book.

Institutional support gave this project its initial impetus, help along the way, and the final assist across the finish line. For a major grant we thank the Spencer Foundation, Chicago, where John Rury was our program officer. Herndon thanks the New England Regional Fellowship Consortium for a summer research grant. We both received sabbaticals from the Departments of History and Economics at the University of Toledo. Herndon thanks the National Endowment for the Humanities and the Massachusetts Historical Society for a long-term fellowship on a separate but related project; during that year in residence at MHS, she was able to see this book through its final phases while launching the new project. We both acknowledge financial support for publication from our universities, through Don Nieman and Roger Thibault at Bowling Green State University and Frank Calzonetti and Mike Dowd at the University of Toledo. Murray thanks his colleague Kris Keith for taking on advising duties for an extra year so he could work on this project.

Most essays in this volume first appeared as papers presented at conferences organized specifically around the topic of pauper apprenticeship in early America. The first conference in September 2001 was hosted by the University of Toledo and underwritten by the Spencer Foundation. All attendees benefited from the efficient work of Debbie MacDonald and Jeannie Stambaugh, both at the University of Toledo, in facilitating the gathering.

The second conference in November 2002, jointly sponsored by the University of Pennsylvania's McNeil Center for Early American Studies and the Spencer Foundation, was facilitated especially well by Amy Baxter-Bellamy. We appreciate Daniel K. Richter's scholarly collegiality in locating the conference at the McNeil Center and giving this project the benefit of a very productive hearing with Philadelphia-area scholars. We particularly thank Farley Grubb, Susan Klepp, and Stephanie Grauman Wolf, who served as commentators of the paper sessions.

Several of the chapters appeared also as conference papers at the annual meetings of scholarly associations. At the Omohundro Institute meeting in Austin (1999), John Demos, Christine Daniels, and Stevie Wolf provided excellent comments. At the meeting of the Society for Historians of the Early American Republic in Baltimore (2001), Irene Q. Brown and Richard D. Brown gave detailed and insightful comments that significantly guided our editing. We also thank participants at the Social Science History Association meeting in Pittsburgh (2000).

At key moments, colleagues lent their support by reminding us of the significance of these children bound to labor in the larger world of early American studies. Billy G. Smith, Lisa Wilson, Peter Potter, Cathy Matson, Lorena Walsh, Farley Grubb, and Howard Bodenhorn have been among the most stalwart and generous friends of this project, and we thank them for their advice and support in seeing this project to completion.

Perhaps the ultimate test of a scholarly project's worth is its reception in the classroom. Many of our students at the University of Toledo and Bowling Green State University read pauper apprenticeship contracts, listened to stories of children bound to labor, and wrote about the children and the system in helpful ways that helped us better understand the past. At the University of Toledo, Mary Patchen produced an excellent M.A. thesis on pauper apprentices in early Ohio; she also read a fine paper drawn from her thesis at the conference in Philadelphia. Although she chose not to include her essay in the book, we appreciate her work and are grateful for her collegial permission to cite and use her research.

Karin L. Zipf and Barry Levy, who participated in this project in its early stages, gave us helpful feedback and insight into the system of binding out poor children in North Carolina and New England.

Bill Pencak, Christine Daniels, and an anonymous reader for Cornell University Press gave us excellent and constructive criticism in their reports.

Cornell University Press has been a pleasure to work with. We particularly appreciated the hard work of Peter Potter, Alison Kalett, Michael McGandy, Sara Ferguson, Karen Laun, and the production staff.

We are grateful that our spouses, Jim Herndon and Lynn Wellage, were so understanding about the time away from home that this project took. We can't thank them enough.

Children Bound to Labor

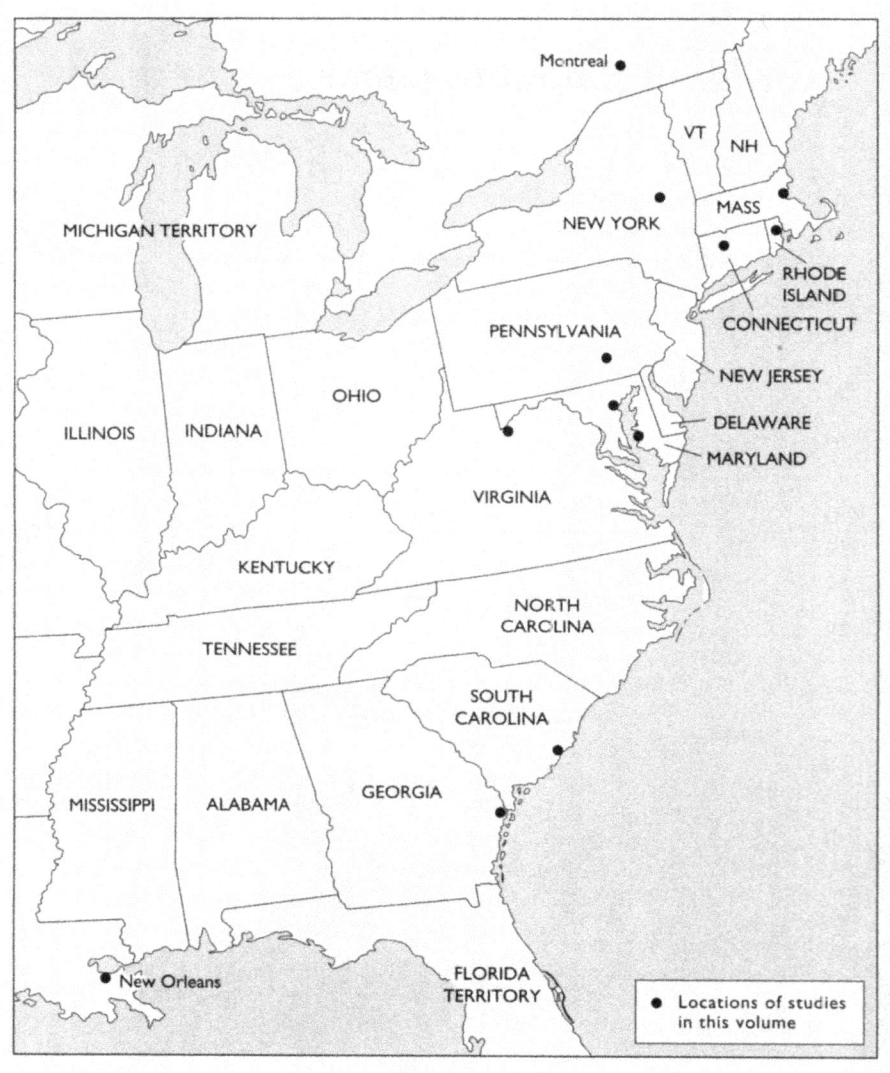

Locations of the studies in this volume

PART I

OVERVIEWS

This book describes pauper apprenticeship, the system used widely in early America to redirect the lives of poor children who were illegitimate, orphaned, abandoned, abused, or otherwise considered by authorities to be at risk. Bound out to masters, these children were raised to adulthood in a legal condition of servitude. Most of these children were poor, without resources and often without advocates. Sometimes authorities intervened because they considered the children's living situations to be "improper." Other times, parents sought the assistance of officials in finding a new situation for their children. Either way, after an interim period with approved caretakers or in a poorhouse or orphanage, the children were formally bound to a master. They lived and worked in the master's household until they reached adulthood, usually defined as twenty-one years of age for boys and sixteen or eighteen for girls.

Indentures were legal contracts that specified the conditions of the apprenticeship. The indentures for these pauper apprentices show that the children received varying degrees of daily "maintenance" (food, shelter, clothing), acquired varying levels of literacy education and skill training, became accustomed to varying intensities of manual labor, and were rewarded with varying amounts of "freedom dues" at the end of the contract term. Local officials calibrated the terms of the contracts to further their own goals, but certain common elements nearly always applied: maintenance, education, and some eventual payment provided by the master; labor and appropriate behavior required of the child; approval of and regulation by some civil authority; and a paper contract to govern the relationship. Supporting the studies in this book are some eighteen thousand contracts or orders to bind out children.

Binding out was practiced in North American communities from colonial settlement forward into the mid-1800s. Rooted in Old World poor laws and customs, it was familiar to colonists and was heavily used in English, Dutch, and French communities in North America. Sometimes it was a clear success: the child's daily life improved significantly and the child acquired skills that promised independence in adulthood. Sometimes it was a clear failure: the child's daily life worsened and the child reached adulthood without acquiring skills necessary to live independently as an adult. Most of the time, however, it was neither success nor failure but rather a holding pattern. It kept vulnerable children alive, it put them in a family setting, it put them to work at some useful occupation, and it familiarized them with the kind of manual labor that was the lot of most early Americans.

Despite its widespread usage in early America, binding out has been neglected by historians. For many years the only focused study was the section of Lawrence W. Towner's 1955 dissertation, "A Good Master Well Served," on children bound out by the Boston overseers of the poor. More recently other scholars have studied specific communities and reported on binding out in its local contexts. These essays, while valuable in describing the experience of particular communities, fail to convey the extent of the institution. In fact, as the essays in this volume show, it was everywhere.

Binding out illuminates three different kinds of human relationship. It was a kind of master/servant relationship that expands our comprehension of labor in early America. Bound-out children were not slaves or immigrant indentured servants or traditional craft apprentices; they were poor, home-grown, young laborers that every community harnessed for economic ends. Binding out was also a parent/child relationship. Because binding out by definition separated parent and child and placed a "substitute" child with "substitute" parents, it focuses attention on the nature of parent/child interactions and on the expectations communities had about such substitutes. Finally, binding out reveals otherwise hidden aspects of the family/state relationship. Local magistrates intended that pauper apprentices should be raised in homes that conformed to official ideas of order. Binding out was in fact the state's declaration and affirmation of what a "proper" household should look like.

CHAPTER ONE

"A Proper and Instructive Education"

Raising Children in Pauper Apprenticeship

RUTH WALLIS HERNDON AND JOHN E. MURRAY

Today, children born to unwed mothers, abandoned children, abused children, and orphans all move through government systems of care. How did early Americans deal with similarly vulnerable children? Orphans and "bastards" (as they were then called) constituted a significant proportion of these unfortunate youngsters, because in those days adult mortality rates and social disapproval of unwed mothers were greater than in our own. Child abuse was not generally recognized as a problem then, because adults were expected to use violence when disciplining their children. But community-constructed ideas about "proper parenting" prompted official intervention then, as it does today. And education to a skill and to a basic standard of literacy was essential then, as it is now. What differentiated early America was the expectation that children would contribute their labor to the households in which they lived.

In early America, "proper" families were places where children learned to serve the larger community by contributing meaningful labor—important in an era when being "useful" to the community was more important than exercising individual rights. In such families children would receive all the necessities of life and not end up on "poor relief" that drained community resources—important in an era when all public welfare was funded by local taxes. In such families children would be well "governed" and would learn their place in

---

The title of this chapter comes from Anonymous, *The Countryman's Lamentation, On the Neglect of a Proper Education of Children; With an Address to the Inhabitants of New-Jersey* (Philadelphia: W. Dunlap, 1762), 44.

society—important in an era when social inequalities were considered God-ordained.¹

A successful childhood meant different things then and now. Today we emphasize children's literacy and education, and we expect children to graduate from high school. Early Americans measured success by acquisition of work skills that enabled children to perform adult labor. Conscientious parents raised their children to carry on the work of their mothers and fathers. In 1750, an orphaned boy who learned the "mysteries of husbandry" so that he could farm his own plot of land was considered a success. So was a "bastard" girl who learned "housewifery" skills so that she could "keep house" for her husband.

Child labor and education were intertwined in early America, as binding out makes clear, but communities differed about what constituted a proper education. Educational provisions in indentures for poor children reflected the various European laws and customs that early Americans had adapted, diverse expectations of children's labor according to race and gender, and the economic and social histories of particular American communities. By the early 1800s, binding out poor children occurred through a patchwork of systems that revealed experiences and assumptions about children held by adults in various regions and localities.

A social critic writing in 1762 under the name "Jersey Man" articulated some of his assumptions in this regard in *The Countryman's Lamentation*. Having observed and lamented over "great Numbers of People in a distressed and starving Condition" whose children were destined to "inherit all their Patrimonies," he had tried to persuade such parents to "let their Children go"—into someone else's household as an apprentice. If parents resisted, then local magistrates should "wrest these poor unhappy Children from under the thick Shades of Ignorance" and bind them out themselves. The Jersey Man was convinced that children would profit significantly from being "put out" and that they would ultimately be grateful for life opportunities they could not find in their own homes. Several morality tales illustrated this conviction. The son of "R. Indolent" grew up under his new master "to be a useful Man as most in the Country." The daughter of "E. Simpel" grew up under her new master to marry well and "become very useful in Society." In the Jersey Man's view, the only way many children would receive a "proper and instructive Education" was for them to be removed from the "Briers and Rubbish" of their natal homes; only then might society might "expect a useful Member in succeeding Periods of Life."²

The Jersey Man was clearly championing pauper apprenticeship, but he never used that term. "Pauper apprenticeship" follows English precedent but does not reflect the diversity of terminology in early America, as the historians contributing to this volume have discovered. Where the children's parents were poor or troublesome, the authorities doing the binding referred to the practice as "pauper apprenticeship," "orphan apprenticeship," or simply "indenture of poor children" in the documents that are our best informants about the system. "Apprenticeship" was used broadly to refer to both poor children and those whose parents had bound them voluntarily to learn a trade, and the term meant very different things in different times and places. In Boston, children bound out by the overseers of the poor were uniformly labeled "apprentices," but in Connecticut, the term was seldom used by selectmen doing the binding. In New Netherland, "apprenticeships" provided vocational training, in contrast to "indentures for service." Although "servant" was applied to many of the bound children, it can hardly cover the case of those bound out by their parents to learn crafts and trades, and in some locations, magistrates avoided calling poor children "servants," even though their indentures bound them to menial servitude. Colonial Maryland law stipulated that children without property be bound "as servants," but in Charleston, South Carolina, prospective masters specifically promised not to treat children as servants (a term that often referred to slaves); they commonly applied for simple "apprentices." In Virginia and New Orleans, magistrates favored the term "apprentice."

Whatever this binding out was called, it was a local institution, and the documents revealing it were generated by local magistrates. One reason for the relative obscurity of this practice is its local nature. Historians of particular localities found records of pauper apprenticeship, which they discussed as a small part of a larger community history. The extent and significance of the institution could not be glimpsed until those scholars brought their work together. Now that these local studies have been aggregated in this volume, it is clear that pauper apprenticeship was an important a source of labor to individual communities. The thousands of contracts underlying this study confirm that a significant share of children passed through this system (see table 1.1). From

TABLE 1.1.
Distribution of records in this study

Place	Time	Number of bound children
England	16th–18th c.	N/A
New Netherland	1639–1674	36
Maryland	1660–1759	1,254
Southern New England	1720–1820	2,114
Montreal	1791–1842	2,691
Virginia	1750–1820	567
Baltimore & environs	1780–1850	7,495
Charleston	1790–1860	2,084
Southeastern Pennsylvania	1800–1830	320
Savannah, Georgia	1817–1860	555
New Orleans	1809–1843	1,152

the mid–eighteenth century onward, the share of children who were bound as pauper apprentices was roughly the same as the share of immigrant indentured servants in the population as a whole.[3]

The records that describe pauper apprenticeship are still located in local (town, parish, or county) archives, many in surprisingly good condition. Inconsistency in record-keeping and subsequent record preservation has resulted in gaps in documentation, so that we cannot provide an accurate count of all children bound out in each area studied. Nevertheless, the existing documentation reveals a distinctive chronological arc of binding out in each case study, and when the studies are taken together, they reveal general trends (see figure 1.1).

Indenturing children began as soon as Europeans organized settlements in North America, as the following chapter shows. In the late eighteenth and early nineteenth centuries local magistrates produced and preserved increasing numbers of indentures. By the middle of the nineteenth century, pauper apprenticeship was no longer practiced in some areas and had significantly declined in the rest. Orphanages and other institutions began to assume responsibility for caring for young people.[4]

When pauper apprenticeship flourished, local civil officials drew their authority to bind children from colonial and state statutes. These laws gave a distinct advantage to public officials in the creation of apprenticeship records. Most of the documents behind the studies in this volume report the viewpoint of those court officials, town leaders, and institutional directors who generated the indentures and the accompanying paperwork. The magistrates have the loudest voices and the greatest advantage in telling their side of the story.

The Jersey Man was probably himself a magistrate, for he promoted the binding out of poor children in language and allegory that take the perspective of civil authority. His *Lamentation* reflects the *mentalité* of these authorities to some degree, revealing what they thought they were doing when they bound out children. If we can believe the self-presentation that looms perceptibly in the *Lamentation* and, more subtly, between the lines of the indentures, the magistrates who bound out pauper apprentices were, for the most part, well-informed, well-connected, and well-intentioned men. They stayed alert to problems in households under their government; they fashioned solutions to those problems with shrewdness and benevolence; and their solutions took into consideration the good of the whole community.

Officials had several strong motivations for binding out poor children, and they probably all worked simultaneously. The first and perhaps the most compelling reason was to relieve the community of the financial burden of poor relief. In the studies in this volume, the great majority of the children bound out had been judged to be "poor" and were therefore the responsibility of overseers of the poor. Supporting the poor was serious business in early America. Lacking consistent external standards to determine whether a family was poor,

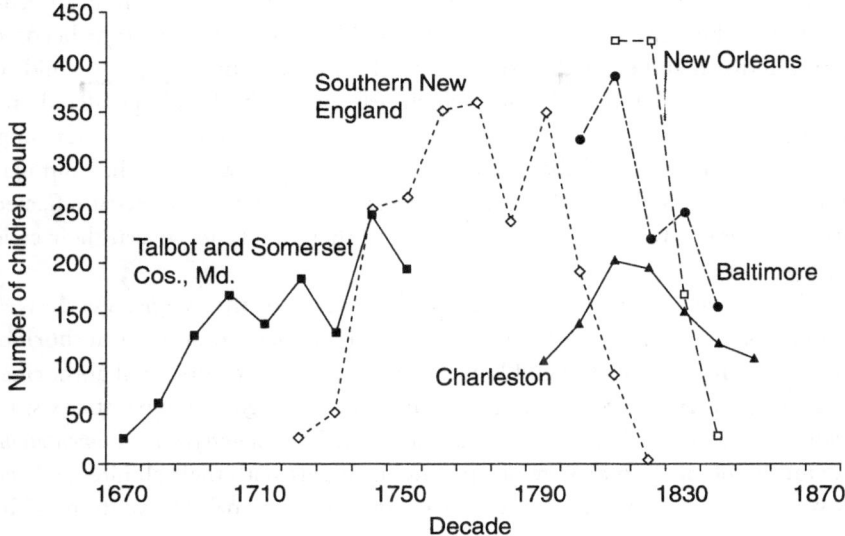

FIGURE 1.1. Numbers of bound children by decade

authorities made subjective decisions based on the custom of the country. Thus, whether a given family would have been identified as poor varied from place to place. Relief funds came from local taxes, and officials and taxpayers alike wanted to minimize those taxes. Binding out took the financial obligation for care of poor children out of public hands and placed it on the children themselves, who had to work for their keep under the direction of their masters.

Binding out was also an effective way for magistrates to shape households under their jurisdiction. In American societies organized along patriarchal lines, the ideal family was headed by an adult male who was recognized as responsible by the authorities; in some cases authorities did not recognize free men of color as sufficiently responsible. The death, absence, or failure of such an authority—resulting in a child who had no parent, guardian, or master—prompted magistrates to intervene. Binding out not only resolved economic problems in the child's household, it also resolved the social problem implicit in a minor not living under the authority of a "suitable" father—it put such a child under the "government" of one who would impose discipline of a kind acceptable to civil authorities. In a few localities, magistrates proactively searched out adverse situations in their jurisdictions; observation was an official task. In many other localities, magistrates expected others to relay information to them. In still other cases, would-be masters approached magistrates and requested an indenture, often because an orphaned or abandoned child was already being cared for in the household, so that the indenture simply formalized an existing living arrangement.

After locating a master, officials negotiated contract terms with him. In general terms, the master was expected to raise his pauper apprentice to become a productive member of the community. This meant socializing the child to the community's culture of work, which was inevitably sharply gendered and hierarchical. Girls were to learn housewifery skills; boys were to learn farming, a trade, or plain manual labor. A satisfactory indenture was thus the culmination of much thought and discussion between authorities and others; it reflected officials' knowledge of their community and their ability to govern their civic family.

The *Lamentation* and the archival documents suggest that magistrates derived satisfaction from a successful binding out. Doubtless some civil authorities had little sympathy for the children they bound out, but other civil authorities looked upon themselves as humanitarians and followed the apprentice's situation with a benevolent eye. One anecdote in *The Countryman's Lamentation*, obviously intended to prod reluctant parents to part with their children, related how an ill child prospered because of magistrates' personal intervention: "The Overseers of the Parish took him home, and all necessary Care was taken of him; but before he got well it was observed he had a bright Genius for Learning and Improvement, and great Endeavours were used with the Parents to put him out for that End."[5] The records suggest that this tale was not pure fabrication. Authorities responsible for binding out poor children often actually lived with those children. Most overseers of the poor and institutional managers received dislocated children into their homes and institutions on a temporary basis, but some went further. Some officials even took indentures of children who had come to their attention.

When civil authorities bound out a child as a pauper apprentice, they were standing in the place of parents, taking actions that many able mothers and fathers often took—finding a "place" for a child to be educated for adulthood. In North America before 1850, it was neither unusual nor remarkable for children to live outside their natal households. Middling sort parents commonly turned to formal craft apprenticeships as a way to prepare their children for adulthood, negotiating sometimes costly contracts so that their adolescent sons and daughters could spend five, six, or seven years living with and learning a trade from a relative or neighbor. Parents with fewer resources frequently resorted to "placing" their children in households where they would receive care and where the parents could keep an eye on them. Many—perhaps the majority—of these arrangements were secured not by contracts but simply by verbal agreement, and the children involved grew up informally as laborers in other households.

Pauper apprenticeship empowered officials to intervene when parents were unwilling or unable to make such arrangements as officials deemed necessary for their children. The Jersey Man directed his *Lamentation* to unwilling parents and proffered his advice in a staged conversation between a "squire" and straw-man fathers bearing names such as "Mr. Shortsighted," "Mr. Weakmind," "Mr. Inconsiderate," and "Mr. Mistrust." In fact, the *Lamentation* presents pauper apprenticeship as necessary because so many parents—fathers in particular—lacked the common sense and self-discipline to relinquish their children to be educated and governed by more able and prosperous persons: "Oh how many serviceable Men, and Women might we have had from amongst your Children, if you had not abstinately stood in their Way: How can you be so unnatural to your own Flesh to confine them to sordid Ignorance and Want, when Preferments waits ready to take them by the Hand."[6]

The documentary record gives us a less prejudicial and more complex view of the pauper apprentice's parents and other advocates. Many of the children bound out had no living parents to see to their interests; instead, magistrates dealt with other relatives, guardians, or friends as they fashioned indentures. In all of the studies in this volume, such nonparental advocates were a significant presence in the process of pauper apprenticeship. Even the Jersey Man acknowledged this reality in his vignette of a child bound out "by the forceable Persuasions of some near Relations."[7]

A child came to the attention of civil authorities for a variety of reasons, including disorderly behavior in the child's family, bastardy, and parental death, desertion, or neglect. The high mortality rates that characterized North America until the twentieth century necessarily entailed deaths of relatively young mothers and fathers. In the documents relating to binding out, magistrates frequently used the term *orphan,* but its meaning varied from locality to locality. The most common usage referred to a child whose *father* had died; even if the mother was living, civil authorities might still consider the child an "orphan." Children designated as orphans constituted one-fifth of the pauper apprentices in eighteenth-century Rhode Island and nineteenth-century Savannah; one-quarter of the cases in antebellum Ohio; between 60 and 90 percent of the children bound out in Talbot County, Maryland, before 1760; and a whopping 95 percent of the instances in Baltimore County, Maryland between 1794 and 1830.[8] In Charleston, as John Murray's chapter shows, mothers brought just over half the children who had been proposed for admission to the Orphan House between 1790 and 1860, while fathers sponsored only a tenth; the remaining third were presumably full orphans. In Montreal, as Gillian Hamilton's chapter shows, in addition to local children who had lost a parent, the Children's Friend Society brought several hundred British orphans to Canada. These children lost all connection with extended family: truly strangers in a strange land.

Desertion by the parents was another problem officials solved by binding out children. Sometimes officials designated abandoned children as orphans even though their fathers (or both parents) might still be alive somewhere. The Jersey Man characterized such a situation in his tale of "R. Indolent," who "absconded" for a few weeks and, upon his return, found his oldest son bound out.

Although the father "did all in his Power to get him back again" and "made a great bluster," the boy stayed where he was.[9] The documents are peppered with similar real-life desertions. In some cases when a seafaring father did not return from a voyage within the expected time, the family sought binding out of younger children to ease their destitution. Other times a father had clearly "absconded" (often to the West), and occasionally a mother deserted her children.

Children born to unmarried parents were a significant problem for magistrates in some places but not others. Illegitimate children were so numerous in Frederick County, Virginia, in the mid-1700s that they constituted a significant subset of pauper apprentices; similarly, in colonial Talbot County, Maryland, they averaged between 10 and 30 percent of pauper apprentices over the period 1670–1760; and they accounted for about 20 percent of indentures in Rhode Island between 1750 and 1800. On the other hand, "bastards" were very few indeed in Charleston. In these cases, the mother—an unmarried woman—did not constitute a proper head of household in a society where the patriarchal family was the prevailing ideal. Indeed, the difficulties faced by single women in earning a living wage meant that a fatherless family really was at increased likelihood of an eventual application for poor relief. Illegitimate children came under the oversight of the civil "fathers" of the community, as illustrated by bastardy laws and other statutes that gave local officials considerable latitude in extracting maintenance from the supposed father and binding out the child.[10]

"Poor" is often the single descriptor of a child's family situation. While this was often a catch-all term that substituted for a more enlightening explanation, other times it referred to real destitution. The Jersey Man declared that he had seen "great Numbers of People in a distressed and starving Condition."[11] The frequent descriptions of poverty in pauper apprenticeship records suggest that his judgment may not have been far off the mark. Other times, children were not in physical distress for lack of food or clothing but were behaving in ways that violated community norms. Sometimes the problem was the behavior of the parents themselves. This was the Jersey Man's theme song. He assured his audience that "all Parents that will bring up their Children in religious Duties carefully, and teach them Industry" were not in danger of having their children bound out. "But Multitudes are Strangers to these Things themselves, and therefore unlikely to bestow it upon their Children either by Example or Precept."[12] In fact, it was the Jersey Man's opinion that the poverty that necessitated pauper apprenticeship was the result of the parents' wasteful and ignorant behavior: "A whole Street of you that there is some Hundred in it, would not keep one good Farm, not even mine, in the same Order one Year not by your own Oeconomy, and this keeps you but a Step before the Animals in your best Appearance, and in some Things much below them."[13] The records verify that some magistrates used pauper apprenticeships as a punitive measure to curb the behavior of the parents, but such circumstances did not apply to the vast majority of children bound out.

Many parents who sought or agreed to indenture their children desired to have control over the conditions of the contract. They saw the advantage of indenture in providing for their children when they could not, and they granted officials the right to disassemble their families, but they wanted to have a say in the way their daughters and sons were integrated into other households.

The removal of children through binding out reshaped the natal family. Sometimes siblings left their families in a staggered fashion, indicating that parents or guardians had made hard decisions about when a child was most ready to leave home or when that child's help was least needed at home. Other times, siblings were all removed from their home simultaneously, pointing to a major crisis that disrupted the family unit. But indenture did not necessarily mean complete separation from parents. Sometimes family members stayed in contact with bound children and monitored their progress and treatment. Nor did relatives hesitate to complain to authorities if they felt something was amiss. In various localities, mothers who married or remarried sometimes tried to reclaim their children from pauper apprenticeship, since the child would return to a male-headed household that conformed to community norms—and enjoyed the new husband's greater income. Parents and other advocates thus demonstrated their concern for their children's welfare and their hope that binding out provide their sons and daughters with some semblance of family life.

The Jersey Man's *Lamentation* was addressed to parents, not masters. It was not a treatise on the good management of pauper apprentices or an advice book for employers of children. Masters of pauper apprentices do not even appear as major characters in the pamphlet. Rather, they are offstage, allegorical figures—negative images raised by fearful parents and positive images raised by magistrates trying to quiet those fears. One of the greatest of those fears was physical abuse, and the Jersey Man addressed it directly. "Mr. Mistrust" raises the issue: "Their Masters or Mistresses sometimes uses them very hardly: You know Mr. Condescending's Son was beat by Mr. Severe and I know not but my Son may be treated in the same Way: I don't choose to venture it."[14] "Esquire John" responded not by denying the existence of such possibilities but rather by declaring that beatings were no barrier to a child's ultimate happiness: Even if a child was "so unfortunate" as to be "treated with Severity for five or six or ten years of his life" and subsequently became "a useful Member of Society" who was "happy in himself" and made his family happy by his "prudent conduct," then that child had "Infinately the Advantage of those that are brought up in Ignorance." Ask Mr. Condescending's son yourself, the squire suggested: "he will tell you, that tho' his Hardship was considerable for Ten long Years, yet the Ballance was greately in his Favour; and that were it to do again he had rather go thro' it than miss of Improvement."[15]

"Improvement." That was the master's task. Running through the *Lamentation* is the assumption that masters were, by and large, better at this task than were the parents of those children. In a master's household, poor children would encounter "good Instruction and Example" so that their "Ideas are enlarged and Judgment ripened."[16] Still, the Jersey Man understood that parents were skeptical about putting their daughters and sons in the care of another family, and he appealed to poor parents' sense of deference to their "betters."

From the perspective of civil authorities, masters were indeed "better" than the parents of the pauper apprentices they took on. Masters had won the approval of local magistrates. In the *Lamentation,* it is clear that masters were trusted *by* authorities to work *with* authorities by binding out children who represented a risk to the peace and prosperity of the community. In a sense, masters were agents who carried out the goals of the magistrates in preparing the youngest and poorest of the rising generation for a useful adulthood of service within the community.

The vast majority of masters were male, white, and middling or upper class. Occasionally a child was bound to a single woman who practiced a trade or to a widow who carried on her husband's business, but such women stand out in the documents because of their scarcity. Even though they were not often legal masters of bound children, women were essential to the administration of indenture in the domestic setting. While under the official "government" of a master, the pauper apprentice was usually under the daily care and management of the master's wife or other adult female. It was assumed that women in the master's household would fulfill the contract terms relating to food and drink, provision and care of clothing, and, in many cases, basic literacy education. When a girl was bound to a master to learn "housewifery" skills, it was assumed that the master's wife, daughter, female relative, or female servant would do the actual instruction. In some cases, the indentures make clear that a child was going to a master "and wife"; in some instances the wife is explicitly mentioned as essential to the success of the indenture.

Magistrates expected masters to do a better job than their apprentices' parents had done in "improving" their offspring. This meant not just putting food in children's bellies and clothing on their backs, it also meant preparing them for a productive adulthood, consistent with the child's status and abilities. The rank and skills of the masters varied widely but always were greater than those of the parents of the child bound out. Masters were also expected to train their apprentices in a skill or trade, a practical and important preparation for adulthood. In most cases, someone in the master's family was already practicing the trade; the child would simply learn by watching the adult. This was particularly true in the case of girls who were to be taught housewifery skills; household business would proceed along familiar lines while the girl watched and learned from the women in the family. Masters were expected to see that their pauper apprentices learned the basics of reading and writing and also (in the case of many boys) arithmetic. While the great majority of masters were literate, there were a few instances of masters marking indentures rather than signing. In those cases, it was the master's responsibility to hire a tutor or send the child to whatever school the community provided. Education in the three Rs was correlated to the skill training pauper apprentices would receive.[17] The goal was that they became literate enough to sell their skills.

A relational commitment between the child and its master focuses attention on the child's place in the master's household. Some children experienced great affection and were treated as one of the family. Other children suffered considerable brutality, as indicated by documentary accounts of abusive treatment and by the Jersey Man himself, who tried to assure the anxious Mr. Mistrust that "these Instances [of severe beating] seldom happen, and I hope they will be fewer still as we have an excellent Law that is well guarded in Favour of such as may fall into severe Hands."[18] Severe masters were in every community, often armed with a whip or rod. For many masters, an extra pair of hands and a strong back were the central motivation in taking on a bound child. Barry Levy has shown that in eighteenth-century Massachusetts, a typical master took a bound child early in the marriage, before his own children could contribute significant labor to the household.[19] Masters' concern for economic benefit can be glimpsed in squabbles between masters and magistrates about bonuses for taking an indenture or about the profitability of a child's labor. Other masters appear to have had a genuine desire to help a child in distress. Whatever their motives, masters were constrained by the terms of the contracts they signed with magistrates. They were bound as much as the children were. Their obligations to provide daily maintenance, literacy education, skill training, and freedom dues probably bore heavily on them at times, as the master's economic fortunes shifted or as tensions developed between master and child. Masters ran the gamut from kindly to vicious, from men prompted by charity and conscience to look after those in distress to men motivated purely by economic greed. It was the unfortunate child who got the latter.

In the Jersey Man's pamphlet, pauper apprentices—"poor unhappy children"—are objects of pity: "It is not easy and pleasant to Children to be confined to stedy Employment, but those of Age and Experience know it to be good and order them a suitable Portion of Labour according to their Age of Ability."[20] They are also implicitly presented as the future of society: it is imperative that they be taught to work well and grow up to be useful members of the community. But the Jersey Man gives them no voice of their own. They do not appear in any of the constructed dialogues. They offer no narratives. The genre of children's literature was well established when the *Lamentation* appeared in 1762, much of it purported to be written by children, but the Jersey Man does not make use of it. Similarly, in the documents of binding out, the children are the hardest to hear. Their voices are the most muted, although their perspective was singularly important. It was they who would experience the dislocation of removal from their natal homes and placement in a new home.

Pauper apprentices were among the least powerful people in a community. In a patriarchal and hierarchical society, they were a form of property. They "belonged to" their parents, and then they "belonged to" their masters. As children, they were dependent people in multiple ways. Historian Stephanie Wolf points out that "The words 'child,' 'boy,' and 'girl' were all derived from Old English derogatory terms for servants, and even the legal word for youth—'minor'—was literally defined as 'less,' a social rather than an age designation."[21] Pauper apprentices, as both children and servants, were at the bottom of the social hierarchy.[22]

These young people were in a difficult place. They came from family situations that were tenuous. Some had no fathers, because those men had died while others had refused to acknowledge their sons and daughters or had abandoned their families outright. Others had no parents at all, because their mothers too had died or abandoned them. Some had witnessed parents being injured or becoming seriously ill. Some had parents who were drunken and abusive or so hopeless at providing for their families that starvation threatened. At critical moments in their young lives, they were being placed forcibly into new households.

Further, few children had any say in the terms of their indentures. Some older apprentices asked to change masters in order to learn a new skill, but most children had to live with whatever arrangements were made on their behalf by friends and relatives or by magistrates and masters. Children might be bound into family situations that were little better than the ones they were leaving behind, or they might find themselves in vastly improved circumstances. The wide range of fates for bound children is suggested in the contract variations that pertained to daily maintenance, literacy training, skill training, and freedom dues. Magistrates did not intend that all children should be treated alike. The system was permeated with distinctions of the basis of the child's sex, race, age, and family background.

In every study, boys outnumbered girls. They constituted 64 percent of the indentures in Charleston, 78 percent in Virginia, 83 percent in Baltimore. This did not mean that girls labored any less in their neighbors' shops, gardens, and houses but rather that their labor was less likely to be protected by formal contracts. This consistent preponderance of males suggests that magistrates and masters were more eager to secure male labor in a formal way and that widowed mothers might have been especially interested in getting boys out of the house.

Another important variable in determining the apprentice's experience was race. The extent to which children of color were targeted for binding out varied greatly. Black children are absent from the Charleston Orphan House indentures and nearly absent from the Boston Almshouse and Chester County Almshouse indentures; apparently, officials in these localities had some other means of placing children of color. Only two of the thirty-six indentures in New Netherland were for "Negro" children, and few indentures in Connecticut were for children designated as other than white. On the other hand, in certain towns in Rhode Island (where slavery had flourished) as well as in Maryland and Virginia, pauper apprenticeship became a highly racialized institution by the beginning of the nineteenth century, increasingly directed to harness the labor of people of color across the generations.

The age at which a child left the natal home and entered pauper apprenticeship, either directly or after a time in an institution or with a temporary caretaker, had a great impact. A child bound out at age three or four literally grew up as a member of another household; a child bound out as a teenager had only a few years to endure—or profit from—the government of the master. The indentures that form the basis of this study show that children were bound out at every age from a few months old to just shy of majority; the average age at binding was anywhere from 6.7 to 15.3 years, depending on the locality (see table 1.2). In addition, girls were often bound at younger ages than boys, and children of color at younger ages than whites. Thus it would be misleading to specify a "typical" age at binding for all American pauper apprentices.

Still, this range of ages generally reflects changing perceptions of the stages of childhood. During the eighteenth century, children were generally considered to be able to labor enough to earn their keep around age six or seven; this rose

TABLE 1.2.
Gender and age of children bound out in England and America

Region studied	Years covered	Girls as % of children bound out	Boys as % of children bound out	Average age of child at binding
England	1589–1750	32%	68%	11*
New Netherland**	1639–1674	19%	81%	n.a.
Maryland	1660–1759	30%	70%	9.6
Southern New England	1720–1820	39%	61%	9.5
Virginia	1780–1820	26%	74%	7.9 to 11.4
Charleston	1790–1860	36%	64%	13
Montreal***	1791–1842	0%	100%	15.3
Baltimore	1800–1870	17%	83%	13.5
Southeastern Pennsylvania	1800–1830	42%	58%	6.7
New Orleans	1809–1843	5%	95%	14.1
Savannah	1817–1860	48%	52%	14†

*Mid-Sussex. **n=36. ***Sample excluded girl apprentices. †Boys only; girls not recorded.
Sources: Essays in this volume; Hindle, "'Waste' Children?" 35 (see bibliography; figures adapted from table 1.1); Mid-Sussex Poor Law Records, passim.

to age eight or nine in the nineteenth century.[23] Masters who took on pauper apprentices younger than that often were rewarded with some kind of bonus, premium, or maintenance payment to compensate for the child's relative lack of productivity. By their early teens, children were considered able to perform nearly-adult labor, and most early censuses counted boys over age fifteen as male adults—ready to bear arms—in the general population.[24] Pauper apprentices bound at age twelve or thirteen were often considered very desirable, capable of bringing a substantial profit to the master's household, because they contributed nearly-adult labor in return for little more than daily maintenance.

Arguably the most significant differences in the contracts have to do with the educational preparation the child would receive: literacy and skill training. White boys were usually promised the most literacy education (reading, writing, cyphering, or equivalent schooling), particularly before the 1800s. They also were more likely than girls to be promised more valuable skill training. Thus they had the best prospects for independent adulthood. Girls generally were promised less literacy training (reading, writing) until sexual disparity in schooling began to disappear around 1800. They also were usually trained only in "housewifery" or female domestic labor, which had less market value than the skilled trades. Thus they were more likely to remain in dependent labor positions as adults. This disparity was emphasized by race. In general, boys of color sometimes were promised more literacy and skill training than white girls, but they usually were promised much less skill training than white boys and were often simply put to manual labor for the duration of their indentures. Girls of color benefited the least from the system, exiting indenture with the least literacy training and fewest work skills. Race proved the stronger determinant over time, as binding out became increasingly associated with children of color after 1800 in places as diverse as Rhode Island and Virginia. Then, more than ever, the system prepared children to take their parents' place in society.

Sharp differences also separated children by race and sex in the matter of freedom dues, the master's payment promised to the child at the end of the indenture, a clause that appeared in most indentures (Talbot County, Maryland, was an exception). This payment usually included an outfit of clothing—*uitzet* in New Netherland—but the amount and quality of the clothing varied widely. Beyond these basics, some boys were promised money, land, livestock, or tools of the trade, and some girls were promised money, furniture, or a cow. In general, boys received more valuable freedom dues than girls: they more frequently were promised something beyond clothing, and the worth of their dues was greater than that of girls. These extra payments sometimes reflected that a boy had been bound for a longer term than other children or at an older age, so that his labor during the term was more productive. Other times, the extra payments reflected societal expectations that certain boys would establish themselves as independent workers as young adults.

Children bound out must have looked forward with great anticipation to the day their indenture ended and they became "free." Children were bound to adulthood, in most cases, but adulthood was defined in different ways. White girls were bound to age sixteen or eighteen. In a few places, girls of color were bound past age eighteen—until twenty-one in some Rhode Island towns; until thirty-one in colonial Maryland and Virginia. White boys almost always were bound to age twenty-one, while boys of color were sometimes bound past this age—until twenty-four in some Rhode Island towns, until thirty-one in colonial Maryland and Virginia. Most indentures prohibited the apprentice from marrying, but in some cases they offered a powerful incentive to marry: freedom. South Carolina law, for example, stipulated that female pauper apprentices would end their time at age nineteen or upon their marriage, whichever came first.[25]

There is frustratingly little evidence by which to measure the consequences of pauper apprenticeship for the children who came through the system. The contracts are prescriptive literature, telling masters and servants how they *should* behave, but there is scant documentation of the gap between prescription and reality.[26] We know in a general way that the relationship between master and pauper apprentice did not end when the indenture ended. Some former apprentices continued to work side by side with their former masters. Some stayed in the same community, claiming residency by virtue of their years of bound labor. Some used the social and business connections fashioned during apprenticeship to set off in a new direction or set up a new occupation. A sense of responsibility and rights lingered for both. But the specifics are elusive. The children themselves—either as bound laborers or as free adults in later years—left little record of their eventual literacy, work accomplishments, and economic welfare. Still, as fragmentary as these records are, they can tell us something important about the lives of pauper apprentices once "out of their time." Timothy Lockley points the way in his study of Savannah pauper apprentices, which follows a significant number of the children into adulthood and finds suggestive patterns of success and failure. This kind of meticulous microhistorical research can bridge the gap between the few "famous faces" and our educated guesswork about the rest.

The core of commonality in pauper apprenticeship is the involvement of these four parties—civil authorities, parents or advocates, masters, children—in an arrangement presumed to be for the benefit of the child. But pauper apprenticeship was a distinctly different institution in different localities. Each system developed under the influences of local social, economic, and cultural concerns, resulting in what Stephen Whitman in his chapter calls "varying local histories" of apprenticeship.

Each community took the process and used it for its own purposes. Therefore, the system of pauper apprenticeship looked different in Boston from the way it did in Frederick County, Virginia, or New Orleans or anywhere else. Until we have more studies of individual communities like the ones presented here, our sweeping generalizations are limited to observations about common clauses in the indentures and disadvantages of girls and children of color. Without those studies, we cannot know the extent of this institution. If it was as pervasive as the essays in this volume suggest, then it may have functioned in some places as a system of bound labor second only in importance to slavery.

This project has taken under consideration thousands of indentures of children bound out before 1850. The numbers alone indicate that binding out was a widespread, accepted, and familiar practice, one that parents recognized and resorted to, one that masters were familiar with before they signed a contract. It also suggests that enterprising scholars could follow a cohort of bound out children and construct a prosopography for them.

Orphaned, illegitimate, abandoned, and destitute children did not disappear when binding out declined in the 1800s. With the information we have now, it appears that pauper apprenticeship was the precursor to several overlapping systems of child-rearing that became commonplace after its decline. Those institutions—orphanages and poor farms, for example—took over the care of children who previously would have been bound out as pauper apprentices. In the latter part of the nineteenth century, the core elements of binding out were revitalized in orphan trains that took poor children from crowded eastern cities to labor-scarce frontier communities, where they lived and worked in foster families, although without formal indentures.[27] After states legalized adoption beginning in the 1850s, the more fortunate of distressed children were made sons and daughters in their new families, rather than being shunted into asylums, orphan trains, and foster homes.

Where does the poor orphan fit in the American historical and literary imagination? Where is Oliver Twist's American counterpart? Has the American narrative so stressed upward progress that a shrewd and savvy poor orphan cannot embody the hopes and aspirations of ordinary people? Perhaps the answer is that there are so many true stories that we don't need fictional ones. The following essays, which analyze pauper apprenticeship in a variety of localities, begin this answer by telling the true stories of ordinary people who were once children bound to labor in early America.

CHAPTER TWO

Recreating Proper Families in England and North America

Pauper Apprenticeship in Transatlantic Context

STEVE HINDLE AND RUTH WALLIS HERNDON

The American colonies did not invent the practice of binding out poor children; they inherited it. From the early 1600s until well into the 1800s, local authorities in both England and North America regarded pauper apprenticeship as an acceptable, even a desirable, way to raise the children of the poor. Communities on both sides of the Atlantic shared similar assumptions about the powers of the local authorities—to decide whether a poor family was able to maintain its children; to identify (and to negotiate terms with) an appropriate master; to place the child in the master's home. There were, however, significant differences in the development of pauper apprenticeship in England and North America. Most striking is that whereas English contracts tended to emphasize the master's responsibility to keep the child off poor relief, American contracts tended to emphasize the master's responsibility to train the child in both work and literacy skills. In this chapter, we show how this and other ideas about pauper apprenticeship persisted or disappeared in North America, as American magistrates adapted the practice to their own particular needs.

In England, parish apprenticeship had developed as part of a centuries-old effort to manage poverty and poor relief at the local level, and its principal purpose remained that of alleviating the burden that an orphaned or impoverished child represented to the local taxpayers. Printed forms became common in England only in the eighteenth century, but both print and manuscript indentures almost invariably included among the master's obligations a standard phrase revealing this purpose. A typical clause stated that the master should "so provide for the said Apprentice, that he be not any way a Charge to the said

Parish, or Parishioners of the same; but of and from all Charge shall and will save the said Parish and Parishioners harmless and indemnified during the said Term."[1] In this respect, pauper apprenticeship in England represented an adaptation of the feudal system: as R. H. Tawney put it, "The poor laws began where villeinage ended."[2]

American magistrates also worried about poor relief, but the contracts they devised indicate that preparing poor children for a useful adulthood remained the dominant rationale for binding out. Many poor children were raised outside their birth homes, but without the protection of a legal indenture. When children *were* legally bound, the contracts stressed practical education (for the child) and labor (for the master). American indentures rarely stipulated the master's obligation to keep the child off poor relief but almost always stipulated the master's obligation to provide skill training and literacy education, however minimal. In this respect, American pauper apprenticeship was less like typical English parish apprenticeship and more like the formal craft apprenticeships that had governed entry to trade guilds in England since the medieval period.

The American colonies shared with England neither the history of pauper apprenticeship nor the economic context in which the practice arose. The practice was transported there by the earliest English colonists as an already accepted element of their cultural heritage. When Anglo-Americans turned to pauper apprenticeship, they did so with one eye on the aspirations of a colonial future—educating the descendants of reform-minded colony-makers; managing race relations with indigenous people bowed by military conquest and with involuntary migrants from Africa and the Caribbean; and supplying cheap manpower in a labor-hungry economy.

Most of the case studies presented in this volume consider the practice of binding out poor children in colonies and states of English origin. They were English administrative units, in which political authority flowed from the king-in-parliament, English language and culture dominated, and English precedent formed the basis for law and legal custom. It is, therefore, imperative to understand the system of pauper apprenticeship as it developed in England in order to appreciate the attitudes and conventions that undergirded Anglo-American apprenticeship. This essay is a first, tentative step in the direction of a genuinely comparative history of social welfare policy as it was transmitted to British North America (see table 2.1).

The English North American colonies were established and their laws codified between the 1610s and the 1720s at the very time that statutory parish relief of the poor, including the compulsory apprenticeship of pauper children, was emerging in England from a traditional bundle of informal practices bound together by patronage, hospitality, and indiscriminate almsgiving. Long into the seventeenth century, the assumption that poverty was a God-given condition that could only be ameliorated, rather than remedied altogether, dominated

TABLE 2.1.
Varieties of bound child labor in England and Colonial America

	England (c. 1598–1814)			North America (c. 1630–1860)				
Form of service	Craft apprenticeship	Pauper apprenticeship		Immigrant indentured servitude	Pauper servitude	Craft apprenticeship	Pauper apprenticeship	*Post nati* service under gradual emancipation
Age at entry	Teens	(By law) 7; (in practice) 8–10		Teens to young adults	All ages	Teens	Infancy to late teens	Birth
Duration of service	7–14 years, varies by trade	To age 24 (boys); to 21 or marriage (girls)		Average 4 years	Varies/ 1 year	Typical maximum 7 years, varied by trade	To age 21 (boys) to 18 (girls; some variation)	Age at emancipation set by state statute (varied from 18 to 28)
Indenture assignable to another master	No	No		Yes	No	No	Conditional	Yes
Premium payments to master	Universal	Uncommon		No	Common	Common	Uncommon	No
Training/education	Universal	No		No	No	Universal	Common	No
Wage paid	No	No		Uncommon	No	Common	No	No
Freedom dues/end payments	Common	Limited (double apparel)		Required by statute	No	Common	Common	No
Who negotiates for laborer?	Parents	Overseer of the poor		Self	Overseer of the poor	Parents	Overseer of the poor	Informal agreements lacked force of law

Sources: Adapted from Murray and Herndon, "Markets for Children"; Farley Grubb, "The Statutory Regulation of Colonial Servitude: An Incomplete Contracts Approach," *Explorations in Economic History* 37:1 (January 2000), 42–75; Hindle, "'Waste' Children?" Cf. Joan Lane, *Apprenticeship in England, 1600–1914* (London, 1996), 82, table 4.1.

English thinking about the poor. Even the statutes in relief of the poor aimed to lighten, rather than remove, the burden of poverty.

From the start, by contrast, Anglo-America was officially portrayed as a place where poverty could be entirely overcome.[3] As early as 1584, projectors such as Richard Hakluyt envisioned North American colonies where the children of "the wandering beggars of England" might be "unladen" and "better bred up... to their own more happy state."[4] A century later, in 1698, Gabriel Thomas described Pennsylvania as a place where "Poor People (both Men and Women) of all kinds, can here get three times the Wages for their Labour they can in England or Wales"; further, food was plentiful and cheap, children were born "beautiful to behold," and inhabitants "live Friendly and Well together."[5] In 1773, on the eve of American independence, Boston printer Joseph Greenleaf's one-volume abridgement of Richard Burn's four-volume legal manual for local magistrates omitted all the information "of no possible use or importance to us in *America*," including the entire 150-page entry on "The Poor."[6] That Greenleaf could omit the very section whose pages were amongst the most well-thumbed in a handbook that lay tossed and tattered on the desk of virtually every magistrate in Georgian England speaks volumes about the different contexts in which this aspect of social policy operated.[7] The journey across the ocean transformed poverty into something else, perhaps even into *potential;* poor people were not poor in America—or were not, at least, acknowledged to be a problem for local magistrates. As Alexander Hewatt put it, with reference to South Carolina and Georgia, in 1779, because "every person by diligence and application may earn a comfortable livelihood, there are few poor people in the province, except the idle or unfortunate."[8]

From the late sixteenth century, on the other hand, the English magistracy was confronted with large numbers of poor people whose poverty was a permanent condition. The authorities regarded the poor at worst as a threat and at best merely as an inconvenience, only gradually accepting the notion that they constituted a "pool of badly-managed labor."[9] The language used on each side of the Atlantic to describe the ways in which the poor might survive is instructive in this respect. The term to "make shift," or "shift for oneself," frequently employed in English sources to characterize the very diverse survival strategies of the poor—including begging, borrowing, and stealing—was rarely used in the English American colonies.[10] Other terms, usually to "provide for," to "support," or to "maintain" themselves, all of them implying more formal and legitimate strategies, were used in the colonies to indicate how the poor made do (or failed to). In both contexts, however, the existence of a tax-based relief system is revealed in the idiom most commonly deployed by local officials to describe the situation of the poor—those who were "chargeable" or, more tellingly still, "likely to become chargeable."

In North America, moreover, social inequality was less marked. As the colonies officially had few poor, so they had, in official discourses at least, few very rich. The underrepresentation of a gentlemanly class in the colonial context implies the underdevelopment of a convention of charitable giving among a landed elite, whose households provided an important context for informal relief in England, where their fabled generosity supplemented, and even may have altogether obviated, local taxation.[11] Perhaps because the charitable resources of the colonial elite were relatively meager, the Elizabethan poor laws, which placed the responsibility for poor relief with the local taxpayers, were very quickly incorporated into legislation in North America. The colonies do not appear to have gone through a transitional period, as was the case in England, where magistrates and inhabitants alike had to be persuaded, sometimes even coerced, to accept the parish relief system in general and parish apprenticeship in particular.[12] The apprenticeship of poor children was therefore codified and put into practice extremely early in North America. The first Massachusetts general laws of 1642 required parents to train their children "in some honest lawful calling, labour or imployment." If parents failed to do this, then the selectmen and justices of the peace were authorized to "place them [the children] with some masters" who would "force them to submit unto government."[13] In 1646, the Virginia Grand Assembly, citing English law that recommended binding out children "for the better educateing of youth in honest and profitable trades and manufactures" and "to avoyd sloath and idlenesse wherewith such young children are easily corrupted," passed a law authorizing Virginia county commissioners to bind out children of "such parents who by reason of their poverty are disabled to maintaine and education them" for the specific purpose of supplying labor for the colony's public flax houses.[14] Colonies established later also explicitly authorized magistrates to bind out poor children; such laws came thick and fast after English legislation of 1697, which resolved once and for all the legal power of overseers to compel masters to accept parish children—Pennsylvania in 1705, New Jersey in 1709, South Carolina in 1712, New Hampshire in 1719, and Delaware in 1741.[15]

Despite their common ancestry, however, these two systems became increasingly differentiated as they were implemented on either side of the Atlantic. This raises a number of related questions, the most pressing of which is the relative significance to the poor themselves of the institutionalized relief provided by taxpayers, on the one hand, and the wider survival strategies practiced by the poor themselves, on the other. Was charitable giving, either voluntarily by neighbors or institutionally by taxpayers, more central to the survival of the poor in England than in the colonies? Did the radical Protestant impulse that, superficially at least, fueled colonial settlement imply that it was undesirable for the charitable to relieve those poor people who were perceived as unwilling to help themselves? Was there a tradition of informal support among the poor in England that did not translate to North America? Was there a collective memory of survival strategies on which the poor might draw as they exploited natural resources, social institutions and the charity of the well-to-do? If so, were these strategies imported to the colonies at an early stage of their historical development, or did they have to be rediscovered as the colonial economy grew? Further research on both sides of the Atlantic is needed to answer these questions. In this essay, we emphasize five central issues on which the comparative history of pauper apprenticeship in the Atlantic world turns: the definition of poverty; the political and institutional contexts in which charitable relief was administered; the availability of alternative forms of support; the identity of those eligible to be bound out; and the strength and nature of the local economy.

First, how was poverty defined, and by whom? Were colonial people as ready as their English counterparts to define or characterize themselves as poor by their willingness to accept charity? Was the sense of public disgrace about indigence and dependency better developed in North America than in England, where even the "shame-faced" were increasingly prepared as the seventeenth century progressed to advertise their need and plead for relief? Were the poor of the colonies less inclined to concede that they were indigent? Or was poverty defined by the authorities as a voluntary condition to which the poor had brought themselves through their own idleness, drunkenness, or disorder?[16] The sense that there might well have been a different set of cultural attitudes toward poverty on either side of the Atlantic is reinforced by the absence in North America of a tradition of ballads or other popular literature on poverty.[17]

The second fundamental issue dividing the two systems is the political and institutional context. In both England and in the colonies, the process of administering poor relief (and thus the binding out of pauper children) was locally based and therefore highly responsive to local conditions. Although English poor relief was administered in the local community on a parish-by-parish basis, these parishes formed part of a broadly based but fully integrated polity that extended from the vestry of the most remote rural community to the central courts of common law at Westminster. Crown, parliament, and privy council made decisions over poor law policy that influenced practice in every county and, in turn, every parish. In North America, however, each colonial court or assembly made its own laws about poor relief, and a centrally coordinated system on the English model was conspicuous by its absence. The potential for local variation was accordingly even greater in the colonies than in England. Furthermore, the very fact that the political unit chosen to administer poor relief in England was the parish, an institution with an ancient history of ecclesiastical jurisdiction, ensured that the ecclesiastical authorities in general, and the parish clergy in particular, had a significant say about the nature and scale of relief. This was true to a lesser extent in those colonies—Virginia, North

Carolina, South Carolina, and Georgia—where Anglicanism was strongest and where the parish relief system functioned on a similar basis to that in England. On the whole, however, ecclesiastical authority in the colonies was fragmented and diluted by assembly. This is not to deny that there were individual congregations, especially Jewish and Quaker, that developed their own traditions of charitable provision but simply to argue that ecclesiastical jurisdiction was less significant in shaping relief in the North American colonies. In turn, the different institutions responsible for administering relief naturally developed divergent bureaucratic practices and documentary forms. These in themselves are highly revealing of differing assumptions about the nature and scale of poor relief in general and apprenticeship in particular. Not until the late eighteenth century did most North American communities begin to use boilerplate forms, suggesting that the volume of indentures was not large enough to warrant the investment of costs in printing. But what might the material form of the contract suggest about the entrenchment of the practice? That pre-printed form suggests the "routinization" and, in turn, the ideological acceptance of the pauper apprenticeship system.

A third set of ambiguities concerns the availability of alternative forms of support for children. Begging, references to which are extremely common in the archives of the English magistracy and vestry, is rare in the official records of the colonies.[18] Perhaps apprenticeship gradually recommended itself to the colonial authorities as a way of avoiding the scandal of begging, reinforcing the image of America as a place where "poor people" did not have a legitimate public presence. The poor children of the colonies and the early Republic were invisible, exported from the streets into productive households where someone took official responsibility for them. In England, although mendicancy was first regulated and subsequently prohibited by statute, begging on the streets or from door to door remained common into the late seventeenth and eighteenth centuries and was generally tolerated in local communities, especially if those seeking alms were the familiar neighborhood poor. Indeed, sending children out begging on behalf of their families was so ingrained and widespread a strategy among the English poor even by the end of the sixteenth century that part of the intention of the apprenticeship clauses of the Elizabethan poor laws was to suppress it.[19]

A fourth factor that complicates comparisons is that of eligibility to be bound out. The identification of those who might legitimately be apprenticed raises one obvious question, that of how the needs and assets of poor laboring households might be measured. In England, that task fell to the "overseers of the poor," unpaid householders of middling status serving on a voluntary basis for a year at a time, responsible in each parish for administering the relief system and for visiting the households of the poor to see "what was wanting." In the townships and counties of the American colonies and states, it also was the responsibility of locally elected officials or their surrogates, the overseers of the poor. In both England and Anglo-America, these local officials had responsibility for a few hundred households at most. The equitable administration of the system also begged other questions about the rights of settlement and the thresholds of belonging, a process of inclusion and exclusion that lay firmly in the discretion of local officials. The English evidence suggests a deep-seated and ubiquitous conflict between long-settled inhabitants—the "ancient poor"—who possessed legitimate rights to communal and natural resources within the parish and the shiftless migrants—the "poor strangers crept amongst us"—who sought to encroach upon them.[20] In America as well, law and custom early established the rights of the poor who "belonged" to a community to use resources held in common.[21]

A fifth factor is the changing economic context in the two societies. In England, parish apprenticeship was conceived primarily as a means of enforcing labor discipline on poor children who would otherwise represent a burden on their families and on local resources of charity and parish relief.[22] It therefore followed that fluctuations, some of them regional or even local in nature, in the demand for labor influenced the willingness and capacity of the local authorities to force the children of the poor into apprenticeships. The imperative to export children from pauper households to those of their more prosperous neighbors seems to have been particularly characteristic of years of high prices and surplus labor. If the binding out of poor children was therefore "generally a feature of hard times" in England, to what extent did the different regional and local labor markets of the colonies have a major impact on the use of pauper apprenticeship?[23] In New England and Charleston, South Carolina, at least, the regularity with which children were bound out was not particularly sensitive to good or bad economic times. John Murray and Ruth Herndon's analysis suggests that specific clauses in the indentures (generosity of premiums, skills to be inculcated, freedom dues) might vary with good or bad times, but the number of indentures themselves hardly fluctuated at all.[24] This suggests that Americans did not, as English ratepayers did, think about apprenticeship as a relief valve for the parish treasury during difficult economic times.

The circumstances in which children were bound out might, in turn, affect the attitudes of their parents. The English evidence suggests that parents were often extremely reluctant to see their children taken away, not only because they feared that masters might prove negligent or abusive but also because the dual economy (manufacture as well as self-provisioning) practiced in many rural households depended on the labor input of children. This is to say nothing of what disdainful authorities condemned as the "foolish pity" of parents who were vain enough to value emotional ties over economic realities. In many cases parents were persuaded, perhaps even blackmailed, into giving up their children; some faced withdrawal of their parish relief if they did not cooperate.[25]

Was economic pressure on parents more severe in England? Were parents more cooperative about binding out in North America? *The Country Man's Lamentation,* discussed in chapter 1, suggests that many parents were reluctant to relinquish their children to apprenticeship. For the most part, however, there does not seem to be strong evidence of concerted resistance on the part of American parents, who were probably more sympathetic to pauper apprenticeship precisely because it promised children some "education" and some "training" in skills that might offer children the possibility of "getting a good living" as adults. The evidence for European American parents resisting or dodging the system is slender; on the contrary, some parents used the apprenticeship system strategically to their own advantage. The coercive elements of punishing English parents and masters who refused were simply not present in American apprenticeship.

English masters were often very reluctant to take on apprentices, especially in dearth years when they were already struggling to meet the expenditure of their own households and there was little work to give the children for whom they were asked to become responsible. Even in years of plenty, however, some masters resisted accepting pauper apprentices because they were suspicious of the noxious aura of pollution and peril with which the poor were clouded. The Hertfordshire clergyman Alexander Strange argued in 1636 that "the young people in these [poor] familyes are brought up so idlye that no honest man will willingly take such ill condicioned people into their howse for servants, hardly upon any termes or conditions, because they have bynne so ill and unprofitably brought up."[26] Commentary of this kind is redolent of social and class division, which seems to have been significantly less marked in the colonies. Perhaps the colonists themselves had a different *mentalité,* regarding themselves so instinctively as natural slaveowners and servant masters that they regarded taking on poor children not so much as a hardship to the family as an opportunity to extract surplus labor.

Scholars of English poor relief have been interested in the apprenticeship clauses of the Elizabethan poor laws since the early years of the twentieth century. So central was the binding out of pauper children to the rhetoric of statutes and proclamations that pioneering historians like E. M. Leonard, Sidney and Beatrice Webb, and E. M. Hampson, interested as they were in the gestation of social policy, could hardly fail to notice that the poor child whose parents were still alive took his or her place alongside the orphan as one of the principal targets of the relief statutes.[27] Even so, there was a general agreement among these historians, as well as those like Ephraim Lipson who followed them into the archives of central government, that the binding out of pauper children, like the setting of the poor on work, was one of the less practical, and therefore less successful, features of Tudor and Stuart social policy.

This assumption seemed to be confirmed in the 1960s and 1970s when the first generation of practitioners of the "new social history" began to explore the parochial archives of poor relief and to offer a more richly contextualized reading of the administration of policy.[28] Especially important to this phase of the historiography was the analysis of the account books kept by those responsible for administering relief across nine-thousand-odd parishes, the overseers of the poor. These books were replete with lists of "transfer payments," usually pensions distributed weekly in cash, targeted at the deserving poor, especially at the elderly and at young families overburdened with children. As scholars began to analyze the pattern of these disbursements, it became clear that the rate at which the parish pension was paid out increased both as paupers grew older, and where they had larger numbers of children. Overseers were, in effect, supplementing the household incomes of the indigent at clearly defined stages of the life cycle.[29] Given that overseers were evidently very sensitive to the household circumstances of the poor, historians were forced to take seriously the possibility that they also paid more attention than had previously been thought to the administration of the apprenticeship clauses. In turn, scholars began to analyze indentures archived by overseers and to investigate the age, gender, and trades of those bound out.[30] Historians of pauper apprenticeship in England are now confident that effective enforcement of pauper apprenticeship fluctuated over time but generally seems to have been associated with years of high prices, especially the early 1630s; that the majority of those bound out were not orphans but still had at least one parent surviving; that boys were far more commonly apprenticed than girls; that the average age at which children were bound was nine; that masters were very rarely if ever paid premia; and that the trades to which the offspring of the poor were bound were primarily menial. As the most significant legal authority on the poor laws pointed out, the apprenticeship clauses were intended "not for the education of boys in arts but for charity to keep them and relieve them from turning to roguery and idleness."[31]

In sum, the historical literature on pauper apprenticeship indentures in England is rich, and the questions that historians are now formulating for North America have already been asked (and substantially answered) in the English context. This book, by contrast, represents only the beginning of the literature for North America, which might profitably follow the agenda set by poor law historians in the United Kingdom.

Pauper apprenticeship in England was governed by the acts for relief of the poor of 1598 and 1601, the two statutes that together have become known to posterity as the "Elizabethan poor laws." The wording of the apprenticeship clauses of the 1598 act, confirmed in this respect as in so many others in 1601, was ambiguous: the children of those parents which *"shall not...be thought"* able to *"kepe and mayntaine"* them were to apprenticed until they reached specified ages (twenty-four for men, twenty-one for women).[32] These clauses were not, it should be emphasized, principally concerned with orphans, since they assumed that at least one of the parents of poor children might still be alive.

The discretionary power of parish officers and magistrates therefore lay in determining whether the parents themselves were "thought able" to bring up their children, either in the present or in the future. Overseers were advised to be circumspect in choosing both which children to apprentice and to whom they should be bound. Parish officers were to distinguish between the child who "by his labour" was "able to keep himselfe and yeelde some releefe to his parents," who must be allowed to remain at home; and the child who was "a burden and charge," who should be bound out. They should also have a keen eye to the "facultie, honestie and abilitie" of the masters, lest they either provoke the apprentices to abscond or fail to provide adequate training and discipline.[33]

These instructions were so vague that the judiciary were frequently required to clarify their implications. By 1607, judicial opinion had declared that poor parents were not *legally compelled* to comply with the apprenticeship of their children, but could easily be *coerced* into doing so, what Chief Justice Popham called "implied compulsion."[34] Persuasion of this kind was the corollary of the powerful discretionary impulse that lay at the heart of all seventeenth-century social policy. Perhaps its most extreme manifestation is revealed in the dynamics of the transportation of vagrant children to the American colonies in the 1618–22 period. Any parents in the City of London who were "overcharged and burdened with poor children" but refused to send them to Virginia were told that they would not receive any further poor relief from the parish until they complied.[35] For the succeeding half-century, however, this orthodoxy was undermined by a series of legal judgments, testimony in themselves to the significance of the English judiciary in reshaping, perhaps even making, social policy. Into the 1660s and 1670s magistrates received conflicting advice about their legal powers to coerce parents or masters; only in 1697 was the issue definitively resolved in favor of compulsion. For over a century thereafter, overseers generated sheaves of indentures, which were stored, alongside account books, with increasing bureaucratic efficiency in parish chests across thousands of local communities. By 1697, therefore, the apprenticeship indenture had taken its place alongside the weekly pension as one of the facts of parish life; both were issued on the discretionary authority of overseers, and both were supervised and audited by county magistrates. In sum, the authority to bind out pauper children in England was statutory from 1598, though subject to substantial judicial commentary and review over the next century.

It therefore seems clear that poor families in England and the colonies were not dealing with officials of comparable social and political status when they were asked to agree to binding out their children. In particular, there were significant differences in the role played by magistrates in issuing indentures on either side of the Atlantic. In England, the magistrate's role was largely one of arbitration and coordination, with active administration and implementation of the policy left to overseers in the parishes. In North America, as the essays in this volume show, apprenticeship was left to the discretion of the local magistrates themselves, who had the power to determine who in their community was considered unable to raise children properly.

Thus far, we have been concerned principally with the legal and administrative aspects of pauper apprenticeship, which are essential to understanding the comparisons and contrasts between the two systems of binding out as they developed over two centuries. In so doing, however, we may lose sight of those very children whose experience of being "bound to labor" we are trying to reconstruct here. To redress this imbalance, we now refocus the discussion on poor children themselves. We might begin by imagining the predicament of the child of tender years about to be bound out. Perhaps she was dimly aware of the visit of the local officials, of the threats and inducements offered her parents, of a journey to the wainscoted parlor of the local magistrate's country seat; of the signing of an indenture that neither she nor her parents could read; of the self-satisfaction of the overseers at having disburdened the taxpayers. The sense of incipient change generated by these machinations might only be crystallized at the moment of removal from her parents; the journey to the household of an unfamiliar master in a distant community would doubtless be one of foreboding, perhaps even one of fear. Exercises in empathy, however, can only take us so far. The experience of pauper apprentices might properly be reconstructed only through an analysis of the indentures in which their rights and obligations, and those of their masters, were inscribed.

On both sides of the Atlantic, there was a significant disequilibrium in the gender distribution of those who were removed from their natal households: the overwhelming majority of poor children bound out were male. In England in the 1630s, over two-thirds of those formally apprenticed under the poor law system were boys.[36] Similarly, boys far outnumbered girls in all of the studies in this volume.[37] The underrepresentation of girls might be explained in several ways. Girls may have been of greater value than boys in the domestic economy, especially in areas where textile production was common. Parents might easily find work for their female offspring in spinning yarn and would therefore be reluctant to let them be bound out. Or parents may have been concerned about the potential for the sexual abuse of servant girls by unfamiliar masters in distant communities. On the other hand, it is likely that girls were being informally "put out" to earn their keep without being thought worth the trouble of a formal contract. If so, this suggests that gender ideology strongly influenced the terms of entry into a life of labor. Most plausibly, however, the preponderance of boys bound out reflects the priorities of masters rather than parents: those who were persuaded to take the children of the poor into their households and workshops surely thought that there was simply more value in boys' labor.

The labor value of a pauper apprentice almost certainly varied according to the age at which the child was bound out. In England, although the statutes empowered the overseers to bind out any child over the age of seven, parish officers generally seem to have waited at least one year, sometimes much longer, before they intervened in the household composition of the poor. The modal age of children apprenticed in West Yorkshire in the mid-1630s, for instance, was eleven; and the Leicestershire bench thought only of "children and youths between ten and sixteen" as "fitt for apprenticeship."[38] Poor children younger than seven in England were much more likely to be *boarded* out informally with relatives or neighbors rather than *bound* out formally with masters, and the vast majority of those involved in this obscure aspect of the poor law system were orphans. At age seven or eight, however, even those who had been boarded were likely to be bound, entailing yet more upheaval. The American pattern was broadly similar, where between nine and eleven years of age was typical for the apprenticeship of a poor child.[39] That the typical binding age was the same on both sides of the Atlantic suggests that the two cultures shared a common ideology about the developmental stages of childhood and about appropriate employments for boys and girls of specified ages.

Premia for pauper apprentices were not frequent on either side of the Atlantic, though the minority of cases in which they were used make possible the sketchiest of statistical analyses. The absence of premia is surprising, especially in the English context where masters were often reluctant and might browbeat the parish officers into offering them inducements. However, the confirmation by the 1697 statute that masters could be legally compelled to accept apprentices gave magistrates an advantage. Indeed, only 18 percent of the 344 indentures drawn up in the parishes of mid-Sussex between 1589 and 1750 specified any premium at all.[40] The average cash value of these premia was approximately £5, but variations around this mean seem to have reflected the length of the indenture rather than the trade to which the child was bound. The same trend can be seen in Rhode Island, where premia accompanied 40 percent of the children bound out when they were under six years of age, compared to only 3 percent of the older children carrying premia with them.[41] In both England and North America, it seems, younger children and those perceived as handicaps were more likely to be bound with premia.

The rarity of premia on both sides of the Atlantic was almost certainly a function of the low-skilled trades to which poor children were apprenticed. The Elizabethan poor laws stipulated only "husbandry and huswifery," the very trades that Gervase Markham, writing in 1613, thought most fitting for "Boyes and Girles, or other *waste* persons" (employing the idiom in the sense of "off-scourings, dregs, worthless people")."[42] There are only occasional hints that there was much variation from this norm, at least not until the late-eighteenth-century development of the factory system in the industrializing towns of the northern counties created a demand for child labor to supply the cotton mills.[43] English apprenticeship indentures very occasionally identify masters as cordwainers or weavers, maltsters or tanners, but poor children overwhelmingly seem to have begun their lives of labor by learning menial tasks in the fields (stone-picking, weeding, bird-scaring) or the households (charring, laundering, water-fetching) of their more prosperous neighbors.[44] Perhaps they might graduate in adolescence to the more labor-intensive tasks of farm or domestic service, but in no sense were they developing skills that might allow them to become masters in their own right. The very best that a male pauper child could hope for was that a particularly charitable master might, in turn, pay a premium on his behalf to enable him to embark on a formal apprenticeship to a craft, effectively giving him a foothold on the ladder of social mobility that was beyond the reach of most pauper children who were "destined for deprivation."[45] A similar situation prevailed in North America, though there the boys who were taught specialized skills formed a slightly more extensive elite stratum of poor apprentices, effectively constituting an aristocracy of child labor. On both sides of the Atlantic, therefore, the universality of husbandry and housewifery suggests that pauper apprenticeship was designed not to raise children above their station but rather to prevent them and their parents from falling into greater deprivation or, indeed, destitution. The children of the poor were almost universally required to perform the menial, marginal work of the community—and to be rewarded for it in the households of their betters—in order to alleviate the burden posed by their youth to their parents and, in turn, to the ratepayers.

The most startling differences between the American and English contracts was the preference for literacy clauses in America, which almost invariably obliged the master to provide instruction in reading and writing for his apprentices. Provision for the education of poor children was, by contrast, conspicuous by its absence from English parish apprenticeship contracts. Some masters did, of their own volition, teach the rudiments of grammar to the children foisted on them by the parish, but most masters cared little for such educational development. It may well be that the children of the poor were taught by parish schoolmasters, clergymen, perhaps even by their mothers, until the age of seven, and that apprenticeship actually interrupted their schooling before they had learned to write, a skill that was generally taught only after the child had learned to read.[46] Whether they went on to do so under the auspices of the parish apprenticeship system owed less to the formal requirements of the contracts to which they were subject, in which writing skills were hardly ever mentioned, than to the conscientiousness of individual masters. The establishment of significant provisions ensuring education for the children of the poor in England, especially through the charity school movement of the early eighteenth century, may well explain why literacy clauses were hardly considered necessary at all in English contracts when they were almost a given in the American context, where public schools were not a commonplace before the early nineteenth century.[47]

A similar divergence occurs over the question of behavioral (or "vice") clauses. Clauses restricting the sociability of apprentices are rare in the English indentures dealing with pauper children, but they are common in the American indentures. In this respect, as we have seen, the colonial contracts resemble the formal trade indentures that had characterized the guild system in England from the fourteenth century onward. This is emphatically not to suggest that magistrates and masters were less concerned with the moral behavior of the poor in England: the discretionary withholding of relief was by no means unknown in English parishes, and paupers who did not conform to the expected canons of social respectability could expect sanctions of social discipline and moral reform.[48] But since the fundamental purpose of parish apprenticeship in England was to remove prospective burdens from the shoulders of the ratepayers, there was much less concern with the behavior of the poor child once bound out. If anything, vice clauses were a hostage to fortune in the English case, since they might easily provide a reluctant master with a convenient excuse to rid himself of an unwanted apprentice. Conversely, of course, it may well be the case that the American vice clauses themselves were merely pro forma, a legacy deriving from the religious zeal of the first colonists, but without real social meaning. It is certainly true that vice clauses began to disappear in Anglo-America in the late eighteenth and early nineteenth century, to be replaced by more generalized statements.[49]

It was, furthermore, universal in the English indentures that the master undertook to keep the community free of any cost associated with the poor apprentice. Especially striking is the frequency with which masters themselves were made to enter into financial guarantees not to evict apprentices once they had agreed to take them. Almost one in ten of those who took parish apprentices in mid-Sussex between 1589 and 1750 were bound in this way, some of them in recognizances of £100.[50] Such clauses were very rare in American indentures. This confirms the impression that pauper apprenticeship was largely designed as a measure of poor relief in England but as one of skill and literacy training in North America.

The more specialized obligations of the masters also varied considerably between England and Anglo-America. The limited nature and scale of the responsibilities English owed to parish children are confirmed by the dues payable to apprentices at the end of their term. In England, the master universally owed the apprentice double apparel, and nothing else. In North America, the range of options was wider, often including money, livestock, tools, and gear. This may suggest more competition for apprentices among American masters or simply reflect the locally designed nature of the Anglo-American apprenticeship system. In their study of indentures from South Carolina and New England, Murray and Herndon found that end payments to apprentices were determined by agreement between local magistrates (who wanted to relieve the community of poor relief expenses) and potential masters (who wanted to receive the fruits of the child's labor and, importantly in this connection, discourage the productive apprentice from running away). Both parties were sensitive to the state of the local economy and understood the worth of a farm-trained, household- or craft-trained apprentice in that economy. Productive apprentices were more likely to receive generous freedom dues where the local economy was prospering but not where it was stagnant.[51]

Equally telling is the age at freedom for English parish apprentices, especially for the girls, whose masters were obliged to keep them only until they reached the age of twenty-one or until they got married, whichever came first. This clause implied that a girl could be exported to an independent household as soon as her husband had the wherewithal to support both her and the children that would doubtless follow soon after marriage. The poor law authorities nonetheless took special care to prevent those unions that were sufficiently improvident to "breed up a charge" on the poor rate.[52] By preventing pauper marriage or delaying it by requiring that male apprentices remain with their masters until the age of twenty-four (until 1768; twenty-one thereafter), overseers and magistrates alike sought to prevent or decelerate the cycle of deprivation in which poverty was transmitted from generation to generation. From the start, the standard in America was for male apprentices to be freed at age twenty-one and female apprentices at age eighteen. Longer indentures were reserved for black and Indian apprentices in Rhode Island, Maryland, and other areas where slavery was commonplace, as the essays in this volume show. In these latter cases, American magistrates seem to have been appealing deliberately to a previous English convention to harness the labor of children of color for a longer period and to restrain the fertility of those they considered uncivilized.

The practice of apprenticing pauper children in England and in Anglo-America derived from a common set of impulses, and it seems to have died out nearly simultaneously on both sides of the Atlantic in the nineteenth century—with the passage of the new Poor Law of 1834 in England; throughout the first half of the 1800s in North America, as states independently developed public institutions to administer care and education to vulnerable children. However, their histories followed radically different early trajectories. For the century or so until the 1697 statute clarified the compulsive powers of magistrates, the early history of apprenticeship in England was characterized by considerable tension, often by outright resistance. Even with the powerful support of the royal prerogative, manifested in the Book of Orders from the 1630s, parish officers struggled to secure compliance with the policy. In North America, pauper apprenticeship commenced almost as soon as the colonies were settled, accepted from the start as an appropriate part of maintaining a community.

From the early eighteenth century on, the English and American trajectories began to converge. Parish apprenticeship began a spectacular rise in North

America and became fully institutionalized, indeed even ubiquitous, in England. Surviving English indentures may even underrepresent the scale of the project of redistributing children from households where they represented a drain on their parents to those where their contribution might be harnessed more productively. After all, since premia were very rare even when pauper children were formally indentured, it is entirely possible that substantial numbers of boys and girls were bound out informally, leaving no trace at all in the archival record.[53] For this reason, it is unlikely that the chronology of the rise and decline of pauper apprenticeship in eighteenth-century England will ever be charted with the kind of precision that is possible in the American colonies, where the practice remained much more closely governed by and recorded in formal indentures.

The practice of binding out poor children was decisively shaped on either side of the Atlantic by the ideological preferences of those local officials serving in thousands of counties, parishes, and townships. This becomes particularly clear when we consider the matter of race, which lay behind much of the apprenticeship story in North America. As the essays in this volume show, the correlations between race and apprenticeship are complex and elusive. Although the issue of race per se was by definition conspicuous by its absence in the English context—at least until the late eighteenth century—cultural divisions of the kind suggested by the American evidence were subtly foreshadowed in England. Both of the groups that were racially marginalized in seventeenth- and early-eighteenth-century England—the Irish and the gypsies—were considered ineligible for parish apprenticeship on the grounds that they were not settled members of the local community. The fate of such highly mobile groups was, however, even less attractive than the compulsory removal of their children, for the vagrancy laws provided that vagabonds were to be punished with the apparatus of social discipline that stood in the streets of so many English market towns: the whipstocks and pillories administered by constables and the manacles and hemp kept by masters of houses of correction.[54]

The institution of binding out poor children was equally shaped by the administrative habits of officials on both sides of the Atlantic. Local magistrates used the apprenticeship of pauper children as a means of relieving the poor without exhausting the funds generated by taxpayers; of training poor children in occupations that they deemed to be useful to the community at large; and of monitoring, and even intervening in, the household composition of poor people, especially by removing children from "improper" households and placing them in "proper" ones. Those same local officials who had oversight of the poor also had a continuing responsibility toward those children who were bound out, but their first allegiance was almost certainly to the taxpayers who provided the relief funds and on whose behalf they decided which impoverished, sometimes even feckless, parents would be the appropriate objects of their attention and action.

The coexistence of traditions of binding out pauper children on either side of the Atlantic into the late eighteenth and early nineteenth centuries suggests at the very least that poverty in North America had become as significant a problem as it had been in England. By that time, binding out had come to be seen as a viable way out of a dreadful economic situation in America, just as it had in England for over two centuries. At that moment, it seems, English and American ideologies of family formation, child-rearing, and child labor had come to mirror each other.

PART II

BINDING OUT AS A MASTER/ SERVANT RELATION

Binding out was a labor relation, for it put pauper apprentices in a legal condition of servitude. Both servant and master were obligated by an indenture that governed the exchange of labor (by the child) for daily maintenance and education (by the master). Binding out was one more means of putting children to work. As the introductory essays show, binding out was also a parent/child relation and a family/state relation. Why should the servant/master relation be featured first? After all, legal commentaries of the 1700s noted that the master/servant relation arose from the even more basic parent/child relation. However, those same legal commentaries viewed pauper apprenticeship as essentially a labor relation, as have historians who have written about it. We follow their lead.

Early American history is full of African and Native American men and women being forced into and held in slavery, and the children born to them usually inherited their parents' status. Immigrant indentured servants, many of whom were young people, have also been studied closely. The same is true of traditional craft apprentices, young teenagers placed by their parents with neighbors or relatives for a few years of skill training, for which the master was reimbursed. Less familiar to present-day Americans is the concept of free children being taken by public authorities from natal homes and put into temporary bondage. Pauper apprentices were not slaves, indentured servants, or craft apprentices. Families did not have to invest in a slave or buy an indenture of an immigrant fresh off the ship from Europe; they could benefit from years of a young person's labor at no greater cost than the "necessities" of life and one or two outfits of clothing. On a continuum of types of labor, binding out fell somewhere between lifelong chattel slavery and the custom of hiring a farmhand or housemaid on a yearly contract. When pauper apprenticeship is factored into our picture of labor in early America, we see that unfree labor was far more widespread and significant than previously thought.

CHAPTER THREE

"Proper" Magistrates and Masters

Binding Out Poor Children in Southern New England, 1720–1820

RUTH WALLIS HERNDON

Records of binding out in eighteenth-century Connecticut, Massachusetts, and Rhode Island show that magistrates and masters cooperatively worked out the terms under which the least powerful members of the community were put to work and prepared for adulthood. Although theoretically on opposite sides of a bargaining table, magistrates and masters shared common assumptions about the proper place of poor children in a hierarchically organized society. To perpetuate that organization and maintain community stability, magistrates and masters joined forces in pauper apprenticeship, placing at-risk children into households that would train them to take up their place in society. Benevolence was not entirely lacking; some magistrates and masters certainly were moved by the plight of poor children and desired to alleviate their distress. But in their disposition of such children through binding out, magistrates and masters served themselves by maintaining the social status quo—in effect, preserving their own social and economic dominance as they preserved community peace and order. In the business of raising pauper apprentices, masters functioned as substitute magistrates, carrying out the aims of good town government within their own households.

To describe pauper apprenticeship in southern New England between 1720 and 1820, this essay draws on 2,114 indentures of poor children and related

---

I gratefully acknowledge research support for this project in the form of a major grant from the Spencer Foundation and short-term fellowships from the New England Regional Fellowship Consortium and the John Nicholas Brown Center for American Civilization.

documents—public records of town and magistrate meetings and official correspondence relating to binding out.[1] At first glance, it may seem unwieldy to combine data from ten different communities in three different New England colonies/states in an analysis of binding out, an institution that reflected local concerns to a high degree. While these ten New England communities developed in distinctive ways over the seventeenth and eighteenth centuries, they nevertheless shared the common ground of town government, through which pauper apprenticeship was administered. Boston, New Haven, New London, and Providence—the most populous towns in the study—all began as seventeenth-century seaports that swelled over the following century with the arrival of shiploads of free, indentured, and enslaved people from around the Atlantic basin. Many inhabitants moved past the seaports to Wethersfield, Bolton, and Tolland, Connecticut; and Westerly, Glocester, and South Kingstown, Rhode Island—the agrarian towns in this study. And wherever they lived, some of these New Englanders fell on hard times, bringing themselves and their families under the scrutiny of officials who did not hesitate to bind out children who might become a social or economic problem to the community. Comparing and contrasting the ways pauper apprenticeship was administered in these ten communities provides a singular opportunity to see local variations within the same region.[2]

The statistical story of binding out in these New England towns follows the general picture presented in chapter 2. The practice waxed in the eighteenth century and waned in the nineteenth century, with the heaviest activity between 1750 and 1800. Gender and race mattered. Boys were bound more often than girls, for longer periods of time, and for greater rewards in the form of literacy education, skill training, and freedom dues. Children of color were bound out in disproportionately large numbers, for longer periods of time, and for fewer rewards. Family background did not matter. The child's situation—orphan, illegitimate, or simply "poor"—did not translate into meaningful differences in placement, education, or benefits. Overall, the descriptive statistics of the children bound out in New England look very similar to those elsewhere in North America.

What distinguishes pauper apprenticeship in New England is the effective cooperation of magistrates and masters in pursuit of community stability. Singular features of binding out between 1720 and 1820 demonstrate how important this partnership was and how the system was shaped to keep the partnership functioning. From the outset, binding out was designed principally to ensure a stable society. The capital laws of Connecticut (1642) mandated that parents should educate their children in the "principles of religion" and in some "honest, lawful calling" deemed "profitable for themselves and the common wealth"; if improperly raised children became "rude, stubborn, and unruly," then magistrates would bind them out to masters who would "force them to submitt unto government."³ Massachusetts law (1648; 1692) similarly authorized magistrates to bind out children who "live idly or misspend their time in loitering."⁴ Rhode Island law (1662) likewise empowered town officials to "put out to service" all "young and able persons" who appeared "likely to become a charge or damage to such town" through their "idleness."⁵ The welfare of the community underlay these early statutes.

This early pattern of community management persisted into the 1700s. Unlike court officials in Maryland, who responded to direct appeals but did not instigate investigations, New England town officials proactively intervened in the lives of at-risk children and deliberately sought out approved household heads to be masters to those children. Together, magistrates and masters acted *in loco parentis* to vulnerable children, taking on what legal commentators of the day agreed were the duties and rights of parents—to maintain, protect, and educate children and to punish children and secure their obedience.⁶ Magistrates and masters expected to reap benefits from pauper apprenticeship beyond the practical profit of the child's labor to the master's household; they expected an orderly society in which the poor labored peaceably for their "betters."

These records show a meaningful pattern of magistrate-master interaction. Meeting minutes show negotiation over contract terms; pre-printed forms show additions, deletions, and amendments in response to these negotiations; official correspondence shows common goals and expectations of cooperation between masters and magistrates. The language in these documents is deliberate and significant, illuminating the culture and context of pauper apprenticeship in New England.

Pauper apprenticeship flourished in New England between 1720 and 1820. Before 1720 it was enacted sporadically and in small numbers; after 1820 it declined sharply. Its peak coincided with a number of other phenomena and can be explained by them. The population of New England grew rapidly in the eighteenth century, through immigration and natural increase of the people already there.⁷ With the increase of population came an increase of poor people. Land ownership—the most reliable way of achieving economic independence in a predominantly agrarian society—became increasingly difficult for new immigrants as well as for the grandchildren and great-grandchildren of original settlers trying to farm successively smaller inheritances, so some of them migrated to more populous towns in search of a living, competing with immigrant newcomers for jobs. Such people lived in an insecure environment where an otherwise minor misfortune could bring the family to the attention of town officials. War and postwar economic depressions were ever-present problems in the eighteenth century; so were weather disasters, poor harvests, disease epidemics, and sluggish trade. When these larger societal problems were aggravated by personal difficulties—disabling injuries, chronic illness, alcoholism, death or desertion by spouse or parent, birth of a child out of wedlock—struggling people had few

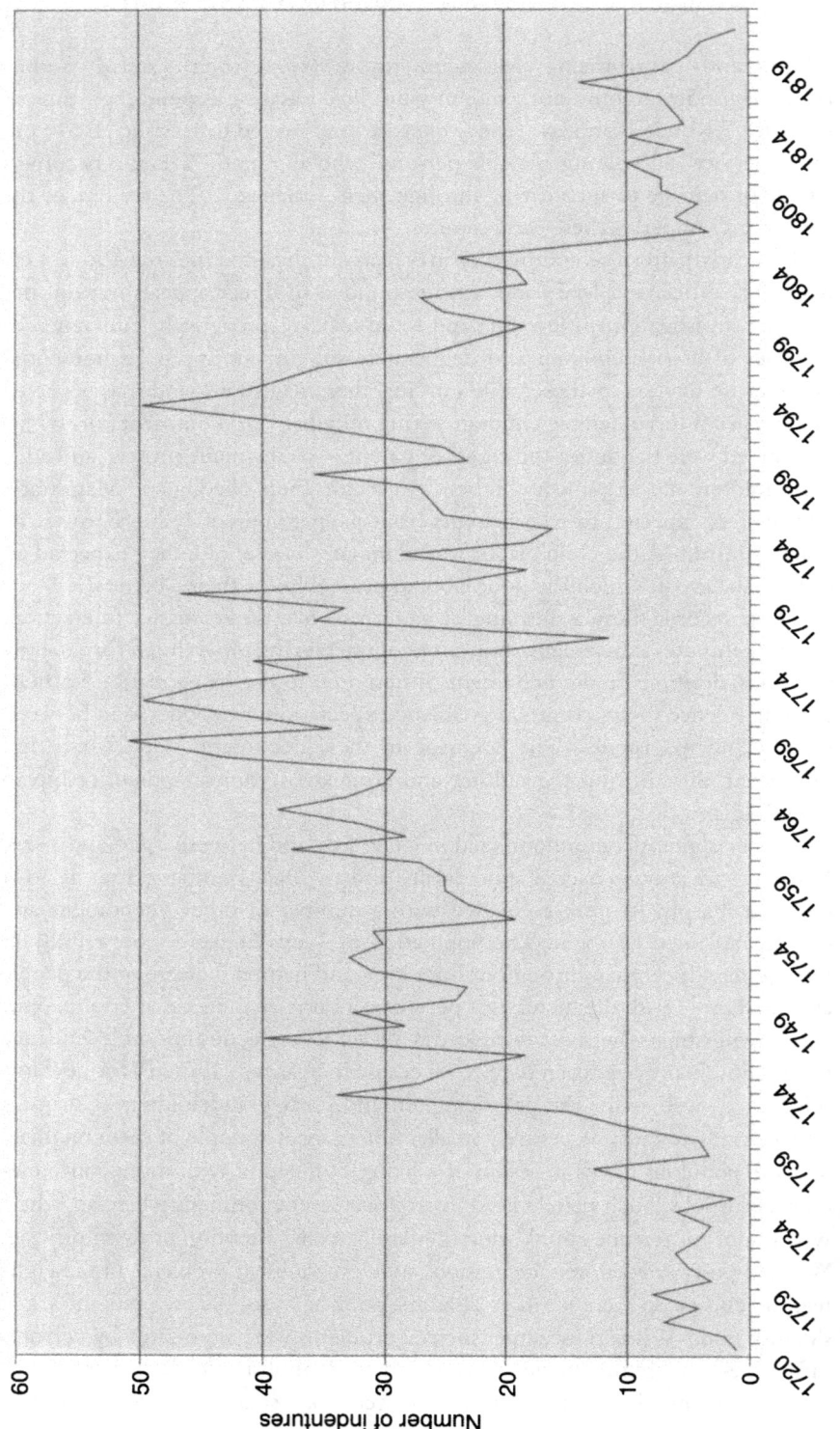

FIGURE 3.1. Pauper apprentices bound out in Southern New England, 1720–1820

resources. Out of such circumstances came many of the children who were bound out as pauper apprentices in eighteenth-century New England.[8]

The trajectory of pauper apprenticeship was also influenced by the decline of slavery in Connecticut, Rhode Island, and Massachusetts. Voluntary manumission of slaves increased, prompted by the rhetoric and ideas of political liberty, even as slave traders based in New England stepped up their importation of slaves, some of whom became inhabitants of the communities in this study.[9] Antislavery activists obtained passage of gradual emancipation legislation in Connecticut and Rhode Island and successfully litigated to free slaves in Massachusetts during and immediately after the Revolutionary War. Gradual emancipation generated a variant of pauper apprenticeship: children born to slaves after March 1, 1784, though technically free at birth, remained under the control of their mothers' masters until adulthood—defined as age twenty-five for both men and women in Connecticut and twenty-one for boys and eighteen for girls in Rhode Island.[10] These children of slaves would grow up under "proper" government, but children of color born to free parents had no such restrictions on their lives—unless town leaders stepped in to control them and prevent imagined disorder. Town leaders turned to pauper apprenticeship to maintain community stability during this time of changing race relations, and binding out became increasingly focused on children of color wherever they concentrated, especially Providence and New London. Even reformers saw pauper apprenticeship as practical protection from chattel slavery during the transition. In 1800, the Providence councilmen heard the appeal of certain "friends" of Peter Sharp, a ten-year-old "black boy," who was bound to Capt. Nathaniel Packard who "has it in contemplation to send him to sea." After listening to Packard as well as to the friends who "pray[ed] the interference of this council," the magistrates transferred Sharp's indenture to Obadiah Brown, who was also present at the meeting and had advocated for the boy's transfer. The clerk noted that Obadiah Brown was "son of Moses," the well-known Quaker and antislavery activist, suggesting that the councilmen feared Peter Sharp might be transported to and sold in another state where slavery was still firmly entrenched; the solution was to bind the child to a master who would keep the boy safely in Providence.[11]

Another factor influencing the rise and fall of pauper apprenticeship was the onset of the Industrial Revolution. Both slave labor and pauper apprenticeship declined in the early 1800s in New England, just as textile mills began to mushroom across the landscape, moving labor out of the household, farm, and workshop and into the factory.[12] In this new order, mill owners and managers became virtual masters of poor laboring children. Magistrates, concerned over peace and order in their communities during this major change in work life, attempted to form common cause with industrial leaders just as they had with individual pauper apprenticeship masters. In 1813, Connecticut lawmakers passed an act directing that "the president and directors of all factories" undertake the education of all children employed by them, whether bound by indenture or not. That education was to include reading, writing, "the first four rules of arithmetic," and "the preservation of their morals."[13] Factory managers were not on their own in this endeavor; public schools were increasingly available in New England communities in the 1800s.[14] Thus keeping children to work and educating them could be easily accomplished outside the individual household, and pauper apprenticeship was no longer the best or only resort in the quest for maintaining a peaceable and well-ordered community.

The years between 1720 and 1820 thus represent a century of enormous change, and pauper apprenticeship reflects that change. Each locality responded uniquely. Boston had a particularly dramatic increase in binding out in 1777, the direct result of the town's liberation from British military occupation; after two years of suppressed activity, the overseers of the poor bound out thirty-two children, some of them doubtless already in place but without legal indentures. The periods of 1766–74 and 1791–96 reflect peaks of binding out in all the study towns. These high points do not correspond to economic downturns, and the postwar depression of the 1780s did not spur binding out. Instead, the practice increased during moments of economic upswing, suggesting that magistrates were more likely to bind out children at a time when local farmers, artisans, and householders were doing relatively well and could envision themselves taking a pauper apprentice into the family.

Changes in statute law governing pauper apprenticeship confirm the arc of activity sketched in figure 3.1. A 1736 Massachusetts law regarding treatment of the poor acknowledged that "the town of Boston is grown considerably populous, and the idle and poor much increased among them" and that "the poor of the said town may, upon the decay of trade, become still more numerous...and very burthensome to the town." This 1736 law, which coincided with the first major rise in binding out in New England, broadened the powers of magistrates so that they could bind out the children of parents prosperous enough to pay real estate taxes yet "unable or negligent" in caring for their offspring.[15] In 1772, following the busiest few years of binding out in the entire century, Massachusetts legislators again broadened town magistrates' powers, this time authorizing them to bind out any children who "shall come, be left, or found dwelling" in their communities, whether or not the children were legally settled there.[16] This law was made retroactive to 1771, but for at least a decade prior to that, Boston magistrates omitted a town in their identification of some pauper apprentices, signaling that these children had no legal settlement there.[17] The 1772 law codified custom, a custom that had sprung up in response to the flood of needy children who had no clearly identifiable home towns. Rhode Island followed. In 1765, during a wave of binding out activity, Rhode Island legislators affirmed local magistrates' power to bind out poor children; in 1798, after another few years of heavy apprenticing activity, Rhode Island town officials received apprenticing powers similar to those enjoyed by Massachusetts magistrates.[18] While Connecticut never granted such sweeping privileges to town magistrates, the law authorizing binding out was strategically renewed and emphasized in 1784, when apprenticing poor children began to rise again after a relatively quiet period during the Revolutionary War.[19]

Over the period of 1720–1820, when pauper apprenticeship was at its height, the process of binding out followed a customary pattern: magistrates decided to bind out a child; magistrates negotiated particulars of the indenture with the master; masters and magistrates signed the physical contract. The decision to bind a child occurred during an officially convened meeting of councilmen in Rhode Island, selectmen in Connecticut and Massachusetts, or overseers of the poor acting on their behalf. These gatherings took place in private homes of magistrates or in local taverns or inns, and potential masters sometimes attended these meetings to make their wishes known. Sometimes a town magistrate was given latitude to seek out a likely master, using his connections in the community. The Hopkinton, Rhode Island, town council, after discussing the case of Jeremiah Crandall's wife and seven children being "in a necessatuous circumstances" because Crandall's property had been seized for debt, ordered the Hopkinton overseer of the poor to "bind out as many of the aforementioned children as he shall think fit."[20]

The second stage, negotiating the terms of the contract, often occurred offstage, in a discussion between one or more town officials and the potential master. Filed with the indenture of Thomas Wallis is a letter from his master, Isaac Stone, dated a few months after the indenture, reminding the Boston overseers of the poor of the agreement they had made with him. Stone asked that the magistrates "fix out the boy as well as you can for cloathing as you proposed."[21] The South Kingstown town council minutes show that the indenture of "Peter a mustee boy" had to be redrawn because of a mistake that the master had caught; in ordering the second indenture, the council noted their original "intent" that the boy "be bound untill he was twenty four years oald."[22] Numerous indentures include language indicating that masters and magistrates had negotiated specifics of the contract. The phrase "if sd apprentice be capable to learn" was occasionally written into indentures, suggesting that at least one party had some question about the child's mental abilities.[23] The phrase "if living" or "if he survive"—referring to the child—was added to some contracts, indicating that master and magistrates had discussed the likelihood of the child dying before the end of the indenture.[24] Occasionally the language of pre-printed forms was altered to show departure from custom, worked out between master and magistrates. Daniel Trudgeon was bound "~~servant~~ apprentice"; Sophia Havens was bound as "~~apprentice~~ servant"; Betsey Colton was bound "~~an apprentice~~ a maidservant."[25] Mary Dennis was to be taught to "read ~~& write~~"; Hannah, daughter of "free Negro" Sampson, was to be taught to "read and ~~write as children of her age are commonly taught~~ to do"; in contrast, Mary Covel, was to be taught to "read, write, and cypher," underlined three times because cyphering was not yet a usual provision for girls and may have been contested by the master.[26] Such alterations illuminate discussions between magistrate and master about what was suitable for the master to provide and the child to receive.

The last stage, the actual signing of the contract by master and magistrates, sometimes occurred in an official setting, other times in piecemeal fashion. Paul Mandell, a selectman in Hardwick who became master of ten poor children from the Boston almshouse in the 1770s, asked a friend in Boston to "take a Small portion of your Leizure time and Step to the Alms house and Ask the Overseer or Master for an Indenture made to me of my Boy William Dun." He explained in his letter that when he first "took" the boy, the Boston overseers "had not had a Meeting & the Indenture on their part Could not be Signd.... I therefore signd on my part and thus it is lain ever since."[27] Mandell had signed the indentures nine years earlier, but the overseers did not put their signatures on for nearly a decade. Numerous indentures show similar back-and-forth conversations between masters and magistrates that culminated in both parties putting their names on paper as partners in an enterprise of governing their inferiors.

The goal of binding out was to place children in "good families," as the 1736 Massachusetts law termed it, and a good master was a valuable partner to town magistrates.[28] In sparsely populated eighteenth-century New England towns, where most inhabitants knew each other personally, local magistrates were well-informed, well connected, and prosperous men who had no problem identifying local families that would make a good home for displaced children.[29] And if a child was bound to a family in a neighboring community, information would flow through friends and relations back to town officials. In densely populated Boston, where leaders did not have such close knowledge of all inhabitants, the overseers of the poor required potential masters to produce written character references.[30]

These character references and the collective profile of the masters themselves tell us that magistrates sought masters as much like themselves as possible—proficient and industrious in their occupations, economically prosperous, and living in well-ordered families with a married couple at the core. Only 2 percent of the indentures in this study were for female masters—widows or never-married women. However, the great majority of those other 98 percent were married men; this was expected by magistrates as essential to maintaining good order in a household. If a master's wife died, young pauper apprentices (especially female ones) would be removed from the home because there was no longer a "proper person" to raise them.[31] It is not likely that Dr. John Chace of Providence instructed Betsey Richmond in "common household business" or that Abraham Bradley of New Haven taught Sarah Smith how to spin, knit, and sew, as these indentures stipulated; the person in charge of training these girls was most certainly Mrs. Chace and Mrs. Bradley—or possibly an adult female relative or servant.[32]

A well-ordered family was sober, peaceable, and well-governed. Occasional horror stories indicate that magistrates sometimes made unfortunate choices, but such tales are rare in the town records, suggesting that most masters did not overstep the bounds of what their neighbors and town leaders considered acceptable treatment of servants. The importance of community standards is conveyed especially well in an endorsement from five men "liveing in near neaghbowrwhood with James Thompson," who had been caring for a boy from the Boston Almshouse. When Thompson applied for an indenture, his neighbors vouched "that we have not seen aney thing a mis in the behavor of himself or his wife towards Cornalius Calahoon his boy or aney of there children whatsoever."[33]

New England magistrates and masters did not intend to treat with equity all children who came under their care. They distinguished one child from another in ways that were reflected in contract clauses stipulating the master's obligation to provide literacy training, skill training, and freedom dues. These clauses were never set in type in pre-printed forms; magistrates and masters had to find the right words to describe the future they envisioned for each child. Variations in contract clauses and trends in those variations sketch a picture of what mattered most to New England magistrates and masters between 1720 and 1820.

Binding out children changed in subtle but important ways over that hundred-year period. The contracts themselves became more formal and bureaucratic, reflecting a certain routinization of the institution. In more commercialized towns, where officials had access to printing presses, magistrates faced with increasing numbers of poor children began relying on indentures with pre-printed sections that reduced scribal labor. As early as 1704, Boston magistrates were using pre-printed forms, even before indentures began to be collected systematically.[34] Local officials were using pre-printed indentures by 1740 in New London, 1747 in Providence, and 1774 in New Haven. Handwritten indentures persisted throughout the period in the other towns in this study, all of them less commercialized communities.

The profile of pauper apprentices changed over the period 1720–1820. The average age at binding rose over the 1700s, starting at less than seven years of age in the 1730s, increasing to nine years of age by the 1750s, and peaking at a little over ten years of age in the 1770s, before declining to 9.4 years old in the early 1800s. This rise in the eighteenth century suggests a growing focus on the labor capabilities of children and an increasing desire on the part of masters for older children's potential contributions to the household economy. The proportion of girls in the pauper apprentice population also fluctuated. When all ten communities are considered together, there appears to be little change over the century, the percentage hovering at around 40 percent throughout. However, when Boston is considered separately, a different picture emerges. There, girls constituted about 40 percent of the pauper apprentice population until the postwar period; then, the percentage of girls climbed to 51 percent in the 1780s and stayed at 50 percent throughout the 1790s, very likely reflecting Boston's role in emphasizing the economic importance of female labor in household textile industries (spinning, sewing, weaving, knitting) in late-eighteenth-century New England.[35]

Promises of skill and literacy training increased over the period, as would be expected in a region where literacy in general was rising.[36] But the racialized and gendered nature of these educational clauses steadily rose as well, thus preserving the comparative advantage of white male apprentices. Masters and magistrates customarily stipulated that boys be taught to read, write, and do arithmetic but that girls be taught only to read and write.[37]

They bound a majority of boys to learn some marketable trade but bound all but a handful of girls to learn only "housewifery." They agreed that boys should receive extra freedom dues far more often than girls. In the Boston and Connecticut indentures, the standard was two suits—one for "everyday," "common," or "working" wear and one for Sundays—and in Rhode Island indentures, the standard was one new suit. A third of the Euro-American boys

TABLE 3.1.
Pauper apprentices in Boston

	Girls of color	Euro-American girls	Boys of color	Euro-American boys
Percentage of total apprentices	1% (11)	42% (474)	1% (14)	56% (624)
Mean age at binding	8.54 (11)	9.47 (474)	11.44 (14)	10.9 (624)
	Percentages below are percentages of particular race/gender group			
Reading only promised	0% (0)*	0.8% (4)	0% (0)	0% (0)
Reading and writing promised	10% (1)*	84% (394)	14% (2)	0.5% (3)
Reading, writing, cyphering promised	90% (9)*	15% (71)	86% (12)	99.5% (609)
Skill training—housewifery	82% (9)	99% (472)		
Skill training—husbandry			21% (3)	38% (248)
Skill training—trade	0.0% (0)	0.4% (2)	57% (8)	47% (293)
Skill training—seafaring			0% (0)	8% (47)
Skill training—servant	18% (2)	0.0% (0)	0% (0)	0.0% (0)
No information about skill training	0.0% (0)	0.4% (2)	21% (3)	6% (36)

*In Boston, all indentures for girls of color except one occurred after 1785, by which time all female pauper apprentices were promised reading, writing and cyphering in their contracts.

Note: N = 1,123. Number of indentures with available information in parentheses.

TABLE 3.2.
Pauper apprentices in Connecticut and Rhode Island

	Girls of color	Euro-American girls	Boys of color	Euro-American boys
Percentage of total apprentices	8% (75)	26% (258)	12% (121)	54% (537)
Mean age at binding	6.94 (47)	9.13 (137)	8.33 (92)	10.9 (347)
	Percentages below are percentages of particular race/gender group			
Reading only promised	25% (19)	21% (54)	6% (7)	1% (5)
Reading and writing promised	9% (7)	34% (89)	10% (12)	11% (58)
Reading, writing, cyphering promised	0.0% (0)	7% (17)	24% (29)	56% (300)
No information about education	65% (49)	38% (98)	60% (73)	32% (174)
Education subtotal	100% (75)	100% (258)	100% (121)	100% (537)
Skill training—housewifery	24% (18)	39% (101)		
Skill training—husbandry			9% (11)	16% (86)
Skill training—trade	1% (1)	5.5% (14)	4% (5)	36% (195)
Skill training—seafaring			2.5% (3)	4% (22)
Skill training—servant	4% (3)	0.0% (0)	8% (10)	0.0% (0)
No information about skill training	71% (53)	55.5% (143)	76% (92)	43% (234)
Skill training subtotal	100% (75)	100% (258)	100% (121)	100% (537)

Note: N = 991. Number of indentures with available information in parentheses.

in Boston received additional cash payments in Boston; 15 percent of the same group in Connecticut and Rhode Island received additional payment—sheep, a horse, cooper's tools, or a gun. No girls received extra payment in Boston; 11 percent of them received some small cash or in-kind payment in Connecticut and Rhode Island. The general picture is consistent with the overview in chapter 1—magistrates and masters designed pauper apprenticeship to give most boys a shot at independent adulthood and to keep most girls in dependent positions as housewives and servants.

The racial profile of apprentices changed over the century. The Boston data are presented separately because of the strange absence of children of color among its pauper apprentices. Only 3 percent of the Boston contracts were for children of color, but this does not mesh with Boston's official activity regarding such children. In 1723, the Boston town meeting ordered that "every free Indian, Negro, or Molatto shall bind out, all their children at or before they arrive to the age of four years to some English master, and upon neglect thereof the selectmen or overseers of the poor shall be empowered to bind out all such children till the age of twenty one years."[38] Further, the Boston Almshouse records show that numerous children of color came into the almshouse and were "placed" and "bound" out of it. Either these children did not receive formal indentures or their indentures were not preserved. The absence of the indentures signals that race mattered to Massachusetts masters and magistrates; they treated children—or their indentures—differently when they perceived them as something other than "white." Magistrates in Connecticut and Rhode Island were more forthright—about 20 percent of the children they bound were described as being of Native American and African ancestry. In Providence, South Kingstown, Westerly, and New London, where the population of color was especially concentrated, the percentage of pauper apprentices with racial labels increased over time, rising from about 20 percent in the 1730s to 50 percent by 1800.[39] Over the entire period, in these four communities, children of color constituted about 40 percent of pauper apprentices, a figure that is significantly disproportionate to the number of people of color in the general population. It suggests that in these New England communities, magistrates and masters increasingly saw pauper apprenticeship as an institution for children they identified as not white, as was the case in Maryland and Virginia.[40]

Magistrates and masters put children of color at a disadvantage in literacy education, skill training, and freedom dues (see tables 3.1 and 3.2). While boys of color sometimes received less education than Euro-American boys, they were still much more likely to learn arithmetic than any girls were. The biggest losers in terms of literacy training were girls of color. In a majority of cases (65 percent), there was no mention of literacy for these girls, either because the clerk forgot to write it in or because magistrates and masters never intended for the child to receive any such training. When girls of color were taught anything at all, it was usually reading and nothing else. Magistrates and masters omitted a promise of skill training in indentures for children of color at a much greater rate than in indentures for Euro-American children. Boys of color were occasionally promised training in farming or a trade, but more frequently they were trained only as servants or as common laborers, without any special skills. Girls of color were less likely than Euro-American girls to be taught housewifery skills, less likely than any other boys or girls to be taught a trade; they were more likely to be trained as "servants." Magistrates and masters also put children of color at a disadvantage in freedom dues. In Boston, a little over 17 percent of the boys of color received money as part of freedom dues; in Rhode Island and Connecticut only 2.5 percent received either money or commodities. No girls of color at all received extra payments in the Boston contracts, and only six girls received any extra payment in Connecticut and Rhode Island.

Regardless of the future that magistrates and masters envisioned for pauper apprentices, what kind of adulthood did these children actually experience? Anecdotal evidence suggests that their fates were as varied and individual as the indentures themselves. A few children were wildly successful, following Benjamin Franklin's well-known path from obscurity to fame. Isaiah Thomas, bound out by the Boston overseers of the poor in 1756 to Boston printer and bookseller Zachariah Fowle, became a renowned printer himself.[41] Less spectacular but still very sturdy success attended Phineas Edwards, bound out as a pauper apprentice to William Thurston, a prominent inhabitant of Hopkinton, Rhode Island, in 1765. As an adult, Edwards married and fathered eight children, was elected to various minor public positions, and helped lead a militia company.[42] Thomas Banks, bound out from the Boston Almshouse in 1760, found a considerate master in William Williams, who transferred his indenture to a local shoemaker when it became apparent that Banks was physically unable to do the heavy labor of farming. As an adult, Banks served for Hatfield in the Continental Army, married a Hatfield girl, and became a permanent, well-regarded resident in the town where he had grown up as a pauper apprentice.[43]

On the other hand, many pauper apprentices failed to prosper. Between 30 and 40 percent of people warned out of Rhode Island towns in the 1750–1800 period testified that they had been bound out as pauper apprentices in their childhood.[44] This correlation between bound labor in childhood and transience and dependency in adulthood (magistrates considered transients "likely to become chargeable to the town") suggests that pauper apprenticeship was not a secure route to independent adulthood, even for Euro-American boys. Nor was it intended to be. Magistrates and masters were less concerned with individual children's fates than they were with the well-being of the community they governed. Maintaining a stable and well-ordered society in which the already prosperous might continue to prosper was their shared concern.

Pauper apprenticeship rescued many children from desperate situations. They received food, shelter, and clothing; they were incorporated into a household. Equally important, from the point of view of magistrates and masters, these children were prepared for a future that was suited to their race and sex. Binding out was not intended to give poor children opportunities "above their station." It was not a progressive system but one designed to maintain the status quo—to train children to labor as their parents had labored, in their appropriate stations. Pauper apprenticeship carried forward the racial and sexual conventions and stratifications that supported the hierarchical nature of town life in southern New England. Together magistrates and masters sought community stability through the business of binding out poor children in indentures that were calibrated to reflect each child's particular place in that community.

CHAPTER FOUR

Orphans in City and Countryside in Nineteenth-Century Maryland

T. STEPHEN WHITMAN

Orphan apprenticeship sprang into being in Maryland in the 1630s and survived into the early twentieth century. It originated as an adaptive response to maintaining families in an immigrant society racked by high mortality. Colonists drew on English apprenticeship in husbandry, pauper apprenticeship, laws regulating orphans' estates, and legal forms governing relations between employers and laborers to cobble together practices to care for parentless children. Orphans' courts monitored estate administration for the fortunate and bound out poorer children to caregivers who benefited from the children's labor. In the eighteenth century, as Jean B. Russo and J. Elliott Russo show in chapter 10, apprenticeship developed into a three-tiered institution, featuring craft training and education for moderately affluent children, and manual labor for the poor and illegitimate children.

This essay looks to apprenticeship in nineteenth-century Maryland. Historians have used declension models for apprenticeship's character as a craft-training process for white boys. But that conceit misses the presence of African Americans as apprentices, and the renewed prominence of farm labor or domestic service. *Specialization* and *particularization* are more useful terms, reflecting the evolution of new practices for different kinds of orphans, distinguished by race, religion, or perceived criminal tendency. Ultimately, *simplification* or *privatization* might best describe the how orphan apprenticeship reverted to its earliest form as an exchange of maintenance of youths for their unskilled labor. Courts, masters, apprentices, and their kin contended and cooperated in reshaping this most elastic of social institutions.

The pace of change varied dramatically according to the local economies in which orphans were found. From the 1780s through the 1820s, Baltimore's use of bound laborers, including orphans, diverged from the nearby counties that were becoming its hinterlands. Strong demand for workers in Baltimore preserved apprenticeship as a trade school for the first three decades of the nineteenth century. Counties within Baltimore's economic orbit, however, such as Kent or Talbot in the Eastern Shore's mixed-agriculture belt or tobacco-growing Prince George's on the lower Western Shore rapidly recast apprenticeship to emphasize marshaling farm labor as early as the 1790s. In another variation, Washington County in western Maryland enjoyed a modest spurt of diversification. Craftsmen there, protected from competition with Baltimore until railroads and canals arrived during the 1830s, also sustained apprenticeship as a trade school.

Race and gender mattered, too, in creating varying local histories of apprenticeship. Black children accepted indentures with less frequent and valuable promises of training, education, and maintenance. By the 1850s and 1860s, orphans' courts rarely mandated craft training, as orphan apprenticeship confronted the challenges of urban poverty and black emancipation. The sources for this study are Orphans' Court indentures from Baltimore, Kent, Prince George's, Talbot, and Washington Counties from the 1780s to the 1860s. In each place apprenticeship declined as a labor institution and as a means of supporting orphaned children, although at different times and at different paces.[1]

Most residents of Baltimore County lived in the City of Baltimore, which by 1810 had mushroomed into a sprawling port with fifty thousand residents. Craft enterprises centered on trades such as shipbuilding, ropemaking, iron founding, and sailmaking as well as clothing, building, and food processing. White laborers, slaves, and free African Americans flocked to town, blacks to find work and income with which to purchase freedom through manumission, for themselves or kin.

Prince George's County remained committed to tobacco-growing by slave-owning planters whose chattels comprised half the population. Both whites and free blacks migrated elsewhere from 1800 onward. Talbot and Kent had shifted from tobacco to grain and mixed agriculture in the eighteenth century. A modest expansion of craft work occurred in the county seats, Easton and Chestertown. But manufacturing stalled as cheap goods from Baltimore squeezed local craftspeople out of the market.[2] The move away from tobacco rendered slavery less profitable and manumission more attractive. In Talbot, about one in three blacks was free by 1820, partly due to manumissions by local Quakers or Methodists and partly from the efforts of free blacks to liberate kinfolk. In such counties, black orphans were frequently apprenticed involuntarily as farm laborers and servants. Washington County had fairly few African Americans, enslaved or free, but could count on steady in-migration of whites taking up new land; this region relied heavily on white apprentices.

All of the rural counties ultimately became satellites of Baltimore, where from the 1780s to 1820, slaves and apprentices helped build the city. With the convict servant trade from Britain ended after independence and the migration of German redemptioners all but eliminated during the Napoleonic Wars, slaveholding and binding apprentices increased.[3]

The presence of slaves in city workshops swayed masters and white bound boys into refashioning apprenticeship; likewise, slaves and their owners renegotiated urban slavery, borrowing aspects of apprenticeship to define manumission and self-purchase. Owners wanted to dangle the bait of gradual manumission to motivate slaves, but African Americans coopted the process, generating the nation's largest free black population, who supplanted both black and white bound workers.

In 1810, two-fifths of Baltimore's taxed craftsmen held slaves. At the same time, half of Baltimore's teenage boys were bound out to crafts. Many masters both owned slaves and bound apprentices.[4] Slaves were most common in trades that featured heavy labor, such as brickmaking, ropemaking, ironworking, and shipbuilding. Apprentices predominated in trades with greater fluctuations in demand or in which strength was less critical, such as carpentry, hatting, painting, and shoemaking.

Parents who chose a trade for their sons favored higher-status crafts relatively free of slaves, while courts commonly bound out orphans to trades in which slaves were numerous, such as nailmaking or cigarmaking.[5] Occupations requiring significant capitalization, such as millwrights and coachmakers, included only a few practitioners, few of whom held slaves. Of eight millwrights in Baltimore in 1813, only one held slaves, while fifteen of seventeen apprentices (88 percent) bound out to millwrights did so under voluntary indentures. None of the identifiable coachmakers held slaves; eight of ten apprentices (80 percent) bound out to them were voluntary indentures.[6]

Parental channeling of sons away from trades with many slaves generated "crowding" in those they favored. As voluntarily bound apprentices thronged to certain sectors of the labor market, they tended to receive less valuable promises of maintenance and training than boys bound out by Baltimore's courts, who were spread across all trades.[7]

Slaveholding craftsmen had other effects on apprenticeship in Baltimore. Early-nineteenth-century apprentices in northeastern states won greater autonomy by shortening indenture lengths or substituting cash wages for maintenance, but they did not do so in Baltimore.[8] Between the 1790s and 1830, indenture lengths remained stable at six to seven years, and no more than a handful of agreements promised wages. Availability of slaves as an alternative may have helped masters to preserve apprenticeship as a maintenance for labor exchange, allowing them to resist demands for wages.[9]

White servitude also modified slavery, particularly with regard to gradual manumission. During the late eighteenth century, Maryland moved from tobacco monoculture to less labor-intensive crops, and slaveholders began to manumit significant numbers of slaves, generally after years of service under a will or deed promising eventual freedom.[10] By the 1790s, slaves thus "entitled to freedom" or "having a term of years to serve" had become common, especially in Baltimore.

Both slaves and apprentices contributed to the tremendous growth of the city. In 1816, the Baltimore County orphans' court registered nearly four hundred indentures promising to train boys in the "art and mystery" of no fewer than eighty trades. Perhaps two thousand boys were then serving apprenticeships, to learn not only shoemaking or tailoring, but also sugar refining, pianoforte making, and bridle and bit making.[11] A strong economy increased the attractions of binding out a child worker. Apprentices made up one-twentieth of the city's entire population, and as many as two-thirds of Baltimore's white males between the ages of fourteen and twenty-one were or had been indented.[12] Nearly all white apprentice boys, whether bound out by parents or courts, were learning a craft or trade.[13] Apprenticeship as a trade school peaked in the early 1800s, two generations after the spread of republican sensibilities that some historians regard as the death knell of indentured apprenticeship.

The ages at which orphans were bound underline the drive for craft trainees in early national Baltimore, as distinct from the simplifying economies of its hinterlands. Between 1794 and 1830, only 16 percent of the city's apprentices were nine or younger, while 58 percent were fourteen or older, as table 4.1

TABLE 4.1.
Age distribution of orphan apprentices, 1794–1830

Age at binding	Percent in age group by county			
	Baltimore	Prince George's	Talbot	Washington
0–1	0	5.2	1.5	.3
2–3	.9	3.9	4.5	2.4
4–5	2.5	3.9	4.5	3.8
6–7	4.3	13	10.5	6.2
8–9	8.1	11.7	23.8	6.2
10–11	11.4	15.6	19.5	7.9
12–13	15.1	7.9	13.4	15.2
14–15	22.4	18.2	9	14.1
>15	35.4	20.8	13.4	43.8
Under 10	15.8	37.7	44.8	18.7
14 and older	57.8	39	22.4	57.9
N =	1687	77	67	290

illustrates. City masters had little interest in maintaining a child until he could work usefully in a craft shop. By comparison, 38 percent of orphans bound out in rural Talbot County were under ten, 45 percent of those in Prince George's County. In rural but diversifying Washington County, as in Baltimore, few orphans took up indentures so early.[14]

As the Russos note for the eighteenth century, few children, urban or rural, were formally apprenticed due to illegitimacy or abandonment. Talbot County had the highest proportion, at 7.5 percent, of bindings attributed to abandoned children. Such cases of abandonment in other counties generally indicated a husband who had deserted a family, perhaps by going to sea or joining the army. In Talbot, different situations obtained. Eli Stevens was bound out because "his mother is dead and his father is a slave." Henry Gassaway, son of a slave father, was indented because "his mother has removed to Baltimore." Gassaway's married sister consented to the indenture; perhaps money sent home from Gassaway's mother had temporarily supported Henry until his binding.[15] Gassaway's story exemplifies the perils of black families' transition from slavery to freedom. In Baltimore, where thousands of free people of color resided, mutual aid rendered cases like Gassaway's rare. In rural counties, where higher proportions of blacks remained enslaved and economic opportunities for free blacks were few, more "abandoned" black children were indented.

Baltimore bindings leaned heavily toward boys. In contrast to Boston, where at times over half of apprentices were girls, typically no more than one-fifth of children bound out in Maryland were female. Whether because employers were uninterested in binding out girls to learn trades or because parents and courts were reluctant to remove girls from parental protection, girls were bound out only infrequently and received only maintenance and basic education.

By the close of the antebellum period, apprenticeship had discarded its role as a trade school. Baltimore was still booming; the 1860 census recorded over 200,000 residents. But the 1858 indenture registers counted only 110 new apprenticeships, just 66 of them for white boys. The likelihood of a teenage boy working as an apprentice had fallen to one in forty.[16] Over a third of this dwindling group were bound to farm labor or domestic service, and some

TABLE 4.2.
Status of children bound, 1794–1830 (percent by county)

	Baltimore	Prince George's	Talbot	Washington
Abandoned	1.6	1.3	7.5	2.4
Illegitimate	.3	3.9	3.0	4.1
Indigent	3.2	7.8	7.5	3.5
Orphaned	94.9	87.0	82.0	90.0
N =	1687	77	67	290

70 percent of these indentures were court-directed, a proportion that climbed to over 90 percent in the 1860s. Most of these apprenticeships promised only to feed and clothe a boy in return for farm labor. Both the voluntary binding of boys by kin and the use of orphan apprenticeship to teach craft skills had all but vanished. Only after these changes had occurred did black children begin to be indented in significant numbers; before 1850, when apprenticeship retained vestiges of its status as a ladder of advancement in the trades, disproportionately few African Americans were bound out in Baltimore.[17]

Many factors contributed to the institution's reshaping. The Panic of 1819, which hit Baltimore earlier than other eastern cities, produced a more profound recession than elsewhere. Prolonged hard times lasted well into the 1820s, and fewer craftspeople or manufacturers chose to bind or purchase labor for long periods. Slaves, who had made up about one-tenth of Baltimore's population and a larger share of its workforce, comprised only 5 percent of the city's residents by 1830; the proportion of craftsmen who held slaves also declined. Apprentice indentures fell even more dramatically: while nearly 400 boys a year were bound before 1820, fewer than 200 a year became apprentices thereafter. An institution that embraced half the adolescent males in the 1810s accounted for only one-sixth of them by 1830.[18]

The dual downturn suggests that employers operating in the looser labor market of the 1820s felt less pressure to assume the obligations of long-term bound labor. Nowhere was this more evident than in the large manufactories that had once relied heavily on apprentices.

When Baltimore investors first established large cotton mills around 1810, they staffed them with bound workers. During the Union Mills's first five years, more than 60 boys were bound to learn "cotton manufacturing, including carding, spinning, and weaving, or any of those trades."[19] The Baltimore Manufacturing Company's agent, Nathan Levering, bound 41 boys; Edward Gray and Company signed up 19; and the Washington Cotton Manufacturing Company more than a dozen.[20] The mills preferred to secure the labor of respectable white boys, and at first had their pick of young hands: *all* of the indentures entered into by the Union Mills and Gray and Company before 1816 were contracted voluntarily with parents.[21]

These firms weathered the post-1815 resumption of British competition but discontinued their use of apprentice boys. By 1820, the two largest cotton manufacturers were chiefly hiring girls. The Union Manufacturing Company had 104 girls tending its bobbins, but only 16 boys and 10 men; the Baltimore Steam Works engaged 50 girls and no boys. Nathan Levering, now the proprietor of both the Powhatan Cotton Mills and the Washington Cotton Factory, no longer indented apprentices, but hired many girls for his mills.[22]

Girls seem almost never to have been indentured to textile manufacturers or promised craft training.[23] Those bound out were generally placed as servants.

In the decades before 1820, the heyday of craft training for boys, an average of only 53 white girls a year were being indentured, compared to more than 300 white boys. A few indentures promised to teach girls millinery, mantua-making, or tailoring, and one young woman was bound to an umbrella maker, but well over 90 percent of girls were to learn housekeeping, household sewing, and needlework.

In the mills, as would later prove the case with free blacks, employers did not find it necessary to offer girls the benefits of apprenticeship. They could obtain the labor of female operatives, to whom most craft occupations were closed, more cheaply than that of apprentice boys. While such putative savings were not large, Baltimore's cloth makers felt the need to economize, and abandoned apprenticeship. They did not, however, commercialize the fictive family relationship that governed their dealings with male apprentices; instead, they turned to girls, who were paid less than white male workers, remained subordinate even while they received cash wages, and did not require the quasi-paternal authority that restrained male apprentices. By the 1830s, Baltimore clothing manufacturers employed more than two thousand persons, a large proportion of them children receiving cash wages. By increasing the ability of girls to contribute directly to families' maintenance, early textile factories reduced the need to bind out their brothers to unmechanized occupations.[24]

Thus, the decline of slavery in Baltimore did not generate a countervailing increase in the number of apprentice girls, white or black, bound out as house servants, although it did do so in well-to-do urban households elsewhere in the upper South. The parents and possibly the girls themselves preferred their daughters to earn cash in the mills. The average number of female apprentices bound each year dropped by 40 percent between 1800 and 1850, even as the city's population doubled and redoubled.[25]

As parents, especially of African-American children, became more reluctant to bind either sons or daughters, the Baltimore orphans' court assumed a gradually increasing share of the business of managing and placing children, as table 4.3 illustrates.

TABLE 4.3.
Voluntary and court-directed bindings in Baltimore
(percent bound voluntarily)

Decade	White boys	Black boys	White girls	Black girls
1800s	62%	64%	52%	50%
1810s	52	56	36	43
1820s	58	39	34	18
1830s	46	19	23	15
1840s	38	20	20	14

Craftspeople who did seek apprentices in later decades sought to reduce commitments to the boys they bound to lessen labor costs. Masters sought to cut expenditures for apprentices' maintenance, education, and freedom dues. Larger-scale employers also tried to control boys' work time more closely and to improve productivity by specializing them in a few tasks. The last aim appeared in indentures promising to teach the "pulling and cutting branch of the hatter's trade" or "making soles and heels for ladies' shoes."[26]

Over the first half of the nineteenth century, a slowly increasing proportion of masters and the adult kin of apprentices framed indentures containing one or more of these modifications. In contrast, the orphans' courts continued to promise the full range of benefits to white boys. As a result, orphans became harder and harder to place, especially in Baltimore, and judges grudgingly began to adopt practices that masters and parents had created informally. By the 1840s and 1850s, many court-bound orphans did not receive a full slate of benefits.

An examination of changes in the freedom dues promised apprentices illustrates the gradual alteration of apprentice benefits. In 1800, over 90 percent of court-initiated indentures simply stated that the apprentice should receive "customary" freedom dues, then understood as a suit of clothes, although a handful stipulated the amount and quality of the apparel. Very occasionally, indentures promised cash, usually between ten and thirty dollars. A variation sometimes allowed the apprentice a choice between a suit of clothes "worth twenty dollars" or that amount in cash. Only two or three percent promised an apprentice the tools of his trade. Before 1830, only a tiny fraction of apprentices, orphaned or otherwise, received no promises of freedom dues (see table 4.4). In the decade 1800–1809, 88 percent of voluntarily bindings and 95 percent of court-initiated ones included freedom dues.[27]

Children who did not receive dues tended to be older when bound: a shorter term meant less profit for the master, which could be redressed by eliminating freedom dues. Some 30 percent of duesless boys were eighteen or older when bound, versus only 10 percent of boys promised dues.[28] The provision of "customary" dues applied most strongly to female apprentices: 95 of 100 voluntarily

TABLE 4.4.
Freedom dues paid Baltimore apprentices, 1800–1830 (percent by category)

	None	Clothing	Cash	Customary	Other
Voluntarily bound					
Male (N = 1820)	14.5%	5.9%	9.0%	68.9%	1.7%
Female (N = 234)	9	6	2.1	82.9	0
Court bound					
Male (N = 1339)	3.5	3.1	4.8	88.2	.4
Female (N = 348)	.3	2.0	4.9	92.5	.3

bound girls were promised freedom dues, as were all of the girls bound by Baltimore's courts in the years 1800–1809.[29]

Masters' willingness to provide freedom dues dropped off during lean times after 1819: the ratio of voluntarily bound children with no hope of dues jumped to about 25 percent.[30] A larger proportion of contracts specified a sum of money or a certain amount of clothing of a given quality. Confidence in "customary" freedom dues was eroding. After 1840, more than four-fifths of indentures for white apprentices in Baltimore promised cash or the right to choose between cash and a suit of comparable value.[31] This late-emerging practice gave apprentices more control and may have made their status seem less servile. Nonetheless, as male apprenticeship ceased to be a trade school, widespread agreement about its terms crumbled. Cash payments rendered masters impervious to upward price fluctuations, unlike provisions for a "customary" suit of clothes.

Similar concerns shaped negotiations over educational promises in nineteenth-century urban indentures. Masters strove to define and minimize obligations, while courts continued to mandate education, at least for white boys. But the diminution of private education benefits was dramatic. During the first decade of the 1800s, 80 percent of voluntarily bound boys in Baltimore

TABLE 4.5.
Education of Baltimore apprentices, 1800–1870

1800–1830	Voluntarily bound		Court bound	
	Male	Female	Male	Female
None	23.4%	22.3%	13.5%	13.4%
R	.9	11	1.2	9.9
R/W	2.5	48.1	2	52.2
R/W/C	38.3	8	67.2	22.1
Term	32.2	10.1	15.4	2.4
Other	2.7	.4	.6	0
	(N=1820)	(N=234)	(N=1339)	(N=348)

1830–1870	Voluntarily bound		Court bound	
	Male	Female	Male	Female
None	53.3%	42.9%	21.5%	19.1%
R	0	10.7	2.2	2.2
R/W	.3	15.5	1.8	38
R/W/C	14.7	25	52.3	27.8
Term	28.3	4.8	14.5	6.1
Other	3.4	1.2	7.6	6.8
	(N=580)	(N=84)	(N=1201)	(N=348)

received a promise of schooling (see table 4.5). By the 1850s, that proportion had plummeted to 20 percent. Meanwhile, courts, orphanages, and related groups insisted that orphan boys learn to "read, write, and cypher to the rule of three," in 80 to 90 percent of their indentures.

Courts of the nineteenth century gradually raised the educational standard for white girls. Before 1820, girls were typically to be taught to read and write, but few were promised training in arithmetic, a skill deemed superfluous. But city life demanded new talents, including the ability to buy, sell, or reckon accounts with a shopkeeper. Between 1820 and 1850, nearly half of female white orphans were learning to cypher "to the rule of three," so they, like boys, could calculate prices and avoid being cheated.[32]

Nonetheless, by the mid–nineteenth century, masters had largely ceased to oversee the education of poor and orphaned children. With the rapid spread of tax-supported, tuition-driven, and charitable schools, apprenticeship shed its educational attributes. Tuition-paid schooling had been available from early in the eighteenth century, even in some rural areas, such as Kent County. But would-be students in nineteenth-century Baltimore could choose from nighttime instruction for working men and boys or Sunday schools sponsored to spread the reading of the gospels: Baltimore created an association to promote and administer Sunday schools in 1816.[33] In 1818 Baltimore witnessed the formation of its first Lancasterian school, following a visit by Joseph Lancaster, whose system relied on senior pupils acting as "monitors," conveying lessons to younger students.[34]

Meanwhile the Maryland Assembly incorporated orphanages as schools and as refuges for abandoned or "unprotected" children. Between 1799 and 1820, the legislature chartered four such organizations, beginning with the Benevolent Society of Baltimore. Protestant orphanages were soon complemented by a Catholic group, St. Mary's Orphan Female Society of Baltimore, which opened in 1818 to care for, educate, and place as apprentices orphan Catholic girls.

The directors of St. Mary's oversaw a two-tiered operation, housing a handful of children and running a day school that catered to tuition-paying or charity pupils. Inmates, sometimes formally bound, lived on the premises until their education was deemed complete. At age twelve or fourteen, they were bound out again by the directors to respectable homes. But most children attended school at St. Mary's without coming under its custody.[35] Early nineteenth-century urban orphanages thus filled a function of kin in preventing very young children from being bound as laboring apprentices.

In the public sector after 1793, county boards called "Trustees of the Poor" operated almshouses and cared for the children of "vagrant" or "worthless" parents. The Trustees of the Poor could bind children out and require their masters to educate them. But the development of schools, orphanages, and juvenile prisons as educational institutions had, by the 1850s, largely eliminated the need for masters to school apprentices.

In the interim, masters, courts, and apprentices and their kin bargained and articulated a diverse range of educational promises. Broadly speaking, the process passed through three stages. Before 1820, most masters were legally committed to insuring male apprentices' competence in reading, writing, and arithmetic. During the 1820s and 1830s, masters sidestepped the demanding standard of education until competence and refashioned their promises to provide a fixed number of months of education.

Between 1820 and 1840, nearly 40 percent of voluntarily-bound boys and about 15 percent of girls had indentures with finely drawn distinctions about the extent, timing, and content of education. George Nailer's indenture conveyed no promise of education, but it did guarantee him the "privilege of attending Sunday school." Thomas Smyth secured an agreement from Abraham Howell that he continue his education, but only "at the apprentice's expense." John Harman agreed to see that Christian Schmidt, age sixteen, be taught to read, write, and cypher, but Harman was accountable only "if the said apprentice be capable of learning."[36]

Other indentures specified "day" or "night" schooling. Masters disliked day schooling requirements, as they lost apprentices' labor thereby, but apprentices prized it. Some apprentices were to receive some education "every year" of their indentures to insure continuity of learning, while others could attend school only in the final year of their indenture or after their eighteenth birthdays.[37] Occasionally, parents or courts stipulated that German-speaking masters provide education "in English" or "at an English school." Some French or German parents sought to insure instruction in a child's native tongue. After 1840, however, bargains over the amount of education gave way in voluntary indentures to the virtual abandonment of schooling. Masters who bound orphans still vowed to insure that their charges could read, write, and cypher but did so in the knowledge that these boys had already been schooled.

While promises concerning education and freedom dues were curtailed during the early nineteenth century, those for basic support were not. Masters still had to provide "meat, drink, lodging, clothing, and washing" for voluntarily and court-bound boys and girls. While consensus about the place of education in apprenticeship might wax or wane, few masters succeeded in chipping away at maintenance obligations, although some tried.

As with other factors, few masters reined in costs before the 1820s. Between 1800 and 1819, barely 1 percent of voluntary indentures and less than one half of 1 percent of orphans' court bindings exempted a master from clothing an apprentice or commuted that promise into a cash payment. Another 1.5 percent of voluntary indentures promised wages in lieu of maintenance. But nearly 98 percent of indentures expressed maintenance obligations in traditional forms.[38] That proportion fell a bit during the 1820s and 1830s, when 88 percent of voluntary indentures and 95 percent of institutional ones promised full maintenance.[39] Even during the 1840s and 1850s, over 80 percent of voluntarily-bound boys received full maintenance promises, although some masters succeeded in monetizing promises of clothing.[40]

Even these insignificant shifts, however, failed to occur in female apprentice contracts. Perhaps masters expected girls to sew their own clothes and were less concerned about expenses. Or they may not have reconceived white females as prospective parties to contracts based on cash. Whatever the cause, virtually no white girls in nineteenth-century Baltimore were offered money in lieu of clothing, or wages instead of maintenance.[41]

These data do not prove that masters were unconcerned about maintenance costs. Unwillingness to feed, clothe, and house child laborers certainly contributed to employers' waning interest in binding apprentices.[42] But the contrast between the relative flexibility of apprenticeship regarding education and freedom dues and its rigidity regarding basic maintenance suggests the limits of the institution's flexibility.

The actions of parents, children, judges, and masters defined apprenticeship within constraints imposed by cultural constructions of child and parenthood. Apprentices' masters assumed the role of surrogate parents and, where feeding, clothing, and sheltering adolescents was a factor, could not remold indentures to their ends. They could abandon the institution altogether by signing private contracts with a boy's father to provide wages rather than maintenance, arrangements that could be enforced via civil law.

By 1850, the attenuation of apprenticeship had reversed a once notable flow of country boys to Baltimore to take up indentures. In 1800, boys migrated from neighboring counties, the Eastern Shore, Pennsylvania, and Virginia to learn from Baltimore craftsmen.[43] By the 1850s, however, Baltimore was exporting apprentices, as the city's new House of Refuge bound out dozens of white boys to farm work in outlying rural areas. In a development that harked back to its seventeenth-century origins, orphan apprentices again exchanged agricultural labor for sustenance.

The recrudescence of apprenticeship in Baltimore was hardly unique. In some rural counties, apprenticeship had already been stripped to its simplest form and had shed its emphasis on craft training, education, or freedom dues as early as the 1780s and 1790s. Rural artisans faced severe competition from the rise of the city's manufacturing sector and the expanding reach of Baltimore's merchants. By the early 1800s, few specialized artisans in Baltimore's hinterland could compete in price or volume with urban counterparts. Silversmiths or coachmakers found it difficult to survive in Chestertown or Oxford, and even blacksmiths, shoemakers, and carpenters found their work reduced to simple repair and maintenance tasks.[44]

In such economies, apprenticeship assumed a two-tiered character during the first half of the nineteenth century. The few white men who indentured sons placed them as blacksmiths, carpenters, shoemakers, or tailors who learned the basic tasks of their trades. Boys did not voluntarily take up farming indentures; in Talbot County, only 4 percent were bound by parents to agriculture, domestic service, or common labor.[45] White boys bound out by the courts, however, wielded hoes and scythes rather than awls or chisels: over 60 percent of orphans served as agricultural laborers throughout the first half of the nineteenth century, a repetition of eighteenth-century practices.[46]

Rural justices, like their Baltimore colleagues, imposed higher educational standards than parents and kin could negotiate from masters (see table 4.6). But fewer country boys received an education, whoever bound them. Only 48 percent of male white orphans in Talbot and 64 percent in Prince George's Counties received any promise of education, compared to 80 to 90 percent in Baltimore. Less than a third of voluntarily bound boys in the countryside were to be educated at all, versus two-thirds in Baltimore.[47] The close bargaining that characterized Baltimore's voluntary apprenticeships largely disappeared in the tobacco and grain counties: only one-sixth of Talbot or Prince George's masters fixed schooling obligations at a certain number of months. Again, Washington County, with its small urban centers and growing craft sector, more nearly resembled Baltimore than the purely agricultural areas. Not all country people were less concerned about formal education; some rural craft masters worried about capping costs or losing apprentices' time to schooling, as the popularity of promising a specific term of education in Washington County demonstrates.[48]

Perceptual shifts about the connection between apprenticeship and education did not follow Baltimore's pattern. Throughout the early nineteenth century, as apprenticeship dwindled in importance, about one-third of parentally-bound boys and half of those indented by courts received a standardized and unspecified promise to be taught to read, write, and cypher or "cast accounts";

TABLE 4.6.
Education promised white male apprentices in rural counties, 1800–1850

	Voluntarily bound			Court bound		
	Pr. Geo.	Talbot	Wash.	Pr. Geo.	Talbot	Wash.
None	57.8%	80.7%	25.7%	36.2%	51.9%	10.7%
R	0	0	0	0	0	0
R/W	2.4	0	0	0	1.9	0
R/W/C	31.3	2.6	15.6	55.1	25.9	40.4
Term	8.5	16.7	58.7	8.7	18.5	48.9
Other	0	0	0	0	1.9	0
	(N=83)	(N=84)	(N=221)	(N=69)	(N=54)	(N=299)

most of the rest were left to shift for themselves. A similar situation prevailed for white girls. Only two-fifths were promised any education, and only 9 percent were to learn math skills: adolescent women learning to be rural "house servants" or "spinsters" would have to acquire arithmetical knowledge on their own, if at all.[49] Specialized public institutions did not arise to supply education either: Talbot and Prince George's Counties erected no orphanages to school poor children during the heyday of Christian benevolence, nor did they create manual labor schools in the 1830s or Houses of Refuge for troubled juveniles in the 1840s.

The handling of freedom dues and maintenance in agricultural counties also evinced an ongoing sense of apprenticeship as an exchange of work for food, clothing, and shelter. Half of the boys bound out by parents in Talbot or Prince George's received no freedom dues (see table 4.7). Courts insisted on such dues more often than fathers; 70 to 85 percent of court-bound boys were promised either clothing or a choice between cash and clothing upon completing their terms. In Washington County, most boys could expect to receive cash or clothing upon turning twenty-one.

Girls, who were nearly all bound by courts, were also to collect freedom dues about three-quarters of the time, although less than a quarter would receive cash.[50] Boys bound to trades were no more likely than those performing farm labor to receive dues, and age at binding did not affect the chances of receiving them.

Rural indentures continued to promise full maintenance to apprentices throughout the first half of the nineteenth century; barely 5 percent of white boys in Talbot or Prince George's and no white girls were given clothing allowances or wages instead of part or all of their maintenance.[51]

Negotiations surrounding apprentices' work in grain harvests further illustrate how local labor markets shaped the seasonal value of apprentices' labor and created tensions in the master-apprentice relationship. Maryland's apprentice law of 1793 authorized masters to put male apprentices to work in the wheat, corn, or rye harvests, regardless of a boy's trade; as the Russos note, promises of

TABLE 4.7.
Freedom dues for white male apprentices in rural counties, 1800–1850

	Voluntarily bound			Court bound		
	Pr. Geo.	Talbot	Wash.	Pr. Geo.	Talbot	Wash.
None	49.4%	58.3%	13.3%	30.4%	14.8%	12.7%
Clothing	44.5	26.2	19.4	40.5	42.6	15.3
Cash	3.6	15.5	66.5	0	42.6	71.4
Customary	0	0	0	26.6	0	0
Other	2.4	0	.8	2.4	0	.6
	(N=83)	(N=84)	(N=221)	(N=69)	(N=54)	(N=299)

craft training did not exclude agricultural employments. Many artisans split time between workbench and grain field and wanted to command apprentices' labor and the prime wages it could generate during the hectic harvest season. Apprentices, on the other hand, yearned to mow and reap for their own gain by hiring out to farmers.

In urban Baltimore, few craftsmen doubled as farmers or harvest hands, and city indentures said nothing about harvest work. Masters kept boys busy at their workbenches and blocked efforts by apprentices to take working vacations in the fields. In tobacco-growing Prince George's, too, the apprentice statute had little application; the law expressly omitted work in tobacco from a craft master's prerogatives. By the nineteenth century, sending an apprentice into the tobacco fields would have stigmatized him for performing the work of slaves.

But in Washington County's mixed economy, some boys were eager to reap wheat or pick corn. They occasionally obtained the right to work for themselves, usually for a week or two. Some masters pared down the release to eight or nine days; as with everything else, when apprenticeship assumed or retained the character of a trade school, even control of a few days' labor elicited close bargaining.[52]

Washington County masters showed little interest in reducing commitments to feed, clothe, and lodge apprentices. Only 3 percent of the indentures omitted promises of clothing, offered wages in lieu of clothes, or promised only shoes and hats (the preference of a few masters in the leather trades). Whether in booming Baltimore, the sluggish tobacco counties, or the modestly prosperous wheat belt of western Maryland, men who bound apprentices could not wriggle out from under the promise to maintain them. If they wished to avoid such obligations, they would have to gravitate toward wage labor. As in Baltimore, apprenticeship in Washington County met the booming labor needs of the late eighteenth and early nineteenth centuries, and, like slavery, had been largely discarded by 1850. When it thrived, however, all parties tried to draw terms to their own advantage.

Bargaining did not end when indentures were signed. Apprentices and kin took a lively interest in the fulfillment of promises for maintenance, training, and education, while masters fretted over boys who failed to learn their trade, defied authority, malingered, or ran off. Court records sketch the outlines of these disputes: none of the parties hesitated to go to court for redress of grievances, real or imagined. Not all disputes were thus resolved, however. Hundreds, perhaps thousands, of boys ended apprenticeships by running away.

The runaway apprentice has long been a tantalizing figure. From Ben Franklin to Huck Finn, boys on the loose were suspected of having fled lawful masters. Craftsmen's autobiographies and runaway advertisements verify that the phenomenon was indeed widespread. Historians have put runaways to work supporting theories about workers and economic development in the early republic. Economic and business historians have assessed them from the firm's standpoint, pondering how flight and strategies to defeat it affected labor costs and the willingness to indent young boys. In examining runaways' motivations, they have sought to measure whether distributions by age or trade correspond to economic models predicting risks and gains of absconding.[53]

Exponents of artisan republicanism have exploited runaways, too. For these political and cultural historians, the post-Revolutionary era runaway exemplifies political self-consciousness suffused by republicanism. His departure can be adduced as evidence of decaying mutuality in the workshop left behind, buttressing the declension model on which many depictions of artisan republicanism rest. Both approaches to runaway apprentices have generated valuable insights, but most deal with urban artisans, who comprised only a fraction of craft workers. Rural runaways remain largely unexamined.[54]

Such teenage absconders were virtually always boys. While 10 to 20 percent of children bound out were female, no more than 5 to 6 percent of runaways advertised in Maryland newspapers were girls.[55] Most boys who fled did so during the summer or early fall, at ages sixteen to nineteen, after two years of service. A runaway was most likely to have been bound as blacksmith, carpenter, shoemaker, or tailor, but so were the boys who stayed put.[56]

Baltimore masters who advertised an apprentice's flight offered substantial rewards. Small-town and rural masters instead disparaged the runaway's character and work habits, by "expos[ing] him to public shame" and offering a token "six cents and no thanks" for his return. Nicholas Willis described Joseph Hutchinson as "young in age but old in iniquity...small in stature but a great scoundrel." A single mini-headline could speak volumes; offers of "SIX CENTS and a BROKEN AWL," or "SIX CENTS and a PINT OF WHISKY" for a runaway conveyed unmistakable messages about his supposed proclivities.[57]

Runaways' motivations, however, are not transparent. The republican artisan paradigm would suggest that runaway rates must have risen over time as egalitarian values spread and apprentices progressively found dependent status insufferable. To the extent that declining workshop mutuality spurred apprentices to flee, we might expect city boys, more commonly employed in large numbers and lacking the surrogate family setting of the idealized apprenticeships, to run more often than boys in the countryside.[58] Economic historians who posit maximizing behavior might expect rates of flight to ebb and flow in tandem with rising or falling opportunity in the economy. Or runaway propensities might have been influenced by the size of the bundle of the noncash benefits of maintenance, education, and craft training promised. Such hypotheses can be tested by comparing runaway rates in Baltimore, Talbot, Prince George's, and Washington Counties and by examining the terms of indenture of those who ran.

The comparisons do not strongly support any of these hypotheses. First, apprentices were not more likely to run away over time. In Washington County, the ratio of runaways to new indentures hovered at 9 to 13 percent per year between 1794 and 1815, peaked at 20 to 25 percent between 1815 and 1830, then fell to 6 percent in the early 1830s.[59] Nor did this pattern suggest that apprentices were maximizing their economic opportunities. The surge in runaways during the prosperous years following 1815 did not abate with the hard times of the early 1820s sparked by the Panic of 1819 but only with the stronger economy of the 1830s. Nor did urban apprentices flee most often; instead, rural Washington and Talbot Counties had higher runaway rates than Baltimore.[60] Nor were the terms of runaways' indentures noticeably better or worse than those of boys who did not run. In Washington County, many runaways had been promised large cash freedom dues, and boys whose indentures stipulated six months of education or fewer were no more likely to run off than those promised a year or more. Nor did a cash nexus between master and apprentice affect the runaway rate. Some runaway indentures specified that masters could pay the boy cash in lieu of clothing, and a few stipulated wage payments, but in both Baltimore and Washington counties such arrangements remained rare throughout the period between 1790 and 1840.[61]

But examination of runaways whose indentures appeared in county samples leads to suggestive findings. Absconding apprentices in Washington County, which had very high runaway rates, had commonly been bound out at an unusually young age. Sixty percent of runaways had been bound at age fifteen or younger, which was true of only 40 percent of boys who did not run. In Baltimore, with its relatively low runaway rates, half of the runaways had been bound at fifteen or younger, but so had half of the boys who did not run.[62] On the other hand, runaway boys in all counties had had a collectively unstable apprentice experience. About one-fifth had been bound at least twice and had run from a second master, after having been bound at age fifteen or younger.[63] Perhaps the combination of leaving parents at a relatively young age coupled with later reassignment to a new master triggered apprentice flight. It was often the case that a runaway boy in this situation had been reassigned from a master that his father (and perhaps he himself) had chosen to a less favored one with a different trade.

Anecdotal evidence provides further clues to the importance of continuing family ties and may account for some of the runaway patterns. First, the support of kin could give an unhappy apprentice an alternative to flight, via a legal release from an apprenticeship negotiated between his master and an adult family member. As minors, apprentices could petition for release from an indenture but could not sue masters if they were mistreated or cheated out of an education or freedom dues. On the other hand, a master with a rebellious or discontented apprentice could not simply send him away without risking eventual legal action for lost maintenance when the ex-apprentice attained his majority. Faced with such a dilemma, Jacob Paulus released William Hulbert from his indenture so long as William's father, Joseph, indemnified him from any future lawsuits by the former apprentice. In a more complicated case, Richard Edwards arranged his brother John's release by standing security for John's debts to his master, James Weitzel. Weitzel in turn agreed to hire John as a wage-earning journeyman, whose wages would redeem the debts.[64] Fathers, guardians, or adult brothers could thus mediate disputes between masters and apprentices.[65]

But a dead or absent father could not smooth a son's departure from a conflict-ridden apprenticeship. That orphans made up a higher proportion of apprentices in rural counties than in Baltimore may help explain the higher incidence of runaways in the countryside. Living fathers who refused to care for their sons were also more common in rural areas.[66] What's more, a larger proportion of Washington County apprentices had moved from another county or state to take up an indenture than their Baltimore counterparts; distance would complicate or even bar the parents from monitoring their son or intervening in a dispute.[67] Runaway advertisements suggest that such apprentices commonly chose flight: Washington County masters who speculated on a runaway's destination more frequently cited flight to a distant relative than did Baltimoreans.[68]

When parents could assist apprentices in unsatisfactory indentures, a rural location could make an amicable resolution more difficult. In Baltimore, a father might seek a second contract in the same trade, so a boy could build on his acquired training. A master weary of a fractious boy might even obtain a fee from the next master for acquiring a partly trained worker. Such transitions were not too difficult in Baltimore, where even an apprentice in watchmaking or silversmithing might find several potential new masters. In Hagerstown or Easton, let alone backcountry hamlets like Funkstown or Boonsboro, far fewer opportunities existed for lateral movement in the same craft, so finding a new master usually meant embarking on a new trade.[69] Of course, some moves reflected a distaste for the first occupation, but others were certainly forced by lack of choice.

Family ties evidently remained important for nineteenth-century apprentices for years after their indentures were signed. Kin resources for resolving conflicts with masters could influence whether a young man ran from his master, and they may have more explanatory power than constructions that rely chiefly on the rise of republican sentiments or on maximizing behavior.

Understanding apprenticeship's trajectory from the late colonial period through the first half of the nineteenth century clearly requires a multi-causal explanation. At the grandest level of generalization, the spread of republicanism, with its emphasis on individual autonomy, correlates chronologically to a diminishing role for apprenticeship and other forms of bound labor for white people. At the same time, the rise of privately negotiated, capitalist relations of labor, wages, and contract accompanied the decline of publicly supervised and regulated forms of bound labor like apprenticeship. But neither of these interpretations is fully satisfactory. Baltimore manufacturers embraced apprenticeship—and for that matter, slavery—at the moment of the city's most dramatic economic expansion, during the heyday of Jeffersonian republicanism. Apprenticeship and slavery flourished in Baltimore, not as obstacles to the development of a capitalist economy but rather as highly plastic institutions that could be articulated and rearticulated in ways suitable to capitalism's advance. Eventually, new labor and social relations rendered both apprenticeship and slavery irrelevant in Baltimore, but only after these very institutions had helped create the new conditions that subsequently drained them of meaning. Or rather, the conditions that permitted apprenticeship to shed its acquired role as a means of craft training and return it to its original, less complex form as provider of step-families.

CHAPTER FIVE

Bound Out from the Almshouse

Community Networks in Chester County, Pennsylvania, 1800–1860

MONIQUE BOURQUE

In 1804, four of Mary Derborough's five children were bound out by the Trustees of the Poor at different times after their ailing mother entered the Chester County, Pennsylvania, almshouse; the youngest child temporarily remained with Mary. The five children's fates were decided separately by the trustees, who considered the children's capabilities, the mother's needs, and the potential masters' suitability.[1] In 1856, N. Linton, a Chester County inhabitant, wrote to almshouse steward Thomas Baker about a "little colored girl" whom Linton and his wife were considering taking on as an apprentice. Baker responded that the girl "has not been raised as I could wish" but asserted that he had "a very good opinion of her working capacities as also of her conduct toward children" and added that he and his wife judged the girl "not vicious and can be reclaimed."[2] The girl's placement involved Linton's request, the girl's family history, and Baker's judgment of the suitability of the girl and the master for each other. Placement of the Derborough children and the Lintons' unnamed apprentice required knowledge and connections, and almshouse officials had both. These two incidents illustrate how binding out poor children remained a central activity of the almshouse over time and also how the practice retained its carefully managed character, with overseers considering multiple factors when placing children into an official master/servant relationship.

This essay examines pauper apprenticeship as mediated by the Trustees of the Chester County Almshouse—just west of Philadelphia proper—in the first half of the nineteenth century. It draws on 320 indentures of children bound out from the almshouse between 1800 and 1825. The original indentures have not survived, but a few contracts were transcribed directly into meeting minutes, and an "Index of Apprentices" contains particulars of all indentures enacted during the period.[3] Reconstructing the stories of individual children (and their families) and the institutional practice of pauper apprenticeship in this locality requires scrutiny of an additional body of documents: admission and discharge records, almshouse stewards' correspondence, annual reports, and trustee meeting minutes. Considered together, these records show that binding out from the Chester County almshouse was a labor transaction that provided a child who would perform work for a master—but it was also an act of local governance, the administration of poor relief, the giving of charity, and a matter of neighborly observation and concern. Binding a child to a local master required a community network of diverse social and economic relationships.

Between 1790 and 1830, virtually all of Philadelphia's satellite counties moved from a traditional system of "outdoor" relief—cash or kind payments to the poor or their guardians—to a system of government-funded county poorhouses. Advocates of the change hoped that the new system would prove more economical, efficient, and effective, thus easing the pressure on local taxpayers suffering from declining household production, decreasing agricultural jobs, financial panics, and high rates of migration to Philadelphia from neighboring counties.[4] The goal was to provide for community members in distress without establishing a permanent class of dependent poor or creating a haven for indigent newcomers. Oversight of the poor remained the province of local officials—now called "Directors of the Poor" or "Trustees of the Poor"—who carried on their work in institutions rather than in their own homes or at town meetings. This strategy appears to have been successful. The relief rates in Philadelphia's satellite counties did not increase dramatically in the first half of the nineteenth century—as doomsayers had predicted—and the administration of relief did not take on an increasingly punitive quality, as it did in urban centers like Philadelphia.[5]

Some historians have argued that this shift to institutionalized relief isolated the poor from their neighbors.[6] However, strong evidence exists to indicate that almshouses remained economically and socially integrated into their communities.[7] Almshouses purchased local goods and produce, employed local labor to operate the institution, and supplied labor to local residents by contracting the work of adult inmates and by binding out poor children as pauper apprentices. Binding out did not isolate the poor; through almshouse trustees, poor children and their parents became connected to county officials first and then to masters and their neighbors. The practice depended upon preexisting community networks and forged new ones, formally tying children to masters and less formally tying community members to each other, through the central institution of the almshouse.

While the poor laws in the greater Philadelphia region varied from state to state (Pennsylvania, Delaware, Maryland), all provided for the indenture of minor children with or without the consent of their parents or guardians, particularly in cases where administrators felt that the family setting was injurious to the child's character or moral and physical development, or when parents were found by the magistrates, justices of the peace, or overseers to be "unable to maintain them."[8] The letter of the law suggests harsh treatment in authorizing officials to break up families maintaining their children in conditions judged by authorities to be inadequate, but local practice seems to have been relatively flexible, and individual boards of overseers made their own rules for monitoring children who had been bound out of the house to masters in the community.[9]

Pauper apprenticeship was an important element of poor relief for two reasons: it removed poor children from an institutional environment that overseers believed was potentially bad for children's moral and physical development, and indenture provided the opportunity for these children to learn skills that would help them to live productive lives outside the institution. Administrators hoped that approved masters would shape apprentices' characters and teach them industrious habits and useful skills, so that they would live independently as adults and stay off the relief rolls. Administrators had other ways of taking care of poor children, but binding out was the most effective and efficient, transferring the responsibility for a child's upbringing to a trusted member of the local community.

Almshouse officials sat at the center of a community network, and the information they received shaped the practice of binding out. They conducted personal interviews with poor parents who applied for assistance; they followed up by corresponding with the parents' friends, neighbors, and relatives (some poor parents were "regular customers" whom officials encountered repeatedly over a number of years). These same officials communicated with administrators in other areas of local government such as the Court of Quarter Sessions or the Orphan's Court; they listened to prospective masters describe their needs, express their concerns, and complain about their charges; and they paid attention to masters' neighbors, who helped monitor the welfare of the pauper apprentice. The almshouse steward—who kept the records—and other officials kept pauper apprentices connected to their families by receiving and transmitting information. While children bound out by Philadelphia's Guardians of the Poor were usually placed in adjoining counties, the majority of children indentured by Chester County officials were bound to members of the local community and nearby townships. Consequently, magistrates and families could more easily monitor the children's welfare once they were in the masters' households, and masters could more easily be held accountable for their behavior. This system worked in part because almshouse administrators had personal or direct knowledge of a network of community members.

Overseers were invested in the apprenticeship system's success as supervisors and as masters. Overseers of the poor occasionally took on apprentices themselves, but masters were often neighbors of the institution and always lived within the county. Masters were not always the most substantial members of the community, but many were active in other areas of civic life in addition to serving on boards of overseers.[10] For many of these men, taking on pauper apprentices was an economic decision, but it also contributed to their larger sense of community responsibility; some of them took on multiple apprentices over a period of years. That sense of responsibility is also revealed in numerous entries for masters taking on siblings in an effort to keep family members together, even when some of the children were too young to be effective help around the house or farm.

While they lacked official power, pauper parents were invested in the business of binding out their children. The almshouse was often part of parents' larger strategy for economic and social survival, and their children were a central consideration. Parents sometimes left children with relatives or friends while other family members entered the institution. Margaret Bradley entered the Chester County almshouse in 1811 with her two-year-old daughter Lydia; her husband John remained outside with their children Daniel and Mary Ann, aged eleven and about ten. The rest of the family did not enter the institution until John's consumption forced the issue.[11]

Mary Derborough, mentioned above, entered the Chester County almshouse only when she could no longer support herself and her five children after her husband Daniel's abandonment of the family. "Sick and in a Suffering State" in 1804, she appealed to the Trustees of the Poor for assistance and officially became a pauper. Her oldest child, fourteen-year-old Daniel, was bound out immediately to Isaac Malin, and nine-year-old Joshua was bound to John Stemple.[12] Thirteen-year-old William and six-year-old Sarah remained with their mother for another month and were then bound to George Goodwin.[13] Two-year-old Isaac, the youngest child, stayed with his mother until he was given to Dinah Willets to keep in spring 1805. In July, Willets was released from the contract by the Trustees because "some of Derborough's family" had taken the boy away from her; the Trustees declared both Willets and themselves no longer responsible for Isaac.[14] In 1807, Isaac appeared before the Trustees again and was formally bound out to Job Masson.[15] Meanwhile, Daniel Derborough's property—land, livestock, grain, and more—was sold or rented out for the benefit of the family, by court order and under the management of the trustees. Mary herself continued to receive practical support; for example, her brother George Garrett was advanced money "for cloathing for her and for no other use" in 1808.[16]

The Derborough and Bradley cases underscore magistrates' power to separate family members, a power that made poor people cautious about putting themselves under officials' authority. When a family applied for assistance, the Trustees of the Poor determined which children would be bound out and whether siblings would remain together. Often overseers showed sensitivity to family relationships by binding out siblings to the same master or mistress; in 1816, for example, Ann Denny took responsibility for both Robert and Presley Raymond, aged twelve and fourteen.[17] But being judged of good character did not guarantee that a mother would be allowed to keep her children with her. Two-year-old Lydia Bradley remained with her mother, even though the Trustees had every reason to believe that the family was a long-term investment because of illness or disability—and this proved to be so.[18] Yet two-year-old Isaac Derborough was taken from his mother a few months after she entered the almshouse, even though the Trustees had access to outside sources of support for the family. It is not surprising, then, that some parents went to considerable lengths to avoid having their children bound out: Moses Pyle, for instance, "stole" his children from the almshouse in 1808.[19]

Children were usually bound out as soon as a potential master expressed an interest in taking on an indenture. Thus the ages at which children were indentured varied widely, from infancy to eighteen years—almost from birth up to eighteen years. Individual children were bound according to overseers' assessment of the family's ability to recover quickly from the circumstances that led them to seek aid, so younger children were sometimes kept with their mother and sometimes bound out.

The records suggest that informal apprenticeships were often arranged by poor parents as part of the family's strategy for avoiding official oversight. An apprenticeship of any kind removed a child from the family's household, but an informal arrangement gave parents more influence in selecting the child's master. More important, informal arrangements allowed parents to remove the child at will rather than canceling the arrangement through the Trustees of the Poor. If the family was admitted to the poorhouse, the Trustees of the Poor would set up a formal apprenticeship for the child and take primary responsibility for monitoring the child's treatment.

When a child was bound out, parents were sometimes able to influence a child's placement and care. Apprentices' parents communicated with their children's masters, wrote to poorhouse stewards about their children's care, and sometimes visited the children. Protests from family members could result in the reassignment of a child's indentures to another master or in the cancellation of indentures. George Sloan's indentures were reassigned to his aunt Lydia "due to the dissatisfaction of the boys Relations" with his first master.[20] James Entrikin appeared at the monthly meeting of the Trustees of the Poor and successfully opposed the indenture of his son Reuben to James Webb, even though

Entrikin's property had recently been seized by the Court of Quarter Sessions, at the instigation of the Trustees of the Poor, to pay for maintenance of his wife and son in the almshouse after Entrikin had apparently abandoned them.[21]

The efforts parents made to avoid putting children under the care of relief administrators and to keep track of indentured family members living in masters' households are strong evidence of sturdy family bonds among the poorer sort and indicate suspicion of arbitrary decisions made by administrators. Almshouse stewards sometimes chose to deny families access to apprentices who had been placed with masters. Noting in a letter to Ellen Pyles's half brother James Courtney that "she is in a very good place and is very well satisfied," steward Thomas Baker dismissed Courtney's request to know Pyles's whereabouts so that he could make arrangements for her return.[22] Decisions like this, which appeared to administrators to protect the master-servant relationship they had carefully contracted, must often have appeared to family members to be capricious, callous, and destructive.

While family members' complaints could result in the child's restoration to the family or reassignment to a new master, this was not always the case, and even the intercession of a well-to-do member of the community was not always sufficient to yield information on the master. When eight-year-old Julia Ann McCullough disappeared into the relief system in 1854, taken out on trial with no record of her placement, her anxious mother sought the assistance of a citizen who knew a board member to intercede with the almshouse steward to gain news of her daughter. The steward's response echoes the case of Ellen Pyles: he stated that he had visited Julia Ann, found her and her master's family satisfied with the arrangement, and declined to provide further information.[23]

Masters were usually the focus of the community network that pauper apprenticeship activated in Chester County. Placing the child with the right master was a primary concern of almshouse administrators. Potential masters were allowed to take prospective apprentices "on trial" for varying periods, usually either one or three months, at the end of which time it was expected that formal indenture papers would be drawn up and signed at one of the overseers' regular (monthly or quarterly) meetings. However, the trial period often lasted much longer than three months, and in some cases, no formal indenture ever resulted. The trial privilege was sometimes abused—this was in fact a chronic problem throughout the first half of the century. Institutional administrators felt that time conferred an official character on trial relationships, carrying legal and moral responsibility. Walker Yarnall, steward of the Chester County poorhouse, tartly noted in an 1841 letter to one delinquent master:

> You have returned to our House John McIlgren who you have had out since 25 of April 1836 *which clearly fixes him on you.* It is expected that persons taking

Children from here should either return them in 1 or 2 months or keep them. If I had been at home I should have refused to take him.[24]

While women were the primary caregivers for the children taken into their households as apprentices, women seldom appear in the records as masters; when they do, it is usually as widows. It seems likely that widows often took over apprentices without formal acknowledgement of the shift in authority but occasionally sought the overseers' approval. Many agreements specified the responsibility and authority of both master and mistress over the apprentice, and some forms allowed for a mistress instead of a master.[25]

Existing social relationships in the master's household often determined institutional arrangements, thanks to the individualized character of apprenticeships. Flora Derry, a "poor Black child" born in Philip Price's house, was bound out to him when she was four months old.[26] When George Bird requested that Thomas McConnell (aged three) and Margaret McConnell (aged two) be bound to him, the children had already been living with Bird for two years, after their father "left them with him and absconded."[27] Indentures also reinforced ongoing economic relationships between the institution and its community. When the Trustees settled their account with George McDowell for work around the institution, they paid a sum to Randal Malin, the master of McDowell's illegitimate son George, for "the use and benefit" of the boy when he came of age.[28] Masters who were personally known to the Trustees were more readily acceptable to them. James Pyle, who took on Andrew Summerville as an apprentice in 1824, had done plastering for the new almshouse infirmary in 1812.[29]

Almshouse trustees mediated the master-servant relationship. Through official supervision, they aimed to protect masters from bad or unruly apprentices as well as to prevent the abuse of indentured children. When Thomas Lewis's "evil practices" were judged by the overseers to make it unlikely that his master Reuben Hayes would "ever... have any benefit from him," they canceled the indentures and bound another boy to Hayes instead. Stewards were often asked to vouch for apprentices' characters, but the almshouse meeting minutes give no detail on what Thomas Lewis's "evil practices" were. Since the "Index to Apprentices" gives his age as fifteen, it seems likely that the adolescent was smoking, drinking alcohol, or indulging in other behaviors conventionally prohibited for under-age apprentices.[30]

Neighbors observed the care of apprentices in others' households and occasionally reported abuses or offered testimony of ill treatment by masters. Apprentices could and did approach overseers or justices who had overseen their indentures to complain about their masters: apprentices to William Corbett and Joseph Clark came to the poorhouse to complain to the steward that they were not receiving the education promised them by their masters.[31]

The investigation of complaints of ill treatment put masters in the spotlight of community information networks and bound almshouses to one another and to their county neighbors. In 1856 Isaac Hall wrote to the trustees of the poor for Chester County about John Ford, who had been apprenticed to Charles Kimble. The boy had complained to several adults in the community about Kimble's harsh treatment, and Hall wrote to the Trustees that he had himself seen evidence of abuse: "I have no doubt that he has been abused for on Sunday last he showed where he had been cut with a brush or as you would call it an ox whip rather till the blood came to the out side of the skin, and he has been in the habit of kicking him and cuffing him with his fist." Hall argued that Kimble had failed in the most important role of a master: "The boy says he was to have a trade of some kind but has not got any yet, and he wants to go to a trade and his master will not let him. he has not even learned him the mysteries of farming as he should have done." Kimble kept a tavern and Ford had been kept largely idle and "potter[ing] about as a Horstler."[32]

Hall, the observant neighbor, advised the Trustees that the boy "ought to be seen to" and asked the Trustees to investigate the abuse and to clarify the terms of the original indenture as to whether the boy was to learn a trade or farming. "If the boy is abused any more it must be seen to by some body for it will not do in a Christian land," Hall wrote, adding that "since he has got to be Horstler he has got into the habit of using to much intoxicating drinks."[33]

The steward located Ford's indentures and informed Hall that the boy had been indentured at age five and was to learn farming. Noting that the boy had three years and five months yet to serve on his term, the steward suggested that Hall attend the next Trustees meeting to discuss the situation.[34] Surviving records do not indicate whether Hall did appear at the Trustees meeting, or whether John Ford was removed from Kimble's service; what is significant is that a neighbor felt justified in lodging a complaint on the boy's behalf.

Examining and settling complaints like this often involved relief administrators from more than one county or, more usually, multiple neighborhoods within a county. When John Miller ran away from his master in Chester County and was "taken up" and placed in the Philadelphia almshouse, his master came and took him home. Chester County's Trustees of the Poor were notified of the boy's flight and removal by the Philadelphia authorities and undertook an investigation of the boy's case. The boy had been indentured for nearly four years to James Peoples, who was "blamed for Str”king him, the Boy taken from him and sent to the Directors" of the Chester County almshouse. Peoples had a longstanding relationship with the institution, having done tailoring for the paupers for more than ten years; Miller had been apprenticed to Peoples in order to learn the trade.[35] Peoples's ongoing connection to the poorhouse did not earn him special treatment from the directors, however; they demanded that Peoples pay the reward he had offered for the boy's return, along with "some other expense," and then cancelled Miller's indenture to Peoples and kept the boy at the almshouse "to be disposed of by the Directors."³⁶ He was bound out to Jesse Webb several months later.³⁷

The cases of John Ford and John Miller demonstrate that a strong sense of community was vital to poor relief administration and that the definition of community and the place of the poor in it were more complex than the rhetoric of "worthy" and "unworthy" poor would suggest. Neighbor Hall's argument that abuse of apprentices "will not do in a Christian land" and his inquiry into the matter indicate that he felt responsibility for such children and considered them members of his community. Miller's rescue from an abusive master illustrates that forces like economic self-interest and class loyalty were not always more important than the welfare of individuals; the story is also a reminder that relief officials were always conscious of being accountable to a public that kept a watchful eye on the administration of their poor taxes and appropriations and also that the boundaries of community responsibility were negotiable.

The complex and highly personal relationships among institutional authorities, masters, and neighbors are especially poignant where apprentices and administrators had multiple interactions over extended periods; these cases remind us of both the necessity of negotiating placements and the ways in which institutions profoundly shaped the lives and bodies of the children who received assistance. One such story is that of Temperance Howard, a black girl who became physically disabled while in the poorhouse. Four-year-old Howard first appeared in the institution's records when she boarded with Isaac Carpenter in 1819.³⁸ Carpenter returned Howard to the almshouse in 1824, "in Exchange" for Susan Williams, who would (it was hoped) suit Carpenter better.³⁹ While an inmate in 1825, Howard suffered an accident or illness such that the almshouse physician had to amputate one of her legs and fit her with a wooden replacement.⁴⁰ Twelve-year-old Howard was taken out by Isachar Mann in June 1827 for a month's trial. Two days later she was back, rejected because her mistress was unable to tolerate the girl's disability.⁴¹

The almshouse clerk in the minutes and the steward in his accounts book took the opportunity to express disapproval of Howard's mistress as they recorded events. This Quaker woman (in the clerk's words) "could no longer bear the sound of her wooden leg." The steward put it this way: "Temperance Howard (Negro) returned. She states that her mistress was a Quaker woman and could not bare the noise of her wooden leg on the floor."⁴²

The clerk's note is more easily read as disapproving of the cavalier way the mistress treated the girl (and of the subsequent inconvenience to the institution). The steward's note, presented as a report of Howard's own account, is more ambiguous because it hints at a more complex perspective. Can the girl's account be understood as a simple explanation of her mistress' religious affiliation as evidence of a need for a peaceful household, one in which a servant's wooden leg thumping on the floor as she went about her work was too jarring to the nerves?

Howard's situation may provide an example of the trustees making decisions contrary to the master's wishes—they apparently declined to provide the Manns with another apprentice. Howard left the almshouse three months after her return from the Manns' household, "with leave" but no recorded purpose or destination. She returned to the institution again at some point and was discharged in 1832; she was back again in 1835, listed as aged twenty-three.[43] Then she disappears from the records.

Temperance Howard's case is one of many that underscore the importance of negotiation in the placement of apprentices, especially difficult children. Throughout the first half of the nineteenth century, Chester County's masters did not hesitate to return apprentices who were unsatisfactory for any reason. Emmor Carter returned George Thompson because "he is not Harty."[44] Emeline Jacobs's master returned her because "her temper is very unpleasant."[45] Rejected children were placed with someone else; some were not formally bound until their second or third placement, and some were never successfully bound. Temperance Howard appears to have been one of these unfortunates; the overseers of the poor never offered a monetary incentive that would tempt a master to take her with her disability.

Masters who took small children did not necessarily expect to put them immediately to work. When Isaac Martin took charge in 1821 of Sarah and Jeremiah Gatchell (aged three and one), he clearly expected to play a custodial role for some years.[46] However, the amount of work to be expected from an apprentice during the term of the indenture could be important in evaluating a youngster for an indenture. For some masters, the child needed to be young enough that the labor obtained during a term of service would outweigh room and board costs. When S. E. Dickey returned from a business trip to Philadelphia to find that indenture papers had been delivered for Louisa Bush, a young black girl in the household, he was dismayed and angered to find her age stated as nearly fifteen. Arguing that there must have been a recordkeeping mistake, he threatened: "If you still adhere to her age being 14 *or anything like it,* I shall not like to keep her, though she weeps bitterly when she thinks she will be sent away. I took her, believing she was 8 or 9 years of age, and *under this belief,* we wished her bound."[47] Responding that the girl's age was correct, Baker recommended that Dickey bring the girl back to the poorhouse for the next Trustees meeting to have the indentures canceled.[48]

The children bound out from the Chester County almshouse provide a collective profile that fits the general pattern described in chapter 1. White boys constituted 51 percent (163 children) of the pauper apprentices; white girls, 35 percent (112 children); girls of color, 7 percent (22 children); boys of color,

7 percent (23 children). Boys were bound more often than girls: 58 percent (186 boys) to 42 percent (134 girls). White children were bound more often than children of color: 86 percent (275 white children) to 14 percent (45 children of color). The ages at which children were bound ranged from four months to eighteen years, but some 75 percent of the children in these records were under nine; the modal age at which children were bound out was four years old, and this age does not differ according to either race or gender.[49] The records do not provide the reason for each child's binding; thus it is impossible to tell what proportion of the children were orphaned, illegitimate, or abandoned by their parents.

The index does not provide sufficient information to compare the terms of indenture statistically, but anecdotal evidence from other records indicates that just as ages of indentures were fairly similar across race and gender, the terms apprentices received were not widely different between races and were consistent for gender with indentures in other North American communities. Regardless of the age at which they were indentured, boys were usually bound to age twenty-one and girls to eighteen. Nearly all girls (95 percent of girls of color and 96 percent of white girls) were bound to learn "housewifery"; the majority of boys were bound to learn "farming" or "husbandry" (96 percent of boys of color, and 84 percent of white boys).

Both sexes were to receive a certain amount of formal schooling, including learning to read and write; boys often were promised enough instruction to be able to keep simple accounts. Chester County's trustees revised the institution's bylaws in 1807 to standardize schooling requirements for bound children; under the new rules, boys were to receive somewhat more schooling than the girls (two and a half years compared to one year and eight months). The records are too incomplete to assess how consistent the trustees were in applying their own regulations.[50] Freedom dues typically were clothing only (usually two suits; sometimes one was to be new). Few documents made any reference to cash, and only one of the surviving indentures offered cash instead of clothing on the expiration of the apprentice's term. The greatest variance in contract terms was in the amount of schooling the child would receive and in the amount of clothing to be provided at the end of the contract.

Race was not a powerful factor in Chester County pauper apprenticeship, as it was in other localities in North America.[51] Children of color were not strangely absent from the Chester County almshouse binding out records, as was the case in Boston and Charleston. But binding out was not focused on children of color, as it was in Rhode Island and Maryland, and bound children of color did not serve longer terms or receive less education and freedom dues. While adult persons of color were overrepresented in the population of institutionalized poor in Chester County, children of color were underrepresented, constituting only about two percent of almshouse inmates under age twenty-one.[52]

But neither were children of color a disproportionately large group in those apprenticed by the relief administrators. Young adults and children old enough to work were a relatively small proportion of almshouse inmates regardless of their race, precisely because administrators bound them out when possible both to save money and to protect the children from the bad influences of institutional life. While direct evidence is lacking, the small proportion of children of color in the apprenticeship records may reflect more frequent informal placement of children of color.

The links connecting race, poverty, and "belonging" to the community were complex: race and poverty were integral components of individuals' experience of community. At the same time, these characteristics were markers used in determining poor persons' status as community members or outsiders and in determining paupers' treatment if accepted as aid-worthy. Inmates of color in the Delaware Valley's poorhouses were usually housed in separate and inferior quarters, and applicants of color were less likely to receive outdoor relief than to be admitted to the institution. Gender ratios for persons of color were much more nearly equal than for whites, among both poorhouse inmates and apprentices.

Surviving stewards' correspondence from the 1850s sheds considerable light on the complex negotiations between institutions and communities over the fate of individual paupers, suggests the importance of race in at least some agreements, and shows that apprenticeship was alive and well as part of Pennsylvania's relief system even as it declined elsewhere.[53] Admission and discharge statistics do not, however, support an argument that race was a more important factor in poor relief by the mid-1800s. It is possible that children of color became more "visible" to relief administrators as the century advanced; in the absence of more information, all that historians can say is that in Chester County, race was an important variable for some masters when making indenture arrangements. The experiences of particular children like Temperance Howard, Louisa Bush, and Hall Nash, however, suggest that while race could be a factor in placement, the fit between child and master and the child's ability to work (or perceived potential) were more important than the child's color.

Children bound by the Trustees of the Poor received terms much like those of children bound out by fathers, other male relatives or "next friends," or both parents. Hall Nash, a four-and-a-half-year-old "poor Black child" bound by the Trustees of the Poor in 1830 to Lewis Morton, was to serve his master until he was twenty-one and to learn the "art and Mystery of Farming." At the end of his term, the boy was to receive the customary two suits of clothing. Even his education, two years total to be distributed evenly through the term of his indenture, did not place Nash in harsh contrast to his white contemporaries.[54] Jefferson Worthington, for example, bound with the consent of his "next friend" Eber Worthington in 1822 to Joseph Jones to be a painter, was to receive one month of schooling for each year of his four-year term and two suits of clothing.[55]

A prospective master named Thomas Holton wrote to the almshouse steward, Thomas Baker, in 1855, outlining his interest in a female apprentice: "We would like to have a little girl to bring up and thinking that there were likely to be some under your charge of a useful age—I take the liberty of requesting you to inform me whether I could obtain a white girl—say from the age of eight to eleven." Locating himself in the area for the steward's benefit, he added, "I am a son of Alexander Holton, Russelville."[56] Seeing the "useful" as more important than the girl's race, Baker wrote back that at the time he had "no white girls of any age, but there is a Black Girl here of about eleven years of age, which I think would suit you."[57]

This exchange perfectly illustrates the values central to the administration of apprenticeship as a part of the poor relief system. Holton felt it necessary to establish himself as a member of the community and to provide verifiable information about himself as a claim to respectability in order to enter a request for an apprentice. At the same time, as an established member of the community, Holton felt entitled to specify the sort of apprentice he would like to have. Just as Mr. Linton had relied on the steward's judgment of the girl he was considering as a potential apprentice as "not vicious," Holton counted on Baker to evaluate the suitability of the apprentice. For his part, the steward had to take stock of the available apprentices, evaluate their suitability and judge the relative importance of age, gender, race, and usefulness when offering an alternative to the type of child requested. The girl's opinion of the arrangement was neither sought nor important. The records do not indicate whether Holton accepted Baker's recommendation, or looked elsewhere for an apprentice.

There seems to have been remarkably little change over time in binding out in antebellum Chester County; while difficult to support with statistics because so few records have survived, the lack of trends in the practice of apprenticeship parallels the statistically demonstrated lack of significant change in admission and discharge trends for antebellum poorhouses. The practice itself showed no tendency to decline, as it did in New England; it was as useful a measure for relief administrators in 1860 as it was in 1800. It did not become focused in gendered or racialized ways over the period, as it did elsewhere. Surviving contracts between 1800 and 1830 show no trend toward less schooling, as was the case in nearby Baltimore. Overall, pauper apprenticeship remained a reliable strategy for overseers of the poor to meet persistent needs in their community—households that needed labor, children that needed homes. In 1860 as in 1800, pauper appreciation remained a complex system, forged by almshouse officials, focused on fitting the right master to the right child, and activating an entire network of community members to mediate and monitor that master/child relationship.

PART III

BINDING OUT AS A PARENT/CHILD RELATION

Binding out took children from their birth homes and placed them in other households. As Ruth Herndon and John Murray show in chapter 1, a child's parents were replaced with overseers of the poor and then with a master. Because binding out separated children from their parents and created new relationships between children and substitute parents, it is a good prism to observe the nature and expectations of the parent/child relationship—through the replacement of one set of parents with another. This is an elusive topic in early American studies, because there is such sparse documentation on the family, particularly for non-elites.

In the last few decades, historians have begun to investigate in earnest the experience of children of all races and classes in early American history. Still elusive, however, are answers to questions about the link between children's experiences and the formation of culture in the early modern era. How did parents raise their children to embrace and carry on their values and beliefs? What did communities consider to be the essential elements of successful parenting? Were literacy education and skill training equally important elements of childrearing in North America? What were considered appropriate ties between parent and child, and how were those ties to be maintained? Analysis of pauper apprenticeship engages these questions directly.

High mortality rates in early America meant that many children were raised at some point by someone who was not their biological mother or father. Pauper apprenticeship, widespread and deeply rooted in early America, gives us documentary evidence of the frequent dislocation of children from their birth homes. It indicates how commonplace it was for children to grow up with people who were in fact (if not in law) step-mothers, step-fathers, and step-siblings. It reveals family structures as flexible and diverse, with parents maintaining contact with children who were no longer under their direct control.

Pauper apprenticeship also clarifies the prevailing expectation that parents and substitute parents alike would transmit literacy and work skills to the next generation. For the great majority of early Americans, learning to work was an essential element of growing up; "education" meant primarily the acquisition of work skills for all but the elite. But literacy acquisition was also extremely common in apprenticeship indentures, indicating a widespread assumption that children should learn to read and write.

"Reading" and "writing" were acquired as separate skills in early America. Learning to write was a more significant accomplishment, as it prepared the student for "the world of letters." "Cyphering," or basic arithmetic, was usually reserved for boys. It was an educational accomplishment quite separate from reading and writing, and it was not taught to any significant extent in early America until the late seventeenth century. Basic math became important for the conduct of a trade in the eighteenth century and entered pauper apprenticeship indentures accordingly.

CHAPTER SIX

Preparing Children for Adulthood in New Netherland

ADRIANA E. VAN ZWIETEN

In their daily lives, the children of seventeenth-century New Netherland were expected to contribute to the household economy at an early age, thereby emulating their counterparts in the Republic of the Seven United Provinces of the Netherlands.[1] Current opinion dictated that it was good for children to work (according to their strength) from their seventh year onward. Child labor without some element of training was frowned upon, however, for the primary goal of work was to prepare children for the future so that, as adults, they would make a positive contribution to the community.[2]

Preparation for a lifetime of labor was essentially a family affair, for Dutch mothers and fathers shared joint responsibility for the physical and mental development of their children. They were obliged not only to bring their offspring through infancy and childhood but also to provide them with "food and drink, . . . clothing, housing, comfort, ease, discipline, teaching and learning of various arts and crafts, according to each one's condition and opportunity." Conversely, children owed their parents honor, gratitude, and submission.[3] Such attitudes also shaped the practice of apprenticeship and binding out, for masters and mistresses took over parental responsibilities when they added indentured youngsters to their households. Their charges were required to act diligently, faithfully, and obediently, while masters and mistresses, as substitute parents, were admonished to treat them as if they were their own children. New Netherland's

---

I want to thank Firth Fabend and Martha Shattuck for their comments on an earlier version of this chapter.

provincial, municipal, and village leaders protected and regulated the customs and laws that defined apprenticeship and binding out as well as the relationship between children and their parents, masters, or guardians. Furthermore, the community aided parents and substitute parents in rearing future generations by providing schoolteachers and ministers, who strove to impart literacy, learning, and the fear of God.[4] The parental and communal effort to provide New Netherland's children with a wide variety of skills is examined in this chapter, thereby presenting a Dutch colonial perspective as a cultural alternative and comparison to the English studies encountered elsewhere in this volume.

New Netherland's parents of European origin used various strategies to prepare the most vulnerable members of the family to enter the community; and the choices parents made were rooted in Old World institutions. Transplanting and replicating a European system of apprenticeship in a colonial place was a practical solution for organizing their children's lives. This study is based on an analysis of the customs and laws that regulated child labor, as well as an analysis of thirty-six apprenticeship or service contracts binding children to masters and mistresses under various conditions and ninety court cases that specifically concerned children at work or children in service or apprenticeship. The contracts and law suits were compiled from New Netherland's provincial, municipal, and village court records and from notarial protocols and church registers for the years 1638 through 1674. The evidence presented here is among the oldest for the American colonial period. The only other data from the seventeenth century in this volume can be found in the study of colonial Maryland by Jean B. Russo and J. Elliott Russo.

The number of contracts and court cases is relatively small when it is compared to the studies in this section by John Murray and Timothy Lockley; and when it is compared to the number of youngsters present in New Netherland for the period under consideration. Although the actual total is difficult to determine, there were certainly more children present than those considered in this chapter. In 1654, a New Amsterdam (now New York City) resident mused: "Children and pigs multiply here rapidly and more than anything else."[5] From 1639 through 1674, more than 2,500 baptisms were recorded by the ministers of the New Amsterdam Reformed Church, yet again this register reflects but a small part of the total number of the colony's children.[6] For example, the baptismal records of infants born within other religious denominations are no longer extant for this period, nor are the baptismal records of many villages and towns, including Beverwijck (now Albany, New York). The births of some children were simply never recorded, and some immigrated to the colony with their parents but remained nameless on ships' registers. The total number of children is decreased, of course, by infant mortality rates, which were high in the seventeenth century. Many children died in infancy or youth, never reaching the age of apprenticeship or service.[7]

The New Netherland data may suggest, however, that binding out was considered a less important way of maintaining and training children than other systems, such as informal agreements between neighbors and friends or education and training within the home under parental guidance. In fact, it has been shown that 37.5 percent of the sons born to New York City men, who were in the city at the time the Dutch capitulated to English rule in 1664, performed the same work as their fathers, while 42 percent did so in the following generation.[8] Take, for instance, the five sons of the surgeon Hans Kierstede, four of whom entered the medical profession; and Maria Van Cortlandt, who learned her entrepreneurial and brewing skills in her parent's home. In 1665, her husband, Jeremias van Rensselaer noted that in her father's house, she always managed "the disposal of the beer and helping to find customers for it." Van Rensselaer established and Maria Van Cortlandt managed a brewery in Rensselaerswijck (now part of Albany).[9] The knowledge imparted to children by their parents required no formal contracts. However, once a decision was made to continue a child's training beyond the household environment, other arrangements were made.

As is true of children in any era, those living in New Netherland were a mix of mischievous sprites and dutiful youngsters. When they appear in the colonial record, they are most often associated with some form of work. Their labor could be as simple as delivering beaver skins or as strenuous as hauling heavy logs with a four-horse team.[10] Work was closely allied to the success and prosperity of the colony, and as early as 1625, children were encouraged to labor alongside their parents for proper compensation in order to hasten the establishment of a permanent settlement. While the surveyor staked out the site for New Amsterdam, the first order of business for the carpenters was to make an enclosure for the valuable cargo of cattle that was "guarded night and day by some boys."[11] As the colony matured, children were born into a society that was both urban and commercial in its administration and organization. In fact, the ordinances and customs of the commercialized Maritime Provinces of Holland and Zeeland and "the common written law qualifying" them were used as guides for the administration of New Netherland.[12] Consequently, contract law was well defined and developed. In legal treatises, contracts for hire or service warranted a separate category that was identified as *huur,* or *hire. Huur* was a situation whereby a person agreed to put his own service, or the services of another person, animal, or thing, at the disposal of a second party, who in turn promised some form of compensation. The agreement could be oral or written, and the terms and recompense were stipulated. The contract was considered complete if it was freely entered upon and all conditions were met. Concerned parties had to be competent and could be represented by letters, messengers or agents. A valid contract was enforceable by civil law.[13]

The key word for contracts concerning the children of New Netherland is *competent.* Legally defined, minors were children under the age of twenty-five (the age of majority) or those with mental or physical disabilities, regardless of age. Orphans were minors of whom one or both parents had died. Minors and orphans were further classified as persons of limited capacity who were incapable of managing their own affairs and were therefore in need of tutelage.[14] They could not bind themselves, nor could they litigate in their own names. Any contract made independently by a minor was not binding; however, it was valid if it was made with the assistance of a parent or guardian. Young men could make their own arrangements once they attained majority or upon marriage, whichever came first. Majority also released young women from parental guidance, but marriage put them under their husbands' supervision no matter what their age. Minors could also gain their emancipation either through judicial decree or tacitly, if they were permitted to establish their own homes or business. Thus liberated, they acquired the administration of their property and judicial capacity.[15]

Parents had the right to bind their children to perform anything that they might undertake themselves by contract—for example, let out their services for hire. Guardians were authorized to bind out their wards and make contracts on their behalf.[16] Parents and guardians in New Netherland exercised this right on at least thirty-six occasions and bound out the minors for whom they were responsible by visiting the office of a local notary or secretary accompanied by intended masters or mistresses. Written before two witnesses and signed by all parties between 1639 and 1674, the contracts are of two types: apprenticeships for vocational training or indentures for service. They average about one indenture per year. It seems a paltry sum; however, many parents and guardians made oral or casual agreements with neighbors and friends, arrangements that were never recorded. Countless contracts have also been lost along with other invaluable documentation concerning the Dutch colony.[17] We know this because of the frequent mention of parents and masters presenting copies of indentures as evidence to court magistrates. Hundreds of children must have worked as apprentices but left no trace of their existence as they diligently fulfilled their obligations. The thirty-six extant contracts contain specific information such as the names of the contracting parties and of the child involved. A contract might or might not also contain a reference to the intended vocation, the length of apprenticeship or service, the child's age, the recompense, or whether the master would impart some form of education besides vocational training.

The earliest contract was an uncomplicated agreement between Hendrick Harmansen and Cornelis Jansen in 1639. Jansen bound his son Jan for a term of seven years. Harmansen owned a farm on Long Island, but no mention was made of Jan's duties or the training he would receive. Both parties promised to fulfill certain conditions customarily found in the contracts of indentured children. Harmansen would "take care of the boy as if he were his own," and Jansen could not break the contract by taking his son back before its expiration. For what was written, neither party could "claim or demand whatsoever against the other at the expiration of the aforesaid years." Both men signed before two witnesses in "good faith, without fraud or deceit," an oft-used phrase in Dutch obligations.[18]

Despite the variety of crafts and professions practiced in New Netherland, only 17 contracts (47.2 percent) specifically state the intended occupation of the apprentice, including glazier (glassmaker), shoemaker, smith, tailor, gunstock maker, carpenter, millwright, tile maker, bookkeeper, sewer or needle worker, surgeon, and turner.[19] For example, Evert Duyckingh was to teach the six-year-old orphan Cornelis Jansen "the trade of a glazier or such [other] trade as Evert" knew in 1648. Jansen finished his training, for in 1659 he sailed for Holland to claim an inheritance for himself and his siblings. He was seventeen at the time, and it was noted that he was "by trade a glazier."[20] Likewise, in 1665, Gijsbert Schuyler, then about thirteen years old, was to learn "the art of surgery and all that appertains thereto" from the surgeon Cornelis van Dijck. Schuyler probably began his apprenticeship, but he may have died at a young age for he was not mentioned in his father's will in 1683.[21]

Although vocational training is not explicitly expressed in the other nineteen contracts, some children undoubtedly learned the trade of their masters. Consider the boy Dirck Jansen, who came to the colony under indenture to Andries Hudde, a landowner, surveyor, provincial counselor, and trader. Neither the date of Jansen's contract nor the date of his arrival is known, but in 1641, his master transferred him to Willem Adriaensen, a cooper, "on the same conditions as...Hudde had made with the boy's mother." The document was unsigned; again the mutual obligations of apprentice and master remained unstated. Nevertheless, as late as 1674, the record notes a Dirck Jansen, a cooper.[22] If this is indeed the same individual of the earlier contract, then the boy learned the cooper's trade from his master, though not stated, and practiced it as an adult in the busy colonial port town of New Amsterdam.

Seven contracts (19.4 percent) bound out girls, but little is known about the training they received. Research into the daily activities of girls residing in seventeenth-century Dutch orphanages demonstrates that they mastered textile work (sewing, knitting, spinning, mending, and darning) and domestic work (cleaning, washing, ironing, cooking, and preserving food)—in short, the necessary skills for future wives or servants.[23] Some colonial girls also learned such arts, for Madelene Blanchan taught knitting in Kingston, New York, in 1669. She organized the lessons in her home and charged seven schepels of wheat for the instructions, or about 17½ guilders per student.[24] Two contracts binding out girls stipulate that the apprentice learn the art of sewing. The most detailed is the 1653 apprenticeship of Marritje Jans, a fourteen-year-old orphan. Her guardians apprenticed her to Isaac Kip and his wife Catelyntie Hendricx, who agreed "to teach, or have her [Jans] instructed in sewing bonnets, linen and other articles, which... Hendricx herself performs and doth belong to her trade."[25] When Jans joined the Kip household, the couple was newly wed and Kip was a young trader in New Amsterdam. During her four-year stay, two children were born. Undoubtedly, her days were well occupied. As she learned to sew bonnets and linens, she also acquired knowledge of caring for infants and children, running a vital enterprise and managing an active household. Whether she earned a living with her sewing skills is not known, but she did employ the business acumen and domestic skills learned from the Kips. She married the trader Cornelis Langevelt in 1657, participated in his trading enterprise and bore him two sons and a daughter.[26]

Marritje Jans's contract and twenty-nine others (83.3 percent) state the term of service, which ranged from one to eleven years with an average length of about four—younger children serving longer apprenticeships than older children. For example, Jans, at fourteen years of age, served four years, but two eight-year-old girls apprenticed in 1662 and 1674 were bound for six and eight years, respectively.[27] Other children were hired for shorter periods, like Jan Stevensen, who worked for a tile maker in 1661 for "two summers, as long as the season is suitable." In 1649, Thomas Keuningh's son labored during the harvest and was paid according to time served and the number of mowers with which he could keep up in binding bales or sheaves.[28] Girls were also hired for shorter periods, but evidence of this appears in the court cases, not in their formal contracts. Take Anneke Pia's daughter, who cleaned a house in New Amsterdam for a total of four days in 1659, while Eechie Ariaen's daughter worked on a farm in Kingston from May to All Saints' Day (November 1) in 1666.[29]

Despite the length of service, masters and mistresses as substitute parents were obliged to provide certain necessities for young New Netherlanders, like food, clothing, and housing. These were required in Old Amsterdam by a proclamation of 1597.[30] Twenty-nine contracts (80.5 percent) specify a master's obligation to provide some combination of food, drink, board, clothing, housing, or lodging. A few also included washing. If additional recompense was agreed upon, it was given at the end of service and typically included an outfit of new clothes. For boys, this usually comprised a combination of coat, breaches, shirts, stockings, shoes, hat, and handkerchiefs. Some received a new Sunday outfit as well as one for everyday, which was called fitting the child out "burgher wise" or "burgher fashion." When the mother of Johanna Hans agreed to bind her daughter in 1674, she noted that at the end of eight years, the child was due "a new black grosgrained mantle and a black apron, a new skirt, three new chemises, three new aprons, a pair of new shoes and a pair of new stockings and furthermore other trifles which may be needful for her body, together with her old clothes which she then may have."[31]

Several boys were paid a monetary sum at the end of service ranging from 40 to 300 guilders. They were older at the beginning of their apprenticeships and probably more experienced.[32] In 1660, Hendrick de Graaff's master agreed to give him two hogsheads of "choice Virginia leaf tobacco, each hogshead weighing at least 300 lbs. net," for three years of service. However, if his master had to return to Holland, De Graaff would receive instead 150 guilders in Holland currency.[33]

Only two contracts stipulate that the master be paid to impart his knowledge to an apprentice. The guardians of Marritje Jans paid 4½ good merchantable beavers (about 36 guilders) annually to learn the art of sewing in 1653; in 1665, Gijsbert Schuyler's father paid 100 guilders a year to learn the art of surgery.[34] Schuyler's father was a successful merchant in Albany at the time of his son's apprenticeship and could probably afford the fee. In the Netherlands, the children of the elite were often apprenticed at the cost of the parents. The sums varied in Old Amsterdam between 45 and 300 guilders, a range not unlike that of the colony.[35]

The costs of apprenticeship were increased if a contract obliged a master to teach a child reading or writing or to send him or her to school. Providing an education was an important part of parenting, and "schools were regarded as critical for propagating religious creeds and literary skills needed to read God's Word and write bills of lading."[36] Sending a child to school, however, was a personal choice; if an occupation did not warrant reading, writing, or arithmetic, parents were not admonished for withholding instruction. In colonial indentures, school charges were on occasion paid by parents or guardians, perhaps to ensure that the child would be educated.[37] Boys and girls attended the elementary schools of New Netherland, generally at their parents' expense, and the poor were taught for free. Parents in New Amsterdam paid 30 stuivers per quarter to have a child taught "the a b c, spelling and reading," 50 stuivers for reading and writing, and 60 stuivers for reading, writing, and cyphering.[38] It took about three years for children to read satisfactorily in the city of Utrecht. They progressed to writing at about age eight or nine; therefore, they began their schooling at age five or six.[39] The small number of colonial contracts requiring schooling (11 contracts, or 30.5 percent) may indicate that some children had already learned to read and write at the time of their binding. Nine of the contracts that specified some form of learning mentioned the age of the children, which on average was 11½ years.

Contracts requiring literacy or schooling allowed masters and mistresses various options to fulfill the agreement. For instance, in 1663, Jan van Campen could teach Annetje Prae himself or send "her to school during the winter evenings"; meanwhile, Wophert Webber agreed to teach Jochim Anthony Robberts reading and writing in 1661 "or cause him to be taught" these skills. Robberts was bound for three years by his sister Susanna Anthony Robberts, "free Negress" and his guardian. His contract is one of two pertaining to children of African origin. Robberts' duties were not recorded, but he would receive "board and clothes," and his master's obligation to teach him reading and writing was an "express condition" of the contract. At "the expiration of the apprenticeship," he would be "decently clothed, be fitted out without anything more."[40] Jochim Robberts may have been the son of Anthony Portugues. In February 1644, when Jochem was perhaps six months old, the provincial court manumitted his father along with ten other West India Company slaves and their wives. Their children, "at present born or yet to be born," remained "bound and obligated to serve the... Company as slaves."[41] That Robberts was not identified as a slave in the indenture indicates he was probably free like his sister, evidence that some manumitted parents were able to release their children from the stipulations of the decree of 1644, which in turn afforded them a better opportunity for advancement and an education.

Jochim Robberts was undoubtedly an orphan in 1661 when his sister Susanna, as guardian, bound him to Webber. Seventeen of the thirty-six contracts (47.2 percent) involved a *wees,* or an orphan. Five of the seventeen had lost either mother or father, and the other twelve were full orphans. Orphans with some property were maintained from the residue of parental estates, but children deprived of parents and property became wards of the Reformed Church. Other denominations cared for their own orphans, but no records remain for this period in New Netherland. The deacons of the Reformed Church were generally charged with providing custodial care and occupational training for the community's orphans.[42] The case of eight-year-old Anna Tielemans is an example how this was achieved. When her mother Teuntje Straetmans died in 1662, Tielemans came under the guardianship of the consistory—minister, elders, and deacons—of the Reformed Church of Breuckelen (now Brooklyn, New York), for her father was also presumed dead. Two consistory members were present at Straetmans's deathbed and promised to look after the child. This they did, in part, by binding her out to Gerrit Cornelissen van Niekerk, who lived in Midwoudt (now Flatbush, New York) on Long Island. Tielemans would live in his house and serve him for six years. He promised to provide board and clothing, to send her to school during the winter evenings, and "to treat her in a proper way." In 1664, it was noted that under Cornelissen's care she was "getting plump and fat, an indication that she is thriving better there than she did at home." The household liked the little girl "as much as their own children," and she was certainly not "a burden to us [the consistory]."[43] Tielemans grew to adulthood on Long Island, married, had children, and was reunited with her father, who had remained in the Caribbean in the 1650s after Tielemans and her mother traveled from there to New Netherland.[44]

The contracts made for Tielemans and sixteen other orphans and half orphans may signify that a formal agreement, rather than an oral or casual one, was a better way to ensure proper care and treatment of children who had lost their parents as advocates, should things go awry. Placing such orphans in an apprenticeship or service provided occupational training and maintenance, demonstrating the custodial function of such contracts.

Certainly, the report on Anna Tieleman's condition two years into her contract was proof that her master had upheld his obligations according to seventeenth-century Dutch civil law. However, the records of New Netherland document sixty court cases from 1638 to 1674 in which contracting parties appear because something had gone wrong during the apprenticeship term, and an additional thirty miscellaneous suits mentioned a child or children in service or apprenticeship or performing specific tasks. The sixty court actions were divided into four categories: in twenty-three cases (38.3 percent), parents or guardians claimed unpaid wages or end-of-service clothes due to their children or wards; in eighteen cases (30 percent), masters and mistresses sued parents or guardians for children who had run away or left service before the end of the contracted time, or parents sued masters for discharging children early; in thirteen cases (21.7 percent), some form of mistreatment or abuse upon a child by the master is mentioned; in six cases (10 percent), a child is accused of a crime or misdemeanor. An analysis of such suits and the thirty miscellaneous cases increases our knowledge of the relationships among masters and indentured children and their parents or guardians. Parents had to ensure that their children serve out the stipulated time faithfully and satisfactorily, and masters had to keep children in their service for the length of the contract, treat them as their own children, and pay the stipulated compensation. Both parties were held accountable. Magistrates weighed the evidence, examined documents, and heard and questioned contending parties and witnesses before pronouncing their judgments. Unfortunately, the children involved often remained nameless and were designated merely as the sons, daughters, wards, apprentices, or servants of the adults bringing in the actions. The ninety court cases must be seen within the context of New Netherland's court system, for the provincial, municipal, and village courts met on a weekly basis. New Amsterdam's municipal court had an especially busy roster from 1662 through 1663, when approximately 1,200 cases were presented, of which only thirteen (1.1 percent) concerned children and their work. Again, such small numbers may suggest that children learned their trades from parents or that problems with children bound to friends or neighbors may have been settled outside the courts.

The compensation that children received at the end of their contracts was a concern in twenty-three court actions. Such recompense was an important contribution to a household's total annual earnings and could not be missed, especially by families living on the edge of poverty. The average annual cost of maintaining a child has not been established for New Netherland, but the amounts some masters calculated to support their young charges were noted in the 1650s and 1660s. By way of illustration, a wealthy New Amsterdam merchant, Allard Anthony, claimed 5½ guilders a week (286 guilders per year) for expenses incurred to train the son of another merchant in 1656, a sum that included the costs of raw materials or goods spoilt by his untrained apprentice. Jacob Corlaer required 2½ guilders per week (130 guilders per year) to board and clothe the bastard child who was indentured to him in 1658, while Marritje Claes received 150 guilders in one year (1658-59) to board a ward of the deacons of the Reformed Church of Beverwijck.[45] The annual outlay, then, to maintain a child in New Netherland could range from 130 to 286 guilders per year. If unskilled and skilled laborers in the colony worked six days a week all year round and if they earned 1 and 2 guilders a day, respectively, their earnings would have amounted to 312 or 624 guilders a year.[46] Certainly, the higher amount may have been adequate for a family of four with little left over for extras, but 1 guilder a day would not. Buying shirts and shoes for growing children undoubtedly strained the family budget when a loaf of bread and a pound of butter already cost a guilder each.[47]

The numbers indicate, therefore, that children had to contribute to the household by earning their daily bread as soon as possible. New Netherland's parents and guardians sued dilatory masters for their children's dues or wages, but by law, "the year, month or day, named in the contract" had to have passed before a demand for compensation could take place, unless otherwise stipulated.[48] Many of the twenty-three suits for recompense are similar to the action Wolphert Webber brought against Albert Albertsen, a ribbon weaver. In 1654, Webber demanded 91 guilders for his son, who was bound for two years, and complained that Albertsen had not clothed the boy according to the contract, had set him free on three different occasions, and had finally sent him home. Albertsen denied the charges and professed that their contract had not yet expired, therefore the boy had to complete his time and then he would pay. After examining the submitted documents and questioning the parties and witnesses, the court sided with the plaintiff, Wolphert Webber. Albertsen was ordered to pay "according to the last verbal agreement."[49]

Proving one's assertions in court could be difficult. In 1659, the shoemaker Jan Snedingh sued the farmer Matthijs Boon for the balance of wages earned by Snedingh's son, being ten guilders, stockings, and shoes. Boon's wife produced a written contract in court and complained that the plaintiff had "forcibly taken his son away" while her husband was sick. Snedingh denied this and offered to drop the suit if Boon could verify his claim. Apparently, the defendant's witnesses were not forthcoming, one was living in the Esopus (now Kingston) and the other had died. Without their testimony, Boon was ordered to pay.[50]

If proven, the accusation made by the wife of Matthijs Boon would have been a serious breach of contract. A parent who took a child out of a master's service without lawful reason, or a child who left service without the consent of his master, could lose half the agreed-upon wages stated in a contract.[51] Certainly Jan van St. Obin adhered to this right in 1659 when he demanded that the court dock half the wages of Saartje Pieter's boy, because he ran away, leading St. Obin to hire another in his place. The court ordered Pieter to return the boy to serve out his time according to the agreement.[52] St. Obin's suit was one of eighteen similar actions concerning runaway apprentices or young servants.

Albert Lenaertsen is the first child on record to run away, from his master Jan Damen in May of 1638. Damen owned and leased farmland north of New Amsterdam and sued Lenaertsen's father for his return. Why he ran away is not stated, nor is his age. In 1645, his father Lenaert Arentsen testified that he had arrived in New Netherland in 1638, making it possible that his son be hired out shortly after their arrival. Perhaps it was his strange surroundings that made Lenaertsen long for the companionship of his family. The court ordered the parties to adhere to their mutual obligations. The boy was "to fulfil his [contract of] service," and his master was to treat him "as his own son." Should he "run home" again, his father was bound to return him "each time, on pain of making good the loss and damage" that Damen would suffer.[53] Runaways apparently had no trouble reaching the home of their parents or guardians. The proximity to home could also be a detriment to their training, however, as it was for Hendrick Obe Jr. in 1665. When he ran to his parent's house, his master Thomas Tiddeman demanded that his father return him to serve out his five-year term and confessed that the child would do better if his "father's howse Was not soo nye" to Tiddeman's.[54] The court's final decision was not recorded.

While masters could withhold half the pay of runaway youngsters, they could, on the other hand, be charged the full wage for dismissing them without lawful cause before the end of their terms.[55] Anna Webber quoted this law almost verbatim in the court of New Amsterdam in 1658, having hired out her daughter for a year to Johannes Nevius. She declared that Nevius's wife had ordered the girl to leave the house and added "that in law if a master or mistress bid a maid or man servant leave the house before the expiration of the time without weighty reasons, he is bound to pay the full wages."[56] In this case and many others, the magistrates ordered recalcitrant masters to pay for the time their charges served rather than the full wage. Asser Levy also received this judgment in 1665 when Aucke Jansen sued him for releasing his daughter without cause. After her discharge, the girl, whose name and age were not recorded, had gone to see the wife of Balthazar Bayart to ask for employment. Bayart's wife had given a cautious answer. Yes, she would hire the girl only "if she were free from her mistress, other wise not." The customs and laws of Amsterdam obliged masters or mistresses to inquire about potential servants: Were they already bound? Had they been fired from service? Negligent parties paid a 20-guilder fine to the city's coffers and enjoyed no future service from the person hired.[57] There is no evidence that fines were charged in New Netherland, but Bayart's reluctance to hire Jansen's daughter if she was still bound to her employer indicates that some of the colony's denizens were well aware of the possible consequences of taking on such help.

Following the letter of the law was not always possible in so new a society and, at times, colonial magistrates used a certain degree of discretionary authority in deciding when and how to apply rules concerning children and their work. A case in point is that of the widow Femmetje Westerkamp. On her husband's deathbed in 1654, she had promised that she would take their daughter away from her master, Andries Herpertsen. She asked the magistrates to break the contract, and they agreed. A deathbed promise had to be carried out, on the condition that Westerkamp allow her daughter five more weeks with her master so that he could look for another servant.[58]

Upon commencement of a contract, parental rights and authority were transferred to a master, including the right to discipline and punish. In 1674, when Barentie Stratmans bound her eight-year-old daughter Johanna to Richard and Elisabeth Pretty for eight years, she asked them to be "as a father and a mother" and to bring her up "in the fear of the Lord as if she were their own child." Stratmans gave them "the right to properly punish her [Johanna] for wrongdoing and disobedience, giving them full power to do so and trusting them to do all that is good." The obedience and submission that Johanna once gave to her mother was now due her master and mistress. Stratmans promised that Johanna would, "with the help of God Almighty," serve her eight-year apprenticeship "with all diligence and faithfulness."[59] But what could the Prettys do if Johanna failed to comply? Historians have noted that children learned to make their own choices and to distinguish goodness from evil, diligence from sloth, and duty from disloyalty through a combination of family counsel and education (either in the workplace or in school).[60] To achieve such goals, Dutch moralists recommended that parents not spare the rod and avoid spoiling a child. However, Johannes van Beverwijck, a noted seventeenth-century physician in Amsterdam, advocated "that fear of the rod was better than its use since it was likely to harden the child into expectations of brutality and wickedness. At the other extreme, it was thought foolish to allow children's willfulness to go unchecked and unpunished." The "humanist emphasis on giving some rein to the natural instincts of the child and cajoling it into learning" was prevalent in the Netherlands, while the "notions of 'breaking the will,' apparently strong in more intensely Puritan and evangelical cultures, were almost wholly absent in the Netherlands."[61]

Some colonial Dutch parents apparently shared similar tendencies toward leniency. In 1661, the magistrates of New Amsterdam admonished Alexander Curtius, the master of the Latin school, for not keeping "strict discipline" among his pupils. Curtius claimed his hands were bound, "as some people do not wish to have their children punished."[62] However, it was perhaps the punishment administered by others to which parents objected, not the discipline they themselves meted out. The insolence or disobedience displayed by an apprentice could be rewarded with a swift kick in the rear or a knock on the head, punishment that one master said was as "his own child" would receive for similar behavior.[63] The parents or guardians of children on the receiving end of such punishment, however, responded differently. They presented their cases (thirteen in all) with concern for their children's welfare. Some children appeared in court to display the scars on their heads or the bruises on their bodies. Some parents produced a surgeon's report. Although corporal punishment was considered a necessary part of discipline, it was not permitted, of course, to be life-threatening.[64]

A case in point took place in 1656 in Beverwijck, where the court decreed payment of 30 guilders for the pain suffered by Jan van Hoesem's daughter, who was bound to Geertruy Jeronimus. Jeronimus declared that she had admonished the girl "to mend her ways as she was a young maiden," whereupon the girl made "some retort." Outraged, the mistress chastised and kicked her charge "with her foot in the behind." Van Hoesem claimed that his daughter was kicked in the groin "when she stooped over, so that she discharged much blood contrary to nature and for a long time was confined to her bed, suffering great pain," making her unable to do any work. He exhibited a surgeon's report as proof. Jeronimus had to pay the fine along with the costs of the suit. Whether van Hoesem's daughter remained with her mistress to serve out her time is not stated.[65]

The son of Wolphert Webber suffered no physical abuse, nor did he endure hunger or lack of care, yet Webber feared for his son's life in 1657. He sued the boy's master Claes Kos in the court of New Amsterdam for breaking their contract. Webber declared that he had hired his son to Kos "to dwell with and serve him in this City," but Kos employed him "not here but mostly over at Pavonia [across the Hudson River, in today's New Jersey] and in journeying to and from that place, where much danger is to be expected both by water as from the Indians etc." He demanded that Kos not "employ his son there and thus, but in truth within this City, or else to send him back home." If he refused, Webber threatened "before God and the Judge that he, in his capacity as Father, protests against the deft. [defendant] that if any misfortune happen [to] his son, either in passing over, or from the Indians or otherwise, he had done his duty [by bringing the suit], and shall avenge himself on him." Kos denied the conditions of the contract, whereupon the magistrates ordered both parties to bring in their evidence.[66] It is apparent that Webber kept a watchful eye on his son and was prepared to go to any length to protect him. Whether he broke the contract and took his son back is not known, for the men did not appear again in court concerning this matter.

A father's desire to protect a treasured son was matched by the community's willingness to guard against the unnecessary wrath of a master or mistress upon bound children, especially those who had no parental advocates. Four women filed evidence in 1662 against the wife of the farmer Aert Cornelissen, who beat and kicked an orphaned boy bound to him by his guardians. Their evidence and the boy's own testimony ended the indenture, and the child was bound by the Orphan Masters of New Amsterdam to one of his guardians.[67]

As the minutes of the New Netherland's courts chronicle the violence of masters or mistresses, they also record the crimes and misdemeanors of indentured children in six court actions. Several received punishment more severe than the kicks and beatings given for disobedience or sloth. False accusation and lying earned one twelve-year-old boy a whipping "with rods in the presence of an alderman" in 1665. "Consideringe his Youngeness," he was eventually handed over to his master with a recommendation that he correct the boy for his committed faults and "Warn him Seriously for the future to take heed for to Commit Such faults any more."[68] Two nameless indentured orphans, a boy and a girl, "transgressed with unfaithfulness in their masters' house" and were disciplined aboard the warship *de Waagh* (the Scale). No other details were given, and the case is obscure. The boy was "punished discretely at the capstan in ship's manner by boys" and was ordered to "work on board until further orders." The girl was forced to watch the boy's chastisement and, "after threatening her," was allowed to return to her master.[69]

The system of apprenticeship and service that was established in New Netherland in the seventeenth century was based on Old World institutions. It provided vocational training for colonial children. The directors of the West India Company supplied the initial guide that local authorities and residents implemented and used. The system regulated the relationships between masters and parents and their children. Children learned the skills required for a productive life of labor. Labor was, after all, expected of all members of society, infants and invalids being the only exceptions. Contracting parties, parents and masters—not children—had the authority to hold each other to the terms of the indentures. Their agreements, both oral and written, were binding. They sued if one or the other was found in neglect. Local magistrates enforced the laws but used their discretionary power when necessary to serve the needs of the colony's children. As graduates of the system, former apprentices, now skilled workers, earned their daily bread, thereby becoming valuable additions to the community.

The apprenticeships of young New Netherlanders developed into a system that required both parental and communal effort to achieve its goals. Its analysis adds a Dutch perspective to an institution that affected and shaped the destinies of colonial children, and it allows a comparison with the English and French institutions presented elsewhere in this volume. Such comparison reveals enduring similarities between the customs and laws of indenture and of apprenticeship upheld in the Netherlands, elsewhere in Europe, England, and North America. In 1664, New Netherland ceased to exist in name but continued in culture and spirit. English law gradually altered Dutch lives. By 1665, the Duke of York's

Laws instructed parents and masters to "bring up their Children and Apprentices in some honest and Lawful Calling, Labour or Employment," which must have sounded hauntingly familiar to inhabitants of Dutch origin.[70] They had, after all, been applying similar standards since their arrival in New Netherland and had lived by the same system before they came to their new home.

CHAPTER SEVEN

Mothers and Children in and out of the Charleston Orphan House

JOHN E. MURRAY

Destitute, abandoned, and orphaned children faced grim futures in early America, as the essays in this volume testify. But not all poor children were equally vulnerable, and not all futures were equally grim. For poor white children in Charleston, South Carolina, the Orphan House provided some promise of a better life. The Orphan House's walls were not an impermeable barrier that sealed young residents off from the outside world. Rather, the Orphan House, the first public orphanage in America, was the site of numerous interactions among children, surviving parents, city officials, and masters. Most children who entered were eventually bound out to local tradesmen and housewives, but these apprenticeships were frequently negotiated by watchful and concerned relatives. The ongoing and loving bonds between surviving mothers and the children they had relinquished stand out in the story of the Charleston Orphan House. Care and advocacy given by these mothers to their children after surrendering legal authority over them offers a rich new perspective on poor white families in the antebellum South.

When Charleston established the Orphan House in 1790, it was the richest city in the nation. Studies of probate records indicate that the per capita wealth

I gratefully acknowledge financial support from a major grant from the Spencer Foundation; archival assistance of James Barkley at the South Carolina Department of Archives and History, Elizabeth Newcombe at the South Carolina Room, Charleston County Public Library, and especially Harlan Greene at the College of Charleston Library; and comments by Ruth Herndon and David Mitch on an earlier version.

of Charleston was twice that of New England and the middle colonies, even after including the substantial slave population. Nobody knew it at the time, but the city was near the peak of its prosperity. Indigo production was in decline following withdrawal of British subsidies. Combined with the rise of short-staple cotton production, the economic heart of the Old South would soon shift westward. Within the old city, planters who saw Charleston as a pleasant residence contended with merchants who wanted to revive the city's economy. Symbolic of planter victory, the rail line from the cotton-growing upcountry ended at the city's boundary, well short of the old residential district—and of the wharves from which that cotton was shipped to textile manufacturers across the Atlantic world. But the planters could not hold this line forever. The devastating Panic of 1819, combined with a worldwide decline in cotton prices, led to increased interest in industrial and mercantile activities. By 1850, grist mills, rice mills, iron foundries, turpentine distilleries, and saw mills were all operating within the city. By the eve of the war, Charleston's wealth had declined dramatically, relative to that of the great northern cities, but in southern terms it was still quite prosperous.[1]

In 1790 the first census proclaimed that Charleston was the fourth city of the new nation, behind Philadelphia, New York, and Boston. The city's population did grow afterward, but so slowly that the 40,522 Charlestonians who appeared in the 1860 census made it the twenty-second-largest city in the country, less than a quarter the size of Boston. Racially, whites had been in the minority from the onset of record-keeping right up to the 1850 census. White fear of black insurrection led to legal restrictions on black movement that in turn caused the total population to fall in the 1830s and 1850s. During the 1850s, large numbers of Irish and German immigrants settled in the city, many of whom struggled unsuccessfully to keep out of the Poor House. Private efforts to care for the poor focused on particular segments of the population. Over the antebellum period were founded the Hebrew Orphan Society, the Brown Fellowship Society (for free men of color), and a Catholic orphanage to look after impoverished and unfortunate children of deceased brethren.[2] For the rest, there was the Orphan House.

The Orphan House's benevolence was aimed at Charleston's poor and working-class whites, groups that have for the most part avoided the attention of historians. On the rural South, Frank Owsley's well-known *Plain Folk of the Old South* sought to rehabilitate the yeoman class: those who may have owned a little bit of land but few, if any, slaves.[3] His work influenced later historians such as Stephanie McCurry, who found in her study of the South Carolina yeomanry a strong element of patriarchy even at the lowest levels of material wealth.[4] Charles Bolton and Bill Cecil-Fronsman each examined poor whites through census, tax, and court records. They described people who, without much to live on, sought self-respect through belief in racial superiority.

Although these historians used the few available sources on poor whites skillfully, the overrepresentation of court records among those documents may have biased our picture of this group, since much of our understanding of their behavior arises from their misbehavior.[5]

Poor families have featured in histories of other aspects of the South. Bertram Wyatt-Brown considered southern childraising patterns in the context of honor. Mothers felt ambivalence toward their children, he proposed, but still permitted themselves to form emotional bonds with their offspring. The evidence for these assertions, though, was of questionable quality, depending as it did on secondary literature on planter families plus assumptions that the poor acted pretty much the same as their betters. Peter Bardaglio described how southern jurisprudence seemed to lack the notion of "the child's best interests" in adoption and public apprenticeship (as in the North after midcentury) due to their commitment to upholding blood ties (in particular, the father's) as established in the common law. Finally, Barbara Bellows's sensitive study of charitable activities considers, for the most part, the same part of Charleston examined in this essay but primarily from the perspective of the benevolent white elite. This essay aims to show, in part, what family life was like for those on the receiving end of that benevolence.[6]

In the colonies, binding out poor children to masters who could support them, masters who in turn kept the usufruct of the child's labor, carried over from the English Poor Laws of 1601.[7] As in England, overseers of the poor in South Carolina enjoyed the legal authority to seize children of poor families and bind them out, but Charleston officials did not use such legal powers to bring children into the Orphan House.[8] Because English and South Carolinian laws were intended to make each parish care for its own resident poor, an applicant had to prove that he had gained a settlement in the parish to be eligible for poor relief. From the early eighteenth century, that meant the Poor House for settled residents of Charleston, but few who could live on their own voluntarily entered it. It was part hospital, part insane asylum, and part homeless shelter for those who had hit bottom. Included among Poor House denizens were children too young to leave their mothers. Poor House children from the ages of nine to twelve or so were boarded out and enrolled in a charity school, and those slightly older were bound out directly to masters. Creation of the Orphan House promised to insulate the youngest and most impressionable from the despair of the Poor House. In addition, city fathers believed, a centralized and dedicated Orphan House could reduce "expenses on the parish" that ratepayers found so burdensome.[9]

So many poor white families wanted to place their children in the Orphan House that not all could be accommodated. Commissioners of the Orphan House investigated families and guardians of prospective residents to see whether they were legally admissible by age and residency criteria—and how well their claims of poverty stood up to close scrutiny. When the commissioners "enquired into and determined as to the propriety of their admission," as their charge read, they created a body of records that describes the lives of the very poor in antebellum Charleston—a remarkable collection.[10] Documents include the standardized indentures, as the legal documents that bound the child to the Orphan House were called. Letters and reports from parents, guardians, Poor House officials, and the commissioners reveal in some detail the life experiences of these children prior to the time of their application. While court, census, and tax records yield some information about the poor, the Orphan House documents provide a rare glimpse into the experiences of the poor in early America in their own words.[11]

The numbers of children who depended upon the Orphan House varied over time. The resident population rose steadily to nearly two hundred in the mid-1820s and then declined until waves of immigrants appeared in the 1850s, when it increased sharply. The share of local poor white children who lived in the Orphan House paralleled its overall population levels. In the later eighteenth century, historians have estimated that about a fifth of Charleston's white population belonged to the ranks of relatively poor nonslave owners.[12] Assuming that the share of the white population that was poor remained about one-fifth over the period in question, the ratio of children in the Orphan House to one-fifth of Charleston County's white population under the age of fifteen was 9 percent in 1800, 12 percent in 1810, 11 percent in 1820, 9 percent in 1830, 8 percent in 1840, 6 percent in 1850, and back up to 10 percent in 1860.

In common with other American cities at that time, the increase in needy children at the end of the period was in part due to ever greater numbers of European immigrants landing in Charleston. The last two decades before the war saw steady population growth, with the 1850s registering the greatest jump of any decade between 1770 and 1870.[13] By the mid-1850s, about 40 percent of white Charlestonians were recent German and Irish immigrants. Not all of them attained prosperity right away, and as a result the Poor House population doubled between 1850 and 1856.[14] Orphan House officials believed that waves of immigration could overwhelm relief institutions. In rejecting the application of one visibly destitute family, an official wrote that acceptance would lead to numerous similar applications from Irish and German laborers "who would...greatly increase the burthen of the citizens," a clearly undesirable outcome.[15]

To ensure that their children qualified for admission to the Orphan House, families described themselves in some detail. Most fathers were drawn from the lower ranks of laborers and artisans. They toiled as building tradesmen, shoemakers, and the occasional mechanic. Usually these men could support their families, but they enjoyed little room for error. When epidemics, particularly of yellow fever, struck down mothers of young children, surviving fathers brought their children to the Orphan House.¹⁶ A father who took ill might lose his capacity to support his family. James Boswell could not work due to his "tedious lingering sickness," which his physician diagnosed as "painter's cholic"—that is, lead poisoning.¹⁷ Nor could a disabled or imprisoned father support his family.¹⁸

As in all Atlantic port cities, families of men who worked on the sea barely scraped by.¹⁹ In Charleston, they constituted a large share of those seeking the Orphan House's aid. A sailor on a longer-than-expected cruise might return to find that his wife had remedied the family's financial distress by leaving a child or two at the Orphan House. Sophia Campbell anxiously begged the Orphan House to take her two sons because her husband had been at sea for six months and the family was destitute without his continued support.²⁰ A widowed seaman named John Hanson had hoped to continue boarding his children with the neighbor lady who had taken them in upon his wife's death in 1825. "But," he explained, "the wages of a sailor are not adequate to do this." Indeed, this neighbor testified, Hanson had left for the sea without ever paying her, so it was she who applied to send the children to the Orphan House.²¹

The need for widowers to continue working prevented them from caring for their little ones during the day. In an 1803 case, neighbors declared that a widowed father of four "has used every means to board these children out, but with all his exertions cannot pay for the same."²² Bereaved fathers who drowned their sorrows in alcohol left their children to depend on the kindness of strangers. The Reverend John Bachman, a Lutheran pastor, reported that in the days after one mother's death, the father was "too far gone to hold up his head." Bachman feared that the man would not sober up long enough to testify to the family's destitution before a city alderman, as the rules for admission required.²³

In several ways, mothers were in a different situation than fathers. Although debilitating illness seems to have been equally prevalent between the sexes, relatively few of the women drank to excess. In one unusual case, a child was orphaned by the state of Georgia, which executed her mother for the murder of her stepfather.²⁴ Meddlesome neighbors recommended to commissioners that certain mothers be dispossessed of their children, because they worked as prostitutes or left their children in the care of blacks.²⁵

The single most common reason given by women for relinquishing their children was poverty, which they pled in two different ways. Some women claimed that their financial problems stemmed from a trough in the business cycle. For example, many applicants in the 1820s (but not before or after) reported that "the extreme pressure of the times" or "the times being so hard" had driven them to offer their children to the Orphan House.²⁶ And in fact, these were hard times in the low country. From 1815 to 1818, rising relative cotton prices formed a tide that lifted all free boats in Charleston, but beginning in 1819 they sharply declined. The downturn surprised and swamped debtors and led to the Panic of 1819, a nationwide economic slump that nonetheless fell especially heavily on cotton-growing regions. Histories of the Panic of 1819 have concentrated on business failures and suspension of note redemption by banks, but real deprivation among the very poor was another consequence. In Charleston, poor families unable to care for their children ensured that the number of children entering the Orphan House in 1819 would be greater than in any other year from its founding to the mid-1850s.[27]

Other mothers and female guardians reported that they were unable to earn much of a living no matter where they found themselves in the cycle of boom and bust. To emphasize how dire their situation was, many described their sole means of support as needlework, a sure sign of near-destitution. A man who supplied a reference for Elizabeth Clarke explained why she could not support the youngster in her charge: "Her only dependence for self and another child being the needle, which you all gentlemen must be convinced is not sufficient ever to pay for room, rent, & the most common food."[28] All understood that a woman who claimed to be "without any dependence but what arises from my own exertions" faced a meager existence and likely could not support her children.[29] Needlework did carry one great benefit, the ability to work at home while keeping an eye on young children.

Those who toiled in another common occupation of the poorer sort, household service, were not so fortunate.[30] Perhaps surprisingly in a slave-based economy, it was common for poor white women to work in household service. They "scoured" and cooked in kitchens and watched and nursed the children of the well-to-do.[31] This work paid poorly. A hotel washerwoman in Charleston might earn $6 per month at a time when a common laborer there made over a dollar a day.[32] A few employers permitted mothers to bring their young children to work. That possibility was all one commissioner needed to reject Ann Fitzpatrick's application to admit her daughter. He claimed that the girl would be better off going to work with her mother, who was a housekeeper in a hotel, than living in the Orphan House.[33] Most well-to-do families found children of domestic servants to be intrusive, so it was common to require a domestic to rid herself of her child as a condition of employment. Many applications pleaded for the Orphan House to receive a child or children so that the mother could take a "situation." A commissioner observed of Catherine Blake in 1857, "She is in entire poverty & is desirous of going out to service as a washer or seamstress, but is unable to procure employment while incumbered with her child."[34] As we shall see, this was a particularly persuasive argument.

Many new mothers worked as wet nurses. The going rate for wet nurses around 1840 was a penurious six to seven dollars per month.[35] Southern women of the middle and upper classes believed that breastfeeding was a vital duty for a new mother.[36] Notwithstanding the stereotype of the "mammy" wet nurse, many white women breastfed their infants and did so out of a well-reasoned ideology of health benefits and maternal obligation. For a variety of reasons, not every mother suckled her child. While some women of the slaveholding class did turn their babies over to black nursemaids, in other cases they advertised for white wet nurses to enter their households. A few advertisements specified that blacks only need apply, and others solicited women of either race. One announcement that did not mention race required the wet nurse to report for work without child.[37] Since, as in the cases of domestics, children of wet nurses were usually not welcome in the employer's household, many ended up in the Orphan House. One such mother made her case to the commissioners in economic terms she thought they could understand:

> I have within the last few days got a place as nurse but I must pay out of my wages for my baby whom I have been obliged to put out to Nurse. If I have also to pay for my two boys, I shall not be able to retain a cent, but if thro' your humanity I am permitted to place them in the Orphan House a few months earlier than the usual time I shall then have it in my power to save something.[38]

Thus did older children of wet nurses make their way to the Orphan House. After Eliza Cregier started work as a wet nurse to Thomas Napier's family and accompanied them on a trip to the North, two of her children entered the Orphan House.[39] When Mary Creamer was widowed, the wealthy planter Henry Izard hired her to nurse his infant. Izard allowed her to bring her own baby into his household, but to take the position she had to place her other four children in the Orphan House.[40] Relinquishing one's own child in order to nurse the child of another for pay must have been a difficult decision, although the documentary evidence does not reveal the mothers' feelings about it.

A woman who had hit absolute bottom might move into the Poor House, a dreary fate indeed. Not just paupers but also the insane and criminals inhabited the Poor House, making it no place for children. So believed the Commissioners of the Poor House, perhaps in part because each additional child added to their budgetary concerns. To move a child from the Poor House to the Orphan House lifted one burden, and if the mother then went out to service, officials had killed two birds with one stone. As a Poor House commissioner explained, transferring a child out of the Poor House "would relieve this house of both trouble & expense, as we have at present both mother & child, whereas if the child was sent to the Orphan House the mother could be discharged & would be able to maintain herself which she is not capable of doing while her children are with her."[41] Civic duty called for the Orphan House to accept one five-year-old boy, argued a commissioner of the Poor House, because "as the city will probably be thereby relieved of its mother as a pauper, your honorable body will perceive that granting this application will not only be an act of benevolence to the parties but a benefit to the community."[42] An unhappy choice for the mother, perhaps, to say nothing of the newly institutionalized child, but to move a woman from the Poor House into the ranks of the employed was a happy bargain to city fathers operating on a tight budget.

Most inmates had been brought to the Orphan House by a widowed parent. Full orphans and abandoned children were nominated for Orphan House admission by three different sorts of adults: stepparents, more distant blood kin, or strangers who took them in. Stepparents, especially stepfathers, seem most likely to have abused these children, either through violence or neglect. Some stepfathers banished their new wives' children. Mary Anne McDermott sought admission for her two sons by her late husband because "the present step father Ed. McDermott will not allow them near the House or premises for sustenance."[43] Where exactly these children obtained their sustenance before coming to the Orphan House is not clear. A mother's death could reveal how in life she had protected her children from their stepfather's wrath. After his mother and half sister died from fever, Joseph Ringland's intemperate and poor stepfather simply kicked him out of the house, forcing the boy to fend for himself.[44] More distant relations took in some of these children, but often not for long. "Connexions" who were kin to the child only through marriage were rarely enthusiastic about a strange youth entering their household. The Visiting Commissioner reported in one such case that "the aunt says she has done all in her power but that her husband objects to the keeping the children, as he cannot support them."[45]

The Orphan House documents recorded remarkable acts of love by Charlestonians who were virtually destitute themselves. These women, never men, opened their doors to homeless children who were not their kin. These applicants were variously described as a "a poor Irishwoman," "a lady," and "a poor woman receiving a pension herself from the poor house." The extent of their invisibility was emphasized by one woman who wanted to fend off orders to collect corroborating statements. She was, she said, "a poor woman having no acquaintance with any one whose recommendation would be of any consequence," an arresting statement in light of the commissioners' extensive contacts in poor areas through many dedicated clergymen and their wives.[46] These women sheltered strange youngsters "through motives of charity alone" for a time, but eventually they wanted to move them into the Orphan House.[47] Some claimed indigence and asked to be relieved from caring for someone else's child, in effect saying that she had done her part and now it was time for the city to do its part. Others found the disciplinary demands of raising an older boy too great. For four years Mary Byrd had raised a widowed acquaintance's sickly son so that she could go out to service. Now at age six, she complained that "the older he gets the more ungovernable." She hoped that the Orphan House would "protect him from ruin which a female cannot do."[48]

Many children suffered from a distinct lack of permanency in their relationships with others. John Bowman lived a particularly unstable childhood, which apparently began with the loss of parents not long after his birth. According to his guardian,

> John Bowman was born at sea, when he came here (an infant) he was taken charge of by Mrs Walker. She died and then he went to Pemberton with whom he stayed until about 4 years ago, when he discharged him, having no use for him. He then went to a Mrs Myers on Gadsden Wh[ar]f, where he has been staying since; she discharged him a few days ago, saying she could support him no longer. Mr Jameson finding him destitute took him & presents him to the charity of the Institution.[49]

One aspect of instability was separation from siblings upon entering the Orphan House. While a relatively young mother with two or three children may have been able to get all of them admitted, it was unusual for the Orphan House to accept all children in families of four or more. More typical was the case of Eliza Laurence, who applied to get her six children admitted. The Commissioners took two, explaining that their limited resources restricted the number of children they could aid.[50] Some women, anticipating this response, incorporated it into their pleas to turn the tables in their favor. She might tell commissioners that she would manage a few of the children if they would take the rest. As with the arguments from the altruistic ladies implying that it was time for the city to do its part, we can see a negotiation of duties between the private/family and the public/corporate sides to perform necessary acts of charity. Someone had to care for these children, who were unable to care for themselves. Just who that adult would be for particular children emerged from interactions between officials and family members.

In some cases responsibility for childraising actually fell to older siblings who were not themselves fully grown yet. Sixteen-year-old Mary Tierney was an apprentice tailor, "learning to make vests & pantaloons," when her mother died unexpectedly. She left her master's household and returned home to care for her three siblings: a brother aged eight and two sisters aged six and three. Unable to pay the rent from his work as a city guardsman, their father turned to drink. Out of his mind with drink and rage, he regularly tossed out Mary and then beat the young ones. After he passed out, she returned to care for the younger ones. After seven months of this, she finally turned to the Orphan House, which took in all three young Tierneys.[51]

Given stories of abandonment and mistreatment by parents and stepparents, it is natural to wonder about emotional bonds that may have formed between children and the adults who cared for them. Most applicants were unable to support their children due to poverty and did not coldly (or permanently) abandon them. The more spectacular cases of domestic violence or child abandonment were relatively uncommon among the thousands of applicants who described their lives. Parents were painfully aware of their own straitened circumstances and believed the Orphan House promised a better childhood than they could provide. Such textual evidence of loving relationships as can be gleaned from the letters must be interpreted with some care, given our lack of understanding how impoverished whites in the South might have expressed feelings of love, or whether feelings were discussed at all. Most letters do not address the topic of emotional attachment, instead noting in straightforward fashion that an application was motivated by the destitution facing a widow or the limited resources of a household whose head had decided that a particular child was one too many.

Some letters to commissioners did describe qualities of parent-child relationships. Mothers related the distress they felt at leaving their little ones. A widow named Catherine Shelbock described how "grievous it is to me indeed to part with so young an infant who was a solace to me even in distress."[52] A letter attributed to the barely literate father of six-year-old Joseph Carson observed simply that "now gentlemen you no that they aint one of you that would like to part with your child."[53] A widow successfully petitioned the commissioners to return her son to her following the death of her infant. Despite sending the boy to the Orphan House, "her heart and affections" continued to "yearn with the love of a mother for him."[54] The commissioners sympathized with these parents and understood the bond between them and their children. That was why they allowed surviving parents to retrieve children from the institution in nearly every case.

Actions of parents and other family members suggest loving attachments to their children. Rather than turning to the Orphan House immediately after being struck by calamity, widows and guardians persisted in keeping children for months, even years, before seeking help. Susan Adams did not seek admission for her two sons for two years after her husband was lost at sea, during which time, she wrote, "for their support I have sold all that I had." Before turning to the Orphan House, Eliza Cregier supported not just her own four children but one of her husband's from a previous marriage with only her earnings as a wet nurse for a year and a half after he abandoned them. Not just mothers but other blood relations attempted to raise the children in their charge. Ellen Burkley's parents both died in the yellow fever epidemic of 1854, before Ellen could be weaned. The family physician, William Pettigrew, advised her aunt to place the infant in the Orphan House. However, wrote Pettigrew, "Her affection for the little destitute girl was too great, she could not think of such a thing." After caring for Ellen for several months and marrying, the aunt did send her to the Orphan House, but not immediately, even when advised to do so by a trusted physician.[55]

Once children were admitted into the institution, they did not lose contact with surviving parents. Evidence of parental, especially maternal, interaction appears in their correspondence with Orphan House officials.[56] Many adults continued to inquire about their children after the youngsters had moved into the Orphan House and become its responsibility. One father berated the institution for the "unmerciful floggings and whippings" his son endured at the hands of a schoolmaster.[57] Sometimes a mother took things into her own hands. When Mary Shedy determined that her daughter was getting too little food as a matter of course and too little attention when sick, she simply took her out of the House.[58] Such continuing advocacy suggests warm and loving ties between parents and children.

Beyond the occasional emergencies or holidays, some parents saw their children on a regular basis. Into the 1820s the Orphan House did not allow Catholic priests to teach children of Catholic parents nor to deliver the sacraments, which could explain why Mary Anne Carroll arranged to take her children to Mass every Sunday.[59] For some children, contact with a parent was a rare consolation in a life of pain. Several mothers expressed their desire to see children who would otherwise "fret" if left without maternal contact.[60] After her husband left her, Sarah Wray arranged for her six- and nine-year old sons to enter the Orphan House in September 1823; the elder one, James, died soon thereafter. She requested permission for her younger son to visit her in these terms:

> My son Henry who is in his seventh year of his age & who you so kindly received into the Orphan House has been in the habit of coming to me once a week for a long time past. I would therefore esteem it a favor if you would have the goodness to continue this indulgence, as he is so much a child that he mixes with no boys but comes to me and then returns in quietness. He having lost his elder brother there [he] seems to be quite lonesome and lonely.[61]

An appeal from a mother who had been denied permission for such a regular visit illustrates how important such ongoing contact was to her, as well as how the commissioners valued the appearance of propriety. After Ann Zylks unknowingly accompanied a woman of low reputation along the walk from the gate to the main building, she was denied permission to visit her children. Perplexed, she explained to the commissioners that the woman was a stranger to her and that she anxiously desired to see four-year-old Thomas and seven-year-old Margaret, whose blindness required "all the assistance I can give her as a mother."[62] Many poor women of Charleston who had entrusted their children to the Orphan House continued to fulfill their maternal obligations as best they could.

The indentures signed by each child and the responsible adult bound the child into the Orphan House only temporarily, until the institution arranged an apprenticeship. Many children left to learn a skill from a local tradesman, while others were bound to merchants from the upcountry. The rules of the

Orphan House called for boys to be apprenticed at age fourteen and girls at age thirteen, but in practice both sexes were bound in a range of ages of several years on either side of those targets.[63] The indentures required boys to work for their master until age twenty-one, or about seven years, while girls were bound to age eighteen, or for five or so years.[64] All together, just over half of the children were bound out and one-fifth returned to their parents (table 7.1), but these proportions changed over time (figure 7.1).

Of those children who left the Orphan House in the decade beginning in 1800, about 85 percent were formally bound to new masters. This proportion steadily decreased over time, and the proportion returned to a surviving parent increased, until by 1860 nearly as many were returned as were bound. These different trends suggest that deep changes were taking place in the underlying structure of the poor white Southern family—or stepfamily, to be precise.

All parties in the binding out process—child, parent, master, and commissioner—participated actively. A master who wrote to the institution seeking a particular child would carefully note that he had discussed the situation with the child's parent or guardian. A master described a typical process of gaining the consent of all parties: "One of the boys of the institution by the name of George King wishes me to take him as an apprentice to the tin-plate worker's business. I have consulted his mother on the subject and she consents that he should come to me. I am willing to take him if it meets your approbation."[65]

Not all masters passed this test. John Fairbrother's request for Charles Reyes to be bound to him was thwarted by Reyes's mother, who found painting "an unworthy trade" for her boy.[66] An application to the Orphan House by

TABLE 7.1.
Descriptive statistics of children in Charleston Orphan House sample

Sex	
Boy	64%
Girl	36%
Average age at entry	7 years
Average age at binding	15 years
Identity of responsible adult who brought child to Orphan House	
Mother	57%
Public official	28%
Father	12%
Other family	3%
Both parents	1%
Outcome	
Bound out to new master	55%
Returned to parent	22%
Died in Orphan House	8%
Returned to other family member	4%
Other	11%
N	2084

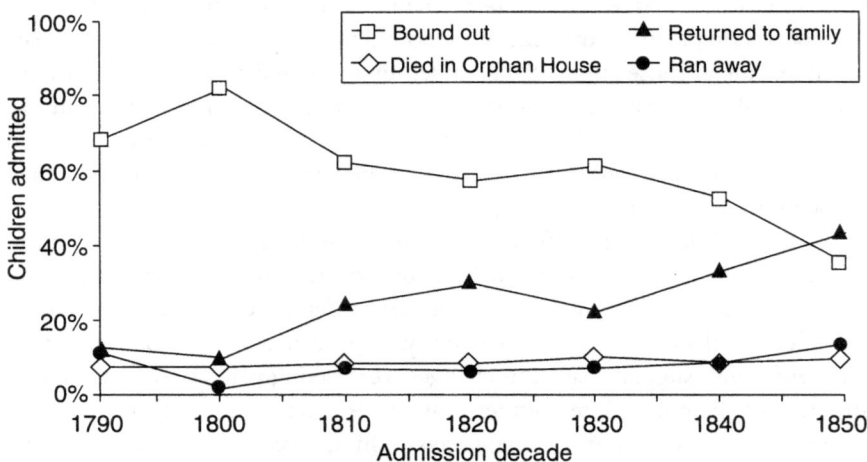

FIGURE 7.1. Outcomes for Charleston Orphan House residents, 1790–1860

a well-qualified and vetted prospective master who wanted to take on an apprentice could be rejected by the child, and Orphan House residents frustrated plans of hopeful masters from time to time. In one case commissioners approved an application by an out of town master in part because it was "the choice of the girl," while regarding another girl named Mary Mitchell, who "having changed her mind, and expressed her dis-inclination to go to Mrs. Belin, the Board agreed not to force her inclinations." Mrs. Belin received another girl, and Mary Mitchell was immediately bound to another mistress of whom she approved.[67]

Commissioners themselves rejected applications by some masters. One of the Visiting Commissioner's duties was to investigate prospective masters who lived in Charleston or review letters regarding masters who lived out of town. If the master appeared not to offer a respectable setting for the child, Commissioners rejected the application. When John L. E. W. "Doc" Shecut founded the South Carolina Homespun Company, he applied for six boys by name. The commissioners noted that most of the boys requested by Shecut were not yet of age. As for the others, "It would not conduce to their benefit to place them to learn that business," and so the commissioners declined to bind any of them out to Shecut.[68] A mistress who operated a boarding house was unlikely to receive a child, but no other characteristics of masters consistently induced the commissioners to deny their applications. They did, though, reject applications for children who were too young or who had not attained an educational level commensurate to the work the master proposed to put them to. Children sought as apprentices in an apothecary shop, for example, were expected to have had a better than average educational background to gain the commissioners' consent to their indenture.[69]

Parents actively worked to get their children into some trades and out of others. When William Milligan sought the return of his son, also called William, he explained that he had "return[ed] to my business with advantage" and pledged to provide "instruction in the branches of my employment."[70] Parents also sought tradesmen—and tradeswomen—and arranged for them to take their children as apprentices. Margaret Moles, a shopkeeper, applied for Sarah Fields after "being solicited by her mother Mrs. Clipper to make application for her daughter." She specified that Sarah would "attend in a dry good store or rather a fancy store where there is no kind of grocerys"—i.e., liquor.[71] Stepfathers made such arrangements for their wives' children, even going so far as to offer to pay for the schooling that the master was legally obligated to provide.[72]

As time went on, it became more common for a child to return to his natal family. Mothers began to inform commissioners that it was now in their power to support, maintain, and even educate the child, hence the petition to restore custody.[73] If a mother had been unable to maintain a child at one point, and thus applied for the child's admission to the Orphan House, and then claimed at a later time that she was in fact able to support the child, what had changed in between? Increasing numbers of widowed mothers appear to have remarried to men who were willing to support their new stepchildren. The record is thin, since documents usually describe the person receiving the child as "mother" or "father" rather than by name, but it appears to have become increasingly common for the mother to sign with a different surname when she petitioned for restoration of custody. Of the 266 children bound into the Orphan House in the 1790s, eighteen (7 percent) were eventually returned to mothers. Four of these women had new surnames, and no doubt some of the unnamed others had remarried as well. Two children were returned to still-married parents, but in no cases did a father come back to retrieve his offspring. The share of mothers who had remarried seems to have increased over time. Of the 518 children bound in during the 1850s, 130 (25 percent) were returned to mothers and 12 to fathers. Here all fourteen mothers who were listed by name had remarried.

Remarried women undoubtedly fared better materially than they had as widows. It became increasingly common for the new husband to permit his wealth to be spent on his new bride's offspring. Alexander Ballard informed the Board "that he had married Mrs. Margaret Jackman the mother of Elizabeth Jackman, whom he now requests from the Orphan House as he is able to maintain and educate her."[74] While Mrs. Jackman was unable to support Elizabeth, not only was the new Mrs. Ballard able to care for her daughter, she also chose to do so, and there are many such cases in the records. Despite the legal doctrine of coverture, in which the wife's legal status was hidden behind that of the husband, some remarried mothers directly addressed the Orphan House rather than applying for their child through their new husband: "I respectfully beg that he may be restored to me," wrote one.[75] Martha Deliessiline anxiously wrote the commissioners: "I have taken to myself a husband, I now feel capable of taking care of my sons, John & Isaac, I would wish to take them from the Orphant Asylum if this meets your approbation. Please send me an answer as soon as possible."[76] All such cases of restoration illustrate how bonds between mother and child persisted after the child's institutionalization.

Petitions for restoration of custody also give a fuller picture of the roles of stepfathers in a high mortality regime. Widows were numerous, so their legal and financial quandaries were not unusual. When they remarried, the fates of their children were heavily influenced by the attitudes of their stepfathers. In the early republic, it was common for the new husband to deny his wife's children access to family resources and force them to the Orphan House. In the antebellum era, many a new husband enabled a widow to regain custody of her children by allowing them access to the new family's resources. The transformation of step-patriarchy in this way indicates subtle shifts in the structure of white southern families of the lower classes.[77]

Even after a child was bound out and living in the new master's household, a parent or other relative often continued to follow him and look out for his best interests. Just as the process of binding out aimed to please all parties, once bound a youth who changed his mind about his prospective trade would also be accommodated—if his parents approved. A gunsmith informed the commissioners about a transfer of indentures: "William Arnold whom you apprenticed to me about six months ago shows no taste for the trade of a gunsmith. He and his mother have consented to a transfer of his indentures to Mr E Merker blacksmith."[78] Mothers responded to child complaints that the master had failed to provide clothing as he had promised or was putting the apprentice to work at menial labor rather than training him in a specific skill. Fearing that her son would "go to ruin," Elizabeth Rhodes petitioned the commissioners to remove him from Thomas Yates, a carpenter, who, she claimed, was neither providing him with clothing nor washing what he brought with him. After her son was re-bound to J. C. Stecher, a blacksmith, Mrs. Rhodes complained again that Stecher too was failing to fulfill the indenture and reported that she had found yet another prospective master, one who would provide for her son as the indenture required.[79]

Boys and their mothers seemed eager not to put too many miles between each other. One anxious mother, who insisted that her son's indentures to a master in faraway Anderson District (today County) be revoked, succeeded in having him re-bound to a local iron foundry.[80] Children evinced a desire to remain close to their parents as well. One merchant offered to transfer the indentures of his apprentice to another master in a location that would suit the boy, who "don't wish to go so far from his mother." Wyatt-Brown proposed that sons and mothers in yeoman families drew together out of fear of the violent husband-father. The recurrence of such comments in the Orphan House letters might raise doubts as to whether that was the full story in the Charleston setting. Mothers and sons formed loving bonds in natural course of family life, and these bonds may well have been strengthened by their joint suffering as widow and half orphan.[81]

The unwillingness of the commissioners to force children into apprenticeships they did not want and their willingness to return the child to his or her family at almost any time before being bound out suggest an ongoing concern for the child's welfare. This has implications for proper terminology. The role of consensus in the arrangements for a child's future suggests that the terms *involuntary* or *compulsory apprenticeship,* common in other regions, do not really describe how the Charleston Orphan House bound out its children.[82] The commissioners nearly always approved of a request by a family member to restore a child to the family. While this apprenticeship institution operated as a quasi-public agency (the Orphan House received both tax funds and private donations), making the apprentices public rather than craft apprentices, little in the entire process occurred involuntarily. For these reasons, "public" apprenticeship might best describe system governing the Charleston apprentices.

An assessment of the Charleston Orphan House's significance might focus on three interrelated aspects of the institution: necessary and sufficient conditions for its founding, and its success in executing its charge. To the extent that its goal was to educate poor and distressed white children who would otherwise have gone uneducated, the Orphan House was successful. Many of the children who received a basic education while resident would likely have learned very little otherwise. Certainly not enough even to write their names, to judge by signature patterns at entrance and exit, among same-aged children.[83]

To the extent that its goal was to coopt the poor whites of Charleston, the Orphan House also succeeded. The ongoing role of mothers in children's lives was part of a larger social process that enshrined consensus among white Charlestonians. However upset Catholics and Jews may have been when local Protestant ministers preached a particular kind of Christianity to their children in the Orphan House, city fathers believed that it contributed greatly to white unity.[84] Just so, the paternal (and paternalist) care offered by the commissioners could only take effect when all parties agreed to it, not just master and commissioners. Children were asked for their consent not once but twice, to enter to the Orphan House and then to be bound out to a particular master. Mothers who wanted their children returned or who wanted them moved to a different master were easily accommodated. The emphasis on harmony of interests raises the question why Charleston's white elite went to such lengths to accommodate the city's white poor.

In part, they did so because they were able to. To build benevolent institutions required substantial resources, and Charleston had that wealth; by many measures it was the richest city in newly independent America.[85] The city's leaders also wanted to make that accommodation. They explicitly noted their desire to practice Christian charity, they wanted to manage the affairs of the city more efficiently, and they did not see any conflict between these goals.[86] Perhaps, as Henry Laurens claimed, Charlestonians were more sensitive than other Americans to the needs of the suffering poor.[87] This leaves unaddressed their motivation to aid the white poor in such a public way, long before similar charities operated in the North.

All parties discussed in this essay were white, but half of all Charlestonians were black. A recurring theme in South Carolina historiography is the recognition by the white elite that racial unity was necessary to preserve the political and social order.[88] The Orphan House, I suggest, was also seen as a means to maintain racial unity in Charleston. Through this institution, the elite class could offer insurance to the city's poorest whites in case of disaster as well as, for many, hope of upward mobility. By contrast, public policy to provide for needy blacks tended toward incarceration. Immediately after the trial and execution of Denmark Vesey in 1822, for his alleged role in leading a potential slave revolt, the pundit James Gregorie urged that the city invest in a "stepping mill" for the Work House and then collar as many blacks as needed to grind grain for the city's institutionalized population. And in 1825 such a treadmill was added to the municipal Work House.[89] In antebellum Charleston, it was important for that elite class to address the situations of the white poor and the black poor differently, and to do so publicly.

The Orphan House was a benevolent institution, to be sure, but disinterested it was not.[90] It was an institution with a charitable aim, to care for destitute, orphaned, and abandoned white children, and that charge it fulfilled with diligence. It was also a political institution that provided self-assurance to white leaders of their goodness, and it reminded the white poor of the paternal concern of the white elite. The Orphan House bound together all strata of white society in ways that made Charleston the only city in America that would have thought to create such an institution at such an early date. Distressed parents and guardians sought its charity. Commissioners from the wealthy elite spent considerable hours enacting their magnanimity. Masters from the artisanal classes obtained the labor they needed while providing homes to luckless little ones. And the destitute children who hardly appear anywhere else in Charleston's rich history found some degree of compassion. Webs of white cooperation reached across class lines among these groups, as if the other half of Charleston's population wasn't there at all.

CHAPTER EIGHT

The Extent and Limits of Indentured Children's Literacy in New Orleans, 1809–1843

PAUL LACHANCE

Literacy is a special dimension of the general topic of children bound to labor in early America. The studies in this book reveal that removing poor children from their natal home and placing them in another household or institution where they were expected to work was as variable a practice as it was ubiquitous. In some settings, it was little more than a means to supply employers with cheap labor from a particularly vulnerable element of the population and offered scant protection from exploitation or abuse. In other situations, it represented a genuine attempt to provide children of the poor with skills and opportunities that their own parents could not or were not likely to provide. Whether or not the court orders or legal contracts binding children out to other households stipulated literacy training is one indication of the potential impact of pauper apprenticeship on children's lives.

In places where children were asked to indicate by a mark or signature their acceptance of terms specified in the legal documents by which they were bound, it is possible to measure and analyze their literacy directly. Over a thousand indentures made in New Orleans in the early nineteenth century provide such data. They were endorsed by three parties: the person who was bound, in most cases a child; his or her sponsor, usually a parent but not always; and the master or employer. Their signatures, or marks in lieu of a signature, are all that is needed to measure literacy. Calculate the proportion of persons who could sign their names, and you have an indication of the ability to read and write.[1]

Secondly, clauses in over half of indentures promising from two to forty months of schooling offer a means of measuring the importance placed on literacy training by parties to the agreement. In all but three of those that specified how it was to be provided, it was at night school. Masters very rarely allowed time off from work to attend school. The phrasing of educational clauses often gave basic literacy as the goal to be achieved. Since 44 percent of provisions for schooling were for children already capable of signing their indentures, they suggest that signature rates provide an optimistic estimate of acquisition of competence in reading and writing.

Investigation of popular literacy in New Orleans through the indentures responds to the need for analysis of children's literacy where evidence exists. In a 1990 survey of studies of literacy from 1630 to 1840, the author remarked that studies of "literacy among children and young teens are virtually nonexistent."[2] Since then, the subject has begun to receive attention, but more case studies are needed to expand the base for answering basic questions about the acquisition of literacy before compulsory primary education of virtually everyone in public schools.[3] What proportion of children learned to read and write in the pre-public-school era? At what age? Where? In the home, in church-run schools, or in private tuition–based schools? Where various methods of transmitting literacy existed side by side, what was their relative importance? What roles did the mother and father play in the literacy training of their children? How much did race, class, and gender differences affect transmission of literacy and illiteracy from one generation to the next? Did public schools attenuate their effect? In their absence, did clauses in apprenticeship contracts requiring the master to provide basic education contribute to the same result?[4]

This chapter addresses these questions with the New Orleans indentures. It will show that popular literacy was relatively widespread in New Orleans, among adults and children. By age fifteen, about three-fifths of apprentices could sign their indentures. Since that proportion did not change in the later teen years, it seems that if children had not learned to write by age fifteen, they would never learn to do so. Girls were less likely than boys of the same age to sign their names, but the difference was small. As in other studies, the mother seems to have played a greater role than the father in the acquisition of literacy by the child prior to apprenticeship. The establishment of the first public schools in New Orleans in the middle of the period covered by the indentures (1809 to 1843) provides a possible explanation of why literacy signature rates of white children increased after 1830, but not those of free persons of color whom the educational reform did not benefit.

Founded by the French in 1718 and ceded to Spain in 1763, New Orleans was purchased with the rest of Louisiana by the United States in 1803. On the one hand, several contemporaries described the French-speaking Creole, or native-born, population of Louisiana as largely illiterate at the time of the Purchase. According to Daniel Clark, American consul in the late Spanish period, "Not above half the inhabitants can read or Write the french, & not two hundred in the country with correctness."[5] On the other hand, marriage contracts and wills, two sources frequently used to study literacy, reveal fairly high signature rates for the New Orleans elite from the beginning of the nineteenth century.[6] Over 90 percent of white bridegrooms and brides were already able to sign their names to marriage contracts drawn up between 1804 and 1820. Wills were made by a wider cross section of the population than marriage contracts, although they, too, are usually said to overrepresent the elite. Excluding testators too weak to sign, the proportion of white males who signed their wills rose from 69 percent between 1804 and 1812 to above 80 percent after 1820. White female literacy rose from 53 percent in the first period to 80 percent between 1835 and 1840 but then fell back to 63 percent between 1858 and 1860.

The most dramatic improvement in literacy during the antebellum period, judging from the same elite sources, was among free persons of color, who made up 44 percent of the free population of the city in 1810, 23 percent in 1840, and 7 percent in 1860.[7] In marriage contracts for free persons of color, almost two-thirds were already able to sign in the 1804–20 period, and almost all free men of color and three-fourths of free women of color by the late 1830s. From around 10 percent who could sign their wills between 1804 and 1820, 60 percent of free men of color did so by the end of the antebellum period, while the percentage of free women of color able to sign climbed from 12 to 50 percent during the same span.

Did these improvements in elite literacy extend downward to popular classes of the free population? Indentures provide data to answer this question. The vast majority were apprenticeship contracts involving master artisans, working-class children bound to them, and their sponsors. Just over half of bound children in New Orleans were free persons of color, a higher proportion than in any of the localities examined in other essays in this volume.

In general, demographic and economic conditions in New Orleans during the period covered by the indentures, 1810 to 1840, seem conducive to growth in popular as well as elite literacy. The decades following the Louisiana Purchase have been aptly labeled the "Glamour Period" of New Orleans history.[8] By all indicators, the city's increase in population and commercial activity was spectacular. The number of inhabitants of the city and suburbs multiplied sixfold, from 17,242 in 1810 to 102,160 in 1840.[9] Steamboats operating on the Mississippi River and its tributaries increased from 17 in 1817 to 536 in 1840. The value of exports, the two major commodities being cotton and sugar, rose from $2 million in 1810 to $34 million in 1840; imports from $3 million in 1821 to a high point of $17 million in 1835.[10] By 1820 New Orleans was the largest city in the Old South, and it advanced from the seventh to the third largest city in the nation in federal censuses taken between 1810 and 1840.[11]

Another reason to expect an increase in popular literacy in New Orleans between 1810 and 1840 is the decision made by the Louisiana state legislature in 1826 to use some of the funds that had previously supported the College of Orleans to start two elementary schools and one high school. The first public school opened in 1828. It was tuition-based but free for indigent children. By the mid-1830s, as many as three thousand students, approximately the number of whites aged ten through fourteen enumerated in Orleans parish, were enrolled in these schools. In 1832, 150 of 200 places reserved for poor students were filled; in 1836, 260 of 300 places.[12] This experiment in public education collapsed in 1836 but restarted in 1841 when the Louisiana legislature approved a school tax for New Orleans and developed to the point that its public school system in the 1850s compared favorably with those in other cities. Their most notable limitation was exclusion of free and enslaved blacks.[13]

Although indigent, orphaned, mulatto, and illegitimate children were indentured in New Orleans, the practice there did not have the negative status implications that binding out had elsewhere as a result of targeting marginal elements of the population as, for example, Herndon demonstrated in chapter 3. Nearly all New Orleans indentures provided for training in a specific skill or craft and offered terms that do not seem overtly exploitative. At the same time, they were not explicitly benevolent, unlike the charitable institutions for orphans and indigent children in Charleston (as in Murray's chapter 7) and Savannah (as in Lockley's chapter 9).

As van Zwieten's chapter 6 describes for New Amsterdam and Hamilton's chapter 11 does for Montreal, New Orleans had a legal system based on a civil code rather than the British common law tradition.[14] Nineteenth-century indentures reflected notarial precedents from the eighteenth century in their contractual form.[15] They were entirely voluntary, differing substantially in this respect from official orders in American colonies by which a government magistrate—at the town, county, or institutional level—bound out a child to a master, if need be against the wishes of his or her parent and often not subject to the agreement of the child. In New Orleans, there was no prior investigation of the circumstances prompting application for indenture, nor of the suitability of the prospective master, unlike procedures for binding children elsewhere described in this volume. Louisiana law limited the role of the state to registration of a private contract, thereby attesting to its conformity with the statute regulating apprenticeship and indentured servitude, and to adjudication if a party to the contract complained that its provisions were not being respected.

In 1806, three years after the Louisiana Purchase, the legislature of the Territory of Orleans, whose boundaries corresponded roughly with those of the state of Louisiana today, enacted a law regulating apprenticeship and indentured servitude, with a model indenture in standard notarial format.[16] Five years later, indentures began to be copied into a register maintained by the office of the Mayor of New Orleans. The first entry dated from 1809, and the last was made in 1843. Since notarial records from these years contain few apprenticeship contracts, the service provided by the mayor's office for a fee of five dollars appears to have deprived notaries of part of their business. If so, their loss is the historian's gain. The mayor's records contain the full text of indentures for 1,152 individuals covering without gaps the years from 1809 to 1843, with the signatures and marks needed for analysis of literacy.[17]

The number of indentures per year in New Orleans rose quickly in the second decade of the nineteenth century. Interrupted in 1814 when the War of 1812 most severely curtailed business in New Orleans and again in the recession following the Panic of 1819, sixty-three indentures were made in 1822. However, this year also marked the beginning of an extended, almost uninterrupted decline in the number of indentures per year over the next two decades.[18] From over fifty in every year but one between 1816 and 1823, the annual number fell to less than fifty from 1824 to 1827, less than thirty in every year but one from 1829 to 1832, less than twenty from 1833 to 1840, and less than ten from 1841 to 1843. The decline was also relative. In the age cohort born between 1794 and 1810, somewhere between a fourth and half of free males were formally indentured. The ratio fell to less than one in twenty for the cohort born between 1816 and 1839.[19] Some fathers, of course, continued to teach their trades to their sons, and unregistered agreements continued to bind other youth to masters to learn a trade.[20]

New Orleans indentures had a variety of functions and were not entirely limited to children. Approximately 7 percent were contracts of temporary servitude that used general terms, usually *servant* or *laborer*, to describe the work of indentured persons, three-fifths of whom were young adults in their twenties. The purpose in these cases was to reimburse the costs of transportation from Europe to Louisiana, obtain release from prison, or repay personal debts. A few indentures involved whole families or groups of laborers rather than individuals. Another 2 percent assigned children under the age of eight to foster parents well in advance of the usual age of apprenticeship. The remaining 91 percent of indentures (93 percent including young children younger than eight to be taught a specific trade) were apprenticeships of one sort or another, for the most part in artisan crafts. Around 4 percent of indentured persons were adults, 3 percent were slaves, and 6 percent were females. The statistical analysis that follows excludes adults and slaves. Children are defined as persons under the age of twenty-one at the moment of indenture.[21] This subset consists of 1,018 cases, 88 percent of all indentures in the database.

New Orleans children were somewhat older at binding than other children in this volume. The average age of indenture in New Orleans was 14.1 years.[22] The average duration of New Orleans indentures was 4.7 years. In addition to age at the start of indenture, the length of the contract also depended on the degree of responsibility of the master for the care of the indentured child.

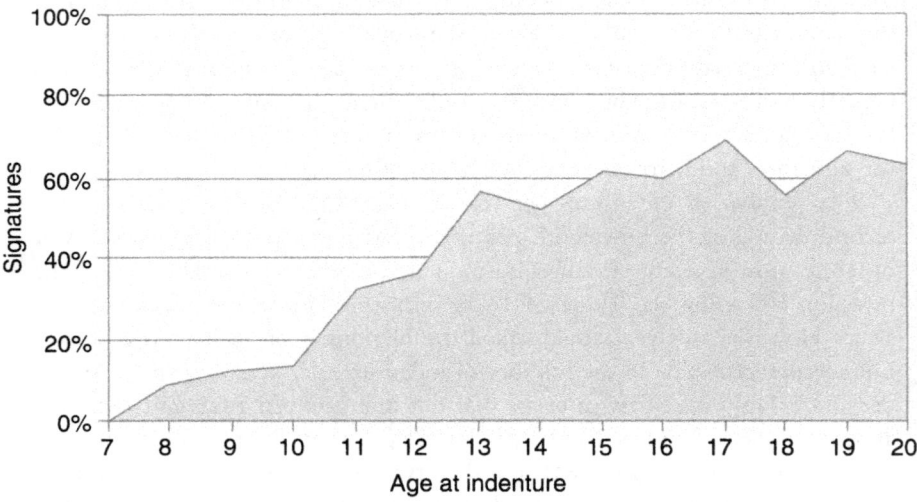

FIGURE 8.1. Proportion of signatures by age at indenture

Indentures assigning him full responsibility for food, lodging, and other basic needs of the apprentice were twelve to eighteen months longer on average than arrangements delegating daily maintenance partly or entirely to the sponsor or even the indentured person. Over time, shared or delegated maintenance increased, as did monetary payments to the child during the period of indenture or at the end in the form of a bonus. In general, indentures in New Orleans appear to be fair contracts with a mix of clauses in which a term of special advantage to one party was offset by another provision favorable to the other party.

Counting each individual only the first time he appears in the subset of 1,018 indentures, 94 percent of masters, 54 percent of sponsors, and 51 percent of indentured persons were able to sign their names rather than make a mark to show acceptance of the terms of the contract. Since most masters were artisans, their literacy rate may be considered high for that social class. In the city of Quebec, the signature rate of independent artisans was 70 to 80 percent in the same decades as in the New Orleans data.[23] The sponsors' literacy rate of 54 percent, by comparison, indicates much lower literacy in the social class from which apprentices were recruited.

A certain number of children indicated their consent to the terms of indenture by a mark rather than a signature because they were too young to have learned how to read and write. The increase with age in the proportion of children who signed, shown in figure 8.1, reveals when literacy skills were typically acquired. No children younger than eight signed their indenture. Around 10 percent of children between the ages of eight and ten could do so. From there the proportion of signers increased to a third at ages eleven and twelve, over half at ages thirteen and fourteen, and a maximum of two-thirds at age seventeen. The signature rate from seventeen to twenty, the age range of the oldest fourth of indentured children, was 63 percent.

The sharpest increase in literacy was between the ages of ten and fourteen, the age range used earlier to estimate the percentage of white children enrolled in public schools by the 1830s. Provisions for education in indentures reflect diminishing expectations of literacy if beyond age twelve. While schooling was offered to four out of five children eight to twelve years of age who could not sign, it was promised to only two out of five illiterate children between the ages of seventeen and twenty. Provisions for education of literate children also diminished with age. Comparison of the literacy rates of children at the age of indenture with the proportion promised schooling suggests that being bound to labor may have actually increased the chances of older teenagers receiving some formal education.

The gender difference in literacy among adults in the social milieu from which most indentured children came was greater than that observed among the children themselves. Only 33 percent of female sponsors were able to sign the indentures, compared to 81 percent of male sponsors. This difference is based on over 400 cases for each sex. At the apex of the artisan hierarchy, among masters and mistresses, the gender gap narrowed. The signature rate of 26 females to whom children were bound was 81 percent, compared to 95 percent of their male counterparts.[24]

Although only 52 girls were indentured, the number is sufficient to describe gender patterns in acquisition of literacy. While 52 percent of male children could sign, only 27 percent of females could do so. This difference, however, was in large part the consequence of an average age at indenture of 9.7 years for females, toward the beginning of the age range during which literacy was typically acquired and almost five years younger than the average age of males at indenture. From ages ten through thirteen, the proportion able to sign increased from roughly 10 to 40 percent for both sexes. Then it leveled off for females at around 45 percent while it continued to rise for males. Although this pattern suggests equal gender exposure to primary education of some sort up to the age of twelve or thirteen, it also indicates that males who were not immediately indentured continued to be given the opportunity to learn to read and write, presumably in school, while most females were not. The low level of female literacy past the age of fourteen could mean that only around half of working-class girls received some primary education in their early teens or that it was of such poor quality that it did not teach half of them how to read and write. It confirms and helps to explain the large difference in the literacy rates of female and male sponsors.

New Orleans had a very cosmopolitan population. Over 40 percent of its inhabitants were foreign-born in 1850.[25] It had a larger slave population than any other city except Charleston and a larger free black population than any other city except Baltimore.[26] The proportion of Catholics was much larger than elsewhere, and the first language of a majority of the population was French rather than English into the 1830s.[27] The heterogeneity of the population is reflected in characteristics of parties to indentures. Almost half the bound children were born outside Louisiana. Half of the children, 45 percent of their sponsors, and 20 percent of masters were free persons of color. Two-thirds of the contracts were written in French.

The signature rate of indentured children and youth was exactly the same in English and French indentures.[28] It did, however, vary noticeably by race and place of birth. Only 40 percent of free children of color could sign their indentures, compared to 63 percent of white children. The racial difference in the literacy of sponsors was even greater. Only a fourth of free sponsors of color signed the apprenticeship contracts, compared to three-fourths of white sponsors. As for birthplace, the signature rate of indentured children was around 40 percent for "Creoles," the term designating in the early nineteenth century anyone born in New Orleans or Louisiana regardless of race or language, and 59 percent for immigrants of all origins.[29]

The cross-tabulation in table 8.1 provides a more precise picture of the way in which race and birthplace intersected to produce an ethnically differentiated apprentice class. Literacy rates in the table range from 20 to 82 percent. Both the highest and lowest rates were for natives of other states who immigrated to New Orleans. Fifteen free persons of color born in nine different states were noticeably less literate than free persons of color born in Louisiana, while fifty-eight whites born in an equally wide variety of states were much more literate

TABLE 8.1.
Nativity and literacy rate of apprentices by race

Nativity	Whites			Free persons of color		
	N	%	Literacy rate	N	%	Literacy rate
Creole						
New Orleans	93	22.6	40.2	172	39.7	38.4
Louisiana	61	14.8	50.8	111	25.6	33.0
Subtotal	154	37.5	46.3	283	65.4	36.2
Immigrant						
Other state	58	14.1	82.1	15	3.5	20.0
Europe	139	33.8	67.7			
Saint-Domingue	51	12.4	72.3	127	29.3	55.7
Other	9	2.2	77.8	8	1.8	37.5
Subtotal	257	62.5	72.4	150	34.6	51.0
Total	411	100.0	62.4	433	100.0	41.6

Source: Subset of craft apprenticeships in New Orleans indentures database. Literacy rate is defined as the proportion of apprentices who signed indentures.

than white Creoles, who in turn were more literate than Creole free persons of color. Among whites, foreign-born immigrants were slightly less literate than natives of other states, but the signature rate of foreign-born free persons of color was markedly higher than that of other indentured free persons of color, whether born in Louisiana or in another state.

For every birthplace except one, the proportion of whites who were literate was greater than that of free persons of color, and in each race, immigrants were more literate than Creoles. There is one striking aberration from this hierarchical pattern. The literacy rate of immigrant free persons of color, 51 percent, was not only higher than that of Creole free persons of color, 36 percent, it also surpassed the 46 percent of white Creoles who were literate. This anomaly was mainly due to the 56 percent literacy rate of free persons of color born in Saint-Domingue (today's Haiti) and Cuba, children of refugees from the Haitian Revolution who fled to New Orleans in 1809 when they were expelled from Cuba, where they had first sought asylum. Their literacy rate was higher than that of natives of Louisiana, whatever their race.

What might explain the relatively high literacy of the Saint-Domingue refugees of color? We can reject the hypothesis that they benefited from opportunities for education in their place of origin that were superior to those that existed in New Orleans. A third of the 175 refugee children were indentured between 1809 and 1814, and the other two-thirds between 1815 and 1828. Those born before 1815 could have learned how to read and write elsewhere before arrival, but the others passed through ages 10 to 14 in New Orleans. These refugee children faced the same situation as Creoles up to 1828—the need to learn to read and write in private schools or at home in the absence of free public education. If schooling in New Orleans had lagged behind Saint-Domingue and Santiago de Cuba, refugees indentured in 1815 or later should have been less literate than those indentured between 1809 and 1814. On the contrary, controlling for age and race, a larger percentage of refugee children educated in New Orleans after 1815 signed their indentures than those who could have been educated prior to arrival in the city.

Over time, though, the literacy rate of white Creoles improved more than that of other groups. Figure 8.2 shows the trends in literacy of the four ethnic groups defined by the combination of race and nativity. The literacy rate of both Creole and immigrant whites increased over the three decades covered by the indenture data. For white Creoles, it was 27 percent higher in the 1830s than in the 1810s, well above the 10 percent rise in adult while male literacy in the United States in this period.[30] The literacy rate of immigrant free persons of color, four out of five of whom were Saint-Domingue refugees of color, also rose in the second decade that they were present in the data set, and it surpassed the literacy rate of white Creoles in both decades. An increase in literacy of Creoles of color in the second decade of indentures paralleled that of refugees

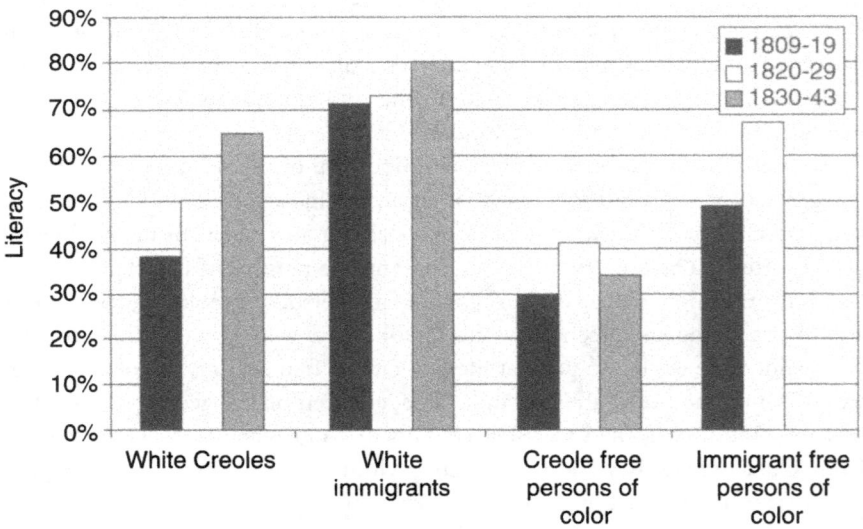

FIGURE 8.2. Percent literate by birthplace, race, and period

of color and was to some extent due to it, since it was in this decade that Creoles included refugee children born in New Orleans. Among Creole free persons of color, however, literacy fell in the 1830s relative to the level attained in the 1820s.

The unexpected arrival in 1809 of free persons of color from Saint-Domingue whose children were more literate than those of white Creoles may have prodded the latter's interest in schooling. From 1809 to 1819, 93 percent of the indentures for illiterate white Creole children had educational clauses. After 1820, as white Creoles had to compete less and less with the refugees of color, provisions for schooling fell to 78 percent of indentures for their illiterate children and then plummeted to 38 percent after 1830. Much of the decline in educational clauses, from 67 percent of all indentures before 1820 to 48 percent after 1830, was due to their diminution in the indentures of illiterate white Creoles. Thus race affected the level of popular literacy in New Orleans, but in a convoluted way due to the arrival of a contingent of immigrants of color more literate than whites native to Louisiana.

The final factor whose effect on literacy can be measured with data found in the indentures is the family situation of children bound by these agreements. Four out of five apprentices were sponsored by kin. In slightly more than half of these cases, the sponsor was the apprentice's mother; in 30 percent it was his father; and in the remaining 20 percent, an uncle, aunt, sibling, grandparent, cousin, or in-law. One out of ten apprentices was accompanied to the mayor's office by non-kin who were identified in the contracts by such terms as guardian, benefactor, tutor, friend and well-wisher, and patron. In a few cases, a former employer, government official, or director of an orphan asylum served as sponsor. Finally, one out of ten indentured children appeared alone before the mayor and sponsored themselves.[31] The signature rate of self-sponsored children, whose average age at indenture was 15.7 years, a year and a half above the average for all children, was 61 percent. Next highest was the signature rate of 54 percent of children sponsored by non-kin, followed by 51 percent for children sponsored by parents and 46 percent for children sponsored by kin.

Much more important than the nature of the relationship of the sponsor to the child was the sponsor's gender. Only 33 percent of female sponsors were literate, compared to 81 percent of male sponsors; only 46 percent of children sponsored by females could sign, compared to 55 percent of those sponsored by males. In each type of relationship to the child—parents, kin, or non-kin—male sponsors were more literate than females, and children sponsored by males were more literate than children sponsored by females. Since females sponsored a higher proportion of free persons of color than whites, gender was an additional factor contributing to racial differences in literacy.

The proportion of indentured children who could sign their indentures varied by every characteristic examined thus far: age, gender, race (white, free person of color), birthplace (Louisiana, Saint-Domingue, United States, Europe), and sponsor's relationship, gender, and literacy. Logistic regression reveals that the three most significant predictors of an indentured child's literacy, controlling for other variables, were age, the sponsor's literacy, and birthplace (figure 8.3). The signature rate increased with age of indenture up to the age of seventeen. Relative to the age group seventeen to twenty, apprenticeship before the age of thirteen reduced the probability of literacy by 43 percent. Having a literate mother increased the probability of a child signing the indenture by 28 percent over the relatively high signature rate of self-sponsored apprentices. Being sponsored by a literate father increased the probability by 21 percent. Birthplace was also a highly significant predictor of literacy. Compared to being born in Louisiana, being born elsewhere in the United States increased the probability of signing by 33 percent, birth in Europe by 29 percent, and birth in Saint-Domingue or Cuba by 23 percent.

The most dramatic improvement in literacy over time, in elite sources, was among free persons of color. In the indenture data, by contrast, the literacy of free children of color, after increasing from 39 percent in the 1810s to 46 percent in the 1820s, declined to 36 percent in the 1830s. The boost received from Saint-Domingue refugees arriving in 1809 was not sustained. The discrepancy between the trend in literacy of free persons of color in indentures and in marriage contracts and wills could be indicative of a gap between popular and elite elements of the group that widened over the antebellum period, slowing down the general advance of literacy in the city.

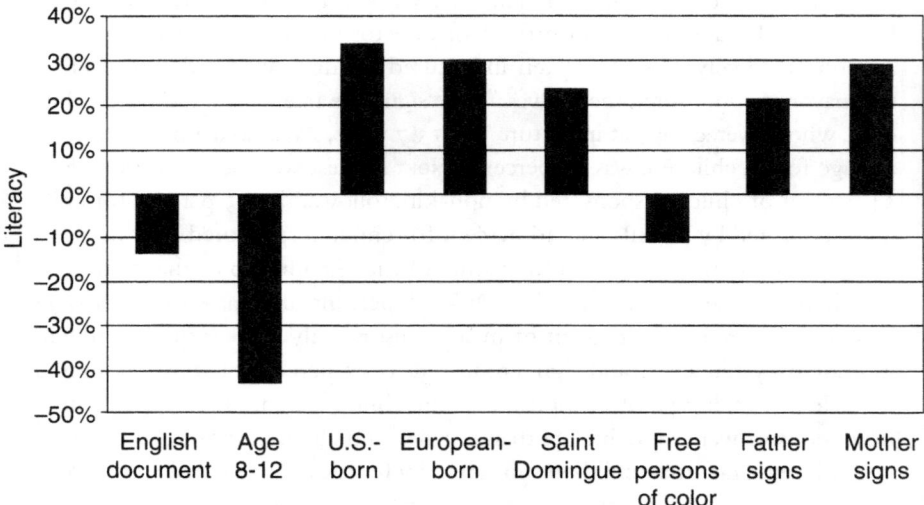

FIGURE 8.3. Effects of significant variables on children's literacy

The decline in the level of literacy among children of color indentured in the 1830s is in direct contrast to the trend among indentured white Creole children. The most evident improvement in literacy in the indenture data was among white Creoles. Although the literacy rate of white children born in Louisiana never equaled that of white immigrant children, it did increase from 38 percent in the 1810s to 50 percent in the 1820s and 65 percent in the 1830s. The indentures do not report the birthplaces of the parents of Creole children, many of whom were immigrants, but marriage patterns permit one to assume that two-thirds of their mothers were also Creoles.[32] The literacy rate of mothers who sponsored white Creole children fell from 50 percent before 1820 to 40 percent in the 1820s but increased to 63 percent after 1830. The clearer upward trend in literacy of their children is indirect evidence that it was acquired more often in schools rather than at home. White Creole children were the most likely to have benefited from the public school initiative in 1826.

The ability of only 38 percent of white Creole children to sign indentures between 1809 and 1819 shows there is an element of truth in disparaging comments about Creole illiteracy at the time of the Louisiana Purchase, especially relative to the signature rate of 71 percent of white immigrant children in the same decade. Nevertheless, even at its low point in the 1810s, the white Creole literacy rate in New Orleans was as high as the 37 percent literacy rate of apprentices in Montreal. The most detailed statistics on the literacy of apprentices and their sponsors in another Francophone city of North America are presented in a monograph on artisan apprentices in the city of Quebec. Between

1790 and 1815, only 19 percent of French Canadian apprentices and 15 percent of their parents could sign, even lower than the signature rates on indentures of Creole free persons of color in New Orleans. In Quebec, 54 percent of British apprentices and 61 percent of their parents could sign, less than white immigrants and their sponsors in New Orleans.[33] Compared to cities in British North America, the level of popular literacy in New Orleans was high from the beginning of the nineteenth century.

Revealing is the proportion of children sponsored by literate parents who still had not learned to read and write at the moment they were indentured. If these skills were routinely taught at home when possible, that is, when the child lived with a literate parent, this proportion should be small. It was in fact quite high. Among children thirteen and older, 17 percent of whites sponsored by literate parents could not sign their indentures, nor could 31 percent of free children of color sponsored by a literate parent. That so many children who could have been taught to read and write at home were not able to sign their name by the age of thirteen is evidence that, for many youngsters, if they were not taught to read and write at school, they were not going to acquire these skills at home either.

The most likely explanation of the significance of mother's literacy as a predictor of the child's literacy in regression analysis (a child with a literate mother was 28 percent more likely to sign than a self-sponsored apprentice, controlling for other variables) is her role in providing basic literacy training at home. If the signature rate of children with literate parents was higher for whites than for free persons of color above the age of thirteen, the opposite was true among children eight to twelve. In this age range, 60 percent of free children of color sponsored by a literate mother could sign, but only 26 percent of white children with literate mothers. This finding is consistent with education at home playing a more important role in the acquisition of literacy by free persons of color than by whites before the age of thirteen. The role of literate free women of color in transmitting literacy skills to their children helps to explain how the signature rate of free children of color could be practically the same as for white children between the ages of eight and twelve (27 and 28 percent, respectively). Greater educational opportunity, whether in the first public schools or in private schools, is the most likely explanation of the higher literacy of white children indentured at the age of thirteen and older (47 percent for free persons of color, 68 percent for whites). However, many more free persons of color were handicapped by their mother's illiteracy than profited from her literacy. Mothers sponsored 54 percent of free children of color; and only 18 percent of free mothers of color were literate.

In these ways, the New Orleans indenture data demonstrate how important it is to expand studies of popular literacy in the pre–public school era beyond the focus on white adult males. When home instruction, usually by mothers rather than fathers, was one of the means by which literacy was transmitted from one generation to the next, literacy growth depended in part on the opportunity of women to acquire basic literacy skills. In antebellum New Orleans, literacy training by the mother, especially among free persons of color, produced a higher level of literacy among indentured children than in Quebec and Montreal. At the same time, large gender and racial differentials in literacy in New Orleans imposed limits on the increase in the proportion of children who could sign indentures between 1809 and 1843. Public schools subsequently overcame these constraints on literacy growth, but only after the Civil War, when they began to educate all children, regardless of gender and race.

CHAPTER NINE

"To Train Them to Habits of Industry and Usefulness"

Molding the Poor Children of Antebellum Savannah

TIMOTHY J. LOCKLEY

To suggest that the antebellum elite conceived of benevolence as a tool that would help to control the behavior of the poor no longer raises eyebrows among historians of antebellum reform movements. The debate sparked by the work of Clifford Griffin in the 1950s and continued by historians such as Lois Banner and Lawrence Kohl seems to have run out of steam. Griffin and others argued that "social control" was the main motivating force behind nineteenth-century benevolence as elites sought to check poor people's "rampant propensities to low and vicious indulgence." Banner countered this by stressing the genuine desires of the benevolent to assist the poor by opening up new opportunities for them and denying that the elite had a program to mold society into any sort of predetermined shape. In this sense, the elite were only aware of the directions that society should *not* go. Kohl rightly pointed out the imprecision with which the term "social control" was used, noting that it could mean a variety of things in different contexts, and questioning scholars' "excessive concern with motive at the expense of results."[1] Since 1985, historians of antebellum reform have continued to amass evidence as to the motivations of the benevolent, and most agree that a desire to control the behavior of the poor was certainly an important element. There is a crucial difference between "social control" and a desire for reform, however. "Social control," as Kohl pointed out, is widely understood as being "elitist, conservative and repressive," and no doubt many of those involved with benevolence thought that the poor needed to be controlled, sometimes institutionalized, for the benefit of wider society.[2] Reformers, on the other hand, hoped to give individuals the skills they needed to support themselves and their families—to foster eventual self-reliance. The process of imparting skills might involve a degree of physical control, to break former habits, but ultimately the control would be lifted so that the reformed individuals could take their appropriate place in the social fabric. While "control" and "reform" might be understood to be competing influences on benevolent men and women, in reality they were complementary. Successful reform produced the best form of control—self-control.

To have the most beneficial effect, reformers quickly realized that their energies would be best concentrated on poor children who, once reformed, would be useful and productive citizens for the rest of their lives. Moreover, children had not usually fallen into the vices of drunkenness and prostitution that older paupers often had and were therefore perceived to be less fixed in their course and more capable of reform. Historians have not been insensible to this, with case studies of orphanages in Charleston and New Orleans, among others, exploring this aspect of benevolence in detail.[3] What has never really been tested, however, is whether the reform of children actually worked. It is reasonably straightforward to document the motives of the benevolent and their desires for the future lives of poor children, but no one has tried to trace the lives of poor American children once they left the care of benevolent societies. Did the children follow the paths mapped out for them by the benevolent elite, leading virtuous lives and becoming useful citizens? Or were their lives seemingly unaffected by the assistance they received as children? In order to test the efficacy of "social control" and "reform" ideas and to answer the above questions, I have taken three benevolent societies from Savannah that were exclusively concerned with poor children—the Union Society, the Savannah Female Asylum, and the Savannah Free School Society—and traced the later lives of many of the children they helped.

The city of Savannah, founded on philanthropic principles in the 1730s, was a significant port by the antebellum era. While the city had its fair share of wealthy merchants and planters, the overall population was actually very mixed. The employment opportunities offered by the city attracted hundreds of immigrants, mainly from Ireland and Germany, who joined an existing native-born poor white population, a concentration of free blacks, and thousands of slaves in the urban throng. As one might expect, the lives of the non-elite varied considerably, with age, ability, gender, race, and fortune all playing their part. More than half the white population had no access to enslaved labor, and hundreds did not own land or other property, renting rooms in boarding houses while they sought whatever work they could find.[4] With so many living a marginal existence, it is unsurprising that a complex network of charitable societies arose to aid the unfortunate, though, as in other southern slave societies, assistance was only available to whites. The Union Society was the oldest benevolent society, founded in 1750, though records only survive from 1783. Originally designed to be a mutual society whereby paying members received the security of knowing that their relatives and widows would be cared for in the event of an untimely death, the mission of the Union Society gradually expanded to include assistance for any poor or disadvantaged child, regardless of whether their parent had been a member. After 1810 their attention was reserved solely for boys. Managed exclusively by men, the Union Society could claim nearly eight hundred of the leading merchants and planters resident in the city as members in 1860. The Savannah Female Asylum was founded in 1801 on the model of similar institutions founded in Baltimore and Boston to assist orphan girls. Seen as a female counterpart to the Union Society, young girls were housed with a matron in a purpose-built institution from the age of five. The third major benevolent institution concerned with "indigent" children was the Savannah Free School, a day school founded in 1816 that educated both boys and girls, including some on the rolls of the Union Society and the Female Asylum. Both the Female Asylum and the Free School drew support from the female members of elite families; in the 1820s both societies had about three hundred subscribers. For the remainder of the antebellum era, these three benevolent societies maintained their focus on the poor and orphan children of Savannah, and they were eventually joined in the 1840s by a Catholic orphanage, an Episcopal orphanage, and, in the 1850s, by a public school system.[5]

This article focuses on the children who were assisted by the Union Society, the Female Asylum, and the Free School. The surviving records of the Union Society were published in 1860 and contain the names of 246 boys and 22 girls who were assisted by the society between 1779 and 1860. This list seems reasonably comprehensive, though there are some significant gaps in the minutes in the 1820s. The records of the Savannah Female Asylum are not so complete, starting only in 1810 and ending in 1843 for instance, and only occasionally do they list all of the girls living on the bounty of the asylum. Nevertheless, the names of 220 girls can be gleaned from the surviving minutes, mainly from before 1830. The minutes of the Savannah Free School Society are complete between 1816 and 1856, but names of the children only appear occasionally since the school was not involved with apprenticeships like the Union Society or the Female Asylum. Therefore, despite educating roughly two thousand children between 1817 and 1860, the names of just forty boys and twenty-three girls can be found in the Free School records, mainly dating from before 1820.[6] In addition there were two boys and two girls who attended the Free School while being assisted by the Union Society and the Female Asylum, respectively. This article is based on these 555 poor children (288 boys and 267 girls) and the paths they followed as adults.

As figure 9.1 illustrates, there was no long-term trend in the admissions of poor children to the care of these benevolent societies. The undulations in the chart can, in part, be explained by the records that survive. The small number of boys admitted to care of the Union Society in the 1820s, for example, is

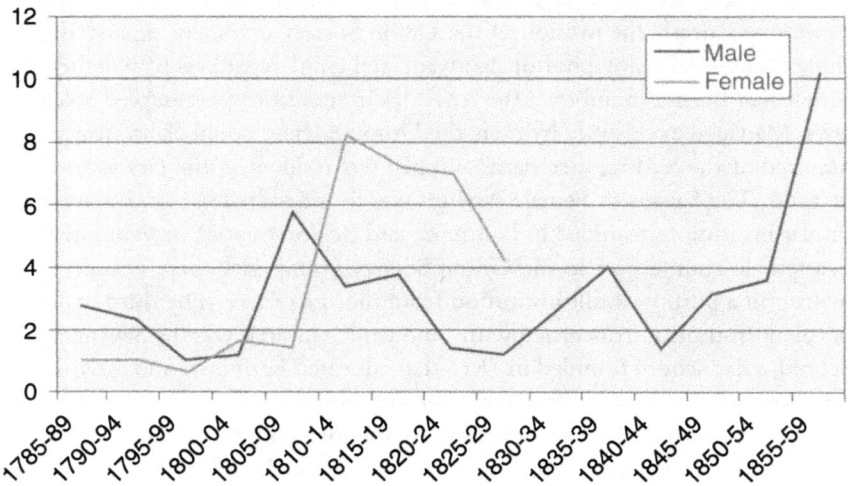

FIGURE 9.1. Five-year moving average of admissions

most likely an underestimate due to record loss and not a reflection of a genuine trend. Similarly, the rapid increase in the number of girls admitted to the Female Asylum around 1810 merely reflects the fact that the earliest surviving minute book dates from this period.

For most of the antebellum period, there were roughly thirty girls under the protection of the Female Asylum at any one time and a broadly similar number in the care of the Union Society. There was, however, a rapid increase in the number of admissions to the Union Society in the 1850s, and this was mirrored by other benevolent societies offering residential care for poor children. In 1850 there were 97 children being cared for in orphanages in Savannah, by 1860 that number had doubled to 197. Over the same period, the number of white children in the county aged five through nineteen had increased only 63 percent, suggesting not only that child poverty was a growing problem in the city in the years before secession but also that institutions were sufficiently flexible to accommodate the increase. John Murray notes a similar phenomenon in Charleston during the 1850s elsewhere in chapter 7, and increased immigration to the urban South during the decade was probably the cause.[7]

Only about a fifth of the children admitted to the Female Asylum and Union Society were full orphans: nearly two-thirds of the children were indentured by their mothers, with a further 15 percent indentured by their fathers. Single parents sometimes used orphanages as a form of emergency child care so that they could go out to work, but on other occasions children were indentured just to reduce the household bills. The Female Asylum admitted one child "whose father is in the habit of locking up his child when out at work himself" and another from "a large family" because her father could not afford to keep all his children.[8] In order to secure their control over the children, the Union Society and the Female Asylum each demanded that living parents or relatives sign indentures legally binding the children to institutions, just as they did elsewhere in the South.[9] The managers of the Union Society were absolutely explicit in their justification of this position: "Whereas it may happen that children who have been schooled by the funds of this society, may afterwards be taken away by their parents, guardians or friends, and instead of being put to some useful trade, or occupation, may be permitted to pursue vicious courses, whereby both they and the community, may be deprived of those advantages, which it was the design of this institution to procure."[10] On several occasions, mothers who had been prepared to send their children to the Female Asylum changed their minds at the last moment when they heard they would be forced to "relinquish all claims" to their children and be refused visiting rights.[11] While mothers were able to make applications for the return of their children, the managers of the Union Society and the directresses of the Female Asylum made individual moral judgments as to the suitability of parents to take their children back. Those who were thought to have a "bad character" or be otherwise unsuitable to act as parents were refused permission to receive their child; only those who had undergone a material change in their circumstances, perhaps through remarriage, were likely to regain control over their children.[12] Mrs. Mulryne, for example, was permitted to take her daughter back, but only if she would "promise, by her future good conduct and example, to deserve the charge entrusted to her." In order to give the board some guarantee of this, Mrs. Mulryne had to "sign a bond authorising the directresses to take the child back if they hear any thing prejudicial to the future welfare of the child."[13] It is noteworthy that the Free School, which did not have powers of indenture, continually complained about the failure of parents to "compel their children to attend more regularly at school."[14]

Once under their legal control, the managers of benevolent institutions began the task of molding and shaping the characters of the children. The Union Society, the Female Asylum, and the Free School shared broadly similar benevolent objectives: each aimed to take disadvantaged children from meager backgrounds and to give them the tools to enable them to become independent adults. Boys taken in by the Union Society were expected to "learn habits of industry and usefulness, become familiar with the use of tools, and with farming and mechanical operations and...receive strict attention in their schooling."[15] The directresses of the Free School sought "to dispense the benefits of education, religion and morality, to a number of children of both sexes...to train them to habits of industry and usefulness," while the directresses of the Female Asylum were in the business of "protecting, relieving and instructing orphan children of their own sex."[16] Numerous elements of the rules and regulations of the three societies reflected a desire to control, mold, and shape the bodies and personalities of poor children. The girls at the Female Asylum were to go to church every Sunday "to impress their minds with a becoming sense of God and religion, and the great importance of a modest and virtuous behaviour." Those attending the Free School were also to receive the "important advantages" of religious instruction, while the teacher of the Union Society boys was told to pay particular attention "to their morals."[17]

The easiest aspect to change was the external appearance of the children: the girls at the Female Asylum were to be "all dressed alike, in a plain, and simple attire," while the directresses of the Free School insisted that the children should always be "neatly attired." When Andrew Low donated white cotton dresses to the Female Asylum, the ladies decided not to give them to the girls as such clothing might give "them a taste for dress which the board deem it proper to discourage." Those, such as Mary Shearman, who failed to maintain standards of dress were reprimanded.[18] Since cleanliness was next to godliness, the children at the Female Asylum were bathed twice a week, while the teachers at the Free School were instructed "to take notice of every neglect in this particular."[19] Of course, altering the external appearance of the children did not alter their personality, and those providing charity found that reprimands were often not sufficient to elicit reformed behavior. The matron of the Female Asylum brought Amelia Butler and Diana Kirkland before the board of directresses because of their "impertinent conduct." When the girls refused to apologize to the matron, the board ordered that they should be locked up and only fed bread and water, at which point Amelia apologized, but Diana took her punishment rather than submit. The following year Diana, along with two other girls, was again brought before the board on account of her "improper conduct." This time "the board conceived it their duty to reprove them in the presence of the matron, when they presented her with a whip with directions to use it, whenever their conduct made it necessary."[20] The teacher at the Free School made a similar judgment about "the necessity of using coercion" upon "a few obstinate characters of both sexes" and was happy to report later that the children were now under a "regular discipline."[21] The attempts to refashion the children of the poor into model and useful citizens did not always proceed smoothly. The imposition of regulations concerning behavior, dress, and attitudes did meet a degree of resistance from some children, suggesting that the control and reform sought by the elite was not merely passively accepted. Some children went so far as to flee the asylum, often returning to the parents who had been refused official permission to take them. Elizabeth Thrower took just such a course of action in 1823, leaving the board of directresses no choice but to apply to a city magistrate to recover her.[22] The number of children, according to the surviving minutes at least, who persistently rebelled against the rules and regulated life of an institution was actually very small. Only about fifteen of more than five hundred children assisted fled to their previous homes or a new life elsewhere. Nothing is known of what happened to these fifteen in later life, since they apparently did not remain in Savannah. The children who remained at the Union Society and the Female Asylum continued their regimented days, rising at five or six in the morning, and retiring between seven and nine at night, depending on age.[23]

While instilling a proper moral ethic in the children was understood to be vitally important, all three benevolent societies also tried to impart the rudiments of literacy and numeracy to the children in their care since education would equip the children with many of the skills necessary for adult life. As one city Alderman put it, "it [education] is a companion which no misfortune can depress, no clime destroy, no enemy alienate, no despotism enslave, at home a friend, abroad an introduction, in solitude a solace, in society an ornament, it chastens vice, it guides virtue, it gives at once a grace and government to genius."[24] The studies of other southern societies in this volume confirm that Savannah's elite were not alone in placing an emphasis on the educational role of benevolence. If Savannah's poor children were anything like their counterparts in New Orleans and Charleston, they would certainly have emerged from the institutional experience with far better literacy skills than they went in with, though the sources that would allow us to test this conjecture are not extant.[25] Most boys were taught reading, writing, arithmetic, and perhaps grammar, but for girls the educational opportunities were far more restricted. Girls at the Female Asylum were to be taught to "read, write, sew and do all kinds of domestic business," while those at the Free School were also taught sewing and other domestic pursuits, only receiving basic tuition in academic subjects.[26] The reason for this differential treatment lies in the different expectations that managers and directresses had for the children. Boys who were intended to become carpenters, blacksmiths, and tailors would need to know how to understand written instructions from employers, how to draw up and sign contracts, how to keep accounts to ensure payment, and how to pay bills and taxes: girls, conversely, were not perceived to need such skills since their lives were supposed to revolve around their future husbands and children. The small amount of formal education given to girls was judged sufficient for them to fulfill their duties as "Republican Mothers" giving their infant children a solid start in life.[27]

Education of the poor also had wider public benefits beyond the individual child. One correspondent to the *Savannah Gazette* stressed the importance of education as the one thing which could safeguard the achievements of the American republic. By ensuring that children were inculcated with the "principles of integrity and virtue," the legacy of the Founding Fathers would be maintained and even extended "to the latest posterity."[28] As the antebellum period wore on, education was perceived to have an increasingly political importance. The subscribers to the Free School were reminded in 1839 that "education is the vital principle, the key stone in the arch of our political fabric, the essential aliment [element] of our national existence. If education thus thoroughly and generally diffused is the conservative principle of our invaluable inheritance it requires no laboured reasoning to shew that, that class for who[se] sakes and in whose behalf more especially we are now assembled should be the last to be passed by or neglected." Three years later, the directresses reiterated that education "alone can elevate the minds of our people and teach them to think and support the principles bequeathed by our noble and cherished ancestors." By the 1850s, proper Southern teaching was understood to be the best way to ensure that Savannah's children were not taken in by "Woman's Rights, Spiritualism, Abolitionism, Black Republicanism and Political Demagogism."[29]

On reaching their teens, most of the children in institutional care were indentured to local citizens to learn a trade.[30] The mechanics of indenturing involved the employer and the benevolent society entering into a signed agreement for a set period of time, usually until the child in question reached majority. Since boys averaged fourteen years of age when indentured by Union Society, the average indentured boy would remain in this condition for seven years, until he was twenty-one. The average age of girls indentured by the Female Asylum is not recorded, but as they became free agents at eighteen, it is possible that they did not spend as long in indentures as boys. The "suitable trade or profession" was evidently understood by the managers of the Union Society to mean artisan work. Of eighty-nine boys known to have been indentured to a trade, fifteen were taken as apprentice printers—no doubt valued for their nimble fingers as typesetters—eleven as apprentice carpenters, and the rest as apprentices to cabinet makers, blacksmiths, saddlers, tailors, and other such trades. Seven were apprenticed to merchants, probably to learn the skills of a clerk. The Union Society managers took their responsibility seriously, genuinely trying to find positions for their charges that would lead to a sustainable employment in later life. Concerned in 1817 that "the printing business was not of sufficient importance," managers recommended that boys should instead be apprenticed to "some respectable carpenter, bricklayer or some other mechanic," perhaps recognizing that Savannah was unlikely to support enough newspapers to give work to so many apprentice printers.[31]

The involvement of the Union Society did not cease abruptly when a boy was apprenticed, since on several occasions the boys were later re-bound to a different master to learn a different trade. The minutes do not record, however, whether these moves were due to the death of the original master or to the dissatisfaction of either the boy or the master with the existing arrangement.[32] As figure 9.2 demonstrates, the number of boys indentured in any single year was usually one or two, and the number indentured in the 1850s was slightly below the long-term trend. This latter development was most likely a reflection of the relocation of the orphanage to the old Bethesda site in 1855, about twelve

"TRAIN THEM TO HABITS OF INDUSTRY AND USEFULNESS" 141

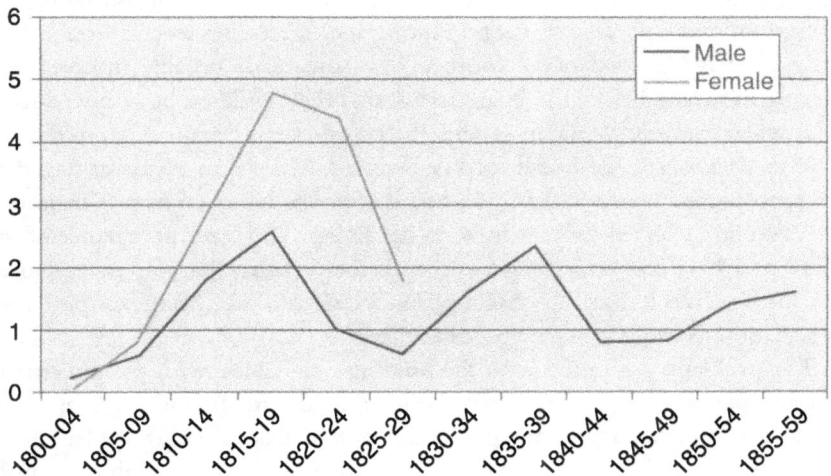

FIGURE 9.2. Children indentured, 1800–1860

miles from Savannah, where the boys were able to gain experience of a variety of agricultural pursuits without the need for an apprenticeship.

The girls attending the Female Asylum did not have the same opportunities for training open to them. Older girls were bound out, hopefully to be taught "millenary, mantua-making, or some business of a similar kind," but otherwise "they shall be placed in good families until the age of eighteen years."[33] Unfortunately the directresses made little progress in finding skilled women to take girls. Only two girls from the Female Asylum were apprenticed to a mantua-maker, and one of those places was arranged by a girl's mother rather than by the board.[34] More than sixty other girls were sent out as domestic servants to live with prominent white families and to cook, clean, nurse, and generally work as directed by the mistress.[35] While work like this was often arduous, real misapplication and abuse of the girls was not tolerated. The directresses took one girl "again under their protection" because "upon information that she had been cruelly whipt, the directresses thought themselves justified in taking her away"; they removed another girl who was "never allowed to go to a place of worship" and was only employed caring for a small child.[36] Moreover, some girls did not wait for intervention from the board before proactively taking matters into their own hands when dissatisfied with their placement.

It is not known if the prior consent of the girls to their placements was sought, as it was by the commissioners of the Charleston Orphan House, but several girls found ways to express their views on their indentures. Sarah Suares, bound by the Female Asylum to Mrs. Plumb, wrote to her mother declaring that she found her work "not agreeable" and that she had decided to leave.

Similarly, Susan Hutchinson refused to be bound to Mrs. Williams and then refused to return to the asylum, prompting the directresses to take legal action against her blatant defiance.[37] Mothers also sometimes became involved, appearing in person before the board to ask that their children be removed from a particular mistress. While in general the board of the Female Asylum did not wish its decisions to be questioned or reversed, Mary Ann Flynn managed to get retrospective approval from the board after she removed herself from one employer and selected another more to her liking. The meek acceptance of the board may have had something to do with the fact that Mary's new employer, Mr. Hutson, was a man. To challenge his decision to take Mary was perhaps a step that the board was not prepared to take.[38]

The problems associated with the binding out system, with the directresses meeting periodic opposition from the girls, their parents, and the employers, led to a complete suspension of binding out in December 1825. Resolving "to keep the children in the asylum... until they were old enough to support themselves," the board instituted a "plan of instructing the children in spinning and weaving, where their services would be turned to more account by being kept in the asylum, learning the habits of regular industry, and thereby saving to the institution the expense of purchasing stocking, thread, frocks &c, &c."[39] For unstated reasons, however, the board returned to binding out within a year with the indenture of Nelly Gill to Mrs. Bears in December 1826, though, as figure 9.2 illustrates, without the same enthusiasm of a decade earlier.

The lives of the five hundred or so poor children assisted by the Union Society, the Female Asylum, and the Free School were meant to be clearly mapped out. All had received a basic education to equip them with some of skills needed to be successful adults, and many had also benefited from job training that would, it was hoped, give them lifelong earning potential. As Paul Lachance demonstrates in chapter 8, education was a crucial factor in social mobility for the poor, and thus equipped, did Savannah's orphan children seize their chance for self-advancement? More importantly, to what extent had poor children absorbed the core message of benevolence—that they should become "useful members of society"—and taken up suitable artisanal trades that would maintain them in life, while shying away from the "degradation and vice" that might otherwise have tempted them?[40] Had they come out of institutional control with the self-control that would make them genuinely reformed citizens, firmly set on a different course than they might otherwise have been? Tracing the adult lives of former orphans through tax, census, marriage, death, and court records allows us to answer these questions, to measure the effect that benevolence had on poor children in Savannah.

Of the 555 poor children assisted by the Union Society, the Female Asylum, and the Free School, a third of boys and nearly half the girls never appeared again in any type of Savannah city record. In itself this is not very surprising.

Beneficiaries did not ordinarily become heads of their own households immediately upon leaving the care of charitable institutions at eighteen or twenty-one years old: they were more likely to rent a room with a larger family or in one of Savannah's numerous boarding houses. As boarders or lodgers, they did not appear in the city tax records as possessing taxable property, nor were they named individually in federal censuses before 1850. So long as they remained alive, single, out of the criminal justice system, and did not belong to a church, nobody would have kept a record of them. The historical anonymity of many southern poor whites is well known, and can in part be explained by the nature of record collection. To modern historians it is as if they never existed. As years went by, no doubt many former orphans left Savannah for new opportunities in Alabama, Mississippi, and Texas or even just across the river in South Carolina or elsewhere in Georgia, where they became untraceable. Many received free land in western Georgia in one of the seven land lotteries held between 1805 and 1832, since orphans were automatically entered into the draw. In 1827 alone, nine of our sample held winning tickets and probably left the city soon afterward.[41] Nevertheless, nearly two-thirds of our children did leave traces of their lives after childhood, a significant and representative sample, allowing us to gauge how far the benevolent aims of managers and directresses were carried into effect.

Former male beneficiaries of the Union Society and the Free School who remained in Savannah long enough to be enumerated in the federal censuses of 1850 and 1860 were generally engaged in a wide variety of artisanal work. This was in line with the intentions of the managers of the Union Society, who believed that "all well regulated communities must have their mechanics."[42] The evidence suggests that there was a strong correlation between the trades to which boys were apprenticed and their eventual careers. More boys were apprenticed as printers than to any other trade, and more former orphans were working as printers than at any other occupation. This held true for other trades as well. William Smith, for example, was bound to a painter by the Union Society in 1839 and continued the same trade through to 1860: Leander Moore was apprenticed to a harbor pilot in 1846 and was still working as a pilot in 1860.[43] For these boys, the training they received as apprentices had equipped them with the skills to sustain themselves and their families in adult life: Moore was married with two children by 1860, while Smith and his wife had five children. Perhaps because of the education they had received, very few boys were working as unskilled laborers competing for work with slaves and immigrants, and two of the three that were had been taken away by their mother before the Union Society had apprenticed them.[44]

The modest fortunes of most of the former Union Society boys can be demonstrated further by looking at the city tax records. About half of all former orphans who paid tax in Savannah never owned any property and paid only the poll tax. This tallies well with data from the 1860 census demonstrating that about half of the former orphans did not possess either real or personal estate. Those with personal estate in 1860 rarely had more than a few hundred dollars, suggesting that true financial security was beyond the reach of most of them. There are occasional examples, however, of poor boys achieving far more for themselves than a modest subsistence. Howell Cobb, on the bounty of the Union Society from 1809, was apprenticed for two years in 1813 to Frederick S. Fell, editor of the *Savannah Republican*. On reaching his majority, Cobb became a teacher and by 1827 was a lawyer and a part-time Methodist preacher in upcountry Georgia. In the 1830s he became a state senator, served as a presidential elector, established the *Cherokee Gazette* and wrote a penal code for the state.[45] With such a prominent career, it is no surprise that Cobb was invited to Savannah to give the Anniversary Address to the Union Society in 1834. In a similar vein, Anthony Suares was apprenticed by the Union Society to Crane and Baker, a firm of bricklayers in 1817. He did not remain in the trade for long but set out for Louisiana, where he evidently became successful. In recognition of the moral debt he owed the Union Society, he sent a $500 donation in 1833. Both Suares and Cobb were made honorary members of the Union Society.[46] Among those who remained in Savannah, perhaps the most successful was Solomon Sheftall, a former pupil at the Free School. By 1850 he was a working as a doctor in the city and possessed property valued at $3,000.[47] These men were the exception, not the rule, but in general it is true to state that most former orphans had skilled trades, reflecting their ability and training, that allowed them to earn enough to live on and that only a few boys lingered in true poverty or left it far behind.

While many former orphan boys can be found in later historical records, tracing the future lives of poor girls assisted by the Female Asylum or the Free School is not an easy task, since among women only widows paid city taxes, and female occupations were not recorded in the federal census until 1860. On the limited evidence available, it seems that few girls who were apprenticed as domestic servants continued in that career for long. Former occupants of the Female Asylum were listed in census records as boarding-housekeepers, milliners, seamstresses, even as a brass and iron foundress, but only once as a domestic. This was not because there was a racial barrier to white women working as domestic servants in Savannah. In 1860, for instance, 266 white women were employed in this manner, but the vast majority of them were young Irish girls newly arrived in the city. Native-born women generally worked at better-paying occupations, though of course, the skills learned working as a domestic to a wealthy family were useful for the girls' own households when they married and had children.[48] No doubt many young women continued to contribute to their household's income by taking in sewing, washing, and ironing or doing childcare without such work being formally acknowledged or recorded. The degree of financial security obtained by young single working women, however, was limited. According to the census, unmarried women who had benefited from the bounty of the Female Asylum or the Free School as children owned very modest personal property as working adults, usually no more than $50.[49]

A possible route to greater financial security open to former orphan girls was a good solid marriage. In general the girls married artisans—butchers, bricklayers, wheelwrights, shopkeepers, and shoemakers, men who were of a fairly similar social status to themselves. About half of these men did not own land or slaves, so although they probably would have been able to provide the basic essentials of food, clothing, and shelter for their families, the husbands of former orphan girls were not a ticket to a life of leisure. Wives married to these men would most likely have had to continue to work in whatever capacity they were able, bringing in vital wages to the household. Some girls had the good fortune to marry property-owners or slaveholders. For these few, marriage was the step that elevated them into a higher social class. Mary Ann Kemp, who had been admitted as a "really indigent" pupil at the Free School in 1817, married lumber merchant Augustus G. Boulineau in 1829. Boulineau's business grew only slowly, but by 1860 he owned real estate in Savannah valued at $11,000, and Mary herself was credited with owning $7,000 of real estate. Another indigent girl, Missouri Loper, had been sent to the Female Asylum by her mother at the age of six in 1824 and was apprenticed in 1827 to Mrs. Jones, a manuta-maker. In 1838, twenty-year-old Missouri married Philip R. Douglas, a man of some property: in 1833 he had owned four slaves and farmed two hundred acres in Chatham County; considering her background, this was an advantageous match for Missouri. Marrying a landowner and a slaveholder gave her a measure of economic security that many of her fellow asylum inmates never acquired.[50]

Missouri Douglas did not enjoy the benefits of marrying a property-holder for long, dying in 1845 at the age of twenty-seven. Premature death was not unknown among Savannah's orphans: one in ten died before reaching the age of eighteen, mainly of "dropsy," a condition today known as edema in which water collects in various body cavities, or of consumption. However, only four orphans succumbed to the 1820 yellow fever epidemic, and none to a later outbreak of the disease in 1854, a very small number considering the mortality the two events caused in the city overall.[51] In part this was because the disease was far more virulent among immigrants, and orphans were generally native-born, but it was also the result of a deliberate attempt to reduce mortality by moving the children to safer climes. In August 1820, for example, the girls at the asylum were moved, on doctor's advice, to a healthier part of the city, and in 1854 both the Union Society and the Female Asylum procured medical treatment for the children in their care. Actions such as those taken during the yellow fever epidemic probably ensured that death rates were actually lower, or at least no worse, for orphans than for children who had parents living.[52]

It is clear, therefore, that most former orphan children survived the institutional experience to enter into the workplace, making themselves "useful" by "prosecuting the various mechanical arts of the day."[53] Of course, work led to wage packets, and one might argue that orphans were no different from the other citizens of Savannah in wanting to have more than merely enough money to stave off starvation. Where one can test more rigorously if poor children imbibed the message of moral reform thrust at them by the benevolent is by examining the court records of the city. The managers of benevolent societies claimed to "prevent the effects of ignorance and error by imparting that early moral culture which alone insures a life of rectitude and consistency" and to save children "from the temptations, the expedients and the crimes of poverty," creating instead "upright, valuable and intelligent citizens," but how successful were they?[54] The jail and court records for Savannah show that only one former orphan was ever imprisoned; as he was released without charge within a day, his confinement for "rioting" can probably be attributed to youthful high spirits.[55] Six of the Union Society's boys did transgress city ordinances as adults and were fined either for "entertaining Negroes on Sunday," an offense that characteristically involved providing a place for slaves to drink and socialize, or "retailing liquor without a license." These were fairly minor transgressions, none of the offenders was fined more than $30, and each only appeared once before the council. Since one of the aims of providing benevolence to Savannah's poor children was to put a brake on antisocial behavior and the "pernicious consequences that spring from ignorance and idleness," it seems it was remarkably successful.[56] In general the orphans conformed to a standard of behavior that the poor usually found beyond them. Hundreds of poor residents of Savannah were brought before the Mayor's Court for transgressing city ordinances, and hundreds more spent time in the city jail for various crimes, both violent and nonviolent. Yet the drinking, gambling, trading with slaves, and other unseemly and sometimes criminal activities in which the poor seemed to engage with depressing regularity were eschewed by former orphans.[57] While the children might well have stayed on the right side of the law, they did not necessarily follow the paths laid out for them to the letter. For example, the children received regular religious instruction while under institutional control, yet the membership records of Savannah's churches show that few orphans actually became full members in later life. If the benevolent hoped to bring poor children into the church discipline network that penalized communicants for offenses such as drunkenness, swearing, adultery, and bastardy, they failed.[58]

Although former orphans seemed to have had enough self-control to keep themselves out of trouble, how far were their views on key political questions shaped by their institutional experiences? As mentioned earlier, an increasingly important element of the education offered to poor children was intended to shape their attitudes toward the South in general and slavery in particular. One correspondent to the *Savannah Republican* urged all parents to have their children "indoctrinated with your own views and principles, then you will have a fortress against which may swell and lash the waves of Black Republicanism, but all in vain for 'Just as the twig is bent, the tree's inclined, 'tis education makes a fortress of the mind.'"[59] As we have seen, very few former orphans transgressed city ordinances regarding trading with slaves. In fact, among those beneficiaries of charity who owned any form of property, the most likely form to hold was enslaved persons—usually just one or two, but sometimes as many as six. Choosing to own slaves was partly an economic decision: having enslaved labor to assist in day-to-day work tasks significantly enhanced the amount of work an artisan could do and hence the amount of money he could earn. But that these former orphans elected to purchase slaves, often before they purchased land, shows how far they had imbibed the established social attitudes toward African Americans in the South. Howell Cobb even published his thoughts on the institution of slavery in 1856, defending it as having scriptural authority and describing is as a "great providential enterprise" and as "beneficial to the slaves."[60] As native-born southerners who had also received guidance as to the proper way of thinking about the South, it is not surprising that at least twenty former orphans fought on the Confederate side during the Civil War, with Thaddeus Fisher reaching the rank of captain in the First Georgia Infantry Regiment. Among those to serve was Cornelius Long, who as a twelve-year-old had spoken on behalf of the boys at the anniversary meeting of the Union Society in 1857: "I hope we may appreciate the many blessings we enjoy here, and that we may never disgrace it by our conduct, but rather, that we may live to do honor and credit to those who have sustained us." The managers of the Union Society would indeed have seen Long as "worthy of the care bestowed"—he was killed in action during the Civil War.[61]

The managers and directresses of the Union Society, the Female Asylum, and the Free School had therefore achieved many of their ambitions for the indigent children of Savannah. Not only were most working in suitable professions, they were also living sober and decent lives without disturbing the peace of the community. The managers of the Union Society and the directresses of the Free School and the Female Asylum were confident that their work had made a real difference to the lives of indigent children. Thomas U. P. Charlton, one-time mayor of Savannah, believed that "the Union Society hath given... citizens to the republic, and sent them forth with minds imbued with the principles of piety and the elements and benefits of a practical education. The Union Society has snatched them from the thraldom of ignorance, and it saved them from the temptations... and the crimes of poverty... [making them] upright, valuable and intelligent citizens"[62] A historian of the Female Asylum noted in 1854 that "among the number of beneficiaries many have been worthy members of the community, have married respectably, and reared up families who have done them credit.... Some (but very few in proportion to those that have done well) have gone astray, and even among these very few, some have erred only for a short season; the seed, early sown, had been for while overgrown by the tares of temptation, but have finally borne good fruit."[63] The directresses of the Free School knew there was real pleasure to be taken from "the delight of rescuing a fellow creature from error and ignorance" and especially "by imparting that early moral culture which alone insures a life of rectitude and consistency."[64] This wasn't simply a one-way street however; the poor children who had been given education and training free of charge were well aware of the helping hand they had been given and were suitably grateful for the assistance. Solomon Sheftall offered his "sincere thanks to Mr Cooper for his kind, indulgent and tender treatment to me," Howell Cobb acknowledged the debt he owed the Union Society "for any usefulness I may be of amongst my fellow men," and Anthony Suares also did not forget the "education which was the basis of his fortune."[65] It became increasingly common practice for managers and directresses to bring the children to the annual meetings of the subscribers so that the results of their work could be publicly displayed. At the annual meeting of the Savannah Free School Society in 1860, the teacher "introduced to the audience Mr John W. Kern, a former beneficiary of the society and pupil of the school, who delivered an appropriate and eloquent address in the course of which he made a very feeling allusion to the debt of gratitude which he owed the society, who, in his early orphanage, gave him all the education he had ever acquired at school. The address was listed to with profound interest by all present."[66] Given the success of their work, the benevolent elite of Savannah could afford to feel justifiably proud.

PART IV

BINDING OUT AS A FAMILY/STATE RELATION

As Steve Hindle and Ruth Herndon show in chapter 2, pauper apprenticeship descended from English poor law and gave local magistrates explicit authority to rearrange a family. The practice of binding out thus reveals the relationship between the family and the state as represented by local authorities in early America. Community magistrates intended that pauper apprentices should be raised in homes that conformed to their ideas of order. Binding out was in fact the state's declaration and affirmation of what a "proper" household should look like, and masters were expected to provide such households to the children they took in.

Colonial and state laws illuminate this expectation, that masters would act *in loco parentis* for pauper apprentices, doing what good parents should do for children—"maintain," "protect," "educate," "discipline," and "govern" them. Delaware magistrates, for example, were authorized to bind out children of any parents "who shall not by the said Justices and Overseer or Overseers be thought of Ability to maintain and educate them" ("An Act for Relief of the Poor"). Such statutes make clear that the state took very seriously the business of childrearing and intended for all children to grow up in a "proper" home; if the children's own parents were not capable, then the state would provide masters to do the job.

In early America, "proper" homes were places where children were provided with all the necessities of life and were trained in the practical responsibilities of adulthood. Children should receive proper food, drink, clothing, shelter, and medical care. They should learn to work, so as to contribute to the welfare of the larger community. They should receive necessary discipline, so as not to become idle and "useless" in later years. Binding out thus drew on children's dependency (they should be protected) and their productivity (they should be trained to work). Binding out also illuminated mutual responsibilities of state and family: the family was responsible to raise a child properly; the state was responsible to see to it that the family carried out that task.

CHAPTER TEN

Responsive Justices

Court Treatment of Orphans and Illegitimate Children in Colonial Maryland

JEAN B. RUSSO AND J. ELLIOTT RUSSO

In November 1734, concern for James Taylor's orphans prompted John Murray to petition the court of Somerset County, Maryland. Murray told the court that Taylor's three sons "have been hitherto neglected as to learning and... he thinks it is his duty to inform your worships who are the father of orphans that care may be taken for their education." The court responded by calling the masters of the Taylor orphans into court and instructing them to put the boys to school by the following March. The justices emphasized that the children would "be removed if there is any further complaint."[1]

Murray's petition and others like it served to keep the county court mindful of its responsibilities as "the father" of orphans and other vulnerable children. From the earliest days of settlement, Maryland's colonists needed to care for children who lacked parental support. Whenever possible, households coped with this challenge through informal arrangements, but if such measures proved inadequate, colonists sought assistance from the county court. Each year the November court sessions concluded with a calculation of the year's tax levy, based on a list of expenses that included monthly or yearly stipends paid to householders who were looking after needy members of the community. In addition, the yearly round of court business generally encompassed the binding out of orphans and illegitimate children for extended periods of maintenance on terms that could include skill training, schooling, or freedom dues.

This essay examines the courts' treatment of orphan and illegitimate children in two of Maryland's Eastern Shore counties, Talbot and Somerset, during the first century of European settlement, from 1660 to 1759.[2] Our study deals exclusively with children placed by the justices in nonparental households. Colonial Maryland communities had no poor houses or alms houses where children in need could be accommodated; the court made all arrangements for care with individual heads of household. In this area, Maryland's county justices held powers of supervision that were similar to those exercised by parish vestries in Virginia and by selectmen in southern New England, but they wielded those powers much less intrusively. Although given considerable authority by Maryland's legislature, the county courts generally exercised that authority only in response to petitions from the community.[3]

Justices could have exerted power on their own initiative to reinforce judicial authority and to ensure that all households conformed to a patriarchal structure. In practice, however, justices never actively endeavored to identify fatherless children, whose lack of paternal care theoretically required intervention. Rather, they limited their involvement to ratification of decisions made within the community. As county residents brought children to the courts' attention, the arrangements made for their care generally conformed to a patriarchal ideal of domestic authority, with the child's master fulfilling the father's role as head of household. Petitioners sought placements for orphans and illegitimate children that were considered appropriate and reasonable within the social and economic structures of the community. Arrangements thus replicated existing hierarchies but not through any deliberate action by the justices to ensure that result.[4]

The surviving records forcefully indicate a dynamic in which county residents, through their petitions and supplications, required the justices to be mindful of their responsibilities *in loco parentis*. Unlike their counterparts in Virginia vestries and New England town governments, who actively sought out children in need of oversight, the justices took action only when circumstances brought children to their attention. This limited involvement reflects the overall character of the courts' administration of county affairs. As Lois Carr notes, "Justices were weak administrators. They did little planning for public services. Instead they responded to petitions."[5] Despite the reactive nature of their role, Carr and others argue that colonial local governments effectively served the interests of their constituents and generated little call for reform.[6] Thus, with few exceptions, county residents initiated supervision of children by bringing their requests to the court. Potential masters made up the largest group seeking judicial assistance, but petitioners also included mothers, other relatives, and the children themselves. In making their appeals, residents invoked the courts' authority to sustain arrangements for the care of orphan and illegitimate children that benefited both the children and the community.

We begin our study with a review of the categories of children subject to the authority of the justices, the means by which children came to the court's attention, and the varied patterns of care prescribed by the court. We then consider more closely the treatment accorded to children bound by the court, including skill training, education, and freedom dues, with attention to differences related to gender, race, and status. This comparative study reveals that justices in different counties, although mindful of local economic and social circumstances, exercised their authority within the broad framework of a shift from concern with the welfare of orphans without family or kin to a practice of maintaining the social status quo by providing children with the normative education and training suitable to their status. Court proceedings contain no evidence to suggest that justices actively removed children from situations considered undesirable or inappropriate and no evidence that justices or petitioners sought to elevate children by providing training and education beyond what they could have expected under the care of their fathers.

Demographic characteristics of Chesapeake settlements in the early colonial period dictated that community stewardship of children was critical for their survival, as many were orphaned at young ages and had no family networks to support them. Maryland's county courts soon acquired both the authority and the responsibility to oversee the welfare of any child lacking a recognized father, including children whose mothers were still living and children of unwed mothers. As colonial society developed, the character of the child population became correspondingly more complex. Although white children were increasingly likely to be positioned within extended family groups and kinship networks, the ongoing migration of settlers into the region and between communities resulted in the continued presence of some children with few sources of support or ties to other residents. Expanding numbers of enslaved Africans and African Americans added further complexity, as county courts became responsible not only for the illegitimate children of white residents but also for bastards of mixed race.[7]

Over the course of ten decades, the Talbot and Somerset courts each oversaw the care of more than a thousand children.[8] Although in rare instances the justices administered foster care or apprenticeships for children whose parents were both alive and married, the vast majority of children for whom the justices acted were those without a recognized father. The legal system considered a legitimate child an orphan upon the father's death and therefore subject to the courts' authority. Yet even a cursory reading of judicial proceedings coupled with a survey of probate records demonstrates that only a small fraction of eligible children came before the court for supervision. Widows, stepparents, or collateral kin provided care for most orphans.

Treatment of illegitimate children, whether white or of mixed race, even more strikingly demonstrates the limited involvement of institutional authorities in providing for the needs of children not part of father-headed families. A minimum of eleven hundred illegitimate children were born in Talbot County between 1660 and 1759, but the court placed only 124 such children, just 11 percent of the total. Somerset records similarly document a minimum of eight hundred children, of whom only seventy-six (9 percent) were bound out. Even allowing for the high mortality rates that these children undoubtedly experienced, it is clear that most illegitimate children were raised by their mothers, by relatives, or by the maternal master without recourse to formal judicial action.[9] Table 10.1 provides an overview of the orphan and illegitimate children whose care did become the responsibility of the Talbot and Somerset county courts between 1660 and 1760 (excluding orphans only assigned guardians, whom we discuss briefly below). As the low percentages of eligible children bound out by the county courts suggest, Talbot and Somerset justices did not aggressively exercise their authority over fatherless children.

Mothers who found themselves unable to supply appropriate care for their orphan or illegitimate children occasionally requested that the justices provide a suitable home for their offspring. Elinor Ennit petitioned the Somerset Court in June 1691 to have two of her children bound to Anthony Bell, describing herself as a "widow woman [with] five children and...not of ability to keep them." The justices bound her son Edmund for a term of sixteen years and three-year-old daughter Anne until the age of sixteen, with Bell agreeing to teach Edmund to read and to give him a yearling heifer when he turned twelve. Mothers who wished to have their fatherless children trained in a useful craft also invoked the courts' authority. In 1741, for example, John Britt's widow Attalanta bound their two sons to Somerset resident Samuel Adams to learn the trade of a shop joiner.[10] Women thus could turn to the court for assistance to support and educate their children, but in no instance in Somerset or Talbot did the court unilaterally remove a child from a parental home on grounds of inadequate care.

TABLE 10.1.
All bound children by county, gender, status, and decade (row percents)

| | Talbot County | | | | | Somerset County | | | | |
| | Male | | Female | | | Male | | Female | | |
Decade	Orph.	Bast.	Orph.	Bast.	N	Orph.	Bast.	Orph.	Bast.	N
1660–69	–	–	–	–	0	–	–	–	–	0
1670–79	37.5	18.8	37.5	6.3	16	50.0	12.5	12.5	25.0	8
1680–89	60.0	2.2	24.4	13.3	45	53.8	7.7	38.5	0.0	13
1690–99	62.0	2.0	30.0	6.0	50	60.8	8.9	26.6	3.8	79
1700–09	48.9	3.2	42.6	5.3	94	64.3	10.0	22.9	2.9	70
1710–19	29.6	7.4	50.0	13.0	54	57.3	7.3	28.0	7.3	82
1720–29	40.0	14.3	27.1	18.6	70	69.2	8.4	20.6	1.9	107
1730–39	64.3	7.1	23.8	4.8	42	76.5	7.1	16.5	0.0	85
1740–49	50.9	17.3	25.5	6.4	110	77.0	8.9	11.9	2.2	135
1750–59	49.1	11.3	37.7	1.9	53	78.0	6.4	13.5	2.1	141
Total	49.3	9.4	33.0	8.4	534	70.0	8.1	19.0	2.9	720

Intervention by relatives provided another avenue through which children came to the court's notice. The Talbot court learned in 1720 that resident Patrick Macway had died intestate but had left verbal instructions concerning his children. According to his father-in-law, John Bradshaw, Macway had asked that the children be left to the "disposal" of his widow and her father, but Bradshaw "thought it his Duty to bring them to Court to be bound by your Worships." Bradshaw proposed that he take Patrick, the only boy, and that Macway's widow take Mary, one of the daughters. As for the other two girls, Bradshaw "thought fitt according to the will of the deceased to dispose of them as followeth, Elizabeth to Mr. Loftis Bowdle who was a peculiar friend of the deceased, and Anne to Morris Orem." The justices bound the children as Bradshaw requested, with the requirement that Patrick be taught the trade of a tight cooper.[11]

Justices also responded to requests from children themselves, particularly those nearing the age of majority. Talbot resident John Cooke's son Thomas, for example, was apprenticed to William Benstead to learn the trades of shoemaker and tanner, but in June 1715, when he was nineteen years old, Thomas petitioned the court because Benstead kept him laboring "in the grounds at the hoe" and had beaten, abused, and starved him. Cooke desired to be set free or placed with a new master "where I may gett my trades." After the court ruled that he could choose his own master for his remaining two years of servitude, Cooke selected Thomas Hankin, to whom he was bound to learn the trade of a shoemaker.[12]

Most commonly it was potential masters who brought children to court to request that they be bound out. In 1706, for example, Somerset resident John Lamme appeared with orphan John Miller to ask that Miller "be put an aprentis," an appeal that the justices granted with the stipulation that Lamme teach Miller the trade of a weaver and at the end of his service give him "a loome and tacklyn." In March 1719 the Talbot court similarly bound Margery Cooke to Thomas Browne after hearing his "humble motion and petition" to have the child placed in his care. Not infrequently potential masters were also relatives, as was the case for Somerset resident Nathaniel Wyatt, who informed the court in 1709 that the children of John Farrell were "lyable to come on ye Parish as Orphants" and requested that they be bound to him "as being ye nearest of relation."[13]

Illegitimate children theoretically comprised the group of children most readily brought to the courts' attention because their mothers faced criminal prosecution. Talbot justices, for example, bound the illegitimate daughter of Anna Maria Gotchawoodlan to Thomas Laws, her master, during the same 1706 court session in which Gotchawoodlan was tried for bastardy.[14] In practice, however, justices did not automatically assume responsibility for children born to the mothers whom they punished for bastardy. The court's primary concern in its treatment of illegitimate children was to ensure that they not be a burden on the county's taxpayers. Generally, if a free woman or her partner could arrange surety to "save the county harmless" from the costs of raising her illegitimate child, she retained custody. Most instances in which the justices did bind out illegitimate children occurred after the child had survived infancy and, as was the case with orphan children, in response to a county resident's petition or request. Thus in 1703 Mary Burk asked the court to bind her son John to the service of Somerset resident Rebecca Price, three years after she received twenty-five lashes as punishment for bastardy.[15]

Although the means by which children came to the attention of the courts varied, the most salient feature of the process was the passive role initially played by the justices. Unless someone, whether a concerned relative, a watchful neighbor, or a potential master, appeared during court days with a request for action concerning an orphan or bastard, informal arrangements for care continued in effect. Only when county residents called on the justices to fulfill their responsibility for fatherless children did the court exercise its authority to place children in nonparental households.

Once county justices became aware of a child needing supervision, they could choose among a range of options for the child's care. In their choices the men seated on the bench followed guidelines set by several legislative acts of the General Assembly, particularly those regulating their role as the orphans' court. In her study of this court, Lois Green Carr identified the two primary motivations that led to its establishment: "nurture of the child and protection of his inheritance."[16] For children with property, legislation required the court to appoint guardians for the child's property, take guardian bonds for safekeeping estates and delivering the property when requested, order regular appraisals of the real property, and monitor guardians' and administrators' performance. Of nearly eight hundred children supervised by the Talbot court, 20 percent came before the justices only for guardianship purposes, while in Somerset guardianships accounted for 30 percent of court-supervised children.

Children without property adequate for their maintenance required different treatment. For these children the legislature directed justices to bind them out as "Apprentices to some Handi-craft Trade or other p'son."[17] Although most children without property who came to the court's attention found homes through the binding out process, not all took this path to adulthood. Justices occasionally exercised the option of placing some children with individual householders and providing compensation for their maintenance, thus supplying shelter in the absence of a work or alms house to perform this service. Most children received this form of care for a relatively short period of time, often less than a year, until suitable arrangements could be made for binding them out until the age of majority.[18] But some children probably lived their entire lives in foster care because they suffered from physical or mental disabilities that made it unlikely for a master to recoup his maintenance costs through work. The 1697 Talbot levy included payments to widow Katherine Winchester for keeping Mary Cartwright, "a poor decriped girl," and to Thomas Hopkins for "keeping a lame girl."[19] For disabled children provisions made for their support at county expense provided vital assistance. Lacking kin who could offer care and unable themselves to labor in return for maintenance, they were entirely dependent on welfare supplied by the county.

For the larger group of illegitimate children and orphans with small or nonexistent estates whom the court supervised through a formal process of binding out, the justices specified what benefits beyond sustenance, if any, the child would receive and required a bond from the master guaranteeing that he would fulfill the court's conditions. The court's responsibility to place a child in a position suitable for his or her status within the county's social hierarchy is implicit in the governing legislation, which required justices to ensure that children were "kept mainteyned and educated according to their Estates."[20] In exchange for the child's labor, the master typically contracted to provide lodging, clothing, and diet in addition to whatever mixture of skill training, education, and freedom dues the justices stipulated. Patterns established over time in treatment of children of differing status suggest that the justices generally employed a set of standard terms crafted to meet the needs of different categories of children, although the requirements of the master or intercession by family members could result in modifications to suit particular circumstances. The justices ostensibly monitored the master's performance and could levy fines or remove the child if their instructions were disregarded. In practice, however, the court took such action rarely and only in response to petitions from the child, his or her kin, or a concerned neighbor.

The placement of orphans and illegitimate children by the court and their acceptance by masters represented a convergence of interests for at least two parties. The justices discharged their responsibilities to both the community and the children by arranging for maintenance during their minority and by providing an opportunity to learn skills for their support as adults. A master who accepted a child, on the other hand, acquired a household member from whose labor he expected to benefit, as petitions to the court often revealed. In June 1707, for example, Richard Dudley informed the Talbot court that John Hodgins, a runaway, had left a son whom Dudley's father, Richard Sr., had brought up and "cured of a scall'd head." Since Richard Sr.'s death, the child had lived with Richard Jr., "and now [that] he is capable of doing some service the neighbours Intices him to leave your petitioner." Dudley wished to have the child formally bound to him to protect the investment already made in the child through the care given by both Richard and his father, their expected return in the form of the child's labor being at risk through lack of placement by the court. Competition for a child's labor similarly moved Edward Bennet to complain to the Somerset court in June 1706 that sixteen-year-old orphan William More, whom Bennet had raised "from his mothers brest," had been persuaded by his stepfather to leave Bennet's service just when his work could compensate Bennet for his "care & charge in bringing up." In response the justices formally bound More to Bennet until age twenty-one and required that the child receive livestock and instruction in reading and writing.[21]

In most cases, although not all, benefits also accrued to a third group, the children themselves, in the form of skill training, education, and freedom dues. Broadly speaking, changes over time in the benefits that the justices required masters to provide reflect the shift from simply accommodating orphan and illegitimate children, with no stipulations beyond the standard food, clothing, and lodging, to a more overt effort to place children in a "suitable" position whereby they would receive the degree of craft training, education, and material goods deemed appropriate for their position in the counties' hierarchical society.

Legislative guidelines that required justices to bind to a trade any orphan with an estate "soe meane & in Considerable tht itt will not extend to a Free Educacon" applied to both male and female orphans, but justices in the two counties distinguished by gender as well as by status (legitimate or illegitimate) in assigning training (see tables 10.2 and 10.3).[22] Courts specified training for less than a third of female orphans bound in the seventeenth century but by the middle of the eighteenth required most masters to teach orphan girls in their care "housewifery work" or to "sew, Spin, Knitt and other Housewifery work." Although justices could choose from a broader range of skills when binding out male children, for much of the period under study, boys were *less* likely than girls to have the court specify any training. During the late seventeenth and early eighteenth centuries, only one-half to two-thirds of the orphan boys

TABLE 10.2.
Percent of male children with skill training by county, status, and decade (cell percents)

Decade	Talbot County		N		Somerset County		N	
	Orphan	Bastard	O	B	Orphan	Bastard	O	B
1660–69	–	–	0	0	–	–	0	0
1670–79	16.7	0.0	6	3	25.0	0.0	4	1
1680–89	55.6	0.0	27	1	28.6	100.0	7	1
1690–99	71.0	0.0	31	1	22.9	0.0	48	7
1700–09	52.2	33.3	46	3	24.3	0.0	45	7
1710–19	68.8	0.0	16	4	31.9	33.3	47	6
1720–29	89.3	40.0	28	10	67.6	0.0	74	9
1730–39	88.9	66.7	27	3	89.2	33.3	65	6
1740–49	92.9	5.3	56	19	96.2	75.0	104	12
1750–59	73.1	0.0	26	6	96.4	88.9	110	9
Total	73.4	16.0	263	50	70.2	37.9	504	58

TABLE 10.3.
Percent of female children with skill training by county, status, and decade (cell percents)

Decade	Talbot County		N		Somerset County		N	
	Orphan	Bastard	O	B	Orphan	Bastard	O	B
1660–69	–	–	0	0	–	–	0	0
1670–79	0.0	0.0	6	1	0.0	0.0	1	2
1680–89	18.2	0.0	11	6	20.0	–	5	0
1690–99	26.7	0.0	15	3	28.6	0.0	21	3
1700–09	85.0	40.0	40	5	6.3	50.0	16	2
1710–19	96.3	42.9	27	7	0.0	0.0	23	6
1720–29	94.7	61.5	19	13	63.6	0.0	22	2
1730–39	100.0	100.0	10	2	92.9	–	14	0
1740–49	96.4	42.9	28	7	87.5	100.0	16	3
1750–59	100.0	0.0	20	1	100.0	33.3	19	3
Total	80.1	40.0	176	45	49.6	23.8	137	21

bound in Talbot and less than one-third of boys bound in Somerset were to receive training. The courts did include training more often by the middle of the eighteenth century; the trend is particularly striking in Somerset, where the percentage rose steadily from just over 20 percent at the beginning of the century to well over 90 percent by the 1750s.

Justices in each county rarely stipulated training for illegitimate children. Of the twelve illegitimate boys bound out in Talbot before 1720, the court required craft training only for John Cullen, whose master contracted in 1705 to teach John to be a carpenter or cooper but not to read or write.[23] The Talbot court placed thirty-eight illegitimate boys with masters after 1720 but ordered that only seven (18 percent) be trained in a craft: two as coopers, two as shoemakers, two as tailors, and one as a weaver. Illegitimate boys fared better in Somerset but still received training in less than half of the cases; most of the boys who were to learn a skill appeared before the court during the last two decades of the period.

Masters who agreed to provide craft training for their male charges generally practiced trades that fulfilled three criteria: they utilized readily available raw materials, they provided for basic needs of local residents, and they did not as a rule require a large capital expenditure for equipment (see table 10.4). Woodworking, leather, and clothing crafts, using the wood, skins and hides, and wool and flax found in abundance on the planters' land and in their fields, accounted for nearly half the craft placements made in Talbot and over two-thirds of those in Somerset. Carpenters and coopers formed the bulk of the woodworking apprentices, while shoemakers accounted for almost all of the leather workers and represented the largest single craft group, claiming 27 percent of the boys with trades in Talbot and 20 percent in Somerset. Within each county, a diverse array of artisans, such as blacksmiths, bricklayers, and shipbuilders, became masters of

TABLE 10.4.
Male children bound to a trade by decade, county, and craft group (column percents)

Craft Group	Decade									
	1660–69	1670–79	1680–89	1690–99	1700–09	1710–19	1720–29	1730–39	1740–49	1750–59
Talbot										
Basic wood	—	100.0	66.7	22.7	54.2	36.4	52.0	37.5	34.6	21.1
Complex wood	—	0.0	0.0	0.0	4.2	0.0	0.0	16.7	3.8	10.5
Ship construction	—	0.0	0.0	0.0	4.2	0.0	0.0	4.2	1.9	0.0
Leather	—	0.0	13.3	45.5	16.7	36.4	32.0	25.0	34.6	36.8
Cloth and clothing	—	0.0	0.0	13.6	8.3	18.2	12.0	4.2	11.5	26.3
Metal	—	0.0	6.7	0.0	4.2	0.0	0.0	8.3	7.6	5.3
Maritime	—	0.0	0.0	0.0	0.0	0.0	4.0	0.0	0.0	0.0
Miscellaneous and unspecified	—	0.0	13.3	18.2	8.3	9.1	0.0	4.2	5.8	0.0
N	0	1	15	22	24	11	25	24	52	19
Somerset										
Basic wood	—	0.0	0.0	45.5	18.2	29.4	30.0	25.0	33.1	33.4
Complex wood	—	0.0	0.0	0.0	0.0	0.0	4.0	1.7	13.7	9.6
Ship construction	—	0.0	0.0	9.1	0.0	0.0	0.0	0.0	10.9	7.0
Leather	—	100.0	33.3	9.1	27.3	35.3	38.0	26.7	22.1	19.3
Cloth and clothing	—	0.0	0.0	36.4	54.5	23.5	18.0	25.0	8.3	10.5
Metal	—	0.0	0.0	0.0	0.0	11.8	0.0	1.7	3.7	10.5
Maritime	—	0.0	0.0	0.0	0.0	0.0	8.0	11.7	7.3	7.0
Miscellaneous and unspecified	—	0.0	66.7	0.0	0.0	0.0	2.0	8.3	0.9	2.6
N	0	1	3	11	11	17	50	60	109	114

Basic wood: carpenter, cooper, sawyer, wheelwright, house joiner.
Complex wood: shop joiner, turner, spinning wheelwright, chairmaker.
Ship construction: ship carpenter, shipwright, caulker.
Leather: tanner, shoemaker.
Cloth and clothing: weaver, tailor, hatter, glover, one wigmaker.
Metal: blacksmith.
Maritime: navigation, mariner, seaman, plain sailor.
Miscellaneous and unspecified: ten bricklayers, one plasterer, one glazier, two ditchers, two millwrights, ten unspecified.

the remaining boys as they availed themselves in small numbers of the opportunity to acquire a worker for their shops.[24]

In addition to skill training, the justices in Somerset and Talbot counties could, at their discretion, require education for orphan and illegitimate children (see tables 10.5 and 10.6). Given the range of ages at which children were bound, there must have been instances in which the courts placed children who already knew how to read and write, making requirements to teach such skills unnecessary. Age alone, however, does not account for all of the observed variation in education provisions. Loosely standardized practices regarding education evolved slowly, with both courts following the same trajectory in their educational provisions for orphan children, both male and female. Prior to 1680, no placement in either county included an educational requirement. After 1700 the courts began to stipulate that a majority of orphan boys learn to read, but not until 1720 did they make the same provision for writing. For orphan girls, requirements to teach reading increased dramatically after about 1710, while provisions for writing lagged well behind.

TABLE 10.5.
Percent of male children with provisions for reading and writing by county, status, and decade (cell percents)

| | Talbot County | | | | Somerset County | | | |
| | Orphan | | Bastard | | Orphan | | Bastard | |
Decade	Read	Write	Read	Write	Read	Write	Read	Write
1660–69	–	–	–	–	–	–	–	–
1670–79	0.0	0.0	0.0	0.0	0.0	0.0	0.0	0.0
1680–89	7.4	7.4	0.0	0.0	42.9	28.6	100.0	100.0
1690–99	32.3	16.1	0.0	0.0	31.3	18.8	71.4	14.3
1700–09	65.2	28.3	33.3	33.3	84.4	33.3	57.1	28.6
1710–19	87.5	62.5	25.0	0.0	85.1	29.8	66.7	33.3
1720–29	92.9	75.0	50.0	20.0	90.5	55.4	77.8	55.6
1730–39	88.9	88.9	100.0	66.7	86.2	73.8	66.7	50.0
1740–49	100.0	89.3	21.6	5.3	89.4	77.9	66.7	41.7
1750–59	88.5	80.8	50.0	50.0	85.5	74.5	100.0	66.7
Total	70.3	56.7	38.0	18.0	84.3	57.9	70.7	43.1

N	Orphan	Bastard	Orphan	Bastard
1660–69	0	0	0	0
1670–79	6	3	4	1
1680–89	27	1	7	1
1690–99	31	1	48	7
1700–09	46	3	45	7
1710–19	16	4	47	6
1720–29	28	10	74	9
1730–39	27	3	65	6
1740–49	56	19	104	12
1750–59	26	6	110	9
Total	263	50	504	58

TABLE 10.6.
Percent of female children with provisions for reading and writing by county, status, and decade (cell percents)

| | Orphan | | Bastard | | Orphan | | Bastard | |
Decade	Read	Write	Read	Write	Read	Write	Read	Write
1660–69	–	–	–	–	–	–	–	–
1670–79	0.0	0.0	0.0	0.0	0.0	0.0	0.0	0.0
1680–89	27.3	0.0	0.0	0.0	20.0	0.0	–	–
1690–99	40.0	0.0	0.0	0.0	47.6	9.5	66.7	0.0
1700–09	70.0	0.0	40.0	0.0	50.0	0.0	50.0	0.0
1710–19	88.9	3.7	28.6	0.0	82.6	4.3	33.3	0.0
1720–29	94.7	0.0	38.5	0.0	95.5	13.6	100.0	0.0
1730–39	100.0	0.0	50.0	0.0	92.9	21.4	–	–
1740–49	92.9	3.6	42.9	0.0	81.3	31.3	100.0	0.0
1750–59	100.0	0.0	0.0	0.0	84.2	5.3	66.7	0.0
Total	76.2	1.1	28.9	0.0	73.7	10.9	57.1	0.0

N	Orphan	Bastard	Orphan	Bastard
1660–69	0	0	0	0
1670–79	6	1	1	2
1680–89	11	6	5	0
1690–99	15	3	21	3
1700–09	40	5	16	2
1710–19	27	7	23	6
1720–29	19	13	22	2
1730–39	10	2	14	0
1740–49	28	7	16	3
1750–59	20	1	19	3
Total	176	45	137	21

For much of the period under study, the justices of Somerset and Talbot Counties demanded much less from the masters of illegitimate children than they did from those taking in orphan children. Justices in both counties were noticeably less diligent about prescribing literacy for illegitimate male children, particularly before 1730. Standards for educating illegitimate girls were even lower, as the courts rarely required literacy training for these girls and never ordered any to be taught to write. For illegitimate boys, provisions regarding writing show trends similar to those for reading, with more masters agreeing to provide instruction toward the end of the period.

Only Somerset records include stipulations about freedom dues for bound children, requiring them for roughly half of all orphan and illegitimate children. Two trends evident in the Somerset cases are of particular note. First, the court initially specified dues that included livestock for most orphan children, both male and female, as well as many male illegitimate children, but by the last two decades of the period only a handful of children were to be given capital in the form of livestock; this shift could reflect the likelihood that orphaned children would receive livestock from their fathers' estates as the county's society matured.[25] Second, Somerset justices increasingly ensured that male children, both orphan and illegitimate, receive tools as well as skill training. In 1732, for example, the court specified that Richard Wallace would give to Henry O'Day "a broad ax hand saw adz three chizzells of different sises one gouge and two augurs."[26] By the last decade of the period, Somerset masters were required to provide tools to nearly half of the orphan boys and over a third of the illegitimate boys.

Taken together, the evidence regarding skill training, education, and freedom dues demonstrates that justices in both counties established a loose hierarchy for the children they placed, taking into consideration both gender and status. Male orphan children comprised the group most likely to be taught reading and writing in addition to learning a skill and, in Somerset, the group most likely to receive useful property as freedom dues. Illegitimate boys were comparatively disadvantaged, particularly in Talbot, where far fewer entered adulthood equipped with even a modest degree of education. For boys, then, legitimacy appears to have had practical consequences in the extent to which the county court would mandate not only skill training but also provisions for education. For girls, legitimacy had less of an impact. Because Chesapeake society considered routine field labor suitable only for black and mulatto women, white female children in these counties, whether legitimate or illegitimate, underwent similar experiences when bound by the court. Both tended to receive the education that women needed in a rural agricultural society that offered few employment opportunities for free women: they were prepared to be housewives or, failing marriage, to be housekeepers or domestic servants.

For the small subset of bound children in each county who were of mixed race, the data are inconsistent. In Talbot, the treatment of the mulatto boys and girls suggests the justices' unwillingness to educate mixed-race children. The Talbot court bound out seven mulatto girls (all before 1730) but made no provision for education or training. The girls were not formally sold into lifetime servitude but, equipped for no other adult role, they would likely spend their days laboring in tobacco fields. Illegitimate mulatto boys fared no better than their female counterparts. The court bound only one to a Talbot master before 1740 and placed only three boys in the 1740s and 1750s. Like the mulatto girls, none of the four were to be trained or educated for anything but manual labor. In Somerset, however, the rough outlines of the court's treatment of mixed-race children are almost indistinguishable from that of white children, particularly illegitimate white children. All but five of the twenty-six mulatto children bound by the court after 1740 were to be taught to read (81 percent), while all but one of the seventeen boys were to be taught a trade (94 percent); four were to receive tools as freedom dues (24 percent of the boys).[27] This is not to say that mixed-race children were treated "equally" but rather to emphasize that in Somerset, unequal treatment nevertheless included some skill training and rudimentary literacy. For both male and female mulatto children in Somerset, the most salient distinction was not the requirement to supply skills or education but rather the nature of the training stipulated. Thus the boys were to be taught reading and either shoemaking or cooperage but not writing, tanning, or more complex woodworking. For girls the difference in experience had less to do with the requirements set by the court than with the probability that they would work in the fields, as the justices placed no restrictions preventing masters from using mulatto girls for field labor.[28]

By the middle of the eighteenth century, the different treatment of mixed-race children in both counties reveals the extent to which earlier concern simply to provide sustenance and a reasonable future to children in need, most of whom were white and legitimate, had given way to placements of orphan and illegitimate children that worked to maintain the social status quo by educating children "according to their estates." The justices did not specify craft training for every child bound out as a servant, and the children left without training tended to be poor, bastards, mulattos, or a combination of the three. Even as masters of white legitimate children increasingly provided craft training as well as literacy and numeracy skills for their charges, the application of the same standards for bastard children in general, and illegitimate mulatto children in particular, lagged well behind. These children generally lacked kin or other advocates who could invoke the authority of the court to effect a meaningful change in their present status or future prospects. As mixed-race children matured in a society in which most African Americans and mulattoes were held as slaves, they would occupy a place in the social order only nominally different from that of their enslaved kin.

Colonial Chesapeake society conferred on the county courts both the authority and the responsibility to oversee a variety of children perceived as "fatherless." The justices exercised this authority in part because they stood as the only administrative and fiscal body that could provide for insolvent children. Planter Richard Cooper expressed this view of governmental responsibility when he petitioned the Talbot court in November 1722 to grant him an allowance for care of an illegitimate child born to one of his servants. "Not having a father for the said child that is or can be made capable of indemnifying this county, or me your petitioner.... I pray this court allow me two hundred pounds of tobacco p month... satisfaction little enough for itts clothing & tendance of nursing.... *The parent meaning the court is solvent.*" Cooper's request for two hundred pounds was excessive, but the court did accept his view of its responsibility as the "father" of orphans and illegitimate children by agreeing to a sum of to one hundred pounds per month.[29]

In authorizing the county courts to act as a "solvent parent" through creation of the orphans' courts, the Maryland legislature responded to demographic realities of life in seventeenth-century Maryland—short parental life expectancy and an absence of extended families—that threatened to leave orphaned children adrift in society. Ideally, the requirements for care and training provided orphans with a home during childhood and a means of earning a livelihood as adults. With the development of a predominantly native-born society by the early eighteenth century, the original imperatives became less critical for the children of all but the poorest white households. County justices continued to supervise the care of orphans and other children in need but evolved a three-tier system in practice: guardianship for the children of the gentry and for those of the middling sort who left real property, craft training for children of nonpropertied middling householders and a segment of poorer white households, and manual labor for children from society's poorest and least powerful groups.

CHAPTER ELEVEN

The Stateless and the Orphaned among Montreal's Apprentices, 1791–1842

GILLIAN HAMILTON

In early Anglo-America, as other essays in this volume show, official ("state") responsibility for orphaned children rested in the hands of local magistrates such as overseers of the poor. In contrast, families in Quebec had official ("state") responsibility for those children of their relatives who had become orphaned or destitute, until at least the mid-nineteenth century. In that sense, the line between state and family was very poorly defined indeed.[1] Peter Moogk explains: "A council of paternal and maternal relations was convened to determine the future of the orphans. Contributions for their upkeep might be apportioned among the kin who elected a tutor...to record and then manage each child's inheritance as well as oversee the child's upbringing."[2]

If family was not available, widows and other single mothers who were too poor to care for their children took it upon themselves to bind them to another family. To do so, they employed a notary public to draw up an indenture. Notaries kept copies of all of the documents they penned; under French civil law, the terms of these agreements were legally binding. An inventory of the notarial documents of Louis Chambalon, who practiced in Quebec, reveals several such agreements. For example, an adoption agreement signed in 1712 between the mother of a twelve-day-old girl born out of matrimony and the apparently unrelated couple adopting her reads: "*Adoption de Geneviève, fille naturelle d'Elizabeth Lemerle, âgée du 12 jours, par François Savary et Catherine Pluchon, de Québec (7 octobre 1712).*"[3] In another case, a father was ill enough to prompt the mother to find a couple to keep her four-year old child for eleven years: "11 year *engagement* [contractual agreement] of Marie-Suzanne Letellier, aged 4 years, daughter of Pierre and Marie-Anne Lanseigne, her father being sick in the Hôtel-Dieu hospital in Montreal, to Romain Dechambe mason, and Catherine Boismé of Charlesbourg...(26 July 1704)."[4] If a mother could afford to care for her children, even her illegitimate children, she could keep them (unlike the situation in Virginia that Brewer describes in chapter 12) and raise them as she saw fit. For example, Mary Mayez, whose husband was "absent," bound her "natural" (illegitimate) fifteen-year-old son, Alexis Gaudert, to a shoemaker for a four-year apprenticeship in 1812. The boy was to be taught his master's trade and was even allowed to profit from any work he completed after the workday was over.[5] Hence local government administrators played a much smaller role in the placement of orphaned children in Quebec than in many other locations in North America. One question this chapter proposes to answer is whether, in the absence of such governmental supervision, binding out in Quebec proceeded without regard to the family status of apprentices, or if children with family members nearby might have been treated differently from those without.

By the early eighteenth century, government officials in Quebec occasionally were involved in the placement of foundlings (abandoned infants). They embraced the use of notary publics, upholding existing indentures and using private contracts drawn up by notaries to place foundlings with foster families. The king's attorney paid the foster family a fee to take on these very young foundlings (called *enfants du Roi*) typically until the child reached age eighteen or twenty-one. More often than not, however, foundlings were the domain of private religious institutions. Children abandoned and cared for by foundling institutions (such as the Grey Nuns Foundling Hospital, discussed below) often died before they could be placed out. In the second half of the nineteenth century, orphanages cared for more children in part because they discarded their policy of early adoption. Shouldering the burden of childraising themselves, the institutions kept the children until they were able to "gain a livelihood." In fact, these church-based orphanages held on to this policy long after other jurisdictions turned to adoption.[6]

The virtual absence of government or institutions in the care of older orphans (that is, not foundlings) prior to 1850 has implications for the sources of evidence available in early-nineteenth-century Quebec. Systematic records of apprenticeship, from which orphans can be identified, have survived. With the Quebec data, it is possible to compare orphan apprenticeship indentures to those drawn up for boys with parents. It seems reasonable to suppose that surviving family members would advocate for their children in the process of indenture formation, while full orphans would not have had such advantages (and little help from any state authorities). In addition, some of these orphans had been born overseas and sent to Canada by well-meaning reformers. This essay considers how the absence of state intervention might have affected the quality of family advocacy. To examine this question, I draw on notary records from early-nineteenth-century Montreal to determine whether the several types of orphans were disadvantaged in the apprentice market. The principal questions raised are: Were they different from other boys entering an apprenticeship? Were they treated differently in the apprentice market? Surprisingly, despite minimal intervention from local officials, boys from each type of background received indenture terms of approximately equal value. Any advantages that accrued to one group tended to be balanced out by benefits granted to others. Thus the orphaned and the stateless emerged from the binding out process having been treated on a par with the craft apprentices who had been bound by their fathers.

The records examined in this study stem from notary offices in Montreal from 1791 to 1842. They consist of 2,691 apprenticeship contracts, chosen for the sake of consistency on the following basis: the apprentice was a boy (and not a girl), the master was a craftsman (and not a merchant or professional), the contract duration could be determined, and the apprentice's age was available (see table 11.1). A subset of 1,559 contracts, in which any form or amount of compensation was clearly stated, was analyzed more closely (see table 11.3). All contracts involving minors required the presence of an adult sponsor because a child's word alone was not legally binding. Family structure can be inferred from the sponsor's identity. Apprentices sponsored by a parent were the largest group of boys. For the purposes of this essay, all other boys were considered to be orphans, and these fell into three groups: those brought from Britain by the Children's Friend Society ("CFS orphans"), those bound by a nonrelative, called a *tutor* ("tutor orphans"), and those bound by a member of their extended family ("family orphans"). The category called here "domestic orphans" comprises tutor orphans and family orphans together and so excludes the British CFS orphans.

These definitions were based on the identity of the sponsor, from which the child's family status can only be indirectly inferred. Some boys sponsored by extended family members were in fact full orphans, meaning that both parents were dead, but others were the offspring of living parents who were unavailable (not living in the city, for example). A court-appointed tutor sponsored boys for whom no relatives were available in or around Montreal. *Orphans* are therefore defined as those apprentices who were not accompanied by a parent (those accompanied by a tutor or a relative other than a parent). These identifications are reasonably but not perfectly accurate. Half-orphans may have been sponsored by their surviving parent. Boys who migrated to Montreal, had two living parents in their hometown, and were sponsored by local relatives would appear to be orphans in these records. In a few cases, generally when a minor was close to the age of majority (twenty-one) when he signed his contract, an adult sponsor was not present. The parents of these children may well have lived in the city. Only two contracts explicitly identify boys as orphans. Contracts where the apprentice had no sponsor and was under the age of eighteen are also included in

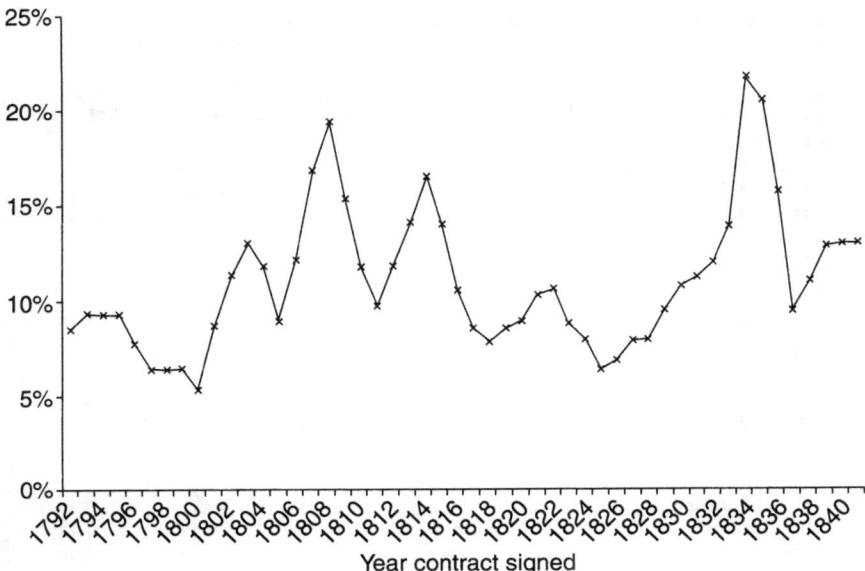

FIGURE 11.1. Share of contracts involving orphans
Source: Archives Nationales du Québec à Montréal (Quebec National Archives—Montreal)

the orphan category. In one such case, three children were identified as orphans and were indented to their uncle.

A distinctive group of orphans appears in these records: boys who arrived in Canada under the auspices of a British philanthropic organization, the Children's Friend Society (CFS). Formed in 1830, this organization undertook the transport of more than one thousand British children to South Africa, Australia, Canada, and Mauritius in the 1830s. The society sent to Canada (New Brunswick, Quebec, and Ontario) roughly two hundred children, most of whom arrived between 1833 and 1837.[7] Their agent in Montreal, John Orrok, claimed to have apprenticed seventy-five boys by early 1836, twenty-one of whom are found in this data set.[8]

The share of orphans among boys who signed apprentice contracts in any given year oscillated over time, with peaks occurring in 1807–8 (21 percent), 1813–15 (17 percent) and 1833–35 (22 percent)—see figure 11.1. The second period coincides with the War of 1812, and the last period overlaps with several severe cholera episodes (see table 11.1). The higher flow of immigrant children in the 1830s also contributed to the relatively high proportion of orphans during this period. Overall, 310 boys (12 percent) signed an apprenticeship contract under the direction of a tutor or relative between 1791 and 1842.

Undoubtedly there were more orphans in the city during this half-century than are represented in this sample. First, children orphaned (or abandoned) at

TABLE 11.1.
Descriptive statistics (percentage of contracts with the specified term)

Sponsor	All	Orphans			Parent
		CFS	Tutor	Family	
Year contract signed					
1791–1803	18.13	0.00	6.98	22.50	18.61
1804–1816	27.68	0.00	34.88	32.50	27.22
1817–1829	27.05	0.00	24.03	18.13	28.06
1830–1842	27.13	100.0	34.11	26.88	26.12
Total	100	100	100	100	100
Sponsor					
Signs his name	41.81	100.0	72.87	57.50	38.56
Apprentice					
Signs his name	36.64	33.33	46.51	39.38	35.95
French last name	57.41	4.76	37.98	50.00	59.43
Age at start of term	15.28	13.99	14.91	15.71	15.29
	(1.80)	(2.56)	(2.15)	(2.20)	
Master					
French last name	46.79	4.76	33.33	38.13	48.47
Signs his name	75.14	100.0	80.62	79.38	74.34
Shop size	2.47	1.33	3.01	2.29	2.46
	(3.68)	(0.66)	(6.42)	(1.72)	(3.58)
Partnership	13.86	4.76	17.83	15.63	13.61
Distribution of master's trades					
Leather	22.33	0.00	13.95	20.63	23.10
Blacksmith	12.86	4.76	10.85	9.38	13.27
Woodworker	14.94	0.00	13.18	18.75	14.91
Builder	15.24	28.57	14.73	16.25	15.08
Clothing	11.26	4.76	13.95	16.25	10.84
Food	7.58	19.05	11.63	5.63	7.39
Manufacturing	2.34	0.00	3.88	1.25	2.35
Bookbinder/printer	4.64	0.00	4.65	4.38	4.70
Miscellaneous	8.81	42.86	13.18	7.5	8.36
Total	100	100	100	100	100
N	2691	21	129	160	2381

Notes: Apprentice's age is expressed in years. Shop size is the number of apprentices the master had under contract in the year the new apprentice was hired. Example: 13.86 percent of contracts involved masters with a partner or company (signed, for example, Smith and Co.). Leather: shoemaker, tanner and saddler; blacksmith: blacksmith, edge tool maker, gunsmith, tinsmith, founder, carriage or coachmakers; woodworker: cabinet maker, furniture maker, turner, carver, chair maker, cooper; builder: carpenter, joiner, builder, ship builder, plasterer, millwright, mason, brick maker, brick layer; clothing: tailor, furrier, hatter; food: baker, butcher; manufacturing: makers of brushes, soap, candles, rope, wheels, or tobacconists; miscellaneous: jeweler (clock maker, goldsmith, silversmith), farmer, gardener, dyer and scourer, barber and wig setter, mariner, miller, brewer, painter, glazier, gilder, potter, unknown.
Source: Archives Nationales du Québec à Montréal (Quebec National Archives—Montreal).

a young age did not always survive to the usual age of apprentice indenture (age twelve would make a very young craft apprentice). For example, of the 2,385 children left at the Grey Nuns Foundling Hospital between 1820 and 1840, just 6 percent (or 138) were indented or "placed into service," because the vast majority of children, at least 87 percent (2,073), died before they could leave the Grey Nuns.⁹ The foundling hospital was the primary repository for illegitimate children in Montreal and the surrounding area. It also accepted legitimate children that were orphaned or destitute, but these children constituted a small minority of the hospital's charges. The younger the child was on arriving at the hospital, the lower the chances of survival.¹⁰

Second, it may have been more common for urban orphans to do other things besides craft apprenticeship. They might have been placed on farms, for example, with no written indenture registered at the notary's office.¹¹ Hence, orphans who undertook craft apprenticeships may have been atypical. Compared to those who became servants, they may have been relatively skilled or otherwise fortunate, because their prospects for future earnings were higher. A comparison to boys who worked on farms seems less clear-cut. The craft apprentices simply may have had a preference for a trade or urban living, or their allocation may reflect demand conditions.

Indentures reveal characteristics of these children, their families, and their masters. Table 11.1 describes the average characteristics of all apprenticeship contracts in this study. Three categories of orphans are defined separately: the CFS orphans from Britain; those sponsored by a tutor act; and those sponsored by a relative who was not their parent (the column titled "family"). The two categories of domestic orphans (tutor and family) were treated separately because presence or absence of family support (albeit nonparental) may have influenced children's choices and outcomes in the apprentice market. All other boys were treated as non-orphans.

Orphans (as a whole) and non-orphans resembled each other in some ways and differed in others. Orphans tended to be disproportionately English: three-fifths had an English last name, compared to two-fifths for non-orphans; these (English-name) orphans were less likely to have extended family in town.¹² Overall, orphans were more likely to have signed their contract instead of simply leaving a mark (42 percent did so, compared to 36 percent of non-orphans). In addition, boys with a parent present (non-orphans) were roughly the same age as orphans when they started their apprenticeships (at an average age of 15.3 years). Thus, the difference in literacy rates must have stemmed from factors other than age difference.

These aggregate means mask considerable variation within the orphan population. For example, half of tutor orphans and one-third of CFS orphans could sign their names, with the proportion of family orphans in between. The average signing rate for the CFS orphans was not much lower than the rate demonstrated by boys with parents, a fairly remarkable finding when one recalls that almost all of the CFS orphans had English last names and signature rates were generally much higher among the English-named apprentices in the sample. In addition, the CFS children arrived late in the period, when signature rates were relatively high for all groups except tutor orphans (figure 11.2). On the

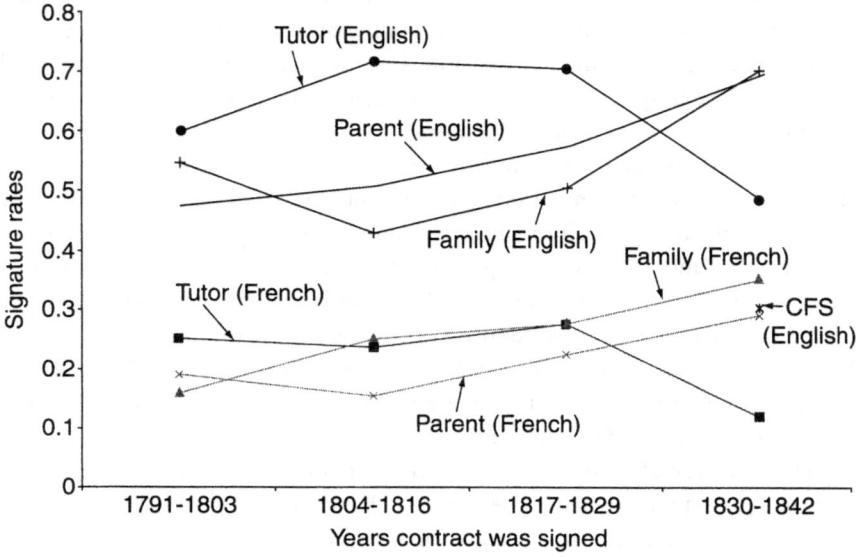

FIGURE 11.2. Signature rates over time, by ethnicity and sponsor
Source: Archives Nationales du Québec à Montréal (Quebec National Archives—Montreal)

other hand, CFS boys may have been less literate because they were one to two years younger on average than the others; as for almost all groups of children, literacy rises with age. In contrast, the relatively high signature rate among tutor orphans may simply reflect the fact that a relatively high share of these boys was English and apprenticed after 1800 (particularly the 1830s).

It is difficult to ascertain whether signature rates were in fact very different for boys with and without parents unless comparison is carefully restricted to like vs. like. The effects of such factors as age, ethnicity, and time period can be controlled with multivariate regression analysis. Regression results will indicate whether signature rates of orphans were statistically and economically different from the signature rates of boys with parents, all else being equal.[13] Figure 11.3 illustrates the value of such an exercise. The raw means indicate the difference in signature rates between boys with parents and the various groups of orphans (as reported in table 11.1). These differences were quite large. The bar chart also shows the relevant differences in signature rates once variation in such factors as age, ethnicity, and time period was statistically taken into account. Once such factors are taken into account, no (statistical) difference in the signing propensities of domestic orphans and boys with parents could be detected. The difference for CFS boys is much smaller, but significantly different from zero. In other words, when comparing the signature rates of domestic orphans and boys with a parent, it is quite misleading to examine differences in the raw or unconditional averages.

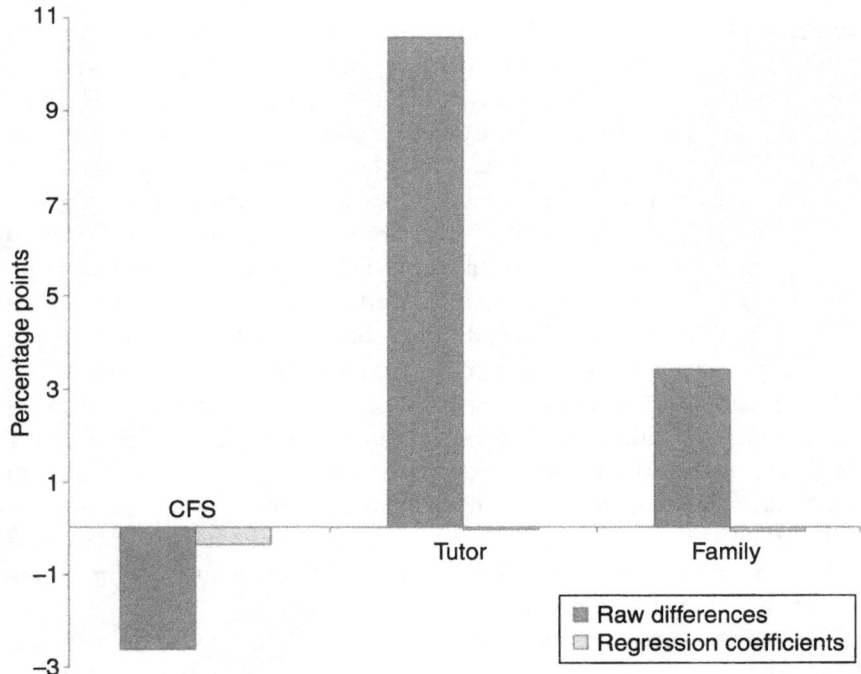

FIGURE 11.3. Signature rates: Raw and conditional mean differences, compared to boys with parents
Notes: Regressors include apprentice attributes (age, age squared, French last name), a dummy variable equal to 1 if the sponsor signed the contract, and dummy variables for the years the contract was in effect. The equation is estimated by ordinary least squares, and the standard errors are corrected for heteroskedasticity (poorly behaved error terms) and any correlation across error terms for apprentices hired by the same master. The sample size was 2,691 (1,204 masters).

Apart from differences in orphan attributes, a particular concern when considering the apprentice experience of the orphan is the trades they typically entered. One could argue that orphans may have been shunted into low-paying trades because guardians had less interest in the future income of their charges.[14] A letter from the Children's Friend Society's Montreal agent, John Orrok, to another agent suggests that the impetus for placements came from employers, with Orrok fulfilling requests for child labor from prospective masters: "I have therefore agreeable to your request sent you a nice little girl named Gwenderlam Israel, enclosed is her character signed by Lady George Murray and her daughter. I also enclose you the Indenture which please to fill in the date and sign, after which please to return to...."[15] Gwenderlam Israel was just ten years old when she was hired to act as a house and nursery maid to a Mr. John Benson of Kingston, Ontario. If Mr. Orrok fulfilled such requests without as much consideration for the future welfare of his charges as a parent might engage, the outcomes for such children may have been relatively poor.

To determine whether trades favored by orphans (or their agents) were especially poor choices would ideally require information on the income of masters in these various trades or the pay of journeymen. Unfortunately information that detailed is not extant, although Robert Margo found that in the mid–nineteenth century, journeymen masons were paid more than painter-plasterers, who in turn received higher pay than either blacksmiths or carpenters.[16]

The cost of setting up a business also might have been an important determinant of trade choice if orphans had fewer resources. Guardians may have steered boys away from trades that required considerable capital investment to begin work as a master. In mid–eighteenth century London (England) the "sums necessary to set up as Master" ranged from £100 to £500 for masons, "[up] to £100" for painters of houses, to £50 to £500 for "carpenters of houses."[17]

If guardians cared more about their charges' current compensation than future income, apprentices' pay may be worth examining. In addition, workers' pay might also reveal something about masters' earnings, insofar as masters in poor trades could not afford to pay their apprentices well.[18] On average, real annual pay was lowest for shoemaking, tanning, and coopering and for contracts with room and board and no clothing. Bakers, printers, manufacturers, and jewelers were the highest-paying trades.[19]

The most important characteristic of the apprenticeship was the trade that the youth was to learn. Table 11.2 illustrates the distribution of trades for children with parents and the various types of orphans. It indicates that domestic orphans and boys with a parent appear to have had fairly similar experiences. For instance, more than one-third of tutor and family orphans and half of boys with parents were employed in the top four trades (shoemaking, blacksmithing, carpentering, and coopering), and around one-tenth of these boys were employed by one of the five least populous trades (jeweler, manufacturer, butcher, tanner, and unknown).[20] There were a few minor distinctions across these groups. For example, only 10 percent of tutor orphans were hired by shoemakers, in contrast with 17 percent of boys with parents, while 6 percent of tutor orphans learned to be butchers, compared to just 2 percent of boys with parents. Butchering was a more remunerative trade than shoemaking and, according to Robert Campbell, required less startup capital, but this minor distinction in the trade distribution of tutor orphans hardly indicates a marked preference for highly prized or low-cost trades.

CFS orphans, on the other hand, had very different experiences from other craft apprentices. None of these boys apprenticed to be shoemakers (the most populous trade) or coopers (likely in part because coopering apprenticeships were on the wane in the 1830s). Instead, an unusually large proportion of these orphans ended up in miscellaneous trades (largely farming), masonry, and the food trades (baking and butchering). As noted, shoemaking and coopering were among the lowest-paid trades, with butchers, bakers, and those in the

TABLE 11.2.
Distribution of master's trades

	Orphans			Parent
	CFS	Tutor	Family	
Shoemaker	0.00	10.08	13.75	16.97
Blacksmith	4.76	10.85	9.38	13.27
Carpenter	14.29	11.63	11.25	11.21
Cooper	0.00	4.65	12.50	9.74
Tailor	4.76	8.53	11.88	7.01
Furniture maker	0.00	8.53	6.25	5.17
Baker	9.52	5.43	3.75	5.08
Printer	0.00	4.65	4.38	4.70
Saddler	0.00	3.10	5.00	4.66
Miscellaneous	28.57	8.53	3.75	4.45
Mason	14.29	3.10	5.00	3.86
Furrier/hatter	0.00	5.43	4.38	3.82
Jeweler	0.00	3.88	1.88	2.60
Manufacturer	0.00	3.88	1.25	2.35
Butcher	9.52	6.20	1.88	2.31
Tanner	0.00	0.78	1.88	1.47
Unknown	14.29	0.78	1.88	1.30
N	21	129	160	2381

Source: Archives Nationales du Québec à Montréal (Quebec National Archives—Montreal).

miscellaneous category all earning substantially higher clothing allowances (on average). While pay for CFS boys is not well represented by this figure (they all received clothing, as discussed below), they appear to have done remarkably well in their trade placement, assuming that these trades were not, in fact, among the lowest-paid. In terms of masters' setup costs, while coopering was relatively expensive, the range of setup costs for shoemaking was no different from those of masonry and baking. Hence the relationship between trade choice and setup costs appears murky at best.[21]

Another way in which apprenticeships of orphans and of children with parents differed was in the type and value of compensation. Table 11.3 details the differences in apprentices' compensation. Comparing orphans to apprentices with a parent reveals that the orphans appear to have signed relatively lucrative contracts. Canadian orphans were more likely to receive all forms of in-kind compensation: room, board, washing, mending, and clothing. In addition, those that received cash payments earned, on average, more pay per year (£5.28 real currency) than non-orphans (£4.94).[22] Orphans' contracts were also slightly more likely to include provision for an end payment and a promise from the master to offer some form of schooling, such as reading and writing (22 percent compared to 14 percent of non-orphan contracts). Finally, orphans served about three months longer than other boys.

TABLE 11.3.
Incidence of contract terms (in percent) and average pay

		Orphans			
Sponsor	All	CFS	Tutor	Family	Parent
Washing	54.14	100.0	71.32	57.50	52.58
Mending	29.80	4.76	43.41	28.13	29.40
Clothing	41.06	100.0	51.16	45.00	39.73
Room	90.45	100.0	93.80	89.38	90.26
Board	92.87	100.0	95.35	95.63	92.48
Teach	92.51	100.0	90.83	91.89	92.57
School	15.35	80.95	20.93	15.63	14.45
Duration (years)	5.11	6.99	5.71	4.87	5.08
Cash	57.93	100.0	45.74	53.75	58.50
End pay	33.11	95.24	35.66	34.38	32.34
N	2691	21	129	160	2381
Annual pay (£)	6.48	0.69	8.36	7.26	6.43
Real annual pay (£)	4.98	0.56	6.49	5.60	4.94
N	1559	21	59	86	1393

Notes: Example: 54.14 percent of all indentures required masters to take care of apprentices' washing; CFS indentures bound children for an average of seven years; tutor orphans who were promised pay (46 percent of them) received on average £8.36, which is reduced to £6.49 in real terms (after adjusting for price changes).
Source: Archives Nationales du Québec à Montréal (Quebec National Archives—Montreal).

In evaluating the compensation in contracts involving the Children's Friend Society, it is first useful to note that they were quite uniform. John Orrok, the society's agent, used a standard form for most of the contracts he signed. Remarkably, a very similar format was employed by the Children's Friend Society, regardless of where the children were being indented (Australia, South Africa, or upper Canada).[23] The apprentice was to receive room and board as well as washing and sufficient clothing (only one contract specified mending). In addition, all of the contracts indicated that the boy would be taught the master's trade (a few non-CFS contracts left this "teach" clause out, perhaps unintentionally) and most (81 percent) included a provision for extra schooling (see table 11.3). This was a much higher proportion than observed among other boys (where the proportions were below 25 percent). Another very unusual aspect of these contracts was the presence of a cash allowance in addition to clothing—something all CFS boys enjoyed. These payments were the same for almost all CFS boys. Specifically, the form stated that the master shall

> pay [to the apprentice] the annual sum of Two Pounds Ten Shillings until he shall arrive at the age of twenty-one years. One Pound Fifteen Shillings of which to be paid annually on the first day of _____ in each year, into the Savings' Bank in arrears, for the benefit of the apprentice, and Fifteen Shillings to be paid in advance annually, to the Tutor, or person authorized by the Children's Friend Society,

in London, to be remitted annually, on ____ in advance, to the Society, the first payment to be made upon the execution of this Indenture.

But in the event of the said __[apprentice]__ absconding, all the Monies invested in the Savings' Bank shall revert back to his Master....[24]

Because the money in the savings bank was to accumulate throughout the term, much of the allowance came in the form of an end payment.[25] Finally, CFS boys served considerably longer terms than other boys—seven years on average.

When examined from the perspective of annual real payments throughout the term, the amount the average CFS boy earned was small (£0.56). This may be misleading, however, since their cash payments were a supplement to clothing, and most of their earnings were realized at the end of their term.[26] The first section of table 11.4 illustrates the distribution of four possible compensation bundles that do or do not involve cash and clothing.[27] As the table makes clear, just 3.5 percent of all contracts involved both cash and clothing. The usual combination was cash and no clothing (54.5 percent), with clothing and no cash a close second (37.6 percent). Just 4.5 percent received neither clothing nor cash. Hence the CFS boys' compensation was both unusual and apparently generous. The second section of the table reports two measures of average real annual pay for each of these compensation bundles. The first excludes end pay and indicates that compared to other boys that received cash and clothing, CFS apprentices' pay was relatively low. This basic ranking does not change when end pay is incorporated into the annual measure of pay, as the last section of the table shows.

Thus at first glance domestic orphans appear to have done well in their apprentice contracts—earning, on average, relatively high pay, more in-kind transfers, and extra provisions such as schooling, although they also tended to serve longer terms. In many of the same respects, CFS orphans also seem to have signed lucrative contracts, although they served especially long terms and their cash compensation may have been relatively low.

From here we turn to the differences in compensation observed between orphans and non-orphans, which actually reflected other attributes, such as ethnicity, that were correlated with family status. For example, family orphans may have been paid well because they tended to have been older when they began their term. The only way to discern these deeper influences is through a multivariate approach, because only such a statistical method will account for these possibilities. Although at first glance it appears that domestic orphans did in fact fare better in the apprentice market—which we might then infer was the result of advocacy by extended family members—the use of multivariate statistics reveals that no great differences existed in the treatment of these boys, orphaned or otherwise.

TABLE 11.4.
Four combinations of compensation

	All	Orphans			Parent
		CFS	Tutor	Family	
N	2691	21	160	129	2381
Incidence (percent):					
No cash & no clothing	4.46	0	3.75	4.65	4.54
No cash & clothing	37.61	0	42.50	49.61	36.96
Cash & no clothing	54.48	0	51.25	35.63	55.73
Cash & clothing	3.46	100	2.50	1.55	2.77
Total	100	100	100	100	100
Mean value of real annual pay (£):					
No cash & no clothing	0	–	0.00	0.00	0.00
No cash & clothing	0	–	0.00	0.00	0.00
Cash & no clothing	5.11	–	5.49	6.58	5.03
Cash & clothing	2.81	0.56	7.94	3.87	3.18
Mean value of real annual pay, end pay included (£):					
No cash & no clothing	0.20	–	0.00	0.00	0.22
No cash & clothing	0.10	–	0.11	0.36	0.08
Cash & no clothing	5.16	–	5.49	6.67	5.08
Cash & clothing	3.08	1.70	8.16	3.87	3.19

Note: "Cash" refers to cash payments during the term (independent from end payments).
Source: Archives Nationales du Québec à Montréal (Quebec National Archives—Montreal).

Figure 11.4 illustrates the differences in real annual pay (for contracts with cash payments) between orphans and boys with a parent present, showing both the raw mean differences and these same differences holding constant such factors as apprentice and master characteristics, the years the contract was in effect, and master's occupations. This exercise demonstrates that the relatively high pay for domestic orphans observed in the raw data disappears when we examine "conditional" pay differences. Hence the pay of both tutor and family orphans was really not that different from the pay received by boys with parents. It just appeared to be high because a higher proportion of these boys had attributes that were well compensated, such as their greater likelihood of being able to sign their name or their higher age (for family orphans). CFS orphans, on the other hand, appear to have been paid relatively poorly, all else being equal. The conditional difference shown, however, does not take account of some of the other differences in compensation (such as clothing), but as table 11.4 indicates, while cash and clothing were an unusual combination, boys who did receive both tended to earn more than the CFS boys.

Undertaking the same sort of exercise to examine the propensity of in-kind compensation in the contracts reveals that in-kind pay (contracts with room, board, and clothing) was significantly more common in both CFS and tutor orphan contracts compared to contracts with a parent (see figure 11.5). Family orphans, however, were indistinguishable from boys with parents.

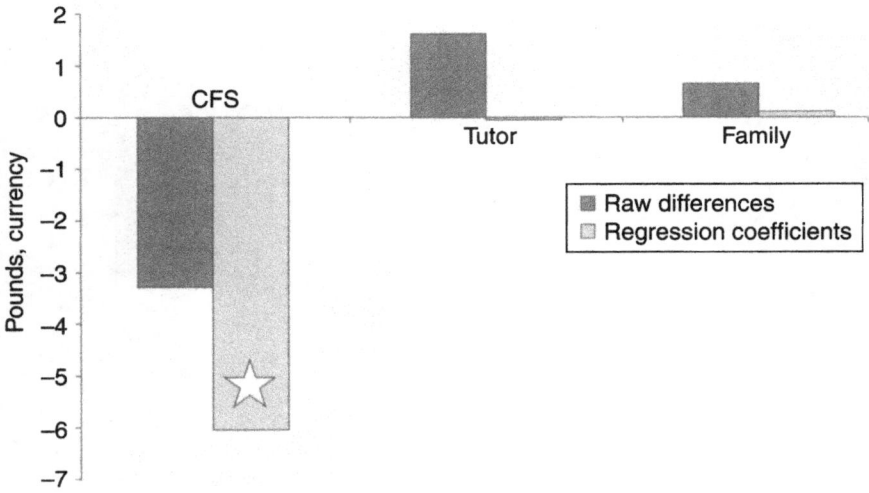

FIGURE 11.4. Real annual pay difference between orphans and boys with parents
Notes: Sample consists of contracts with cash. Regressors include apprentice attributes (signs his name, French last name, a quadratic in age—age and age squared); a dummy variable that equals 1 if the sponsor signed his or her name; master attributes (signs his name, French last name, partner, shop size); dummy variables for the years the contract was in effect and dummy variables for the occupations listed in the appendix. The equation is estimated by ordinary least squares, and the standard errors are corrected for heteroskedasticity (poorly behaved error terms) and any correlation across error terms for apprentices hired by the same master. Pay of CFS boys is statistically significantly different from boys with parents (denoted by star in bar).

The extra time served by orphans also could reflect apprentice or master characteristics and not longer contracts for orphans, all else held equal. Duration is highly dependent on the apprentice's age, for example, so their longer terms may simply reflect differences in age at the beginning of the terms (CFS and tutor orphans were relatively young). Figure 11.6 illustrates the raw mean and conditional differences in duration between orphan groups and boys with a parent. The conditional differences control for differences in apprentice, master, and sponsor attributes as well as the years the contract was in effect and the various trades, which may have had different contract durations because of the different training requirements associated with different occupations. The results indicate that only CFS orphans served more time, roughly half a year more, even after taking account of differences in such factors as the apprentice's age. The raw difference in duration observed between tutor orphans (longer terms) and boys with a parent disappears once we take account of such factors as their younger age. In the same manner, family orphans appear to have served shorter terms (in the raw means), but this disappears once we control for their older starting age (and other factors).[28]

The fate of orphans signing contracts with master craftsmen in early-nineteenth-century Montreal depended on their circumstances. Orphans with

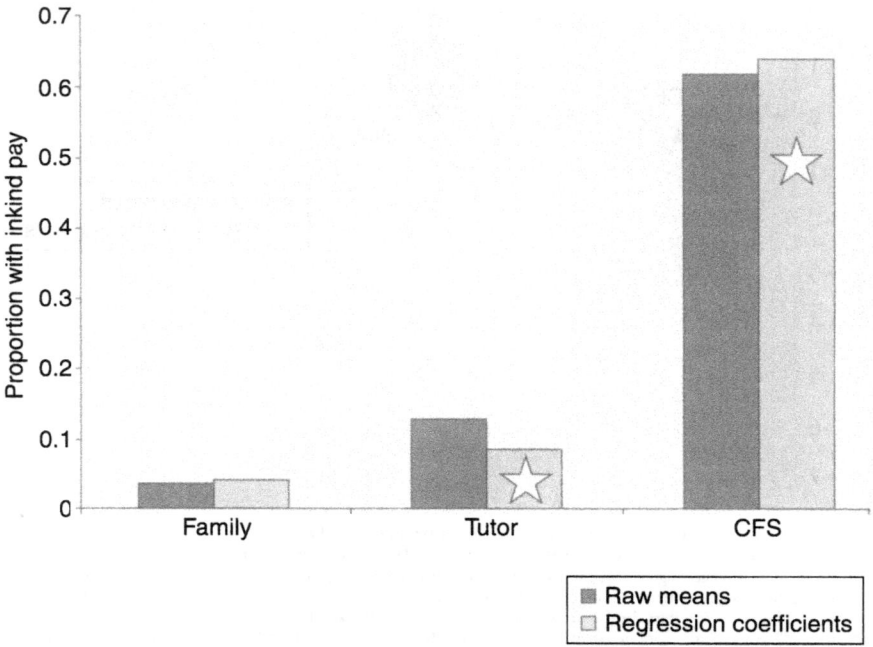

FIGURE 11.5. The incidence of in-kind pay, compared to boys with parents
Note: See figure 11.4

family in the city were more likely to have an English last name and began an apprenticeship when they were a few months older, but their contracts were otherwise virtually indistinguishable from the agreements signed by boys with parents. Once apprentice, year, and master attributes are taken into account, the choices of trade, elements of compensation, and level of pay emerge as more or less the same.

Domestic orphans who relied on a tutor were distinctive. The proportion of English was even higher than among family orphans, and they tended to be younger when they started their term. Controlling for such characteristics as age, their contracts tended to put more onus on the master (or his family) to provide for the boy. Their masters were more likely to provide clothing, room, and board (and other necessities) instead of paying orphans cash and letting them procure these items for themselves. Apart from a heavier reliance on the master's family to provide care, tutor orphans were treated like other boys. Those who received cash were paid comparable wages, and the trades of their masters were not all that different from the trades of masters with non-orphan boys.

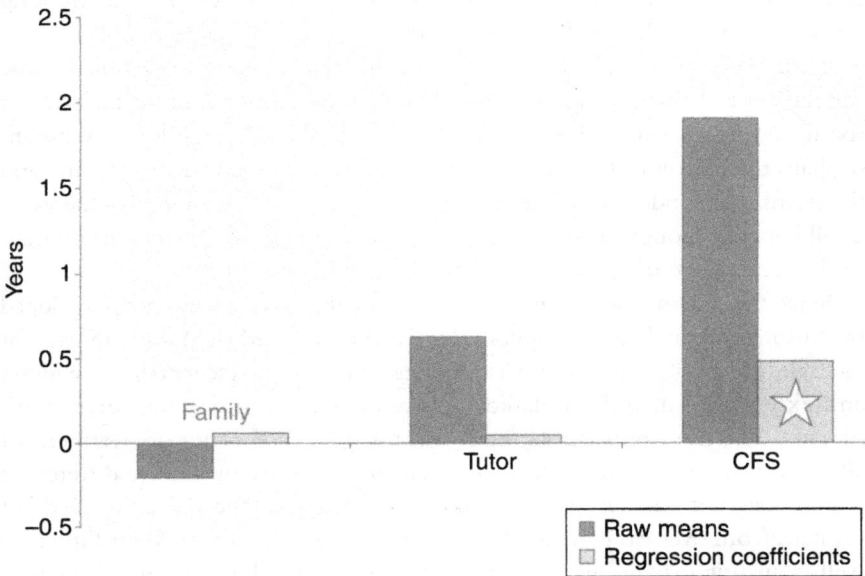

FIGURE 11.6. Apprenticeship duration, compared to boys with parents
Note: See figure 11.4

Immigrant orphans whose voyages were sponsored by the Children's Friend Society, on the other hand, had a somewhat different experience in the urban craft apprentice market. These boys almost all had English last names. They were relatively young and also tended to be illiterate (all else being equal). Even taking account of such factors as literacy and age, their contracts were rather unusual. They tended to match with farmers and builders and ignore (or were ignored by) the more popular trades—leather, woodworking, and blacksmithing.[29] The CFS agent in Montreal, John Orrok, asked for virtually the same terms for all of the boys. As with other orphans without family, these contracts required masters to take a more active role in providing for the apprentice, but the pay Orrok specified was well below that received by other boys who also earned cash. On the other hand, because they received cash in addition to *all* in-kind necessities, it was arguably a relatively generous pay package. Given the uniformity of the CFS contracts, it is difficult to know whether Orrok was simply unaware of (or uninterested in) the "going" wage for apprentices, was responding to the weakened state of the boys, or reacting to prejudices against orphan immigrant children that may have existed. Even if prejudice reduced CFS boys' effective wage, it is unlikely that the same wage was appropriate for all CFS boys, hence some CFS boys likely were overpaid while others, more skilled or educated, were underpaid. In addition, CFS orphans served particularly long terms—almost a half-year longer than other boys, all else being equal.[30]

Thus while indentures of domestic orphans with family resembled those for the general run of boys, those without family relied more on masters for room and board—for who else would provide these necessities? Immigrant orphans themselves differed in their characteristics from domestic orphans, and the terms in the indentures reflected these differences. Accounting for the value of all benefits, though, led to the conclusion that the system treated immigrant orphans no worse than boys with families or tutors nearby.

Since the system that determined the fates of the Montreal orphans developed by custom and civil law, it implies roles for the state and the family by way of contrast. Here, the state stood back and let parents in intact marriages, widows and extended kin, and unrelated sponsors negotiate indenture terms with masters. The most remarkable result was the general equality of treatment of all children, no matter the identity of their sponsor, once qualitative differences in remuneration are recognized. Taking into account the different needs of orphans from overseas compared to boys bound into a trade by their fathers as well as quantitative differences in the value of pay and the duration of the contract, the various groups of boys worked under indentures that extracted similar costs and provided similar benefits. It appears that in the case of Montreal at least, the least the state had to do to order the lives of orphaned children was to enforce these contracts. A specific municipal office to oversee such children would have been superfluous.

CHAPTER TWELVE

Apprenticeship Policy in Virginia

From Patriarchal to Republican Policies of Social Welfare

HOLLY BREWER

In February 1751 the churchwardens of Frederick County, Virginia, bound Hester Ryan, a month-old infant, to the man her mother had declared to be her father—Joseph Roberts. Her mother of the same name was already indentured to Roberts. Hester was apprenticed to him in lieu of his providing a guarantee to the parish that he would reimburse them if they had to pay for her nursing and care in her first few years of life. The churchwardens bound Hester without her mother's consent. Instead of custody of her daughter, Hester's mother received 25 lashes on her bare back. While Roberts could have paid a fine to let Hester avoid that lashing, he refused to help. When she finished her indenture, she had to leave her daughter behind.[1] In fact, the courts left few illegitimate children with their mothers or even with their fathers unless, like Roberts, they were masters themselves. Masters often assumed custody of the illegitimate children born to their servants. The vestry book of Frederick County also gives numerous examples of infant bastard children supported by unrelated families, and the court records reveal that illegitimate children were bound as apprentices at an average age of barely four (4.4) years during the 1750s. Children whose fathers died with little property, if their mother had no broader family to rely on, were also bound soon after their father's deaths. "Poor" children, when their families turned to the county or vestry for relief, were quickly apprenticed, at an average age of 6.6 years during the same decade. All in all, 7.3 percent of all children were bound as apprentices in Frederick County during the 1750s, many at a very young age.

Apprenticeship in colonial Virginia, and especially in Frederick County, was both a way of accessing and controlling children's labor, at the same time that it was the main welfare policy. While it was exploitative—indeed, in its treatment of the poor, it bears some resemblance to hereditary slavery—it was not simply the thirst for labor in early Virginia that shaped this institution. Taking apprenticeship seriously means taking hereditary status seriously in early Virginia, but it also means understanding how patriarchal ideas about family structure shaped the household in the colonial period, such that masters often replaced parents, even for white children. The years after the Revolutionary War marked a decline in masters' patriarchal authority—at least over white children—and a new emphasis both on educating children and parental custody. These new emphases on education and parental custody (for both fathers and mothers) reveal the influence of republican political ideology, which challenged the patriarchal household just as it challenged the patriarchal power of kings. Likewise, children's education—rather than their training and work—became seen as more important in opening avenues for their future equality. It became less acceptable to see white children born to a permanent lowly status. Thus the percentage of white children apprenticed declined sharply.

Richard Morris and William Rorabaugh, among others, have linked the declining use of apprenticeship in the early nineteenth century—both poor apprenticeship and trade apprenticeship—to a declining demand for bound labor in general, and children's labor in particular, as a result of industrialization.[2] There are several problems with applying their argument to this case. First, in Virginia, the demand for bound labor continued to be strong through the mid-nineteenth century. The argument for a general decline in interest in bound labor applies better in the North. Second, Frederick County between 1750 and 1820 was mostly rural and had no direct industrialization yet experienced a sharp decline in poor apprenticeship. Third, the argument that demand for children's labor was declining has been challenged by broad studies that show continuing demand for children's labor throughout the industrial period.[3]

Instead, I suggest that changed attitudes about who should have custody of children, how wealth should be distributed, and when and how it was appropriate for children to be put to work facilitated changes in social welfare policy in the years following the Revolution. One of the changes that accompanied the Revolution was an increased idealization of the bonds between children and their natural parents, particularly their mothers. Thus, more effort was made to keep children with their natural parents, mostly through transfer payments. A second change was the republican emphasis on equality, an emphasis exemplified in the reform of inheritance policy, a shift that led to a somewhat more equitable division of wealth, particularly by the second generation. This meant that more parents could afford to keep their children. A third change was the growing sentiment against the labor of young children, and even the labor of older white girls, such that childhood became perceived as a more distinct phase of life. I argue that this change in attitude toward children's labor grew out of the Enlightenment emphasis on reason—and on an age of reason—that distinguished childhood from adulthood and emphasized formal education. The Enlightenment emphasis on reason was deeply embedded in republican political theory, both in its espousal of formal education and in its assertion that those who consent should be those who exercise reason. It demarcated childhood from adulthood and held that childhood was a distinct period of life and that children had specific needs for education that were on some level different from and opposed to their ability to labor, especially while under the age of about ten. There was a connection between this shift in ideas about childhood and the sharp increase in the average age at which poor apprenticeships began in the years after the American Revolution, the same period that the rate of children apprenticed fell. There were, however, differing gender, class, and race dimensions to this shift.

While this study focuses on only one county, the historical pattern is borne out by other, more general data. First, apprenticeship was the main welfare policy for whites, not only in Frederick County but also in colonial Virginia as a whole: one count of apprenticeship contracts formed by the churchwardens of colonial Virginia, by John Nelson in his massive study of the Virginia Vestry, found that a very large number of white children were routinely bound during the eighteenth century. The surviving records of thirty-one counties between 1690 and 1776 show at least 7,470 such bindings. Given the missing records in so many counties, and that almost half the county records for Virginia were completely burned in the Civil War, this count represents at most half of the actual number of bindings during the period only after 1690. Putting the earlier years, the missing records, and the missing counties back in, it is likely that tens of thousands of poor white children were placed into apprenticeships in colonial Virginia. Translating this number into a rate for white children bound is extraordinarily difficult, given the poor population data we have for Virginia overall, but these numbers suggest that the churchwardens were binding children at a rate similar to Frederick County's rate of 7 percent during the eighteenth century as a whole.[4]

While Frederick County was settled only shortly before the period examined here, that probably had little to do with the broad pattern traced here; the changes in policy that shifted its apprenticeship policy were largely initiated on the state level. Settlers came from a mixed cast—of Virginia tidewater gentry and their African-American slaves in the Eastern half and men and women from Pennsylvania and other northern colonies who practiced small subsistence farming on the Western half; as it lies on the northern border of what is now the boundary between West Virginia and Virginia, it is representative in that sense as well. It was relatively rural and contained seven small towns as well as one bigger town, Winchester, which was a minor trading center and situated on the "great wagon road from Philadelphia" to destinations west. This may have contributed somewhat to the general decline in apprenticeship rates, since the relative wealth of all in the community may have increased.[5] I studied three ten-year periods intensively: 1751–60, 1781–90, and 1811–20—three windows in time from which to gauge changes in practice.

Apprenticeships were the major form of social welfare with regard to white children and free children of color in eighteenth-century rural Virginia. The origins of this policy lie in the English Statute of Artificers of 1562, an example that was followed closely, and elaborated upon, in many colonies/states. This policy reflects what modern lawyers would call the legal doctrine of *parens patriae,* a doctrine that posits that the state is the ultimate parent of the child when parents do not fulfill their parental obligations, either because they will not or, more often in the eighteenth century, because they could not. Many "poor" children and many "orphans" (defined as those whose fathers had died—usually their mothers were alive) and many bastard children were taken from their parents and bound out as apprentices, girls until they were eighteen and boys until they were twenty-one, by the churchwardens, called Overseers of the Poor after 1780 with the separation of church and state in Virginia. The majority of these children were from what could be termed female-headed households.[6] Dozens of children were also explicitly removed from parents for negligence in supplying clothing, food, or education where the parents were not poor.[7]

While the doctrine of *parens patraie* still exists, the meaning of it began to change significantly with the American Revolution. The Revolution initiated a move toward separating the state-as-parent from the natural parent, a shift precipitated by republican political theory. John Locke and Algernon Sydney, whose writings on political theory were widely read and referenced during the American Revolution, and Thomas Jefferson—who rewrote Virginia's entire code of laws during the Revolution—argued forcefully that parental power was very different than state power and that parents should naturally have custody of their children because of the unique bonds between them.[8] Many parents who would have had their children removed from their custody and apprenticed merely because of poverty during the 1750s were enabled to keep their children through the use of state-administered transfer payments by the 1780s and 1810s.

Many people today, when they think of poor apprenticeship, envision the scenes in Charles Dickens's stories that depict children exploited by factory labor. Historians have largely agreed with this scenario. Mason Thomas described the system of apprenticeship as merely exploitative. Walter Trattner, in his summary of the work on social welfare in America, concludes that the system was "full of abuses."[9] Trattner argues that apprenticeship was used for four reasons, three of them associated with social control: the belief that "all people should be attached to a family"; discipline; a desire to minimize public expenditures; and its tendency in reducing "idleness or unemployment."[10] However, apprenticeship was not merely an evil, exploitative, or even "controlling" system. The story is more complicated than that. The law directed magistrates to place children in "fit" homes and stipulated that children receive necessities and not be physically abused.[11] These statutes were enforced: children complained on their own behalf about inadequate diet, excessive punishment, or a failure to educate them. Neighbors, relatives, and the churchwardens themselves also initiated complaints—and the complaints were often heeded. Many children as a result of these complaints were transferred to new masters or, occasionally, returned to their parents or released from their apprenticeships.[12]

Apprenticeship thus resembles modern foster care in that children were supervised and transferred if there were problems. In other ways apprenticeship resembles modern adoption since children were cared for long-term, until they became adults. Adoption itself had been legally prohibited under the Catholic Church in England and had remained illegal after the Protestant Reformation and in the colonies/states, until Massachusetts set a precedent by legalizing it in 1851.[13] That apprenticeship should be seen as a custody arrangement granting rights that in some ways were similar to adoption rights is clear when it is noted that the *average* age of apprenticeship was 7.9 years of age in Frederick County between 1751 and 1760; some children were apprenticed as young as a few months of age or, more often, at two or three, clearly before they could work (see table 12.1). Older children, especially, were given extensive educational guarantees, and accepting an apprenticed child meant a long-term investment, with a loss of the child's labor at precisely the point where the child would have been giving substantial returns—at young adulthood. All poor apprentices were bound in a personal contract to a master and/or mistress, a contract that could not be transferred without the consent of the court.[14] In some cases, apprenticed children could not be removed from the region.[15] Also, the laws—which

TABLE 12.1.
Average age of children apprenticed by Frederick County overseers of the poor

	1751-60	1781-90	1811-20
Bastards	4.4	9.1	9.3
Orphans (fatherless)	10.2	11.6	12.6
Poor/other	6.6	11.0	11.5
Black/Mulatto	5.6	6.8	10.2
Males (white)	8.4	12.0	12.3
Females (white)	7.4	8.9	8.8
White	8.0	11.2	11.6
All	7.9	10.9	11.4

were enforced—required that the master's investment be substantial. Masters were usually bound to teach their apprentices to read and in addition to a trade and to give them freedom dues at the expiration of their terms.

Such restraints on masters to provide education, food, and clothing, to teach a trade, and to refrain from abusing their apprentices indicate that Colonial Virginia society was consciously trying to shape these young people whom they regarded as needing help. This interpretation does not undermine ideas of class-related exploitation or even of social control. Indeed, the whole idea of custody and of directed education embodied patriarchalism and was performed usually without the child's (or parents') explicit consent. But the state did not establish a merely controlling relationship between the master and apprentice. There were careful limitations on the master's power that were intended for the apprentice's good, as that was then conceived. Obviously, it would have been far easier to let the children starve or to hang them for stealing. In allowing such protections for the mostly white children in apprenticeship, Virginia distinguished between their status and those of enslaved children.

Besides apprenticeship, other social welfare policies for children were scanty, although there were a few cases where the state facilitated support payments to female-headed households. If the husband/father were still alive and had money but refused to support his family, wives or churchwardens might bring suit against him to enforce his support.[16] In most cases, however, the few support payments facilitated by the churchwardens aimed not to keep a family together but rather to support an infant being cared for by non–family members. Bastard children, as mentioned above, were often apprenticed at the age of a few months, and while a member of the community might be paid to nurture them for the first year or two of their lives, this payment did not include support for the mother, nor was it paid to the mother. For example, Walter Davidson was given 4 pounds for "supporting a bastard child." Reputed fathers sometimes had to post bond that they would repay the parish for any poor relief it might have to expend on the children, but I found only the case of Hester Ryan, detailed at the beginning of this chapter, in which a father was clearly granted custody, and "reputed" fathers gave no financial support to the mother either.[17] Poor children, if very young, might also be monetarily supported. So William Stewart was given five pounds five shillings for "nursing Ann Nielson a poor child of this Parish." These payments, however, would generally only be given for less than a year, perhaps while the court was making arrangements to apprentice the child, and generally were not given to the natural parent. Apprenticeships of children between younger than six years of age sometimes involved a monetary reimbursement to the new master of amounts up to 15 pounds.[18]

Parental consent to the binding of children, if the courts had decided in favor, was irrelevant. Indeed, parental consent was routinely dismissed during the 1750s.[19] A Virginia law of 1646, still in force a century later, held that the decision to bind children into apprenticeships should rest solely in the hands of judges, who would act for the good of the children and society by teaching them to labor "in honest and profitable trades and manufactures, as also to avoyd sloath and idlenesse wherewith such young children are easily corrupted." Parental preferences about their children's labor were secondary to the needs of society as parents "through fond indulgence, or perverse obstinacy, are most averse and unwilling to parte with theire children." Almost more revealing than this law, however, or the dismissed complaints of parents is a case in which an apparently impoverished father pleaded for the return of his son "praying leave of the court that he may take him under his own care." Although the boy's former master had died, the father, in order to have his son returned to his custody, had to have friends post bond on his behalf that the child and he would never again have to rely on poor relief.[20] Similarly, Margaret Finnichan, whose illegitimate son was bound to her master when he was three, only recovered custody of her son after two complaints that he had been mistreated and a special plea to the court that she and her husband should have custody of William instead of another master, to whom he was initially transferred. He was then twelve, and he had lived separately from his mother since he was about five.[21]

Many more children were affected by these laws than historians have realized. Frederick County, and indeed the whole of Virginia, used apprenticeship extensively during the colonial period (see table 12.2). As noted above, it is likely that some tens of thousands of white children were forcibly bound into apprenticeship—we know now about more than 7,000. During the 1750s, 7.3 percent of children were bound in Frederick County, with disproportionate numbers of girls and boys: 8.2 percent of boys but only 5 percent of girls; if "mulatto bastards," which were a special case, are excluded, along with two free blacks, the percentages were less: 8 percent of white boys and 4.9 percent of white girls.[22]

TABLE 12.2.
Percentage of children apprenticed by Frederick County overseers of the poor

	1750s	1780s	1810s
All children	7.3	3.9	4.5
White children	7.0	3.7	3.3
White males	8.0	5.3	4.7
White females	4.9	2.1	1.4
Black males	n/a*	39	32.1
Black females	n/a*	22	6.4

*In the 1750s, two black children were bound, as well as five mulattos. These numbers probably comprised almost 100 percent of free and mulatto children, since almost none were free in that decade.

The 1780s, however, marked a significant drop in the percentage of children bound in Frederick County. The total number of children bound fell from 7.3 percent to 3.9 percent. Why?

Three new legal policies that began during the 1780s influenced these patterns. The first was dramatically expanded pensions for soldiers and their families when they could show financial need. Previous pensions in Virginia had only been given to the men themselves, and for disabilities only. The various pension laws passed in Virginia between 1775 and 1782, however, consistently equated patriotic service and provision for the family of the soldier, especially where financial need was an issue, marking a broad expansion in pension policy with the biggest changes passed in 1779 under the governorship of Thomas Jefferson.[23] In Frederick County, twenty-three different children of soldiers fighting in the Continental Army were given food and supplies between 1781 and 1783, compared to 151 children apprenticed over the whole decade of the 1780s. During the same decade, eighteen women applied for pensions based on their financial need and the fact that their husbands had died while serving in the Continental Army. Fifteen men applied for pensions based on disability and financial need. Although children were named only when payments were given to the families of living soldiers on the basis of mouths to feed, undoubtedly many of the eighteen wives of dead soldiers were also mothers, and many of the fifteen disabled soldiers were also fathers: and these pensions allowed them to support their families.[24] Otherwise some of these children would have fallen into the categories of "poor orphan" (which, as we recall, meant fatherless) or simply "poor" and would have been bound as apprentices by the Overseers of the Poor.

The second change in policy was not a change in the law of Virginia: but it was a change in legal practice. Judges began to force "reputed" fathers of bastard children to support their offspring by providing payments to the mother. The spirit behind this shift in practice can be glimpsed in Thomas Jefferson's argument for abolishing a law that assumed that the mothers of bastard children had evil intentions toward them. Women who bore bastard children should be seen as their children's best caretakers because of the very strength of the parental bond. Jefferson argued that the mothers of illegitimate children would be unlikely to kill them, and that an earlier law that had assumed that unwed mothers had killed their newborn babies who were found dead should be repealed. "If shame be a powerful affection of the mind, is not parental love also? Is it not the strongest affection known? Is it not greater than even that of self-preservation? While we draw presumptions from shame, one affection of the mind,... should we not give some weight to presumptions from parental love, an affection at least as strong...?"[25]

Indeed, the shift in official policy was dramatic toward unwed mothers and their children. Instead of men providing surety to the churchwardens (later called Overseers of the Poor) that they would refund the parish/county for expenses incurred in the maintenance of their bastard children, by the 1780s the courts began to order fathers to give money directly to the mothers of the bastard children they had fathered, in quarterly payments.[26] Mothers of "baseborn" children, who would have been whipped or fined in the 1750s, ceased to be whipped in 1769 and by the 1780s began instead to receive financial support to keep their children.[27] Although the numbers of paternity suits prosecuted are roughly the same for the 1750s and 1780s (four in each decade), the shift from possible payments to reimburse churchwardens to required payments to the mothers of the children themselves was dramatic. The fathers pledged to make these payments until the children were two or three, under threat of losing a greater sum of money, their bond, by reneging.

These policies were expanded during the 1810s. Further pensions were introduced for soldiers who fought in the War of 1812 and their families, and in 1818 the federal government began offering pensions to all who had served in the Revolutionary War and had financial need.[28] Bastardy suits became much more vigorously prosecuted, with twenty-one fathers having to post bond to provide quarterly payments, and median years for support increased to four years. These suits probably show only a portion of actual paternal support for bastard children: many suits were likely settled out of court.[29]

Thus we should not be surprised that the 1811–20 decade illustrates a relatively stable percentage of children bound, compared to the data for the 1780s. If one excludes free blacks, since binding free black children was a new issue after 1780 and was increasing in proportion to the number of white children bound, only 3.8 percent of white children were bound in the 1810s (see table 12.1). That the drop in the rate of children apprenticed fell from 7.3 percent (or 7.0 percent of white children) in the 1750s to 3.8 percent (of white children) in the 1810s arguably reflects an increased desire to keep children with their natural parents. Bastardy suits and pension plans are examples of these broader shifts in attitudes.[30] This theory is complemented by an examination of the average ages at which children were bound in Frederick County: the age increased from 7.9 years in the 1750s to 11.4 years in the 1810s. Within the different subgroups of bastards and poor children, the ages at which the children were bound show an even more significant increase: the average age at which bastard children were apprenticed increased from 4.4 years in the 1750s to 9.3 years in the 1810s. The average age at which poor children were apprenticed rose from 6.6 years in the 1750s to 11.5 years in the 1810s (see table 12.1).

The significant decline in the apprenticeship rate indicates a shift in policy that placed a higher value on parent/child bonds and sought to provide societal support to enable parents who might lose their children through poverty to keep them for a longer period. In many cases, families didn't have to resort to formal poor relief and thus never fell into the trap of forced apprenticeships. Unwed mothers in particular became perceived as proper parents by 1820, where in 1750 the mere fact that a child was born outside of marriage was construed as reason enough to remove him or her from maternal custody.

The third change was the dramatic revision of Virginia's inheritance laws in 1785, a change that abolished entail (forced primogeniture) and changed the rules such that all children inherited equally where a father left no will, rather than only the oldest son. Thomas Jefferson, who was the author of the two bills that made these revisions, regarded these as two cornerstones of republican government. The effect of this revision of law was probably gradual, since earlier policies, while disproportionate, had rarely completely disinherited all but the eldest son. In one case in the 1750s, John Hog was assigned a guardian to manage the money and property received from his father while his eleven-year-old sister Mary, who received no money or property, was bound to the trade of a mantua-maker. Such extreme cases—where one young child inherited enough to need a guardian while his sibling was so poor that she had to be bound out—were rare, even in the earlier period. The new equal distribution among children is probably best measured by the impact on the second or later generations. Another measure of the impact of these reforms is the dramatic increase in the number of children appointed guardians after their fathers died in comparison to the number bound. In the 1750s, more children whose fathers died were bound out than were assigned guardians, a ratio that shifted dramatically between the 1750s and 1810s. While only fifty-seven children whose fathers had died (and so were called orphans) had guardians and, presumably, could stay with their mother (or a guardian or family member) if they chose, seventy-four orphans were bound out by the churchwardens. Five of the fifty-seven, despite having guardians, were also ordered to be bound out. Thus only 79 of 131 (or 60 percent) were bound. While this ratio does not capture other children who were neither bound nor had guardians, it shows that the rate of children bound was high. Unless the mother remarried, had a trade, or the father/husband left a substantial amount of property, the children were normally apprenticed. This pattern was reversed by the 1810s, when only 33 fatherless children were apprenticed, compared to 185 who were given guardians (185 out of 218, or 15 percent). So the rate of those apprenticed compared to those given guardians dropped from 60% to only 15%. These calculations overstate the actual change since it was more likely, generally, for children to receive guardians by the 1810s because of the changing inheritance laws and norms about custody (in the 1750s, only heirs received guardians). Still, they exemplify the remarkable shift in attitudes.

Opposition to white girls' labor in poor apprenticeships grew more quickly than that of boys. Boys were more likely to be bound than girls in the 1750s, but this gender difference increased dramatically by the 1810s. Between 1751 and 1760, 4.9 percent of white girls were bound, compared to 8 percent of white boys. Girls were also less likely to be taught a trade, were never taught to cypher (while boys were), and by the 1781–90 period in Virginia, there were many cases in which, quite startlingly, girls did not even have to be taught to read and write (although by the 1810s all white girls were taught to read and write) while boys almost always had to be taught a trade and be given a rudimentary education in reading, writing, and arithmetic. The difference in proportions of girls and boys bound is probably explained by two factors. Boys were easier to bind because they served longer (they were bound until twenty-one instead of eighteen), and Virginian authorities were more concerned about boys learning a respectable trade. Still, it is important to note that white boys were bound in smaller percentages and at later ages than earlier.

Black boys, on the other hand, were bound at much higher rates in the wake of the Revolution, when a significant free black population began to emerge. Indeed, the high rates at which black children were bound—and the decreased options within those apprenticeships—reveals it to be both a more exploitative institution for them at the same time that it shows that the ideals of parental custody did not apply to black families. The free black community itself originated with the Revolution, when some white masters freed their slaves. A few blacks and mulattos were apprenticed even during the 1750s. However, the only two free blacks apprenticed between 1751 and 1760 were brothers apprenticed at their mother's request. Under Virginia law until 1765, mulatto children of white mothers could receive very different treatment than white children, since both sexes could be bound until they reached the age of thirty-one.[31] For the free black and mulatto children bound both before and after the Revolution, apprenticeship was not merely some exploitative relationship; they were protected under the same laws as were white children and could (and did) complain that they were improperly treated.[32] They were apprenticed for exactly the same length of time: until age eighteen for girls and until age twenty-one for boys, as is clear from the binding agreements recorded in the Frederick County Minute Books. Like white children, as well, they usually learned a trade, including the trade of a blacksmith, tanner, or barber, albeit many were to learn only "farming."[33] The biggest difference, however, is that in the 1750s and 1780s, the apprenticeship contracts of free black children specified that, like white children, they be taught to read and write. In the 1780s, six out of eleven court orders contained such provisions.[34] However, by the 1810s, there was a conscious exclusion of black children from such skills. The indentures used by the Overseers of the Poor to apprentice children during the 1810s always included reading and writing for white children but never when the contract was for a black child. Such requirements were actually crossed out on the preprinted apprenticeship contracts, indicating the purposeful and systematic way that these children were excluded.[35] It is almost as though there was a sincere attempt at equality during the 1780s that was largely abandoned by the 1810s, perhaps partly in response to Gabriel's Rebellion of 1800, which led to a harsh crackdown on the liberties and opportunities for free blacks.[36]

As shown in table 12.2, during the same decade of the 1780s that the proportion of white children apprenticed dropped, the proportion of free black children soared in comparison to the proportion of whites. This shift did not merely replace white children's labor with that of black children, as the total numbers in table 12.3 show; by far the majority of those bound were still white. The percentages given in table 12.2 make it appear otherwise because the population of free blacks was very small compared to that of free whites.[37] They still reveal, however, that an astounding 39 percent of the population of free black boys were apprenticed after the Revolution, a number that decreased only slightly to 32.1 percent by the 1810s.

A variety of explanations could be offered for such high apprenticeship rates for black boys. As free black children were often born to female-headed households (given that the status of the child was determined by the status of the mother, and slave men, with whom many free black women might form a relationship, could not legally marry), free black children were uniquely vulnerable to the laws that allowed the binding of bastards and of the fatherless. In addition, their relative poverty may have left them more likely than the majority of white families to look to poor relief.

On a deeper level, however, it is clear that Virginia authorities did not idealize the black family in the same way as they did the white. While they apprenticed many fewer girls by the 1810s (see table 12.2), a fact that illustrates that there were some consistencies across racial lines, the shocking difference in the rate of black boys to white boys apprenticed indicates a deeper basis of cultural attitudes. The fact that most black children in Virginia were slaves who belonged not to their parents but to their masters undoubtedly contributed to this devaluation of the black family. Needless to say, any idea that slave parents had custody rights in their children would have interfered dramatically with the slave market. In upholding the idea that slave parents had no legal custody of their children, the Virginia Court probably sympathized with the South

TABLE 12.3.
Net numbers of children bound

	1750s	1780s	1810s
All children	174	203	190
All boys	114	147	151
All girls	57	53	37
White males	110	140	116
White females	54	49	31
Black/mul males	4	7	35
Black/mul females	3	4	6

Carolina Supreme Court, which held in 1809 that "the young of slaves... stand on the same footing as other animals."[38]

Although black children were generally excluded from these broad shifts, the pattern of these changes hint at a shift in attitude toward children's labor, especially that of whites and girls. Not only were children being apprenticed later in life and for shorter periods of time, but apprentices became clearly distinguished from servants in their treatment by the courts, where earlier they had received similar treatment. Christopher Tomlins, who has observed the growing distinction between apprentices and servants at the end of the eighteenth century, a change that is clear in the records of Frederick County, speculates that in the earlier period almost all servants were children, while in the later period many adults were servants.[39] However, many adults were servants in the earlier period too.[40] Instead, I would argue that childhood became a distinct status and that children's labor became perceived as deserving special treatment. In the earlier period, servants and apprentices were lumped together and had a very similar status.

The hypothesis that new attitudes toward children's labor account for some of the changes in apprentice policy in post-1780 Virginia is complemented by shifts in educational policy. Did the new emphasis on formal education (in Virginia as well as the rest of the Republic), an emphasis that in 1788 resulted in the formation of a school in Winchester that was partly supported by public funds, indicate a different attitude toward childhood?[41] That it was a time of play and learning, not primarily of labor? Perhaps more speculatively—and I lay out the groundwork for this argument in detail in my book *By Birth or Consent*—a shift in the place of children in political and legal theory, a shift that emphasized the difference between children and adults and gave great importance to the unique and important place of childhood, also changed attitudes toward children.[42] Clearly, there was a long-term shift in attitudes toward children's labor that relates closely to attitudes about children's education. Michael Katz has explored the simultaneous growth of public education in nineteenth-century America and the decline in apprenticeship, attributing both changes to the growth of merchant-capitalism and ultimately to industrialization. While the connection he draws between the decline of the one institution and the rise of the other is interesting, his hypothesis that public education was started in response to an increasing dislike of bound labor that accompanied industrialization and constituted an effort to control children in alternative ways is unsatisfactory.[43] Comparison with the British policy reveals that while Britain preceded America in industrializing, Britain had no public education system until 1891, while most American states had public education systems a mere thirty years after the Revolution. While Virginia, along with other southern states, did not introduce the universal free public education of the northern states, successive attempts to supply such universal education repeatedly passed the lower house in Virginia, and many counties, such as Frederick County, provided subsidized primary education in the years after the Revolution.[44] Instead of linking both public education and the decrease in apprenticeship of the young simply to industrialization, I would suggest that both the rise of public education and the decline in apprenticeship reflected a shift in attitudes about childhood.

The shift in policy between 1750 and 1820 did not represent, fundamentally, a decreased demand for labor. Most of the county was still rural, and it had not experienced an economic transformation significant enough to have caused the shift in apprenticeship policy. Nor should poor apprenticeship be perceived as merely a way for masters/landowners to maximize their access to cheap labor. It is clear that the policy existed for reasons other than mere exploitation. Significant care was expended on the welfare of children in the earlier period. This shift in policy should be seen as a manifestation of greater concern with keeping children with their natural parents and with giving them a childhood separate from adulthood.

These shifts foreshadowed nineteenth-century programs such as mothers' pensions and vastly expanded military pensions, along with twentieth-century programs such as Aid to Families with Dependent Children and child labor legislation.[45] The roots of both changes were bound up in republican ideology. On the one hand, republican political theory described children as needing a period of education/play such that they should not be forced to labor too young and needed intellectual development that trained them to be future citizens and gave them greater economic opportunities. On the other, republican thought held that there are unique bonds between natural parents and children that should be preserved. The changes in U.S. policy from poor apprenticeship to adoption, foster care, and family-friendly welfare payments and to explicit legal restrictions on children's labor and the provision of public education—should be seen as representing a complex shift in our attitudes toward the relations between the family and the state and toward children in particular. Keeping families together and fostering broad economic opportunity through access to education both democratize, if you will, the family itself, making equality more than an empty legalistic term. The question of what to do for poor children is a fundamental one for any democratic polity; how they are treated is perhaps a crucial measure of general societal mobility. The detailed map of the policy of apprenticeship that the court records of Frederick County reveal suggests that the boundaries between community and family were much more fluid in 1750 than they were in 1820, and the family much less of an inviolable unit in the eighteenth century than in the nineteenth. This implies that such scholars as Christopher Lasch have their progression backwards when they claim that "the history of modern society...is the assertion of social control over activities once left to individuals or their families" or that capitalism first extended its control over the workers and then over the "worker's private life," over his family.[46] Rather, the new republic, with the revision of laws and policies that accompanied the Revolution, accelerated the acceptance of certain elements of Enlightenment thought and saw the implementation of policies that tended to keep families together. This pattern complements the conclusions of Nancy Cott, Linda Kerber, Michael Grossberg, and Ruth Bloch, who have argued that in the new republic, men and women began to be assigned separate spheres, that the community became more separated from the family, and that motherhood began to be idealized.[47]

Still, these new attitudes toward parental custody did not destroy the older system of apprenticeship, at least not initially. What Jefferson called his "republican" revision of the laws, much of which was passed by the Virginia legislature in the 1780s and 1790s, did not altogether dismember the old poor law. Indeed, that would have been an expensive step: for without apprenticeship, assuming that the state should not let these children starve, a system that let many children remain with their parents would have meant substantial transfer payments from the parish/county or the commonwealth of Virginia to each family. Jefferson, instead, supplemented and found substitutes for the older policy, adding provisions for all apprentices to be able to attend the public schools that he was proposing and adding the pension plan discussed above. He still, however, directed that every orphan who could not be maintained out of the estate they were to inherit should be bound out as well as mulattos and the children of those who received poor relief.[48] These legal guidelines were upheld in practice: the children of those who went into the Frederick County poor house during the 1810s, for example, were normally bound out if they were over three. If the family could not support its children and if it did not fall into one of the subgroups that the state decided to aid, children past nursing age were almost without exception (barring serious handicap) bound, probably because of the expense an expanded program would have entailed.[49] The pension plan, equitable inheritance, and paternal child support for bastard children did not completely reform the poor law, yet in providing avenues for children to remain with their natural parents, these shifts in policy were dramatic. They increased the separation between the powers of parents and the powers of the state, putting the responsibility for children ever more fully into the private familial domain at the same time as the state, through educational policy as well as welfare, worked to create broader economic opportunity for white children. These shifts also document the increasing racial divide in early national Virginia. While that divide softened briefly in the 1780s when free black children were also educated in their apprenticeships, that promise was literally crossed out (of the contracts) by the 1810s.

CONCLUSION

Reflections on the Demand and Supply of Child Labor in Early America

GLORIA L. MAIN

Surely the first observation to be made about child labor in early America is that children worked as a matter of course. The vast majority of parents needed their contribution for the household income, and all wanted their children to be active and productive. Society as well as parents worried that children who weren't put to useful labor would get into trouble, go bad, and lose their souls if they weren't kept so busy the Devil couldn't get to them. Even well-off parents sent their teenage children away to work. Commenting on this custom in New England, Edmund Morgan speculated more than sixty years ago that Puritan parents were afraid of *spoiling* their children.[1] The work of Ann Kussmaul and others has shown that the English, and probably the French and the Dutch as well, had the same custom of sending their children away to work as servants for stretches of time. In sum, child labor was not restricted by class but was a broad-based European cultural phenomenon as well as an economic necessity for the poor and middling orders of society.[2]

The supply of child labor in early America, then, was virtually coterminous with the population of children above the age of about seven and was regulated principally by rates of fertility, immigration, and child mortality. Their economic contribution came mainly through the performance of simple agricultural tasks suited to their age and strength, but the growth of household manufacturing in the eighteenth century began to absorb greater amounts of their time. Westward expansion, the agricultural boom of the 1790s, the cessation of immigration during and after the Napoleonic Wars, and the lively burst of manufacturing innovations in the early-nineteenth-century Northeast all affected both the supply and the demand for child labor in complicated ways. We will examine demand first.

Most of the essays in this volume focus on a subsection of the population of all working children in early North America, a fraction of unknown size that varied by place and time: those who were bound out by formal means for a term of years to work for someone other than their parents. Our knowledge of them comes mainly from official records of apprenticeship and indenture that pertain to children who had left, or would soon be leaving, their family of birth. The reasons for separation varied, but the primary purpose of the formal proceeding was to assign legal custody of the minor in question. The documents are usually agreements among three parties: the child entering custody, if he or she was capable of understanding and giving consent; the child's parent, guardian, or sponsor; and the master or employer to whom the child was to be confided. Such agreements were contracts of mutual obligation between child and master in which the child agreed to labor for the master for a term of years and to honor and obey him during that time. The functions performed by masters or employers in return included promises of maintenance for the term of the agreement. The contract might also specify vocational training, vow to teach the child to read and write, and pledge specific rewards for completing the term satisfactorily. The core agreement, however, was the master's promise to maintain the child during the term of the contract in exchange for the child's service.[3]

Despite this uniformity in concept, actual indentures varied widely in their details, as the essays in this collection make abundantly clear. They varied because every locale made its own adaptation of the original institution carried over from the Old World and because of the changing needs of a developing economy and evolving ideas about the nature of children. Indentures served multiple functions in their communities of origin, ranging from the care of orphans to charity for the poor to the use of young servants as agricultural laborers to vocational preparation of children of the propertied classes. More prosperous parents negotiated terms of service for their children at older ages, preferably with kin, and for shorter periods of time. Less prosperous parents bound out their children at younger ages to masters who would adjust their specific demands for labor as their servants grew in years and strength. Contributors to this volume have provided a wealth of detail on these variations, noting the relationship between the age, gender, race, and family situation of the child, on the one hand, and the duration of the term and promised benefits, on the other. Analysis of the records uncovers patterns that indicate that the weaker the bargaining position of the child or its sponsor, the less the master needed to oblige himself in return. Not surprisingly, children of color got the short end of the stick, and white girls did less well than white boys. Among orphans, those with relatives acting on their behalf might or might not receive better terms than did those with an unrelated sponsor.[4]

Given the range of purposes these indentures served, it is useful to distinguish among three kinds: those guaranteeing maintenance to very young children as a form of custodial welfare, akin to foster parenting; apprenticeships designed to employ poor children in farming; and those promising to teach the older child a craft or occupation. The nature and quantity of the three kinds of indenture responded to the ups and downs of the local economy and to the racial makeup of the children to be indentured, but in different ways. Expansion and contraction in local masters' needs for labor actively shaped the scale of indenturing of children in colonial and postcolonial communities, and as Stephen Whitman demonstrated so clearly for Maryland in chapter 4, it is important to distinguish between urban and rural markets for child labor. Although the timing of the onset of the decline in apprenticeships described by Whitman, Gillian Hamilton (chapter 11), Ruth Herndon (chapter 3), and Paul Lachance (chapter 8) varied from place to place, there appears to have been a general nationwide move away from the use of such contracts. Indentured servitude among arriving immigrants, for instance, had entirely disappeared by the early 1830s, craft apprenticeships in northern cities and towns began declining even before 1800, and ever fewer orphan and poor children were bound out in the rural areas studied by volume contributors.[5]

Our pre-industrial ancestors accepted only a qualified responsibility for the poor. Close kin were the first line of support in all the colonies. The expectation in European society was that more prosperous relatives should take care of their own, but English common law did not compel such support outside the immediate family. Sectarian churches often took some measure of responsibility for members, but the principal source of aid in Anglo-American societies since the sixteenth century has been local government. Towns and counties levied taxes in order to provide for those of its respectable citizens who had lost visible means of support. Officially dispensed charity was the main recourse for the down-and-out, and begging was strongly discouraged. In the British colonies, the deserving poor consisted of those whose plight was the result of misfortunes not of their own making: the very young, the old, the sick, and the physically and mentally disabled.[6]

A disproportionate share of those on public relief were, however, none of these. They were widows and single mothers. Their hardship derived from the legal and occupational handicaps imposed on women by Anglo-American legal culture. Custom divided the various forms of labor between men and women and valued male tasks significantly above those of females. So a woman without a husband was much worse off economically than a man without a wife, because for the equivalent number of hours and days worked, women received only one-third to two-fifths the income that men did. A widow without a farm or businesses or savings could marry a man with means, live with relatives, work for wages, or go on relief. If she was without other help and had young children, she could not go out to work, and even if she could go out to work, her wages alone would not be sufficient to support a separate household. That is why, wherever common law prevailed, her children could be bound out against her will by local authorities.[7]

Poverty expands and contracts with the succession of bad times and good, but temporary population imbalances can worsen the hard times and strain public funds and patience. Wars, for instance, disrupt maritime commerce and kill young men, leaving their wives widowed and their children fatherless. These are groups who are otherwise healthy but find themselves suddenly handicapped not only by the loss of an important income-earner but by the operation of gender-based economic discrimination against the surviving maternal parent. Wars also reduce the pool of potential replacements for the lost husbands and fathers of the newly widowed and orphaned. The life expectancy of seamen was, of course, lower than for farmers in peacetime, and the impact of their deaths on public resources can be seen in the records of every port town.[8]

All things being equal, the demand for labor depends on the level of economic activity, and poverty tends to grow and decline as labor demand falls or rises. In early America, economic ups and downs affected employment, income, and poverty levels, although small farmers in the Northeast were more insulated from international markets than were their more export-dependent neighbors to the south. The amplitude of those peaks and valleys grew stronger after 1750, as the North Atlantic economy revved forward. Neither wages nor jobs nor required skills could remain fixed in custom when the pace of production, trade, and technological innovation surged. As the economy became more complex, the demand for labor became ever more finely delineated as occupational differentiation proceeded in manufacturing, but even in the agricultural sector, farming became more specialized at the local level under the growing influence of market prices.[9] All these trends affected the demand for child labor.

The value to the master of a contract binding over a child lay in how soon and for how long the child could perform tasks that would increase the productivity of the master's household beyond the cost of maintaining the child. The value of child labor, in turn, varied not only with the age of the child but also with the nature of the local economy. Thus, in areas specializing in labor-intensive crops with relatively long production cycles, such as tobacco or cotton, there were myriad small tasks that made the labor of even very young children valuable because they released older workers for more productive employment. By the age of eight, for instance, the productivity of slave children in plantation areas of the nineteenth century surpassed the cost of their maintenance.[10] It seems reasonable to infer, therefore, that local officials would not have found it difficult to bind out poor white orphans aged eight and older to tobacco farmers in the upper South or to small growers anywhere in the lower South. Outside of the South, on the other hand, shorter growing seasons constrained farmers' options in finding crops that would appeal to paying customers overseas. Wars and population growth in Europe drove up demand for American wheat in the eighteenth century, but grain growing requires only seasonal inputs of labor. Wherever cities and industries grew, however, residents would pay for milk and butter, fresh meat and garden produce, needs that only local suppliers could meet because of the lack of high-speed, refrigerated transport. And meet it they did, as farm families living near urban markets took up dairying and truck gardening, occupations entailing the reorganization of their schedules and task assignments. Benjamin Rush commented in 1815 on the revolution in diet that had taken place since 1760 with the "profusion of summer and winter vegetables" that had come to make up the bulk of table fare.[11] Intensive farming near cities probably increased the demand for child labor among farm families able to make the switch, but the high cost of land in older settlements along the Atlantic coast posed a barrier to new entrants and encouraged out-migration by youth.

Year for year, pound for pound, children under the age of thirteen were probably better economic investments in the agricultural South than in the rural North for most of the period before the Civil War, although the ups and downs of local farm prices and wages surely affected the truth of this generalization. If similar earnings rates prevailed in earlier times, poor children and orphan teenage girls would have found a cool welcome among strangers in northern farm communities unless non-agricultural tasks suitable for them became abundant.[12] This is precisely why political economists of the period welcomed the innovations in textile manufacturing of the late eighteenth century. Machines promised to utilize more fully the time and labor power of "underemployed" women and children, thereby reducing poverty and raising the level of income and comfort for all.[13] The earliest factories hired families with children or contracted with parents for their young boys. With time, teenage girls in New England, in particular, became targets for innovative manufacturing ideas since they were cheap labor, well suited to factory discipline, and could be hired without contracts.

Formal indentures for child servants were comparatively little used in northern agriculture. This is not to say that there was no market for child labor outside the immediate family. Teenage children, especially boys, were often sent out by farm parents of middling circumstances to work for others in the colonial period, but usually for short terms such as weeks or months rather than for years at a time.[14] True apprenticeship, on the other hand, was a much more formal and extended binding out of the child by the parent or guardian. City officials bound out poor children to rural as well as urban masters, but traditional craft apprenticeship more generally characterized contracts between urban craftsmen and boys in their early teens who promised to stay and work hard for the artisan in return for occupational training.[15] Modern vocational schools still offer such training today in such occupations as plumbing and heating, electrical work, automobile repair, and so on, but students do not live with their teachers' families and are free to leave if they wish. In the pre-industrial past, craft apprenticeship transferred the boy from his family of birth to a master who assumed moral oversight of his wards. Masters were *in loco parentis,* they had full parental rights over the children, had final say over how they were to spend their time, and were, in exchange, to be their teachers, fathers, and spiritual guides. As part of his obligations, the master was to discipline as well as to train the boys in his care. Masters were to keep good order in the shop and make sure their boys did not go out unsupervised at night.

The young apprentice entered the artisan's shop in a dependent, subservient position with the expectation that, in return for his obedience and service, he would learn all aspects and stages of manufacturing a completed final product that customers would want to buy. Judging by the essays in this book, the usual age of apprenticeship to a craft was about fourteen, when boys had reached sufficient size and strength to make their labor immediately valuable to masters, despite their lack of skills.[16] Ideally, an apprenticeship gave a boy the necessary expertise to make a living when his time was up, although he might still have to work for others as a journeyman in order to save the wherewithal to acquire tools, raw materials, and a place to set up shop for himself. Not all crafts were equally difficult, nor did they all require similar outlays of capital for going into business. Hence, the more lucrative or prestigious the craft, the more likely that parents and guardians would pay a premium to the master to take the boy as an apprentice. Crafts requiring few tools and cheap materials, such as shoe-making or tailoring, were usually the easiest and cheapest for poor boys to enter.[17]

Masters also took responsibility for their apprentices' basic education, which in the seventeenth century included only reading. Then in the eighteenth century, writing became a universally desired skill. Most boys entering apprentice contracts in New England could already sign their names, and such seems to have been the case elsewhere. Finally "cyphering"—simple arithmetic—became part of the standard educational package promised by apprenticeship contracts. Boys who had not already acquired these educational tools by the time they entered apprenticeship expected to get time off from work or at night to attend classes.[18]

Craft apprenticeship, then, was a cost-efficient mode of training the small fraction of boys in early America who were not destined for farming. Acquisition of technical skills and basic literacy enabled them to become productive citizens in a pre-industrial world in which educational requirements were minimal and cheap schools were scarce. In reality, of course, boys did not always obey the rules, nor did masters always exercise appropriate fatherly care. In fact, from the very beginning in this country, apprenticeship was a weak institution in comparison to the rigidly structured guilds of European tradition. Labor shortages and land surpluses hampered paternalistic efforts to control and exploit the labor of boys and young men, who grew up knowing there were other options. Events leading up to the American Revolution, the dislocations of the war itself, and the postwar depression all disrupted overseas markets for American-made goods, making contract labor a financial burden to masters who could not keep their workers productively busy. Republican rhetoric and the language of religious revivals may have further undermined ties between urban masters and their apprentices. Contracts substituting pay for maintenance began appearing around the turn of the century in northern port cities and, a decade or so later, in the South. Their growing appearance suggests that fewer and fewer apprentices were living in the master's household. Separate boarding of apprentices gave them greater autonomy by liberating them from the master's oversight after leaving the shop at day's end.[19]

The personal relationship between master and apprentice and the goal of preparing a journeyman craftsman capable of performing every step in the production process had formed the model of pre-industrial manufacturing in great cities and longtime craft centers in Western Europe. But that model, which placed enormous power in the hands of elite masters, had been to some extent subverted in Europe by the movement of market-oriented artisan-businessmen into the countryside, and it never stood a chance in the free air of our own lightly populated continent. Despite the spectacular growth of the white population after colonization, that population remained dispersed and predominantly agricultural until after the middle of the nineteenth century.

The kinds of crafts that flourished in the bucolic pre-industrial countryside of the Northeast and in the non-plantation areas of the South were those that served the needs of local farmers and their families, and many took up such work as a part-time activity in winter. Poor roads and the lack of bridges constricted rural markets, keeping shops small and products crude. Such a system could not support a formal craft apprenticeship program, and most helpers were probably the children or other kin of the artisan himself. But it did create widespread acceptance of handicraft work as suitable employment for independent farmers and their children.[20]

When North American cities began to expand rapidly in the 1790s, the economic and ideological climate further militated against rigid controls over urban business enterprise, particularly how goods were to be made or sold. The expansion of commerce in that decade opened new markets for American-made goods. Ambitious craftsmen became opportunistic businessmen who sought to expand output and satisfy the broadest possible range of potential customers, including slaveowners on southern plantations. Separating the steps of manufacturing and giving the work of each step to the lowest-paid laborer reduced the final cost of the product. Here lay the future of child labor, or so it seemed in the first quarter of the nineteenth century.

Not all manufacturing processes lent themselves to the economizing effects of reorganization like the one that sparked the growth and spread of boot- and shoe-making among teenage boys and girls in eastern Massachusetts.[21] Less visible and striking were the reallocations of labor within farm households that came to include other forms of domestic manufacturing for sale beyond the local community. Making straw brooms became a winter pastime for men and boys in southern New England in the early nineteenth century. A school was established in Baltimore in 1824, "for the instruction of poor girls in the various branches of straw-plaiting from simple plait to finished bonnet."[22] As the century progressed, the fashioning of fancy straw bonnets and cheap palm leaf hats became a part-time occupation of female family members who were supplied with raw materials on credit by itinerant jobbers working out of major cities.[23]

The biggest shift from male craftsmen to female and child labor in manufacturing took place in textile production, but that shift proceeded in stages, and its timing and impact varied by region. Traditional cloth-making in England and the colonies allotted spinning of the yarn to women and children while the adult male weaver produced the cloth on his loom in his shop or on customers' looms at their houses. This pattern persisted in the mid-Atlantic colonies and states even after the appearance of spinning mills in the nineteenth century.[24] In New England, on the other hand, young women living at home began to take up weaving in the eighteenth century, specializing in low-cost plain goods for home consumption and for local exchange, while male weavers took orders for finer cloth. Weaving plain goods for pay gave employment to widows and single women. The female side of production had no masters and used no formal apprenticeships, although there are recorded examples of parents buying the equipment, furnishing the supplies, and hiring a weaver as tutor. After that, sister taught sister.[25]

The introduction of carding mills from England in the late 1780s led to their explosive adoption throughout the Northeast because they simplified a key early stage in the production of both cotton and woolen cloth. Spinning mills produced large quantities of yarn, and improvement in machine design spun a fiber strong enough to permit cotton to be used for both the warp and the woof in its weaving. Sturdy and abundant cotton yarn at a reasonable price drove out flax-growing by northeastern farmers, because making linen from rotted flax was a particularly labor-intensive process. Meanwhile, the beginnings of the westward movement of southern planters and their slaves onto prime cotton-growing land began to increase its supply, and the application of cotton gins to remove its oily seeds greatly eased the most laborious stage in its preparation.

Carding mills also stimulated interest in the production of good woolen fibers suitable for mechanized spinning, leading to the importation of suitable breeds of sheep from Spain and elsewhere in order to improve the fleeces of domestic flocks. As mechanized carding and spinning mills proliferated, households in their vicinity ceased to devote labor time to these stages in textile production. Dairying in the mid-Atlantic states offered a profitable alternative use for youngsters' energies most of the year, but the slack season of winter probably witnessed greater investment in schooling, even for girls.[26] In New England, on the other hand, older girls and young women increasingly filled that time with weaving.

The availability of spun cotton and wool in hitherto unprecedented quantities boosted the demand for commercial weaving. Mills began to "put out" their yarn to female weavers in New England and to male weavers in the mid-Atlantic region. When President Jefferson imposed an embargo on the importation of foreign goods in 1807, domestic manufacturers found ready markets at home for their products. The embargo lasted less than a year, but spinning mill operators had jumped to fill the gap because the American public had shown that they would accept American-made goods as satisfactory substitutes for English goods of lower quality.

When Samuel Slater brought English spinning machines to rural Rhode Island and applied New England's abundant water power to their spindles, he had to assemble a work force for his first mill, completed in 1790. He at first used local children, but there were few available. He then turned to teenage pauper apprentices as English factories did, but he found them difficult to discipline and given to running away. Moreover, their schooling and maintenance (clothing, medical care, and room and board locally) was expensive. Meanwhile he was also hiring children as young as seven on short-term wage contracts, but in order to get them to come, he also had to hire their families and promise them steady work. So he was forced to build residences in which to house them, deducting rent from their wages. Young women and children tended the spindles, while the men took charge of the carding, supervised the spinners, stood night watch, maintained the machines, and carted cotton bales from the docks. By the turn of the century, "indigent families had largely replaced apprentices and had become the primary source of labor."[27] The resulting yarn was then put out to local weavers, in many cases farm women and their daughters, who wove it into cloth and received store credit in return. Slater built more mills, and competitors opened their own. The demand for weavers soon exceeded local supplies, and some mill owners opened stores as far away as Hallowell, Maine, in the hopes of luring farm women there into weaving factory yarn in exchange for store goods.[28]

The beginnings of the Industrial Revolution in America are familiar textbook fare.[29] Manufacturing firms had been small-scale and traditionally organized with respect to age and gender. Larger enterprises were rare until the burst of industrial expansion following the Embargo of 1807 and the end of the War of 1812. Outside of shoe-making districts, cotton and woolen textiles accounted for most of the employment of women and children before 1820. The Federal Manufacturing Census of that year revealed that children made up 23 percent of all manufacturing workers in New England and half of all employees of cotton mills, although their proportions were lesser in woolen mills. The use of child labor in New England, then, had reached levels comparable to Great Britain's, where over half of all workers in cotton manufacturing were under the age of nineteen.[30] During the 1820s and 1830s, girls and young women came to greatly outnumber men and boys in the very large integrated spinning and weaving cotton mills along the Merrimac River, such as those at Lowell and Lawrence, Massachusetts.[31]

In the mid-Atlantic region, the pathway to industrialization was different, because it centered in urban areas where supplies of male labor proved abundant. In Baltimore, the early large spinning mills hired male pauper apprentices, but they, too, came to find long-term contracts burdensomely inflexible when business flagged, and the traditional requirements for maintenance and schooling apprentices expensive.[32]

As a result of the Embargo of 1807 and, later, the Non-Intercourse Act, spinning mills proliferated in the Northeast until the end of the Napoleonic Wars, when the British dumped quantities of cloth on American markets, driving most of them out of business. Yet there were mills that hung on somehow and returned to operation, helped by a succession of tariffs beginning in 1816 that provided increasing protection to the "infant" industry. New mills were built using ever better technology, and the first integrated spinning and weaving cotton mill took shape in Waltham, Massachusetts. Its success led to the development of Lowell and other mill towns on the Concord and Merrimac Rivers, the construction of the Merrimac Canal, and in 1835, the first railway in New England, all projects that brought together unprecedented sums of capital.[33] The choice of machine design at Lowell was deliberately intended to make use of young female labor, and their large-scale employment there is well-known. Older girls and young women were spinners, weavers, carders, and dressers; younger girls worked as doffers in the reeling room.[34]

Manufacturers in New England were tapping into a vast pool of relatively underemployed, low-cost labor. As we have seen, the low productivity of women, girls, and younger boys in northern agriculture made them an attractive resource for manufacturers. The larger the scale of operation, Claudia Goldin and Kenneth Sokoloff argue, the more simplified the tasks, and the easier it became for those of smaller stature and weaker frame to perform productively. It may be, of course, that younger children of both sexes were simply easier to bend to factory discipline, but in any case, the rise of factories greatly increased their employment. Goldin and Sokoloff estimate that their proportion in the nation's manufacturing labor force rose from 10 percent in 1800-1809 to almost 40 percent by 1832, after which it declined but still remained above 30 percent in 1850. Based on their New England samples drawn from a congressionally commissioned survey of manufactures known as the McLane Report (1832), females in manufacturing employment formed an astonishing 27 percent of all females aged ten to twenty-nine then living in the states of Massachusetts and Rhode Island, and 12 percent in Connecticut.[35]

The precise extent to which boys and girls under the age of sixteen worked in American manufacturing, even in New England, is still not clear, however. Henry Carey stated in 1836 that American textile manufacturers hired few children. Using data from the New York Convention of the Friends of Industry in 1832, he claimed that only 7.1 percent of persons employed in cotton manufactures were "children" and that the number of children employed below age sixteen at Lowell was "very small, and none below 12." At Lawrence, he placed their proportion at 8 percent of the whole number employed.[36] In the McLane Report, most textile mills in New England were much smaller operations than Lowell and Lawrence and employed far fewer workers.[37] Woolen mills were generally smaller than those for cotton and typically employed fewer females relative to men and boys.[38] In Connecticut in 1831, for instance, there were 80 woolen mills, employing 796 men, 610 "females," and 278 children, averaging 21 employees per mill and utilizing more men than women. By contrast, 90 cotton mills employed 1532 men, 2717 females, and 496 children "under 12," averaging a little more than 52 per mill and with what looks like a great preponderance of females. The reported categories are unclear about the ages of "females" versus "children." In Rhode Island, where women and children were demarcated by age in the McLane Report, there were many more "children" identified as such, proportionately, than in Connecticut, suggesting to Goldin and Sokoloff that the category of "females" in Connecticut included all ages but "children" there meant boys, and only boys. They reason that the wage differences by age and sex in Rhode Island imply that the lower wages reported for "women" or "females" in Connecticut are due to the diluting effect of numerous young girls. Whether or not this was actually the case, the proportion of children under sixteen employed in textile or any other kind of manufacturing cannot be known exactly. Goldin and Sokoloff concluded that the proportion of boys in cotton manufacturing in 1832 was 6.1 percent of the work force for medium sized firms and 6.7 percent in larger ones. In wool, their proportion ranged from 17.8 percent in small firms to 8.8 percent in large firms. In shoe manufacturing, boys made up anywhere from 3.1 percent to 11.3 percent of employees depending on the size of the firm, and they were below 5 percent for firms of any size in paper manufacturing. All in all, the proportion of boys in the manufacturing labor force surveyed in the McLane Report in 1832 looks to have been in the neighborhood of a mere 10 percent or less. This constitutes an enormous drop from their proportions prevailing in 1820 when the Federal Manufacturing Census shows them making up something like 40 percent. Even if the latter is an overstatement, such reports demonstrate that economic development was moving sharply away from the employment of boys younger than sixteen in the 1820s.[39]

All these numbers raise questions about what happened to the demand for child labor between 1750 and 1850. Based on what we have seen, the preindustrial and early industrial phases of economic development increased demand for child laborers of both sexes in mechanized industries, as it did in Great Britain, but then, in New England, "females" displaced the boys. The feminization of textile manufacturing there made possible by technological and organizational innovations in the previous decades, meanwhile, had virtually eliminated the demand for all children under age twelve in factories and markedly reduced nonfarm employment prospects for boys. These developments apparently did not occur in the more urbanized industrial centers of the mid-Atlantic states, including Philadelphia and northern Maryland, where a steady influx of skilled craft workers reinforced traditional sex and age compositions of the workforce for much longer.[40] Manufacturing employment of females in New England began declining in the 1840s, probably due to the arrival in the region of thousands of unskilled immigrant men willing to accept low wages and factory discipline.

In a demographically stable society, prevailing mortality rates will assure that certain proportions of young and old die every year; meanwhile, prevailing fertility rates will produce a predictable number of births annually. Thus the labor force is perennially refreshed by the private behavior of couples. Wars, natural disasters, and disease epidemics upset these states of equilibrium but given enough time and an absence of intervening events causing further disturbances, birth and death rates eventually return to their previous levels.

There could be no such demographic equilibrium in the colonies or the early Republic, as the Seven Years' War, the Revolution, and the Napoleonic Wars directly or indirectly affected settlers' fortunes. Likewise, immigration from Europe and Africa came in waves between wars, although the numbers of foreign arrivals shrank to almost negligible levels in the early nineteenth century. Westward migration from older settlements on the East Coast largely began after the Seven Years' War and continued whenever and wherever Indian resistance could be overcome or safely circumvented. Agrarian migrants looking for cheap land made up the overwhelming bulk of these human tides between 1750 and 1850. Families on the move to New York and the Midwest raised large broods of children, whereas those who stayed behind faced very different economic prospects. High prices for land barred rising generations from acquiring farms of their own, perhaps forcing young people to postpone marriage and curtail childbearing. On the other hand, did new employment opportunities for child labor, such as those in textile and shoe manufacturing, offer such ample compensation that parents saw no need to curtail childbearing? This question is highly pertinent, because fertility levels in rapidly industrializing Great Britain did not begin falling until the 1880s.

Assume for the moment that married couples in the years before rubber pessaries and condoms became available would not have tried very hard to reduce their fertility below customary levels unless the benefits of doing so significantly outweighed the personal costs of avoiding or terminating pregnancy. One key factor played a role in parental decision-making: the cost of preparing children for adult independence. It was highest in the Northeast in 1860, according to Lee Craig, which undoubtedly discouraged large families. Perhaps not coincidentally, the first public assertions that children younger than twelve had a right *not* to work began to appear around 1830.[41] The costs of raising children in the Northeast and giving them sufficient material and educational resources to live comfortably, therefore, may have come to overshadow whatever income children could earn, even in boom periods like the 1790s. As early as 1800, federal censuses report fewer children aged five and under per woman aged fifteen to forty in the Northeast than in the other regions of the country, and the region's ratios between young children and women of childbearing age continued to decline during the nineteenth century.[42]

This decline in the proportion of young children in the population may indicate that married couples in the Northeast were actively practicing some form of birth control, but it could also have been the result of other factors—rising child mortality, rising age at marriage for women, increasing proportions of women remaining single for life, or some combination of all of these.[43] Recent research in family and town genealogies from New England, however, places the full demographic force of these marriage- and mortality-related factors in the 1830s, whereas lengthening intervals between births began reducing the average completed family size in sample families as early as the 1790s.[44] The time profiles conform with falling child/woman ratios in subregions of New England. If that relationship characterized regions elsewhere in the Northeast, their birth rates were likewise declining.

For reasons not entirely clear, the supply of child labor simply did not expand in response to the new employment opportunities and higher wages of the earliest phases of the Industrial Revolution in America. This is not the place to ponder what was in the hearts and minds of couples in the post-Revolutionary age as they heard about the opening of new territories to the west or the erection of new factory villages closer by, but their decisions about when to marry and when to have children surely shaped the utilization of child labor and the welfare of poor children every bit as much as did the growth of commerce, the expansion of markets, and the rationalization of work regimes.

We have seen that putting children to work served a variety of social purposes in early America: keeping them out of trouble while socializing them to a world of patriarchy and deference; disciplining them to an economy of scarcity in which everyone must work to live; and training them for future careers as competent, productive, and useful citizens. Binding them out to masters relieved impoverished or otherwise incapacitated parents of these duties while reducing the rolls of those on poor relief. In return for accepting the costs of maintaining and educating their apprentice helpers, craftsmen, farmers, and housekeepers benefited from cheap compulsory labor. The rise of orphanages and free schools and the decline of craft apprenticeship were responses to market forces that substituted free wage laborers for bound servants. But the growth of institutions designed to benefit the children of the poor attests to the gradually mounting impact of two sets of new ideas. The first was a new understanding of children, that they were not merely small and poorly socialized versions of adults but rather emotionally vulnerable creatures in need of nurturing as well as good discipline. The other great force at work in early America was the Revolutionary spirit of individual liberty and equal rights. Unfortunately, both these expansionary and liberating forces worked out their impacts on the American people through the medium of a stratified society that favored the propertied over the poor, the male over the female, and the white over the black. We remain optimistic that, despite persistent impediments, these forces continue at work in our own age and will ultimately prevail.

Notes

Chapter 1. "A Proper and Instructive Education"

1. For summaries of the literature on early American thought about children in relation to families and communities, see Carole Shammas, *A History of Household Government in America* (Charlottesville: University of Virginia Press, 2002); Lisa Wilson, *Ye Heart of a Man: The Domestic Life of Men in Colonial New England* (New Haven: Yale University Press, 1999); and Helena M. Wall, *Fierce Communion: Family and Community in Early America* (Cambridge, MA: Harvard University Press, 1990).

2. *Countryman's Lamentation,* ii–iii, 42–44, 46.

3. Compare Whitman's and Brewer's estimates in chapters 4 and 12 in this volume with those of Christopher Tomlins in "Reconsidering Indentured Servitude: European Migration and the Early American Labor Force, 1600–1775," *Labor History* 42 (2001): 5–43. In the Chesapeake of the mid–eighteenth century, Tomlins estimated the share of Maryland's population that was bound in servitude to have been 6.4 percent.

4. David J. Rothman, *The Discovery of the Asylum: Social Order and Disorder in the New Republic* (Boston: Little, Brown, 1971); Timothy A. Hacsi, *Second Home: Orphan Asylums and Poor Families in America* (Cambridge, MA: Harvard University Press, 1997); E. Wayne Carp, *Family Matters: Secrecy and Disclosure in the History of Adoption* (Cambridge, MA: Harvard University Press, 1998); E. Wayne Carp, ed., *Adoption in America: Historical Perspectives* (Ann Arbor: University of Michigan Press, 2002); Adoption History Project website, http://darkwing.uoregon.edu/~adoption/; and Joseph F. Kett, *Rites of Passage: Adolescence in America, 1790 to the Present* (New York: Basic Books, 1977).

5. *Countryman's Lamentation,* 43–44.

6. *Countryman's Lamentation,* 45.

7. *Countryman's Lamentation,* 43.

8. For Rhode Island, see Murray and Herndon, "Markets for Children," 360, fig. 1; for Ohio, see Patchen, "Apprenticeship on the Frontier," 47 (see bibliography). The other figures refer to essays in this volume.

9. *Countryman's Lamentation,* 42.

10. For example, on maintenance see Connecticut (Colony), *Acts and Laws, of His Majesties Colony of Connecticut in New-England* (Boston: Bartholomew Green and John Allen, 1702), 7; on binding out see Joseph Brevard, *An Alphabetical Digest of the Public Statute Law of South Carolina* (Charleston: John Hoff, 1814), 68.

11. *Countryman's Lamentation,* ii.

12. *Countryman's Lamentation,* 47.

13. *Countryman's Lamentation,* 47–48.

14. *Countryman's Lamentation,* 45.

15. *Countryman's Lamentation,* 45–46.

16. *Countryman's Lamentation,* 43.

17. "Cyphering," or basic arithmetic, was usually reserved for boys in pauper apprenticeship indentures. It was an educational accomplishment quite separate from reading and writing and was not taught to any significant extent in early America until the late seventeenth century. Basic math became important for the conduct of a trade in the eighteenth century and entered pauper apprenticeship indentures accordingly. On the shift from a "prenumerate" to a "numerate" culture in America, see Patricia Cline Cohen, *A Calculating People: The Spread of Numeracy in Early America* (Chicago: University of Chicago Press, 1982), esp. ch. 2. For a significant discussion of the importance of cyphering in male crafts and trades and its inclusion in indentures of pauper apprentices in Maryland, see Daniels, "Alternative Workers in a Slave Economy," (Ph.D. dissertation, Johns Hopkins University, 1990), 337, 357–61.

18. *Countryman's Lamentation,* 46.

19. Barry Levy, "Girls and Boys: Poor Children and the Labor Market in Colonial Massachusetts," *Pennsylvania History* 64 (1997): 287–307.

20. *Countryman's Lamentation,* iii, 49.

21. Stephanie Grauman Wolf, *As Various as Their Land: The Everyday Lives of Eighteenth-Century Americans* (New York: HarperCollins, 1993), 108.

22. On the legal status of children as dependents, see Holly Brewer, "Age of Reason? Children, Testimony, and Consent in Early America," in *The Many Legalities of Early America,* ed. Christopher L. Tomlins and Bruce H. Mann (Chapel Hill: University of North Carolina Press, 2001), 293–332; and Levy, "Girls and Boys."

23. Wolf, *As Various as Their Land,* 113; and Sharon Braslaw Sundue, "Industrious in Their Stations: Young People at Work in Boston, Philadelphia, and Charleston, 1735–1785" (Ph.D. dissertation, Harvard University, 2001), 15–58.

24. Plymouth Colony counted males over age sixteen as adults as early as 1643; by the Revolutionary era, all New England colonies/states had followed suit. New York counted persons over the age of ten as adults in 1731 but changed the dividing line to age sixteen in the census of 1746. North Carolina counted sixteen-year-olds among "men" as early as 1761. All states had adopted the sixteen-year-old standard by the 1790 census. John McCusker, "Colonial Statistics," in *Historical Statistics of the United States: Earliest Times to the Present,* ed. Susan B. Carter et al. (New York: Cambridge University Press, 2006), 5:657–64. See also Evarts B. Greene and Virginia D. Harrington, *American Population before the Federal Census of 1790* (Gloucester, MA: Peter Smith, 1966), 11, 20–88, 97–99, 158, and passim.

25. Edgar W. Knight, *Public Education in the South* (Boston: Ginn and Company, 1922), 61.

26. Outcome studies did not begin until the early twentieth century. The first systematic study was Sophie van Senden Theis, *How Foster Children Turn Out* (New York: State Charities Aid Association, 1924). See the Adoption History Project website organized by Ellen Herman, http://darkwing.uoregon.edu/~adoption/topics/outcomestudies.htm.

27. Stephen O'Connor, *Orphan Trains: The Story of Charles Loring Brace and the Children He Saved and Failed* (Boston: Houghton Mifflin, 2001), esp. 95–97.

Chapter 2. Recreating Proper Families in England and North America

1. Indenture of James Toppin by the Overseers of Littleport Parish, Cambridge County, January 18, 1762 (Cambridgeshire Record Office, P109/14/35).

2. R. H. Tawney, *The Agrarian Problem in the Sixteenth Century* (1912; repr. New York: Harper and Row, 1967), 46.

3. Billy G. Smith, ed., *Down and Out in Early America* (University Park: Penn State University Press, 2004), especially the introduction, xii–xiii, and the essay by Gary B. Nash, "Poverty and Politics in Early American History," 1–37.

4. Richard Hakluyt, *A Discourse on Western Planting, Written in the Year 1584* (Cambridge, MA: Press of J. Wilson and Son, 1877), spelling modernized.

5. Gabriel Thomas, *An Historical and Geographical Account of the Province and Country of Pensilvania* (London: A. Baldwin, 1698).

6. *An Abridgment of Burn's Justice of the Peace and Parish Officer* (Boston: Joseph Greenleaf, 1773), quotation from the preface.

7. For the significance of Burn's advice in England, see K. D. M. Snell, "Settlement, Poor Law, and the Rural Historian: New Approaches and Opportunities," *Rural History* 3:2 (1992): 145–72.

8. Alexander Hewatt, *An Historical Account of the Rise and Progress of the Colonies of South Carolina and Georgia* (London, 1779), 2:294.

9. Anthony Fletcher, *Reform in the Provinces: The Government of Stuart England* (New Haven: Yale University Press, 1986), 214.

10. Steve Hindle, *On the Parish? The Micro-Politics of Poor Relief in Rural England, c. 1550–1750* (Oxford: Oxford University Press, 2004), 15–95.

11. Felicity Heal, *Hospitality in Early Modern England* (Oxford: Oxford University Press, 1990); and Hindle, *On the Parish?* 105–9.

12. Steve Hindle, "'Waste' Children? Pauper Apprenticeship under the Elizabethan Poor Laws, c. 1598–1697," in *Women, Work, and Wages in England, c. 1600–1850,* ed. Penny Lane, Neil Raven, and Keith Snell (Woodbridge, UK: Boydell and Brewer, 2004), 15–46; and Hindle, *On the Parish?* 191–226.

13. *The Book of the General Lawes and Libertyes Concerning the Inhabitants of the Massachusets* (Cambridge, 1648), 11.

14. Grand Assembly Act XXVII, passed March 1645–46, reproduced in *Colony Laws of Virginia, 1619–1660,* ed. John D. Cushing (Wilmington, DE: Michael Glazier, 1978), 336–37.

15. The texts of all laws are reproduced in "The Colony Laws of North America" series, edited by John D. Cushing and published in Wilmington, Delaware, by Michael D. Glazier in 1978, as follows: "An Act for Relief of the Poor" [1705], *The Earliest Printed Laws of Pennsylvania, 1681–1713,* 79; "An Act for Relief of the Poor" [1709], *The Earliest Printed Laws of New Jersey, 1703–1722,* 7; "An Act for the better Relief of the Poor of this Province" [1712], *The Earliest Printed Laws of South Carolina, 1692–1734,* 341; "An Act for Regulating Town-ships, Choice of Town Officers, and setting forth their Power" [1719], *Acts and Laws of New Hampshire, 1680–1726,* 156; and "An Act for Relief of the Poor" [ca. 1741], *The Earliest Printed Laws of Delaware, 1704–1741,* 221.

16. Hindle, *On the Parish?* 121, 152.

17. Richard Harvey, "English Pre-Industrial Ballads on Poverty, 1500–1700," *The Historian* 41 (1984): 539–61.

18. Scattered legislation during the colonial period addressed begging—for example, Connecticut passed a law against beggars in the late 1600s—but in 1699, New York's governor, the Earl of Bellomont, noted that the New York General Assembly rejected his proposal to construct workhouses because "there is no such thing as a beggar in this town or country." Quoted in Robert E. Cray Jr., *Paupers and Poor Relief in New York City and Its Rural Environs, 1700–1830* (Philadelphia: Temple University Press, 1988), 34. References to begging and legislation against it become much more common in the post-Revolutionary period.

19. Hindle, *On the Parish?* 66–76, 195.

20. Hindle, *On the Parish?* 27–43, 300–360.

21. Josiah Henry Benton, *Warning Out in New England, 1656–1817* (1911; repr. Freeport, NY: Books for Libraries Press, 1970), 10–11; and Ruth Wallis Herndon, *Unwelcome Americans: Living on the Margin in Early New England* (Philadelphia: University of Pennsylvania Press, 2001), 4–10.

22. Hindle, *On the Parish?* 193–95.

23. Hindle, *On the Parish?* 206.

24. John E. Murray and Ruth Wallis Herndon, "Markets for Children in Early America: A Political Economy of Pauper Apprenticeship," *Journal of Economic History* 62:2 (June 2002): 356–82; and John E. Murray, "Fates of Orphans: Poor Children in Antebellum Charleston," *Journal of Interdisciplinary History* 33 (2003): 519–45.

25. Hindle, *On the Parish?* 209–10, 224, 390–93.

26. *"This Little Commonwealth': Layston Parish Memorandum Book, 1607–c. 1650 & 1704–c. 1747*, ed. Heather Falvery and Steve Hindle (Hertfordshire Record Publications 19, Hertford, 2003), 66.

27. E. M. Leonard, *The Early History of English Poor Relief* (Cambridge, UK: Cambridge University Press, 1900), 237–66; S. and B. Webb, *English Local Government Volume VII: English Poor Law History Part I: The Old Poor Law* (London: Longmans Green, 1927); and E. M. Hampson, *The Treatment of Poverty in Cambridgeshire, 1597–1834* (Cambridge, UK: Cambridge University Press, 1934), 152–64, 268–69.

28. Paul Slack, "Poverty and Politics in Salisbury, 1597–1666," in *Crisis and Order in English Towns, 1500–1700: Essays in Urban History*, ed. Peter Clark and Paul Slack (London: Routledge, 1972), 117–63; Peter Clark, "Migration in England during the Late Seventeenth and Early Eighteenth Centuries," reprinted in *Migration and Society in Early Modern England*, ed. Peter Clark and David Souden (London: Hutchinson, 1987), 213–52; Keith Wrightson and David Levine, *Poverty and Piety in an English Village: Terling, 1525–1700* (1979; repr. Oxford: Oxford University Press, 1995); Tim Wales, "Poverty, Poor Relief and the Life-Cycle: Some Evidence from Seventeenth-Century Norfolk," in *Land, Kinship and Life-Cycle*, ed. R. M. Smith (Cambridge: Cambridge University Press, 1984), 351–404; and A. L. Beier, *Masterless Men: The Vagrancy Problem in England, 1560–1640* (London: Methuen, 1985).

29. Wales, "Poverty, Poor Relief, and the Life-Cycle"; and W. Newman-Brown, "The Receipt of Poor Relief and Family Situation: Aldenham, Hertfordshire, 1630–90," in *Land, Kinship, and Life-Cycle*, ed. R. M. Smith, 405–22.

30. See, for example, Pamela Sharpe, "Poor Children as Apprentices in Colyton, 1598–1830," *Continuity and Change* 6:2 (1991): 253–70; and Hindle, "'Waste' Children?"

31. Dalton's gloss on the judges' resolutions of 1633 is cited in R. E. Leader, *History of the Company of Cutlers in Hallamshire in the County of York* (Sheffield: private publication, 1906) 1:i, 57n.

32. 39 Elizabeth I, c. 3 (1598), secs. i, iv. Emphasis added.

33. *An Ease for Overseers of the Poore Abstracted From the Statutes* (Cambridge, 1601), 27.

34. Historical Manuscripts Commission, *Report on the Manuscripts of the Marquess of Lothian Preserved at Blickling* (London: His Majesty's Stationery Office, 1905), 76; and William Lambarde, *Eirenarcha* (London, 1599), 206ff.

35. R. C. Johnson, "The Transportation of Vagrant Children from London to Virginia, 1618–1622," in *Early Stuart Studies: Essays in Honour of David Harris Willson*, ed. H. S. Reinmuth (Minneapolis: University of Minnesota Press, 1970), 142.

36. Hindle, *On the Parish?* 213.

37. See chapter 1, table 1.2.

38. Hindle, *On the Parish?* 213–14.

39. See chapter 1, table 1.2.

40. Hindle, *On the Parish?* 216.

41. Murray and Herndon, "Markets for Children," 370.

42. Gervase Markham, *The English Husbandman. The First Part* (London, 1613), sig. D4b. Emphasis added.

43. Mary B. Rose, "Social Policy and Business: Parish Apprenticeship and the Early Factory System, 1750–1834," *Business History* 31:4 (1989): 5–32.

44. Hindle, *On the Parish?* 215–16.

45. Christopher Brooks, "Apprenticeship, Social Mobility, and the Middling Sort, 1550–1800," in *The Middling Sort of People: Culture, Society, and Politics in England, 1550–1800*, ed. Jonathan Barry and Christopher Brooks (London and New York: Macmillan, 1994), 52–83. Cf. Sara Horrell, Jane Humphries, and Hans-Joachim Voth, "Destined for Deprivation: Human Capital Formation and Intergenerational Poverty in Nineteenth Century England," *Explorations in Economic History* 38:3 (2001): 339–65.

46. Margaret Spufford, "First Steps in Literacy: The Reading and Writing Experiences of the Humblest Seventeenth-Century Autobiographers," *Social History* 4 (1979): 407–35.

47. Joan Simon, "From Charity School to Workhouse in the 1720s: The SPCK and Mr. Marriott's Solution," *History of Education* 17 (1988): 113–29. On American schooling, see chapter 1 of this book.

48. Hindle, *On the Parish?* 367–80.

49. For example, after 1801, Boston indentures of poor children no longer included a lengthy vice clause—stipulating that the child not play cards or dice games, spend time in taverns, commit fornication, or get married—that had been standard in contracts to that point. From then on, the indenture stated only that the child was bound "after the Manner of an Apprentice to Dwell and Serve." "Indentures of Poor Children Bound out as Apprentices by the Overseers of the Poor of the Town of Boston [1734–1805]," Rare Book Division, Boston Public Library, Boston, Massachusetts, vol. 6, p. 139.

50. Hindle, *On the Parish?* 217.

51. Murray and Herndon, "Markets for Children," 378–79.

52. Hindle, *On the Parish?* 337–53.

53. For this suggestion, see Hindle, *On the Parish?* 219.

54. Beier, *Masterless Men,* 57–65.

Chapter 3. "Proper" Magistrates and Masters

1. The Boston indentures are in a six-volume collection, "Indentures of Poor Children Bound out as Apprentices by the Overseers of the Poor of the Town of Boston [1734–1805]," located in the Rare Book Division at the Boston Public Library; these were the subject of a major study by Lawrence Towner, "The Indentures of Boston's Poor Apprentices, 1734–1805," *Colonial Society of Massachusetts Publications* 43 (1966): 417–68. New Haven indentures are at the New Haven Colony Historical Society. Wethersfield, New London, Bolton, and Tolland indentures are at the Connecticut State Archives. Providence indentures are at the Rhode Island Historical Society and are written into the Providence town council records at Providence City Hall. There are no extant indentures for South Kingstown, Glocester, and Westerly; however, the town council records (housed at the individual town halls) contain orders to bind out children, with specific details about the contracts. These indentures do not constitute all contracts enacted between 1720 and 1820 in the study towns; many others were enacted but not preserved.

2. Of the 2,114 indentures, 53 percent (1,123) come from Boston, the most populous town in the region. See Towner, "Indentures of Boston's Poor Apprentices." Another 19 percent of the indentures (394) originated in Connecticut—New Haven and New London (seaports), and Wethersfield, Bolton, and Tolland (inland agrarian towns). The final 28 percent of the indentures (599) originated in Rhode Island—Providence (seaport), Glocester (inland agrarian town), South Kingstown (coastal agrarian town), and greater Westerly (coastal trading center). As stated, these 2,114 indentures do not constitute all contracts enacted between 1720 and 1820 in the study towns; the town records make reference to other indentures that were enacted, without providing details that allow analysis.

3. Connecticut Code of Laws [1642, 1650], *Public Records of the Colony of Connecticut,* vol. 1 (1636–65), ed. J. Hammond Trumbull (Hartford: Brown and Parsons, 1850), 520–21.

4. *The Acts and Resolves, Public and Private, of the Province of the Massachusetts Bay (1691–1714)* (Boston: Wright and Potter, 1869), 1:67.

5. "Laws Made and Past by the General Assembly of His Majesties Colony of Rhode-Island...Begun and Held at Newport, the First Day of March 1662," *Acts and Laws, of His Majesties Colony of Rhode-Island, and Providence-Plantations in America* (Boston: John Allen, 1679), 10.

6. William Blackstone, *Commentaries on the Laws of England in Four Books* [1765], 1st American ed. (Philadelphia: Robert Bell, 1771), 1:446–60; Tapping Reeve, *The Law of Baron and Femme; of Parent and Child; of Guardian and Ward; of Master and Servant; and of the Powers of Courts of Chancery* (New Haven: Oliver Steele, 1816), 283–89; and James Kent, *Commentaries on American Law* (New York: O. Halsted, 1832), 2:189–208.

7. John J. McCusker, ed., "Colonial Statistics," in *Historical Statistics of the United States: From Colonial Times to the Present*, ed. Susan B. Carter et al. (New York: Cambridge University Press, 2006), 5:651–55.

8. On the underlying causes of poverty and misfortune in eighteenth-century New England, see Ruth Wallis Herndon, *Unwelcome Americans: Living on the Margin in Early New England* (Philadelphia: University of Pennsylvania Press, 2001), 121–25.

9. Jay Coughtry, *The Notorious Triangle: Rhode Island and the African Slave Trade, 1700–1807* (Philadelphia: Temple University Press, 1981); and Joanne Pope Melish, *Disowning Slavery: Gradual Emancipation and "Race" in New England, 1780–1860* (Ithaca: Cornell University Press, 1998).

10. "An Act authorizing the manumission of negroes, mulattoes, and others, and for the gradual abolition of slavery" [1784], John Russell Bartlett, ed., *Records of the State of Rhode Island and Providence Plantations in New England*, 10:1784–92 (Providence Press Co., 1865), 7–8; and "An Act concerning Indian, Molatto, and Negro Servants and Slaves" [1784], Sect. 13, *Acts and Laws of the State of Connecticut, in America* (New London: Timothy Green, 1784), 233–35. For an overview of gradual emancipation enactments in each of the northern states, see Arthur Zilversmit, *The First Emancipation: The Abolition of Slavery in the North* (Chicago: University of Chicago Press, 1967). Zilversmit summarizes the effect of these laws on children of slaves: "Masters could have the services of young Negroes merely for the expense of raising them to working age," 200.

11. Town Council Meeting (hereafter TCM) August 16, 1800, Providence Town Council Record (hereafter TCR) 7:491. On the problem of free people of color being kidnapped and sold as slaves, see Melish, *Disowning Slavery*, 101–6; and Carol Wilson, *Freedom at Risk: The Kidnapping of Free Blacks in America, 1780–1865* (Lexington: University Press of Kentucky, 1994). Wilson discusses the special vulnerability of children to this kind of kidnapping and notes that Rhode Island was one of the few states that never adopted an anti-kidnapping law, 13–15, 67–68.

12. Peter Temin, "The Industrialization of New England, 1830–1880," in *Engines of Enterprise: An Economic History of New England*, ed. Peter Temin (Cambridge, MA: Harvard University Press, 2000), 109–52; Thomas Dublin, *Transforming Women's Work: New England Lives in the Industrial Revolution* (Ithaca: Cornell University Press, 1994); and Jonathan Prude, *The Coming of Industrial Order: Town and Factory Life in Rural Massachusetts, 1810–1860* (Cambridge, UK: Cambridge University Press, 1983).

13. "An Act in addition to an Act, entitled 'An Act relating to masters and servants, and apprentices,'" *Acts and Laws, Made and passed in and by the General Court or Assembly of the State of Connecticut* [May 1813] (Hartford: Hudson and Goodwin, 1813), 117–18.

14. Carl F. Kaestle, *Pillars of the Republic: Common Schools and American Society, 1780–1860* (New York: Hill and Wang, 1983); see also Temin, "Industrialization of New England," 138–41.

15. "An Act for Employing and Providing for the Poor in the Town of Boston" [1736], *The Acts and Resolves, Public and Private, of the Province of the Massachusetts Bay* (Boston: Wright and Potter, 1874) (1715–41): 2:756–58.

16. "An Act in addition to the Several Acts or Laws of this Province, impowering the Selectmen or Overseers of the Poor to Bind Poor Children Apprentices" [1772], *The Acts and Resolves, Public and Private, of the Province of the Massachusetts Bay* (Boston: Wright and Potter, 1886) (1769–80): 5:161–62.

17. See for example, the 1759 indentures of Mary Martin, Ann Ingersoll, John Davis, and Susanna Perraway, Boston OP 2:121, 2:123, 2:125, 2:128.

18. "An Act, directing what shall be a legal Settlement; and for Removal of poor Persons, and the Method of binding out poor Children" [1765], *Acts and Laws of the English Colony of Rhode Island and Providence Plantations* (Newport: Samuel Hall, 1767), 232; and "An Act providing for the Relief, Support, Employment and Removal of the Poor" [1798], *The Public Laws of the State of Rhode Island* (Providence: Carter and Wilkinson, 1798), 348–51.

19. "An Act for Maintaining and Supporting the Poor," *Acts and Laws of Connecticut* (1784), 193.

20. TCM March 29, 1762, Hopkinton TCR 1:78.

21. Letter from Isaac Stone to Boston overseers of the poor, January 1, 1789, with Indenture of Thomas Wallis, Boston OP 5:91.

22. TCM June 11, 1753 and August 20, 1753, South Kingstown TCR 4:233, 4:237.

23. Examples include Indenture of Abner Brown, September 6, 1762, New London; Indenture of John Roberts, June 27, 1781, Tolland; Indenture of Jane Sigourney, October 16, 1788, Boston OP 5:97; Order to bind Thomas Church, TCM January 4, 1796, Providence TCR 7:72.

24. Examples include Order to bind John Seten, TCM May 13, 1751, South Kingstown TCR 4:200; Indenture of Elizabeth Barber, December 9, 1776, Boston OP 4:143.

25. Indenture of Daniel Trudgeon, November 26, 1751, New Haven Indentures, Folder C; Indenture of Sophia Havens, August 7, 1797, PTP 28:48; Indenture of Betsy Colton, November 23, 1804, Bolton.

26. Indenture of Mary Dennis, April 22, 1780, New London; Indenture of Hannah [Sampson], May 3, 1763, Wethersfield 619; Indenture of Mary Covel, June 21, 1786, Boston OP 5:72.

27. Letter from Paul Mandell to Capt. John Hastings, February 28, 1787, filed with Indenture of William Dunn, February 1778, Boston OP 4:181.

28. "An Act for Employing and Providing for the Poor in the Town of Boston" [1736], *Acts and Resolves of Massachusetts*, 2:758.

29. Edward F. Cook Jr., *Fathers of the Towns: Leadership and Community Structure in Eighteenth-Century New England* (Baltimore: Johns Hopkins University Press, 1976); Bruce C. Daniels, "Diversity and Democracy: Officeholding Patterns among Selectmen in Eighteenth-Century Connecticut," in *Power and Status: Officeholding in Colonial America*, ed. Bruce C. Daniels (Middletown, CT: Wesleyan University Press, 1978), 36–52; and Ruth Wallis Herndon, "Governing the Affairs of the Town: Continuity and Change in Rhode Island, 1750–1800" (Ph.D. dissertation, American University, 1992).

30. The Boston OP records include character endorsements from 585 masters who applied for pauper apprentices from the Boston Almshouse. Until the mid-1760s, these endorsements were all written from scratch; after that, most were preprinted with boilerplate language: "_____ is a Man of Sober Life and Conversation...we can recommend him as a fit Person to bind an Apprentice to...."

31. John Langworthy "broke up housekeeping" and gave up his indentures for six-year-old Martha Deake and seven-year-old Mary Deake because "his wife not retaining her common reason," he could no longer provide a proper home for the girls. TCM February 15, 1768, Hopkinton TCR 1:117.

32. Order to bind Betsey Richmond (TCM May 2, 1785, Providence TCR 5:313); Indenture of Sarah Smith (April 14, 1746, New Haven B).

33. Petersham residents' endorsement of James Thompson, master of Cornelius Kellihorn. October 1, 1768, Boston OP 3:136.

34. Indenture of Samuel Hamlin to John Foreland, July 3, 1704, Overseer of the Poor Records, Boston Public Library, BOS W2 Box 3.

35. Laurel Thatcher Ulrich, "Wheels, Looms, and the Gender Division of Labor in Eighteenth-Century New England," *William and Mary Quarterly* 55 (1998): 3–38.

36. E. Jennifer Monaghan, *Learning to Read and Write in Colonial America* (Amherst and Worcester: University of Massachusetts Press and American Antiquarian Society, 2005).

37. Samuel Freeman provides model apprenticeship indentures that prescribe these varying standards of education. Boston officials departed from custom by promising female apprentices reading, writing, and cyphering after 1785, probably because Boston magistrates, themselves highly educated, desired to set a high standard of education for all under their jurisdiction. Freeman, *The Town Officer; or the Power and Duty of Selectmen, Town Clerks...and other Town Officers* (Portland, ME: Benjamin Tiscomb Jr., 1791), 35.

38. Boston Town Meeting, March 11, 1723, Boston Town Records (1700–28), 423.

39. Robert J. Cottrol, *The Afro-Yankees: Providence's Black Community in the Antebellum Era* (Westport, CT: Greenwood Press, 1982); Coughtry, *Notorious Triangle*; Herndon, *Unwelcome Americans*; Ruth Wallis Herndon and Ella Wilcox Sekatau, "The Right to a Name: Narragansett People and Rhode Island Officials in the Revolutionary Era," *Ethnohistory* 44:3 (1997): 433–62; and Melish, *Disowning Slavery*.

40. According to contemporary Euro-American estimates, in 1760 people of color constituted 2.3 percent of the population in Massachusetts, 2.7 percent in Connecticut, and 7.6 percent in Rhode Island. Percentages are extrapolated from statistics provided in McCusker, "Colonial Statistics," 5:651–53; see also Evarts B. Greene and Virginia D. Harrington, *American Population before the Federal Census of 1790* (Gloucester, MA: Peter Smith, 1966), 30, 61, 69–70. Lorenzo Greene calculated that "Negroes" comprised 7.3 percent of Rhode Island's population in 1782 and 6.3 percent of the population in 1790. Greene, *The Negro in Colonial New England* (New York: Atheneum, 1969), 87.

41. Indenture of Isaiah Thomas, June 4, 1756, Boston OP 2:74; see Towner, "Indentures of Boston's Poor Apprentices," 417–18.

42. Indenture of Phinehas Edwards, [March 1765], miscellaneous indentures, Hopkinton Town Clerk's office; Order to bind out Phinehas Edwards, May 21, 1764, June 25, 1764, and October 8, 1764, Hopkinton TCR 1:61, 1:62, 1:67; Hopkinton Town Vital Records 1:117; Town meeting (hereafter TM) October 25, 1781, Hopkinton Town Meeting Record (hereafter TMR) 1:216; TM June 4, 1782, Hopkinton TMR 1:229 and passim; and *Civil and Military List of Rhode Island, 1647–1800*, ed. Joseph Jencks Smith (Providence: Preston and Rounds, 1900), 491, 502, 527.

43. Indenture of Thomas Banks, July 1, 1761, Boston OP 2:169; and Ruth Wallis Herndon, "Children and Masters: Tracking Eighteenth-Century New Englanders through Indentures," *New England Ancestors* 4:1 (Winter 2003): 22–24.

44. Herndon, *Unwelcome Americans*, 20, 206.

Chapter 4. Orphans in City and Countryside
in Nineteenth-Century Maryland

1. Samples of apprentice indentures from these four counties constitute the primary database for analyzing apprenticeship in the nineteenth century. Samples from each county represent roughly a third of all indentures registered with the Orphans' Courts between 1794 and 1870, the ending date of this study. They total 7,495 indentures, of which 6,245 are from Baltimore City and County, 757 from Washington County, 257 from Talbot County, and 236 from Prince George's County.

2. For an in-depth study of Talbot county artisans between 1760 and 1810, see Jean B. Russo, "Chesapeake Artisans in the Aftermath of the Revolution," in *The Transforming Hand of Revolution: Reconstructing the American Revolution as a Social Movement*, ed. Ronald Hoffman and Peter Albert (Charlottesville: University Press of Virginia, 1996), 118–54. Also see Russo, "A Model Planter: Edward Lloyd IV of Maryland, 1770–1796," *William and Mary Quarterly* 49 (1992): 62–88. For Baltimore's impact on rural economies, Christine Daniels, "'WANTED: A Blacksmith Who Understands Plantation Work': Artisans in Maryland, 1700–1810," *William and Mary Quarterly* 50 (1993): 743–67; and T. Stephen Whitman, *The Price of Freedom: Slavery and Manumission in Baltimore and Early National Maryland* (Lexington: University Press of Kentucky, 1997), esp. 8–13.

3. The city's slave population nearly quadrupled from 1,255 in 1790 to 4,672 in 1810. Craftsmen held one-third of these workers and hired more from widows, estate guardians, and others reliant on slave-generated income. As for craft apprenticeship, some two thousand boys and young men were serving under articles of indenture at a single moment in the early 1800s, nearly one in three of the city's adolescent males. On the role of bound labor in early national Baltimore, see Whitman, *Price of Freedom*, 8–32.

4. Whitman, *Price of Freedom*, 13–23.

5. About 56 percent of the apprenticeships in Baltimore between 1800 and 1830 were voluntarily signed by a craftsman and a boy acting with parental consent. But curriers (leather workers) relied heavily on court-ordered indentures: only twelve of twenty-nine curriers' indentures (41 percent) were voluntary. Some 60 percent of curriers with assessable wealth owned slaves, a disproportionately large number. Tobacco manufacturing trades like cigar- and snuffmaking exhibited similar patterns. Only 38 percent of these indentures were voluntary, the second-lowest proportion among Baltimore's crafts, while 92 percent of tobacco manufacturers held slaves. Nearly half of saddlers' apprentices were voluntary, which still placed them among crafts

disproportionately likely to take court-bound apprentices. At the same time, 80 percent of saddlers held slaves, again a disproportionately high percentage. Data drawn from 3,388 indentures registered for thirty-seven trades in thirteen sample years in Baltimore between 1800 and 1830. The thirty-seven trades were those in which an average of two or more bindings per sample year occurred. Of these contracts, 1,913 were voluntary, while 1,475 were ordered by the courts.

6. Millwrights ranked twenty-ninth of thirty-seven crafts in slaveholding propensity, and second in voluntary indentures. No coachmaker on the 1813 tax rolls held slaves, and they were third in voluntary indentures. Data taken from Baltimore County Indentures, registered in the following years: 1800, 1802, 1805, 1808, 1810, 1813, 1816, 1818, 1820, 1823, 1826, 1828, and 1830. On the propensity of craftsmen to hold slaves and bind apprentices, see Whitman, *Price of Freedom*, 24–25, 167–69.

7. Of 1,913 voluntary bindings, 955 (50 percent) lessened the master's obligation in one or more areas, such as maintenance, craft training, education, or freedom dues. The courts permitted comparable leeway in 421 of 1,475 indentures (28 percent).

8. For the monetizing of the apprentice relationship, see W. J. Rorabaugh, *The Craft Apprentice: From Franklin to the Machine Age in America* (New York: Oxford University Press, 1986), 32–75. Rorabaugh's findings are based chiefly on data from northeastern cities.

9. Of 1,913 voluntary bindings of boys, masters made no educational commitments, or something less than the full legal promise of teaching an apprentice to "read, write, and cypher" in 688 cases (36 percent). Freedom dues were eliminated or reduced in 407 cases (21 percent). Commutation of maintenance into wage payments, or elimination of promises to clothe the apprentice occurred in only 86 indentures (5 percent).

10. Of 837 gradual manumissions registered with the Baltimore County court between 1789 and 1830, 85 percent stipulated a term of five years or more; 52 percent a term of more than ten years. Baltimore County Court, Miscellaneous Court Papers, 1789–1830.

11. In the four years sampled in that decade, 1,276 white boys were indented, 319 per year on average, at an average age of 14.6 years and for an average term of 6.4 years, suggesting that 2,042 white boys were serving at any one time. The sample years are 1810, 1813, 1816, and 1818, Baltimore County Orphans' Court.

12. Interpolated census figures indicate that there were an average of 3,287 white boys in the city between the ages of fourteen and twenty-one during the 1810s.

13. Of 2,321 indentures of white boys for sample years between 1798 and 1818, 2,262 promised training in a specified craft, skill, or mercantile occupation. Only 26 bound a boy to learn farming or husbandry and 23 to service or "waiting," while 9 specified no trade, and 1 committed a boy to learn "common labour." Overall, 97.4 percent of indentures promised craft training.

14. Data drawn from a sample of 1,687 boys bound by the Orphans' Courts in Baltimore County between 1794 and 1830 and a sample of 150 such bindings in Talbot County.

15. Talbot County Indentures, Indenture of Eli Stevens, 1830, and Indenture of Henry Gassaway, 1836.

16. Replicating the estimating process used for the 1810s, above, produces an estimate of 330 white boys serving apprenticeships at any one time in the 1850s, about 2.5 percent of the white male population between ages fourteen and twenty-one.

17. In 1858, the Orphans' Court of the city of Baltimore registered 66 indentures of white boys, of which 49 (74 percent) were directed by the court or a surrogate institution such as the House of Refuge. In the 1860s, in three sample years, only 19 of 202 (9 percent) indentures of white boys were entered into voluntarily by a parent or relative.

18. In 1830, the 215 bindings entered suggest that about 1,073 boys were serving apprenticeships, using the estimating procedure described earlier in this chapter. Census data for 1830 suggest that there were 5,772 white males between the ages of fourteen and twenty-one, so the proportion of boys serving would be 18.6 percent.

19. This standardized language appears in virtually every indenture of the Union mills. See Indenture of David Stinchcomb to the Union Manufacturing Company, Baltimore County Court Indenture Records, 1810.

20. All of these indentures occurred between 1808 and 1817 and are recorded in the Baltimore County Indenture records.

21. Altogether, these two firms bound out 82 boys between 1809 and 1815, all voluntarily.

22. See 1820 Census of Manufactures for Baltimore City and Baltimore County.

23. The indenture records reveal only four indentures of girls to cotton manufacturers. In 1810, the Washington Cotton Manufacturing Company bound three daughters of one George Wilson, with his consent, and in 1813, Lewis Lannay, proprietor of a calico printing factory, bound Margaret Scott to learn "those branches of the cotton trade it is appropriate for a female to learn."

24. For an excellent account of Baltimore's economic development, see Gary L. Browne, *Baltimore in the Nation, 1789–1861* (Chapel Hill: University of North Carolina Press, 1980), esp. 55–58, 114–38 on the impact of the textile industry.

25. For a discussion of the substitution of apprenticed servants for slaves, see Stephanie Cole, "Servants and Slaves: Domestic Service in the Border South, 1800–1850" (Ph.D. dissertation, University of Florida, 1994), ch. 4.

26. For an example, see Indenture of Frisby Robbins to Robert Kneeland, Baltimore County Indentures, 1816.

27. Of 657 voluntarily bound white boys in Baltimore County between 1800 and 1809, based on sample years 1800, 1802, 1805, and 1808, 577 (87.8 percent) were promised some kind of freedom dues. Of 390 court-initiated indentures, 370 of 390 (94.7 percent) received such a promise.

28. Of 80 white boys voluntarily bound but promised no freedom dues in Baltimore County between 1800 and 1809, 24 (30 percent) were eighteen or older when bound. The comparable figure for those promised freedom dues was 57 out of 579 (9.8 percent). Average age at binding of the first group was 16.4; the second group averaged 14.6 years of age.

29. Data drawn from Baltimore County, Indentures, sample years 1800, 1802, 1805, and 1808.

30. Of 62 boys aged eighteen or older at binding, 17 (27.4 percent) received no freedom dues, for sample years 1820, 1823, 1826, and 1828 in Baltimore County; 71 of 310 (22.9 percent) younger than eighteen received no freedom dues. The upward trend in duesless indentures after 1820 is a statistically significant movement at the 95 percent level of confidence, as measured by a chi square test.

31. A sample of 742 indentures of white boys in Baltimore during the period 1840–70 reveals that 22 of 210 voluntarily bound boys (10 percent) were promised "customary" freedom dues, while 120 (57 percent) were to receive clothes, money, both, or a choice between the two. In court-initiated cases, 74 of 532 indentures (14 percent) promised customary dues, while 428 (80 percent) specified clothes and/or amounts of money. A similar pattern applied for white girls: 3 of 39 (8 percent) voluntarily bound apprentices and 37 of 248 (15 percent) indented by courts were to receive customary dues.

32. In the period 1800–20, only 30 of 362 (8 percent) female apprentices in Baltimore were promised any math education. Between 1820 and 1850, that proportion rose to 44 percent (136 of 306).

33. For a comprehensive account of this subject, see Anne M. Boylan, *Sunday School: The Formation of an American Institution, 1790–1880* (New Haven: Yale University Press, 1990).

34. Carl F. Kaestle, *Pillars of the Republic: Common Schools and American Society, 1780–1860* (New York: Hill and Wang, 1983), 37–44; and Tina H. Sheller, "The Origins of Public Education in Baltimore, 1825–1829," *Maryland Historical Magazine* 77 (1982): 23–42.

35. *A Hundred Years of St. Mary's Orphan Asylum of Baltimore, being A Historical Sketch*, issued by St. Mary's Orphan Asylum (Baltimore, 1918), passim.

36. See Indentures of George Nailer in 1826, Thomas Smyth in 1820, and Christian Schmidt in 1823, all in Baltimore County, Indentures, for the appropriate years.

37. See Indenture of Hezekiah Bowman to John Kanter, promising "six months day school and eight months night school," or that of Washington Corse to William Armour, promising "six months of school after the said apprentice shall be 18." Washington County, Indentures, 1830 for Bowman, and 1812 for Corse.

38. A sample of 1,323 voluntarily contracted indentures of white boys registered in Baltimore County between 1800 and 1819 revealed 15 (1.1 percent) in which masters avoided promises of clothing or offered cash in lieu of clothing. In the same sample, 18 indentures (1.4 percent)

promised payments of wages to an apprentice or his father in lieu of some or all of the apprentice's maintenance.

39. Between 1820 and 1839, a sample of 710 voluntary indentures of white boys revealed 628 (88.5 percent) that promised full maintenance, while 54 (7.6 percent) fell short of clothing promises in some way, and 28 (3.9 percent) promised wages in lieu of maintenance. Court-initiated indentures in the same sample years numbered 678, of which 645 (95.1 percent) made full maintenance promises, while 22 (3.3 percent) promised no clothes or cash in lieu thereof; 11 (1.6 percent) promised wages in lieu of some or all maintenance.

40. A sample of 210 voluntarily indented white boys reveals 175 (83.3 percent) receiving full maintenance in the period 1840–70 in Baltimore; for institutional indentures the proportion is 96.6 percent, 514 of 532.

41. Two white girls in the sample of 877 nineteenth-century Baltimore indentures were offered money in lieu of clothing.

42. Rorabaugh, *Craft Apprentice;* Charles G. Steffen, *The Mechanics of Baltimore: Workers and Politics in the Age of Revolution, 1763–1812* (Urbana: University of Illinois Press, 1984); and Richard B. Stott, *Workers in the Metropolis: Class, Ethnicity, and Youth in Antebellum New York City* (Ithaca: Cornell University Press, 1990).

43. Forty-three indentures in years sampled between 1800 and 1819 indicated that an apprentice had lived in another county than Baltimore until entering into his indenture.

44. Christine Daniels, "'WANTED: A Blacksmith,'" 743–67.

45. In Talbot County, 81 of 84 voluntary bindings of white boys in years sampled between 1800 and 1850 (96 percent) promised to teach a craft skill.

46. Of 54 white orphans bound by the Talbot County courts and Trustees of the Poor, 34 (63 percent) were to learn farming, husbandry, domestic service, or common labor. The proportions before and after 1820 were 67 percent and 62 percent, respectively. For eighteenth-century patterns, see chapter 10 in this volume.

47. In sample years between 1800 and 1850, 70 of 123 white orphan boys in Talbot and Prince George's Counties (57 percent) had indentures stipulating schooling of some kind. For voluntarily bound boys, 53 of 167 (32 percent) received a promise of education. In Baltimore, 679 of 2,215 boys bound by fathers or kin (31 percent) in sample years from 1800 to 1870 were indentured with no mention of schooling.

48. Of 167 voluntary indentures in Talbot and Prince George's, 22 stipulated a fixed term of schooling.

49. In Talbot and Prince George's Counties combined, only 33 white girls were indented in the years sampled between 1800 and 1850. Fourteen (42 percent) had indentures with educational promises; only three garnered contract language that committed her master to teach her to "cast accounts."

50. A combined sample of 290 bindings of white boys in Prince George's and Talbot Counties yielded 94 of 123 (74 percent) bound by courts and promised freedom dues, compared to 77 of 167 (46 percent) bound out voluntarily by kinfolk. For white girls, 25 of 33 (76 percent) were promised freedom dues, of whom 7 (21 percent) had the option of taking a suit of clothes or an equivalent value in cash, in amounts of five to twenty dollars.

51. Of 290 cases in these counties, 16 (5.5 percent) involved less than full maintenance on the part of the master.

52. Of 564 indentures of white boys between 1794 and 1848, 68 (12 percent) designated an annual number of days of work release for the apprentice, in order to work in the harvest. Both judges and parents entered into such agreements.

53. For a recent example of this literature, see Gillian Hamilton, "Enforcement in Apprenticeship Contracts: Were Runaways a Serious Problem? Evidence from Montreal," *Journal of Economic History* 55 (1995): 551–74. In a related vein for immigrant servants, see Farley Grubb, "The End of European Immigrant Servitude in the United States: An Economic Analysis of Market Collapse, 1772–1835," *Journal of Economic History* 54 (1994): 794–824.

54. The special issue of *Journal of the Early Republic* on "Capitalism in the Early Republic," 16:2 (1996), contains several valuable essays on artisan republicanism and reviewing the literature, in particular Paul Gilje, "The Rise of Capitalism in the Early Republic," 159–82; and Richard Stott, "Artisans and Capitalist Development," 257–72.

55. Runaway apprentice notices in newspapers in Baltimore, Annapolis, Easton, and Hagerstown generated a total of 770 advertisements, of which 44 (6 percent) announced a runaway girl.

56. In Washington County, 66 percent of runaways whose age was specified by masters advertising for them were between sixteen and nineteen (136 of 205); in Baltimore County, 62 percent were in this age bracket (279 of 450). Neither figure deviates significantly from the age distribution of apprentices who did not run. In both urban and rural settings, apprentices were more likely to run in the July-September quarter than at other times: 32 percent of Washington County runaways (81 of 250) and 37 percent in Baltimore County (205 of 550). In neither Washington County nor Baltimore County were apprentices significantly more likely to run from any of the most popular trades than the average runaway rates for all apprentices in the same county.

57. Rewards of one dollar or less were offered by 45 percent of Baltimore masters (241 of 531) who specified a sum payable for the rendition of a runaway apprentice. In Washington County, fully 67 percent of the rewards were under a dollar (164 of 245), a statistically significant difference. Ads placed by James Zwisler seeking Archibald DeButts, *Hagerstown Torch,* January 1830; by Nicholas Willis seeking Joseph Hutchinson, *Maryland Herald,* August 1793; by John Wolford, bootmaker, seeking Henry Keefer, *Hagerstown Torch,* April 1821; and by Joseph Little, wagonmaker, seeking James Furlong, *Hagerstown Torch,* March 1821.

58. For an interpretation stressing growing demands for independence by apprentices and declining conditions in the workshop as an explanation for increased apprentice flight, see Rorabaugh, *Craft Apprentice,* 32–75. For a comprehensive list of artisan studies of recent vintage, see Paul Gilje, "Rise of Capitalism," 18n.

59. Based on a total of 1,768 indentures of white boys and 245 runaway ads over the period 1794–1834. The higher rates for the 1815–30 period are statistically significant at the 95 percent confidence level.

60. In Baltimore, 471 white boys were advertised as runaways between 1798 and 1821, a rate of just under 7 percent of the 7,071 indentures recorded during those years. In Washington, the rate for the years 1796–1821 was over 13 percent (148 runaway ads compared to 1,099 indentures recorded). In Talbot, the rate for white boys was over 12 percent (53 runaways of 427 indentures).

61. Data drawn from 525 indentures of white boys in Washington County between 1794 and 1839, of which 48 could be identified as subsequent runaways. With regard to cash freedom dues, 8 percent of boys promised cash dues of less than $20 ran (5 of 66), while 9 percent of those promised larger amounts (28 of 309) did so. Respecting masters' commitment to educate apprentices, 11 percent of boys offered six months or less of schooling ran (17 of 154), compared to 12 percent of those guaranteed more than a year (2 of 16). On cash payments to apprentices, 3 percent of the Washington County indentures promised same (16 of 525) vs. 4 percent of those in Baltimore (165 of 4,459). Even by the 1830s, less than 8 percent of Baltimore indentures stipulated cash payments in lieu of maintenance, or the payment of wages (56 of 735).

62. For Washington County, 30 of 50 runaways whose original indentures appeared in the sample had been bound at age fifteen or younger; overall 200 of 496 did so. For Baltimore, the comparable figures are 44 of 84 runaways first bound at fifteen or younger, compared to 1,321 of 2,590 of all indentures. In Talbot, 3 of 5 runaways with original indentures in the sample had been fifteen or younger, compared to 45 of 88 white boys overall.

63. Seventeen of 27 runaways from the three counties collectively fit this description. Nine of the 50 runaway ad-original indenture matches (18 percent) in Washington County were from second masters, of whom seven practiced a different craft. Only 6 of 84 (7 percent) of comparable Baltimore County matches fit this description.

64. Washington County Indentures, 1809, Release of Jacob Paulus, and 1812, Release of James Weitzel.

65. The Washington County indenture records list 22 such releases, about 3 percent of the sample of indentures.

66. For the period 1798–1830, 59 percent of the bindings of white boys as apprentices in Baltimore represented voluntary contracts between a parent or guardian and a master; in Washington

only 45 percent of the bindings fell into this category (241 of 532). The difference is a statistically significant one at the 95 percent level of confidence. Remarks in court-initiated indentures also show that a child had a living father who was not caring for his son in 6 percent of the Washington County sample, as opposed to barely 2 percent of the Baltimore County cases.

67. Fathers could be described as absent, absconded, in the almshouse, deranged, enlisted in the army, or simply refusing to support their children. Such cases encompassed 6 percent of Washington County indentures (42 of 684) but only 2 percent of Baltimore indentures (66 of 3,301). Boys or their fathers were described in indentures as from outside Washington County in 19 cases (3 percent), while "outsiders" accounted for 65 cases in Baltimore (2 percent).

These data must be used with caution: it is entirely likely that the courts' notes on these subjects are incomplete. Nonetheless, there is no reason to assume that one county's clerks would be less accurate than another's in noting these circumstances; at the very least, the data do not argue against the inferences developed in this essay.

68. In Washington County, 55 percent of ads naming a runaway's prospective destination (11 of 20) indicated flight to a distant family member. Only 6 percent (3 of 52) Baltimore ads did so.

69. Washington County Indentures, 1815, Release of Joseph Gouss.

Chapter 5. Bound Out from the Almshouse

1. Minutes, Trustees of the Poor, Chester County, October 1, 1804; July 1, 1805; October 7, 1807; and Index to Apprentices, Chester County Archives, hereafter CCA.

2. Steward's correspondence, Linton to Baker, March 4, 1856; and Baker to Linton, March 12, 1856, CCA.

3. The Index is more detailed than many other records of apprenticeship arrangements, including names of apprentices and masters; age of apprentices in years, months, and days; date of indenture; the trade or skill to be learned; and additional information deemed important by the clerk. As with other studies using these records, I have assumed that race was white unless otherwise noted, as clerks were generally careful about making racial distinctions.

4. Diane Lindstrom, *Economic Development of the Philadelphia Region, 1810–1850* (New York: Columbia University Press, 1978).

5. Priscilla Clement, *Welfare and the Poor in the Nineteenth-Century City: Philadelphia, 1800–1854* (London: Associated University Presses, 1985); and John K. Alexander, *Render Them Submissive: Responses to Poverty in Philadelphia, 1760–1800* (Amherst: University of Massachusetts Press, 1980). For the disjunction between urban and rural poor relief in another region, see Robert E. Cray Jr., *Paupers and Poor Relief in New York City and its Rural Environs, 1700–1830* (Philadelphia: Temple University Press, 1988).

6. David Rothman, *Discovery of the Asylum: Social Order and Disorder in the New Republic* (Boston and Toronto: Little, Brown, 1971); and Michael Katz, *In the Shadow of the Poorhouse: A Social History of Welfare in America* (New York: Basic Books, 1986).

7. Monique Bourque, "The Creation of the Almshouse: Institutions as Solutions to the Problem of Poverty," *Journal of the Lancaster County Historical Society* 102:2/3 (Summer/Fall 2000), and idem, "Poor Relief 'Without Violating the Rights of Humanity': Almshouse Administration in the Philadelphia Region, 1790–1860," in *Down and Out in Early America*, ed. Billy G. Smith (University Park: Pennsylvania State University Press, 2004), 189–212.

8. Quotation from "Act for the Relief of the Poor" [1771], 8 St.L.5, Ch. 635. The 1798 Chester County poorhouse-enabling legislation stipulated that the trustees of the poor would bind out "such poor children as shall come under their notice or as may now be bound apprentices by the overseers of the poor" under their new county authority (16 St.L.5, Ch. 1971). An 1804 supplement to this enabling legislation specifically cited the 1771 Act for the Relief of the Poor to reaffirm the authority of overseers of the poor over apprentices.

9. For example, the overseers modified existing rules for apprentices' education requirements in the 1807 revisions to the poorhouse bylaws.

10. See, for example, the 1827 will of longtime almshouse clerk Joshua Weaver. File 8090, Wills, CCA.

11. Annual Reports, Trustees of the Poor of Chester County, filed February 1812, February 1813, CCA.

12. Minutes, Trustees of the Poor, Chester County, October 1, 1804; and Index to Apprentices, CCA.

13. Minutes, Trustees of the Poor, Chester County, November 1, 1804; and Index to Apprentices, CCA.

14. Minutes, Trustees of the Poor, Chester County, July 1, 1805, CCA.

15. Minutes, Trustees of the Poor, Chester County, October 7, 1807, CCA.

16. Minutes, Trustees of the Poor, Chester County, December 1, 1804, January 7, 1805, and October 7, 1808, CCA.

17. Index to Apprentices, December 12, 1816, CCA.

18. Annual Reports, Trustees of the Poor of Chester County, filed February 1812, February 1813, CCA; and Admission and Discharge book, April 23, 1830.

19. Annual Report, Trustees of the Poor, Chester County, Filed January 1808, CCA.

20. Minutes, Trustees of the Poor, Chester County, March 4, 1805.

21. Minutes, Trustees of the Poor, Chester County, March 4, 1805, April 1, 1805, June 3, 1805.

22. Directors Correspondence, James Courtney to Thomas Baker, January 24, 1860, and Baker to Courtney, February 10, 1860, CCA.

23. Directors Correspondence, Williamson to Harlan, February 8, 1855; Baker to Williamson, March 2, 1855, CCA.

24. Yarnall to Gregg Clayton, July 20, 1841, CCA. Emphasis added.

25. Minutes, Trustees of the Poor, Chester County, March 4, 1805, CCA.

26. Minutes, Trustees of the Poor, Chester County, December 5, 1803, Chester County Archives, CCA.

27. Minutes, Trustees of the Poor, Chester County, March 3, 1806; and Index to Apprentices, 1800–1825, CCA.

28. Minutes, Trustees of the Poor, Chester County, September 25, 1809; and Index to Apprentices, 1800–1825, CCA.

29. Minutes, Trustees of the Poor, Chester County, October 5, 1812; and Index to Apprentices, 1800–1825, CCA.

30. Minutes, Trustees of the Poor, Chester County, November 26, 1822.

31. Minutes, Trustees of the Poor, Chester County, May 23, 1826, CCA.

32. Directors Correspondence, Hall to Baker, June 17, 1856.

33. Directors Correspondence, Hall to Baker, June 17, 1856.

34. Directors Correspondence, Baker to Hall, June 20, 1856.

35. See, for example, Pay Books, Trustees of the Poor, Chester County, March 2, 1807, CCA.

36. Minutes, Trustees of the Poor, Chester County, March 24, 1818, CCA.

37. Index to Apprentices, 1800–1825, CCA.

38. Index to Apprentices, 1800–1825, CCA.

39. Steward's Book, vol. 2, 1825–1827, December 28, 1824; and Index to Apprentices, 1800–1825, CCA.

40. Steward's Book, vol. 2, 1825–1827, April 5, 1825, CCA.

41. Steward's Book, vol. 2, 1825–1827, June 26, 1827, June 28, 1827; and Annual Report, 1827, CCA.

42. Steward's Book, vol. 2, 1825–1827, June 28, 1827.

43. Annual Reports, Trustees of the Poor, Chester County, 1832, 1835; Steward's Book, vol. 2, 1825–1827, September 26, 1827; and Admissions Index, CCA.

44. Admission and Discharge Book, Chester County almshouse, June 28, 1827, CCA.

45. Sarah Brown to Thomas Baker, Steward of the Chester County almshouse, April 3, 1856, Directors Correspondence, Trustees of the Poor, Chester County, Box 3.

46. Index of Apprentices, 1800–1825, CCA.

47. Directors Correspondence, Dickey to Baker, March 6, 1856; CCA.

48. Directors Correspondence, Dickey to Baker, March 6, 1856; Baker to Dickey, March 14, 1856, CCA.
49. Children of color were likely to be bound slightly earlier than white children (age three), and girls at the same age as boys. When broken down by race and gender, it appears that the median age at binding for all groups was five.
50. Minutes, Trustees of the Poor, Chester County, May 4, 1807; May 21, 1807; and June 1, 1807, CCA.
51. See also Carole Haber and Brian Gratton, "Old Age, Public Welfare, and Race: The Case of Charleston, South Carolina, 1800–1849," *Journal of Social History* 21:2 (1987).
52. This percentage was about the same for Chester County (1.98 percent) and the Delaware Valley in general (2.22 percent). The total number of children under 21 was 189 (of 1,363 inmates) and 476 (of 2,656 inmates), respectively. These numbers are taken from a database including 2,656 inmates represented in surviving almshouse records from Philadelphia's satellite counties for the years 1790–1860. See Monique Bourque, "Populating the Poorhouse: A Reassessment of Poor Relief in the Antebellum Mid-Atlantic Region," *Pennsylvania History* 70:4 (2003).
53. Lerman, "From 'Useful Knowledge' to 'Habits of Industry.'"
54. Chester County Business Houses, Apprentice and Servants Papers, Indenture Papers, Eighteenth and Nineteenth Centuries, Folder 2, Chester County Historical Society, hereafter CCHS.
55. Chester County Business Houses, Apprentice and Servants Papers, Indenture Papers, Eighteenth and Nineteenth Centuries, Folder 2, CCHS.
56. Directors Correspondence, October 9, 1855, CCA.
57. Directors Correspondence, October 9, 1855, CCA.

Chapter 6. Preparing Children for Adulthood in New Netherland

1. The Dutch Republic comprised the seven northern provinces of the Low Countries that separated from Spain in the sixteenth century and were united under William of Orange. In 1621, the Republic's States General granted a charter to the West India Company, which claimed a domain in North America that included New Netherland and which stretched between the Fresh (Connecticut) River and the west bank of the South (Delaware) River down to Cape Henlopen in present-day New Jersey. On the Company's history, see Henk den Heijer, *De geschiedenis van de WIC* (Zutphen, Netherlands: Walburg Pers, 1994).
2. Rudolf Dekker, *Uit de schaduw in 't grote licht. Kinderen in egodocumenten van de Gouden Eeuw tot de Romantiek* (Amsterdam: Wereldbibliotheek, 1995), 18; and A. T. van Deursen, *Plain Lives in a Golden Age: Popular Culture, Religion, and Society in Seventeenth-Century Holland*, trans. Maarten Ultee (Cambridge, U.K.: Cambridge University Press, 1991), 115.
3. Quotation from Simon van Leeuwen's *Costumen, keuren ende ordonnantien van het baljuschap ende lande van Rijnland* (Leiden, Netherlands: de Hackens, 1667), cited by Van Deursen, *Plain Lives*, trans. Ultee, 115; and Hugo Grotius, *The Jurisprudence of Holland*, 2nd ed., trans. Robert W. Lee (1926; repr. Aalen, Germany: Scientia Verlag, 1977), 1:15.
4. Ronald W. Howard, "Apprenticeship and Economic Education in New Netherland and Seventeenth-Century New York," in *A Beautiful and Fruitful Place: Selected Rensselaerswijck Seminar Papers*, ed. Nancy A. McClure Zeller (Albany: New Netherland Publishing, 1991), 205.
5. Arnold J. F. van Laer, trans., "Letters of Nicasius de Sille, 1654," in *Proceedings of the New York State Historical Association* 18 (1923): 101–2.
6. Thomas G. Evans, ed., "Baptisms from 1639 to 1730 in the Reformed Dutch Church, New York," in *Collections of the New York Genealogical and Biographical Society*, vol. 2 (1901; repr. Upper Saddle River, NJ: Gregg Press, 1968), 9–117.
7. Infant mortality studies have not been done for New Netherland. For seventeenth-century rates in the Netherlands and Tappan, New Jersey, see Dirk Damsma, *Het Hollandse Huisgezin (1560–heden)* (Utrecht, Netherlands: Kosmos-Z&K Uitgevers, 1993), 38–39; and Firth H. Fabend, *A Dutch Family in the Middle Colonies, 1660–1800* (New Brunswick, NJ: Rutgers University Press, 1991), 39–40, 43–45, respectively.

8. Joyce D. Goodfriend, *Before the Melting Pot: Society and Culture in Colonial New York City, 1664–1730* (Princeton: Princeton University Press, 1992), 173.

9. Goodfriend, *Before the Melting Pot*, 174, 231n17; and Arnold J. F. van Laer, trans. and ed., *Correspondence of Jeremias van Rensselaer, 1651–1674* (Albany: University of the State of New York, 1932), 377–78.

10. Berthold Fernow, ed., *The Records of New Amsterdam from 1653 to 1674 Anno Domini* (1897; repr. Baltimore: Genealogical Publishing, 1976), 1:134, 137, hereafter RNA; and Arnold J. F. van Laer, trans. and ed., *Minutes of the Court of Rensselaerswyck, 1648–1652* (Albany: University of the State of New York, 1922), 212.

11. J. Franklin Jameson, ed., *Narratives of New Netherland, 1609–1664* (New York: Charles Scribner's Sons, 1909), 48; and Arnold J. F. van Laer, trans. and ed., *Documents relating to New Netherland, 1624–1626 in the Henry E. Huntington Library* (San Marino, CA: Henry E. Huntington Library and Art Gallery, 1924), 136, 139–40, hereafter DRNN.

12. DRNN, 113–14.

13. Grotius, *Jurisprudence*, trans. Lee, 1:331, 385, 387, 389; Robert W. Lee, *An Introduction to Roman-Dutch Law*, 5th ed. (Oxford: Clarendon Press, 1953), 223; J. W. Wessels, *History of the Roman-Dutch Law* (Grahamstown, Cape of Good Hope: African Book Company, 1908), 614.

14. Gerard Rooseboom, *Recueil Van verscheyde Keuren, en Costumen. Midtsgaders Maniere van Procederen binnen de Stadt Amsterdam*, 2nd ed. (Amsterdam: Jan Hendricks, 1656), 105, 111; and Grotius, *Jurisprudence*, trans. Lee, 1:35, 505.

15. Grotius, *Jurisprudence*, trans. Lee, 1:21, 29, 33, 35, 41, 313, 315, 505.

16. Grotius, *Jurisprudence*, trans. Lee, 1:43, 299, 301; and Lee, *Introduction to Roman-Dutch Law*, 243n3.

17. Charles T. Gehring, "Documentary Sources Relating to New Netherland," in *Colonial Dutch Studies: An Interdisciplinary Approach*, ed. Eric Nooter and Patricia U. Bonomi (New York: New York University Press, 1988), 33–51.

18. Arnold J. F. van Laer, trans., *Register of the Provincial Secretary, 1638–1660*, New York Historical Manuscripts: Dutch, ed. Kenneth Scott and Kenn Stryker-Rodda (Baltimore: Genealogical Publishing, 1974), 1:204–5; for evidence of Harmansen's farm, see 1:63–64, 63n2.

19. For an overview of occupations, see Stefan Bielinski, "How a City Worked: Occupations in Colonial Albany," in *Beautiful and Fruitful Place*, ed. Zeller, 119–36; and Martha Dickinson Shattuck, "A Civil Society: Court and Community in Beverwijck, New Netherland, 1652–1664" (Ph.D. dissertation, Boston University, 1993), 91–100.

20. Van Laer, trans., *Provincial Secretary*, ed. Scott and Stryker-Rodda, 3:64–65; Berthold Fernow, ed. and trans., *The Minutes of the Orphanmasters of New Amsterdam, 1655 to 1663* (New York: Francis P. Harper, 1902–7), 1:32–34, 86, hereafter MONA.

21. Arnold J. F. van Laer, trans., "Albany Wills and Other Documents, 1665–1695," in *Yearbook of the Dutch Settlers Society of Albany* 6 (1930–31): 14–15.

22. Van Laer, trans., *Provincial Secretary*, ed. Scott and Stryker-Rodda, 1:322; and RNA, 7:120.

23. S. Groenveld, J. J. H. Dekker, and Th. R. M. Willemse, *Wezen en boefjes. Zes eeuwen zorg in wees- en kinderhuizen* (Hilversum, Netherlands: Verloren, 1997), 204–6; and Anne E. C. McCants, *Civic Charity in a Golden Age: Orphan Care in Early Modern Amsterdam* (Urbana: University of Illinois Press, 1997), 82–88.

24. Dingman Versteeg, trans., *Kingston Papers*, New York Historical Manuscripts: Dutch, ed. Peter R. Christoph, Kenneth Scott, and Kenn Stryker-Rodda (Baltimore: Genealogical Publishing, 1976), 2:426–27, 432–33. In 1667, the value of a schepel of wheat was 50 stuivers. Versteeg, trans., *Kingston Papers*, 1:355. One Dutch florin, or guilder, was equal to 20 stuivers. In 1650, ten guilders was equivalent to one English pound sterling. Charles T. Gehring, trans. and ed., *Correspondence, 1647–1653*, New Netherland Documents Series (Syracuse: Syracuse University Press, 2000), 241–44; and John J. McCusker, *Money and Exchange in Europe and America, 1600–1775: A Handbook* (Chapel Hill: University of North Carolina Press, 1978), 44, 53.

25. New York City Municipal Archives, no. 134, *Powers of Attorney, Acknowledgments, Indentures of Apprentices, Inventories, Deeds, etc., 1651–56*, trans. Edmund O'Callaghan, 8–9, hereafter NYCMA, no. 134.

26. RNA, 2:101n; MONA, 1:32–33, 2:34–36; and Evans, ed., "Baptisms," 2:36, 43, 51, 59, 68.
27. A. P. G. Jos van der Linde, trans. and ed., *Old First Dutch Reformed Church of Brooklyn, New York. First Book of Records, 1660–1752,* New York Historical Manuscripts: Dutch (Baltimore: Genealogical Publishing, 1983), 196–97; and Jonathan Pearson, trans., and Arnold J. F. van Laer, rev. and ed., *Early Records of the City and County of Albany and Colony of Rensselaerswyck* (Albany: University of the State of New York, 1916–19), 3:415–16.
28. Pearson, trans., and Van Laer, rev. and ed., *Early Records of Albany,* 3:138; and Van Laer, trans. and ed., *Minutes of Rensselaerswyck,* 69.
29. RNA, 3:80; and Versteeg, trans., *Kingston Papers,* ed. Christoph et al., 1:308.
30. Van Deursen, *Plain Lives,* trans. Ultee, 126.
31. Pearson, trans., and Van Laer, rev. and ed., *Early Records of Albany,* 3:415–16, 422–23; for other examples of clothes due and received, 211. See also RNA, 2:247, 5:171; and Versteeg, trans., *Kingston Papers,* ed. Christoph et al., 1:45, 308.
32. For Johannes van Couwenhoven's contract made with the consent of his father in 1662, for example, see Edmund B. O'Callaghan, trans., *The Register of Salomon LaChaire Notary Public of New Amsterdam, 1661–1662,* New York Historical Manuscripts: Dutch, ed. Kenneth Scott and Kenn Stryker-Rodda (Baltimore: Genealogical Publishing, 1978), 207–8.
33. MONA, 1:154–55. For tobacco values, see RNA, 1:251, 289–90, 345; MONA, 2:34.
34. NYCMA, no. 134, 8–9; and Van Laer, trans., "Albany Wills," 14–15.
35. Van Deursen, *Plain Lives,* trans. Ultee, 125.
36. Ronald William Howard, "Education and Ethnicity in Colonial New York, 1664–1763: A Study in the Transmission of Culture in Early America" (Ph.D. dissertation, University of Tennessee, 1978), 106.
37. Van Deursen, *Plain Lives,* trans. Ultee, 116; Van Laer, trans., *Provincial Secretary,* ed. Scott and Stryker-Rodda, 3:64–65; and Van Laer, trans., "Albany Wills," 14–15.
38. William Heard Kilpatrick, *The Dutch Schools of New Netherland and Colonial New York* (Washington, D.C.: Government Printing Office, 1912), 30–31, 228; and MONA, 2:115–16.
39. Van Deursen, *Plain Lives,* trans. Ultee, 122; and Groenveld et al., *Wezen en Boefjes,* 194.
40. Van der Linde, trans. and ed., *Old Dutch Church,* 196–99; and O'Callaghan, trans., *Register of LaChaire,* ed. Scott and Stryker-Rodda, 9.
41. For Robbert's baptism, see Evans, ed., "Baptisms," 15. For the manumission decree, see Arnold J. F. van Laer, trans., *Council Minutes, 1638–1649,* New York Historical Manuscripts: Dutch, ed. Kenneth Scott and Kenn Stryker-Rodda (Baltimore: Genealogical Publishing, 1974), 4:212–13.
42. On orphans and their property in New Amsterdam, see Adriana E. van Zwieten, "The Orphan Chamber of New Amsterdam," *William and Mary Quarterly,* 3d ser., vol. 53 (April 1996): 319–40. On poor relief, see Janny Venema, "Poverty and Charity in Seventeenth-Century Beverwijck/Albany, 1652–1700," *New York History* 80 (October 1999): 369–90.
43. Van der Linde, trans. and ed., *Old Dutch Church,* 50–53, 77–81, 196–97.
44. David W. Voorhees, trans. and ed., *Records of the Reformed Protestant Dutch Church of Flatbush, Kings County, New York, Volume 1, 1677–1720* (New York: Holland Society of New York, 1998), 221, 269, 337, 402, 422; and Van der Linde, trans. and ed., *Old Dutch Church,* 77–81.
45. Charles T. Gehring, trans. and ed., *Council Minutes, 1655–1656,* New Netherland Documents Series (Syracuse: Syracuse University Press, 1995), 6:217; RNA, 7:178–80; and Janny Venema, trans. and ed., *Deacons' Accounts 1652–1674: First Dutch Reformed Church of Beverwyck/Albany, New York,* Historical Series of the Reformed Church in America, no. 28 (Rockport, ME: Picton Press, 1998), 48–51, 53–54, 57.
46. Shattuck, "Civil Society," 108.
47. Prices for necessities are found in Venema, *Deacons' Accounts,* 36, 53, 55, 58, 63–64, 70–71, 75, 83–84; and Van der Linde, *Old Dutch Church,* 179.
48. Grotius, *Jurisprudence,* trans. Lee, 1:327.
49. RNA, 1:162, 168; for Albertsen's occupation, 4:65.
50. RNA, 3:71–72, 75, 86, 95.
51. Rooseboom, *Recueil Van Keuren,* 260, 262.
52. RNA, 3:40.

53. Van Laer, trans., *Council Minutes,* ed. Scott and Stryker-Rodda, 4:9, 12. For Damen's lease of land and Arentsen's testimony, see Van Laer, trans., *Provincial Secretary,* ed., Scott and Stryker-Rodda, 1:2–4, 2:286–87.

54. RNA, 6:149–50, 152–53.

55. Roosebroom, *Recueil Van Keuren,* 261; and Grotius, *Jurisprudence,* trans. Lee, 1:391.

56. RNA, 2:362, 367, 400.

57. RNA, 5:176–77, 183, 188, 191–92; and Roosebroom, *Recueil Van Keuren,* 263.

58. Charles T. Gehring, trans. and ed., *Fort Orange Court Minutes, 1652–1660,* New Netherland Documents Series (Syracuse: Syracuse University Press, 1990), 156–57.

59. Pearson, trans., and Van Laer, rev. and ed., *Early Records of Albany,* 3:415–16.

60. Simon Schama, *The Embarrassment of Riches: An Interpretation of Dutch Culture in the Golden Age* (Berkeley: University of California Press, 1988), 555; and Van Deursen, *Plain Lives,* trans. Ultee, 130.

61. Quotations in Schama, *Embarrassment of Riches,* 556.

62. Berthold Fernow, trans. and ed., *Minutes of the Executive Boards of the Burgomasters of New Amsterdam* (1907; repr. New York: Arno Press, 1970), 76.

63. RNA, 2:247.

64. Groenveld, et al., *Wezen en boefjes,* 222–23.

65. Gehring, trans. and ed., *Fort Orange Minutes,* 278–79, 293.

66. RNA, 2:271.

67. MONA, 1:212, 245–46.

68. RNA, 5:313–14, 317–19.

69. Gehring, trans. and ed., *Council Minutes,* 6:175.

70. Quoted in Howard, "Apprenticeship and Economic Education," 210.

Chapter 7. Mothers and Children in and out of the Charleston Orphan House

1. Ernest M. Lander Jr., "Charleston: Manufacturing Center of the Old South," *Journal of Southern History* 26 (1960): 330–51; Walter J. Fraser Jr., *Charleston! Charleston! The History of a Southern City* (Columbia: University of South Carolina Press, 1989), esp. 178–243; and Peter A. Coclanis, *The Shadow of a Dream: Economic Life and Death in the South Carolina Low Country, 1670–1920* (New York: Oxford University Press, 1989), esp. 125–30.

2. Coclanis, *Shadow of a Dream,* 111–16; Fraser, *Charleston! Charleston!* 227, 235, 253; Robert L. Harris Jr., "Charleston's Free Afro-American Elite: The Brown Fellowship Society and the Humane Brotherhood," *South Carolina Historical Magazine* 82 (1981): 289–310; and Barbara L. Bellows, *Benevolence among Slaveholders: Assisting the Poor in Charleston, 1670–1860* (Baton Rouge: Louisiana State University Press, 1993), 29.

3. Frank Lawrence Owsley, *Plain Folk of the Old South* (Baton Rouge: Louisiana State University Press, 1949).

4. Stephanie McCurry, *Masters of Small Worlds: Yeoman Households, Gender Relations, and the Political Culture of the Antebellum South Carolina Low Country* (New York: Oxford University Press, 1995).

5. Charles C. Bolton, *Poor Whites of the Antebellum South: Tenants and Laborers in Central North Carolina and Northeast Mississippi* (Durham: Duke University Press, 1994); and Bill Cecil-Fronsman, *Common Whites: Class and Culture in Antebellum North Carolina* (Lexington: University Press of Kentucky, 1992).

6. Bertram Wyatt-Brown, *Southern Honor: Ethics and Behavior in the Old South* (New York: Oxford University Press, 1982), 126–37; Peter Bardaglio, *Reconstructing the Household: Families, Sex, and the Law in the Nineteenth-Century South* (Chapel Hill: University of North Carolina Press, 1995), 97–111; and Bellows, *Benevolence among Slaveholders.*

7. 43 Eliz., c. 2 (1601); on applications in colonial South Carolina, see Richard B. Morris, "White Bondage in Antebellum South Carolina," *South Carolina Historical and Genealogical Magazine* 49 (1948): 191–207, esp. 196; and William Simpson, *Practical Justice of the Peace and Parish-Officer of His Majesty's Province of South-Carolina* (Charlestown, SC: Robert Wells, 1761), 16–19, 202.

8. Simpson, *Practical Justice of the Peace*, 16. The 1712 law that formed the basis for this power carried through into the nineteenth century. See Thomas Cooper and David J. McCord, *The Statutes at Large of South Carolina, Edited, Under Authority of the Legislature. Volume Second* (Columbia, SC: A. S. Johnston, 1837), 596.

9. Quotation from St. Philip's Parish Vestry Book, 175, in Walter Fraser, "The City Elite, 'Disorder,' and the Poor Children of Pre-Revolutionary Charleston," *South Carolina Historical Magazine* 84 (1983): 167–79. The process of treating poor children was very similar in Savannah, although there was no centralized institution such as the Orphan House there. See chapter 9 in this volume.

10. Rule 2nd, "Rules of the Orphan House," 1791, *Minutes of the Commissioners of the Charleston Orphan House*, vol. 1, 37–42. Volumes in South Carolina Room, Charleston County Public Library; hereafter *Minutes*. For the early history of the Orphan House, see also John E. Murray, "Bound by Charity: The Abandoned Children of Late Eighteenth Century Charleston," in *Down and Out in Early America*, ed. Billy G. Smith (University Park: Pennsylvania State University Press, 2004), 213–32.

11. Suzanne Lebsock, *The Free Women of Petersburg: Status and Culture in a Southern Town, 1784–1860* (New York: W. W. Norton, 1984), still not surpassed in depth as a community study, found relatively little information on the poor: see xvii. An imaginative work that uncovered lives of the early American poor, to which this essay is indebted, is Ruth Wallis Herndon, *Unwelcome Americans: Living on the Margin in Early New England* (Philadelphia: University of Pennsylvania Press, 2001).

12. Robert Olwell, *Masters, Slaves, and Subjects: The Culture of Power in the South Carolina Low Country, 1740–1790* (Ithaca: Cornell University Press, 1998), 45; and Jackson Turner Main, *The Social Structure of Revolutionary America* (Princeton: Princeton University Press, 1965), 60, both estimate this share to be one-fifth.

13. Coclanis, *Shadow of a Dream*, 116.

14. Fraser, *Charleston! Charleston!* 235.

15. Visiting Commissioner's report of H. A. DeSaussure regarding children of Thomas and Agnes Kelly, November 29, 1855, "Rejected applications to admit" files, Charleston Orphan House collection, South Carolina Room, Charleston County Public Library; hereafter "Rejected applications."

16. Yellow fever was a notoriously urban disease, a kind of counterpart to malaria in the countryside. Joyce E. Chaplin, *An Anxious Pursuit: Agricultural Innovation and Modernity in the Lower South, 1730–1815* (Chapel Hill: University of North Carolina Press, 1993), 94ff.

17. Eleanor Boswell to Commissioners, December 8, 1803; endorsed by physician, Jacob Williman, on reverse, "Applications." Regarding a father who was blind: Visiting Commissioner's report on Z. Y. and Sarah Anderson, May 7, 1846.

18. Regarding a father imprisoned for debt: Richard Boak to Commissioners, March 19, 1818.

19. On straitened circumstances among seafaring families in New England, see Ruth Wallis Herndon, "The Domestic Cost of Seafaring: Town Leaders and Seamen's Families in Eighteenth-Century Rhode Island," in *Iron Men, Wooden Women: Gender and Seafaring in the Atlantic World, 1700–1920*, ed. Margaret S. Creighton and Lisa Norling (Baltimore: Johns Hopkins University Press, 1996), 55–69.

20. S. B. Gilliland to Mr. DeSaussure, February 4, 1858, "Applications."

21. John Hanson to Commissioners, October 13, 1825; Mrs. L. M. Bennett to Commissioners, January 24, 1826 and August 24, 1826, Applications to admit files, Charleston Orphan House Collection, South Carolina Room, Charleston County Public Library; hereafter "Applications."

22. Unsigned letter to Commissioners, November 25, 1803, regarding children of Mr. James.

23. Bachman to H. W. DeSaussure, June 1, 1854, "Applications." On heavy alcohol consumption in the early republic, see W. J. Rorabaugh, *The Alcoholic Republic: An American Tradition* (New York: Oxford University Press, 1979). Bachman was a well-known Lutheran pastor and temperance activist as well as the naturalist after whom Audubon named Bachman's Warbler. See Lester D. Stephens, *Science, Race, and Religion in the American South: John Bachman and the Charleston Circle of Naturalists, 1815–1895* (Chapel Hill: University of North Carolina Press, 2000).

24. *Minutes,* vol. 6, December 17, 1817.

25. J. A. Johnson to Commissioners re: Julianna Barnes, October 14, 1819; H. L. Gervais to Commissioners re: Thomas Richards, 21 July 1856, "Applications."

26. Mrs. Clark to Commissioners, May 18, 1820, "Rejected applications"; Elizabeth Foley to Commissioners, January 7, 1824, "Applications."

27. Fraser, *Charleston! Charleston!* 197; and Murray Rothbard, *The Panic of 1819* (New York: Columbia University Press, 1962), 7–13, 47.

28. B. Quinnan to Commissioners, August 6, 1828, "Applications."

29. Catherine Clements to Commissioners, July 13, 1826, "Applications."

30. References to domestic service appear in later documents, which may have reflected an increased desire to employ white domestics after the Denmark Vesey events; see Archates [Thomas Pinckney], *Reflections Occasioned by the Late Disturbances in Charleston* (Charleston: A. E. Miller, 1822), 18–19.

31. Unsigned report of Visiting Commissioner on Louisa Benton, August 1, 1844, "Applications."

32. Washerwoman: Unsigned report of Visiting Commissioner on Mrs. Pearce, August 24, 1858, "Rejected Applications;" laborer: Robert A. Margo, *Wages and Labor Markets in the United States, 1820–1860* (Chicago: University of Chicago Press, 2000), 33. Presumably the washerwoman's pay included room and board, but the report is silent on this question.

33. Visiting Commissioner report of M. Caldwell, October 17, 1855, "Rejected Applications."

34. Visiting Commissioner de Saussure's report re: Catherine Blake, January 31, 1857.

35. Mrs. W. Johnson to Commissioners regarding Vizzara infant, August 11, 1840, "Rejected Applications"; H[enry] A. D[eSaussure] to Mrs. W. Johnson, August 13, 1840, "Rejected Applications." This refers to a case in which the wet nurse took an orphaned infant into her home.

36. Sally McMillen, *Motherhood in the Old South* (Baton Rouge: Louisiana State University Press), 1990.

37. McMillen, *Motherhood,* 123.

38. I[sabella]. Doyle to Commissioners, April 1835, "Applications." Bernard (age ten) and James (age eight) Doyle were in fact admitted immediately after receipt of this letter. The infant was probably Caroline, born late 1834 (?), who was admitted to the Orphan House in January 1838.

39. Eliza Cregier to Commissioners, November 10, 1824, "Rejected Applications."

40. Miss J. M. Drayton to Commissioners, April 29, 1813, "Applications"; Indentures of Amelia, George, Hannah, and Janet Creamer, "Indentures," Charleston Orphan House Collection, South Carolina Room, Charleston County Public Library; hereafter "Indentures."

41. [Thomas Allen?] to Commissioners, June 25, 1835, "Applications." Letter in file headed "Mark Thomson," but the child in question here was Daniel McQuin.

42. B. Elliott to Commissioners, March 20, 1826, "Applications."

43. Mary Anne McDermott to Commissioners regarding Deignan children, October 29, 1831, "Rejected Applications." Commissioners offered no reason for rejecting this application. See "Minutes," November 17, 1831.

44. Joseph Johnson to Commissioners, July 11, 1844, "Rejected Applications."

45. Report of George Coffin re: Mary and Loretta Darby, June 25, 1857, "Applications." For a few examples from many other cases involving extended family, see William Wish to Commissioners, May 14, 1806, "Applications" (uncle can no longer afford to keep boy); and Rev. Cranmore Wallace to Commissioners, re: James Willis July 18, 1851, "Applications" (aunt cannot discipline nephew).

46. Rev. A. Toomer Porter to Commissioners re: Ann Kain, June 18, 1860, "Rejected Applications;" unsigned Visiting Commissioner report on Louisa Benton, August 1, 1844, "Applications;" Letitia Glen to Commissioners re: Peggy Boyd, December 17, 1803, "Applications;" Lucy Barrett to Commissioners re: John Hutson, January 26, 1842, "Applications."

47. Lucy Barrett to Commissioners, July 11, 1844, "Rejected Applications."

48. Mary Byrd to Commissioners, November 1829, "Applications."

49. John Jameson to Commissioners, November 19, 1840, "Rejected Applications." On November 26, 1840, the Commissioners rejected the application, stating that Bowman was too old and "his habits might be injurious to the Boys of the Institution." *Minutes*.
50. John Dawson et al to Chairman, February 19, 1817, "Applications."
51. Unsigned report of Visiting Commissioner, June 8, 1854, "Applications"; see also *Minutes*, June 8, 1854, for William, Julia, and Sarah.
52. Catherine Shelbock to Commissioners, May 8, 1823, "Rejected Applications."
53. [Mr. Carson?] to Mr. Cornell, Esq., Commissioner, January 29, 1854, "Indentures."
54. Maria Schmidt to Commissioners re: Andreas Schmidt, May 8, 1856, "Indentures."
55. Susan Adams to Commissioners, June 8, 1824, "Applications"; Eliza Cregier to Commissioners, November 10, 1824, "Rejected Applications"; and William Pettigrew to Commissioners, July 27, 1855, "Applications."
56. On craft apprentices, that is, children bound by parents to masters with the intention that the child learn the master's craft, see W. J. Rorabaugh, *The Craft Apprentice from Franklin to the Machine Age in America* (New York: Oxford University Press, 1986), 96–101. Rorabaugh describes the breaking of familial bonds as more decisive than the poor children of Charleston seem to have experienced.
57. James Barry to Benjamin Cudworth, September 5 and 7, 1803, "Applications."
58. *Minutes*, vol. 1, April 28, 1791.
59. Mary Anne Carroll to Commissioners, May 20, 1819 and November 25, 1819, "Applications." On the struggles of Bishop John England with Charleston's civic elite, see Bellows, *Benevolence among Slaveholders*, 28 and 84.
60. For example, Mrs. Jeffries to Commissioners re: Steven Dannals, May 17, 1855, "Indentures."
61. Sarah D. Wray to Commissioners, June 17, 1824, "Applications."
62. Ann Zylks to Commissioners, December 23, 1815, "Applications."
63. *Minutes*, vol. 1, 38.
64. John E. Murray and Ruth Wallis Herndon, "Markets for Children in Early America: A Political Economy of Pauper Apprenticeship," *Journal of Economic History* 62 (2002): 356–82; and John E. Murray, "Family, Literacy, and Skill-Training in the Antebellum South: Historical-Longitudinal Evidence from Charleston," *Journal of Economic History* 64 (2004): 773–99.
65. J. B. Duval to Commissioners, June 18, 1840, "Indentures."
66. *Minutes*, vol. 4, June 30, 1808.
67. *Minutes*, vol. 3, November 7, 1803, June 20, 1805.
68. *Minutes*, vol. 4, August 17, 1809; and Griffin, "Origins."
69. For example, *Minutes*, vol. 3, November 28, 1805.
70. William Milligan to Commissioners, May 1, 1828, "Indentures." Milligan senior was a tallow chandler; and *Minutes*, vol. 8, August 4, 1825.
71. M. Moles to Commissioners, January 7, 1815, "Indentures."
72. Samuel Morris to Commissioners re: Robert Brown, March 7, 1839, "Indentures."
73. Examples abound in the *Minutes*. One is the response to a petition from Magdalena Kohler regarding her daughter and grandson in vol. 4, January 11, 1810. The child was Christopher Memminger, the future secretary of the treasury for the Confederate States.
74. *Minutes*, vol. 6, April 6, 1815.
75. Mary Kirkpatrick to Commissioners re: James Caulfield, February 27, 1834, "Indentures." On coverture in South Carolina, see Robert M. Weir, *Colonial South Carolina: A History* (1983; repr. Columbia: University of South Carolina Press, 1997), 232–33.
76. Martha Deliesseline to Commissioners, February 22, 1855, "Indentures."
77. For more on remarriage at this time, see Susan Grigg, "Toward a Theory of Remarriage: A Case Study of Newburyport at the Beginning of the Nineteenth Century," *Journal of Interdisciplinary History* 8 (1977): 183–220.
78. B. G. Happold to Commissioners re: William Arnold, June 14, 1860, "Indentures."
79. Elizabeth Rhodes to Commissioners re: William Headwright, February 9, 1825 and September 15, 1825, "Indentures."
80. *Minutes*, vol. 8, November 12, 1857.

81. J. A. Stevenson to Commissioners, February 23, 1846 re: Lawrence Hendricks, "Indentures." After reviewing the references for the new master, the Commissioners approved the transfer. Wyatt-Brown, *Southern Honor,* 159–60. For more on mother-son relationships, as applied to literacy acquisition, see chapter 8 in this volume.

82. Michael Grossberg, *Governing the Hearth: Law and the Family in Nineteenth-Century America* (Chapel Hill: University of North Carolina Press, 1985), 259–68; and Carl Bridenbaugh. *The Colonial Craftsman* (Chicago: University of Chicago Press, 1961), 131. For examples of truly involuntary apprenticeship, see chapter 3 in this volume; for a North Carolina focus, see Karin Zipf, *Labor of Innocents: Forced Apprenticeship in North Carolina, 1795–1919* (Baton Rouge: Louisiana State University Press, 2005).

83. John E. Murray, "Literacy Acquisition in an Orphanage: A Historical-Longitudinal Case Study," *American Journal of Education* 110 (2004): 172–95.

84. David Ramsay, *The History of South-Carolina from its First Settlement in 1670, to the Year 1808* (Charleston: David Longworth, 1809), 2:25–26.

85. Walter B. Edgar, *South Carolina: A History* (Columbia: University of South Carolina Press, 1998), 151–53.

86. Rev. William Hollinshead, "An Oration Delivered at the Orphan-House of Charleston, South Carolina, October 18, 1797, Being the Eighth Anniversary of the Institution," in *The Charitable Impulse in Eighteenth Century America: Collected Papers,* ed. David J. Rothman (New York: Arno Press, 1971).

87. Bellows, *Benevolence among Slaveholders,* 19.

88. Robert M. Weir, "'The Harmony We Were Famous For': An Interpretation of Pre-Revolutionary South Carolina Politics," *William and Mary Quarterly,* 3rd ser., vol. 26 (1969): 473–501; in the South more broadly, see George M. Fredrickson, *The Black Image in the White Mind: The Debate on Afro-American Character and Destiny, 1817–1914* (New York: Harper and Row, 1971), esp. 58–64 on *Herrenvolk* democracy.

89. Charles G. Steffen, "In Search of the Good Overseer: The Failure of the Agricultural Reform Movement in Lowcountry South Carolina, 1821–1834," *Journal of Southern History* 63 (1997): 753–802; Maurie D. McInnis, *The Politics of Taste in Antebellum Charleston* (Chapel Hill: University of North Carolina Press, 2005), 82.

90. On benevolence more generally, see Bellows, *Benevolence among Slaveholders.*

Chapter 8. The Extent and Limits of Indentured Children's Literacy in New Orleans, 1809–1843

1. Kenneth Lockridge, *Literacy in Colonial New England* (New York: W. W. Norton, 1974), 7; and Lawrence Stone, "Literacy and Education in England," *Past and Present* 42 (February 1969): 98.

2. Farley Grubb, "Growth of Literacy in Colonial America: Longitudinal Patterns, Economic Models, and Direction of Future Research," *Social Science History* 14 (1990): 477n3.

3. John E. Murray, "Generation(s) of Human Capital: Literacy in American Families, 1830–1875," *Journal of Interdisciplinary History* 27:3 (Winter 1997): 413–35.

4. Grubb, "Growth of Literacy," 476.

5. Daniel Clark, "Queries respecting Louisiana, with the Answers," enclosed with his letter to the Secretary of State, New Orleans, September 8, 1803, in *The Territorial Papers of the United States,* vol. 9, *The Territory of Orleans, 1803–1812,* comp. Clarence Carter (Washington, D.C.: U.S. Government Printing Office, 1940), 38. See also Amos Stoddard, *Sketches, Historical and Descriptive of Louisiana* (Philadelphia: Matthew Carey, 1812), 208–9, 220; and Pierre Clément Laussat, *Memoirs of My Life to My Son During the Years 1803 and After,...,* trans. Sister Agnes-Josephine Pastwa, ed. Robert Bush (Baton Rouge: Louisiana State University Press, 1978), 68. For comparison, see Grubb, "Growth of Literacy," 458–59.

6. Databases entitled "New Orleans Marriage Contracts," sample covering the period 1804–60 created from documents in the Notarial Archives and the City Archives of New

Orleans, and "New Orleans Wills," sample covering the period 1804–60 created from documents in the Notarial Archives and the City Archives of New Orleans. Both databases are described in Charles Patch, comp., *Gulf Coast Historical Database Group* (New Orleans: Historic New Orleans Collection, 1993).

7. Joseph Logson and Caryn Cossé Bell, "The Americanization of Black New Orleans, 1850–1980," in *Creole New Orleans: Race and Americanization*, ed. Arnold Hirsch and Joseph Logsdon (Baton Rouge: Louisiana State University Press, 1992), 206.

8. Albert Fossier, *New Orleans: The Glamour Period, 1800–1840* (New Orleans: Pelican Press, 1957).

9. Third Decennial Census: 1810, *Aggregate amount of each description of persons within the United States of America, and the Territories thereof, agreeably to actual enumeration made according to law, in the year 1810* (Washington, 1811), 82, MSS., 295 [Orleans parish]; Sixth Decennial Census: 1840, *Compendium of the enumeration of the inhabitants and statistics of the United States* [Sixth Census, 1840] (Washington, D.C.: Blair and Rives, 1841), 60–63, 234–39, 256.

10. Fossier, *New Orleans*, 54; and Thomas Redard, "The Port of New Orleans: An Economic History, 1821–1860" (Ph.D. dissertation, Louisiana State University and Agricultural and Mechanical College, 1985), 218, 229.

11. Campbell Gibson, "Population of the 100 Largest Cities and Other Urban Places in the United States: 1790 to 1990," U.S. Census Bureau, Population Division Working Paper No. 27 (June 1998); http://www.census.gov/population/www/documentation/twps0027.html, table 1, "Rank by Population of the 100 Largest Urban Places, Listed Alphabetically by State: 1790–1990."

12. Thomas Conway, "John A. Kennicott: A Teacher in New Orleans," *Louisiana History* 26:4 (Fall 1985): 403–7, 409–12.

13. T. H. Harris, *The Story of Public Education in Louisiana* (New Orleans: Printing Department of Delgrado Trades School, 1924), 9; and Robert Reinders, *End of an Era: New Orleans, 1850–1860* (Gretna, LA: Publican Publishing Company, 1964; repr. 1989), 131–32.

14. Gilles Vandal, "Le système notarial de la Louisiane au XIXe siècle: profil et fonction des notaires," *Canadian Journal of History/Annales canadiennes d'histoire* 32:2 (August 1997): 221. Public notaries played an important role as public officers in the civil law system. As drafters of various types of legal documents from prenuptial agreements, wills, and succession inventories to acts of sale and business and labor contracts, they informed all parties involved of their rights, checked that arrangements conformed to the written code, and kept a permanent record of proceedings in their offices.

15. Apprenticeship records from the Spanish colonial period (1769–1803) are found mainly among acts of notaries in the Notarial Archives of Orleans Parish, Civil Courts Building, New Orleans, Louisiana. See also Kimberly Hanger, *Bounded Lives, Bounded Places: Free Black Society in Colonial New Orleans, 1769–1803* (Durham, NC: Duke University Press, 1997), 68–69; and Thomas Ingersoll, *Mammon and Manon in New Orleans: The First Slave Society in the Deep South, 1718–1819* (Knoxville: University of Tennessee Press, 1999), 168–69. Apprenticeship contracts from the French colonial period (1718–69) are found in the records of the Superior Council of Louisiana housed in the collection of the Louisiana State Museum Historical Center, New Orleans, Louisiana.

16. "An Act for the regulation of the rights and duties of apprentices and indentured servants," approved May 21, 1806, *Acts Passed at the First Session of the First Legislature of the Territory of Orleans* (New Orleans: Bradford and Anderson, 1807), ch. 11, 48–50.

17. Mayor's Office, Indentures (1809–1843), 5 vols., in Louisiana Collection, New Orleans Public Library, New Orleans, Louisiana.

18. This decline is an example of the gradual disappearance of all forms of bound labor except slavery everywhere in the United States in the antebellum period. Sharon Salinger, "Colonial Labor in Transition: The Decline of Indentured Servitude in Late Eighteenth-Century Philadelphia," *Labor History* 22:2 (Spring 1981): 191; Robert Steinfeld, *The Invention of Free Labor: The Employment Relation in English and American Law and Culture, 1350–1870* (Chapel Hill: University of North Carolina Press, 1991), 164; and David Montgomery, *Citizen Worker: The Experience of*

Workers in the United States with Democracy and the Free Market during the Nineteenth Century (Cambridge, UK: Cambridge University Press, 1993) 13, 31–33.

19. The proportion of free males who were indentured was determined by comparing the number of indentures for birth cohorts with the size of corresponding age groups in federal censuses of Orleans parish from 1810 to 1840.

20. Almost to the very end of the years covered by the indenture books, the indentures were handwritten; but printed forms began to be used around 1840. If printed forms were also used for unregistered apprenticeships, their appearance just at the point when the number of indentures fell to less than ten per year would seem less odd, and at the same time be evidence that informal agreements were still relatively numerous.

21. From 1806 to 1825, the maximum age to which a minor could be bound in Louisiana was twenty-one for males and eighteen for females. The Louisiana Civil Code adopted in 1825 lowered it to eighteen for males and fifteen for females, but the state legislature repealed this revision in the following year. "Act for the regulation of the rights and duties of apprentices and indentured servants" (1806), sec. 1, p. 46; *Louisiana Civil Code* (1825), Art. 159, pp. 162–63, in Louisiana Legal Archives, vol. 3, pt. 1, *Compiled Edition of the Civil Codes of Louisiana* (Baton Rouge: State of Louisiana Printing Office, 1940), 99.

22. Excepting nine children "to be educated" whose average age was 11.5 years.

23. Michel Verrette, "L'alphabétisation de la population de la ville de Québec de 1750–1849," *Revue d'histoire de l'Amérique française* 39:1 (Summer 1985), 74.

24. The percentage of literate sponsors and masters is calculated from signatures and marks of individuals when found for the first time in the data set, thus avoiding double-counting. See Lockridge, *Literacy*, 133.

25. Campbell Gibson and Emily Lennon, "Historical Census Statistics on the Foreign-born Population of the United States: 1850 to 1990," U.S. Census Bureau, Population Division Working Paper No. 29 (February 1999); http://www.census.gov/population/www/documentation/twps0029.html, table 21, "Nativity of the Population for the 25 Largest Urban Places and for Selected Counties: 1850."

26. Claudia Goldin, *Urban Slavery in the American South, 1820–1860: A Quantitative History* (Chicago: University of Chicago Press, 1976), 52–53, table 13, "Population Data for Ten Southern Cities, 1820–1860."

27. Paul Lachance, "The Foreign French," in *Creole New Orleans*, 118–19.

28. The signature rate was 51 percent for children and 97 percent for masters in both French and English indentures. It was higher, though, for sponsors in English than in French contracts: 61 and 54 percent respectively.

29. Joseph Tregle, *Louisiana in the Age of Jackson: A Clash of Cultures and Personalities* (Baton Rouge: Louisiana State University Press, 1999), 337–43.

30. Lee Soltow and Edward Stevens, *The Rise of Literacy and the Common School in the United States: A Socioeconomic Analysis to 1870* (Chicago: University of Chicago Press, 1981), 52.

31. For examples, New Orleans indentures database, book 3, indentures 124, April 24, 1819 (John Hadfield), and 263, March 7, 1822 (John Smith).

32. Paul Lachance, "Intermarriage and French Cultural Persistence in Late Spanish and Early American New Orleans," *Histoire sociale/Social History* 15 (May 1982): 81.

33. Jean-Pierre Hardy and David Thiery Ruddel, *Les apprentis artisans à Québec 1660–1815* (Montreal: Presses de l'Université du Québec, 1977), 164.

Chapter 9. "To Train Them to Habits of Industry and Usefulness"

1. Clifford S. Griffen, "Religious Benevolence as Social Control 1815–1860," *Mississippi Valley Historical Review* 44 (1957): 438; Lois W. Banner, "Religious Benevolence as Social Control: A Critique of an Interpretation," *Journal of American History* 60 (1973): 41; and Lawrence Kohl, "The Concept of Social Control and the History of Jacksonian America," *Journal of the Early Republic* 5 (1985): 27. See also C. S. Griffin, *The Ferment of Reform, 1830–1860* (London: Routledge and Kegan Paul, 1969): 17.

2. LeRoy Ashby, *Endangered Children: Dependency, Neglect, and Abuse in American History* (New York: Twayne Publishers, 1997): 17–34; Paul Boyer, *Urban Masses and Moral Order in America, 1820–1920* (Cambridge, Mass.: Harvard University Press, 1978): 1–53, 90–97; Priscilla Ferguson Clement, *Welfare and the Poor in the Nineteenth-Century City: Philadelphia 1800–1854* (Toronto: Associated University Presses, 1985): 38, 50–56; and David J. Rothman, *The Discovery of the Asylum: Social Order and Disorder in the New Republic* (Boston and Toronto: Little, Brown & Co., 1971).

3. Barbara Bellows, *Benevolence among Slaveholders: Assisting the Poor in Charleston, 1670–1860* (Baton Rouge: Louisiana State University Press, 1993), 121–30; Barbara L. Bellows, "'My Children, Gentlemen, Are My Own': Poor Women, the Urban Elite, and the Bonds of Obligation in Antebellum Charleston," in *The Web of Southern Social Relations: Women, Family, and Education*, ed. Walter J. Fraser Jr., R. Frank Saunders Jr., and Jon L. Wakelyn (Athens: Louisiana State University Press, 1985), 52–71; Priscilla Ferguson Clement, "Children and Charity: Orphanages in New Orleans, 1817–1914" *Louisiana History* 27 (1986): 337–52; John E. Murray and Ruth Wallis Herndon, "Markets for Children in Early America: A Political Economy of Pauper Apprenticeship," *Journal of Economic History* 62 (2002): 356–82; and John E. Murray, "Fates of Orphans: Poor Children in Antebellum Charleston," *Journal of Interdisciplinary History* 33 (2003): 519–45. Others to stress the importance of reform rather than social control include Ronald G. Walters, *American Reformers, 1815–1860* (New York: Hill and Wang, 1997): 35; and Jean V. Matthews, *Toward a New Society: American Thought and Culture, 1800–1830* (Boston: Twayne Publishers, 1991), 144–48.

4. See my *Lines in the Sand: Race and Class in Lowcountry Georgia, 1750–1860* (Athens: University of Georgia Press, 2001): 23–28. In 1860 there were about 22,000 people resident in Savannah, one third of whom were enslaved. Of the c. 14,000 free people, about 800 were free blacks.

5. The principal sources for these benevolent societies are: *Minutes of the Union Society being an abstract of existing records from 1750 to 1860* (Savannah: John M. Cooper, 1860), hereafter Union Society Mins.; *Savannah Morning News*, April 25, 1860; Savannah Female Asylum, Minutes of the Board 1810–1843, Georgia Historical Society, Savannah, hereafter SFA Mins.; Savannah Free School Society, Minutes, vol. 1, 1816–1838, vol. 2, 1838–1856, Georgia Historical Society, Savannah, hereafter SFSS Mins.; and *An Account of the Origin and Progress of the Savannah Free School Society* (New York: Day and Turner, 1819).

6. The estimate of the number of children educated by the Free School is based on fifty per year over more than forty years. *Savannah Republican*, November 11, 1856. In its annual report in 1841 the school noted that it had taught 1210 pupils since 1817. SFSS Mins., November 1841.

7. These figures are taken from the 1850 and 1860 censuses. In 1850 the Union Society housed 23 boys, the Episcopal Orphanage 8 boys and 1 girl, the Female Asylum 33 girls and the Catholic Asylum 32 girls. In 1860 the Union Society was home to 69 boys, the Episcopal Orphanage 3 boys and 7 girls, the Catholic orphanage 15 boys and 74 girls and the Female Asylum 29 girls. The number of children aged five to nineteen in the city rose from 2,712 in 1850 to 4,254 in 1860. On immigration, see Dennis C. Rousey, "Aliens in the WASP Nest: Ethnocultural Diversity in the Antebellum Urban South" *Journal of American History* 79 (1992): 152–64 and idem, "From When They Came to Savannah: The Origins of an Urban Population in the Old South," *Georgia Historical Quarterly* 79 (1995): 305–36. The Irish constituted the largest immigrant group in Savannah in the 1850s.

8. SFA Mins., December 1, 1840, August 7, 1823.

9. See Bellows, "'My Children, Gentlemen'"; and Murray, "Fates of Orphans."

10. "An ordinance to regulate the terms on which children are to be schooled on the funds of the Union Society," Union Society Mins., 28–9—April 23, 1795.

11. SFA Mins., February 6, 1840; June 4, 1840; August 7, December 4, 1834.

12. SFA Mins., April 7, 1825; January 2, 1827; October 1831 (refusals), January 2, 1827; August 5, 1835 (success).

13. SFA Mins., November 14, 1822.

14. SFSS Mins., May 4, 1831; see also September 5, 1817; November 24, 1851; April 1855.

15. Union Society Mins., 156—April 26, 1856.

16. SFSS Act of Incorporation, December 19, 1818. *Acts of the General Assembly of the State of Georgia, passed at Milledgeville, at an annual session in November and December, 1818*

(Milledgeville: S. Grantland, 1819), 106; SFA Act of Incorporation, December 15, 1810, *Acts of the General Assembly of the State of Georgia, passed at Milledgeville, at an annual session in November and December, 1810* (Milledgeville: S. Grantland, 1810), 58.

17. Rule 5 of the SFA, Rule 27 of the SFSS, Union Society Mins., 77—September 9, 1817.

18. SFA Mins., Rule 2, December 3, 1818; February 3, 1820; April 13, 1840; and SFSS Mins., November 1842.

19. [Savannah] *Daily Morning News,* May 11, 1854; Rule 23 of the SFSS.

20. SFA Mins., July 9, 1827, March 6, 1828.

21. SFSS Mins., July 7, 1817.

22. SFA Mins., July 29, August 7, 1823; see also July 29, August 7, 1811; and October 6, 1842; for Union Society runaways, see the lists of beneficiaries in the Minutes.

23. [Savannah] *Daily Morning News,* May 11, 1854.

24. *Savannah Gazette,* January 14, 1817.

25. See John E. Murray, "Literacy Acquisition in an Orphanage: A Historical-Longitudinal Case Study," *American Journal of Education* 110 (February 2004): 172–95, and chapter 8 in this volume. No indenture forms survive from Savannah.

26. *Georgia Analytical Repository* 1 (July 1802): 69. SFSS Mins., November 28, 1825; January 5, 1820. John E. Murray has found a similar gender differential among the children at the Charleston Orphan House. John E. Murray, "Bound by Charity: The Abandoned Children of Late Eighteenth-Century Charleston" in *Down and Out in Early America,* ed. Billy G. Smith (University Park, Penn.: The Pennsylvania State University Press, 2004), 219–23.

27. On republican motherhood, see Anne Firor Scott, *Natural Allies: Women's Associations in American History* (Urbana: University of Illinois Press, 1991), 13; Lori D. Ginzberg, *Women and the Work of Benevolence: Morality, Politics, and Class in the Nineteenth-Century United States* (New Haven: Yale University Press, 1990), 11–35; Suzanne Lebsock, *The Free Women of Petersburg: Status and Culture in a Southern Town* (New York and London: Norton, 1984), 204–5; Nancy F. Cott, *The Bonds of Womanhood: "Women's Sphere" in New England, 1750–1835* (New Haven and London: Yale University Press, 1977), 96, 141–46; Anne Boylan, "Women in Groups: An Analysis of Women's Benevolent Organizations in New York and Boston, 1797–1840" *Journal of American History* 71 (1984): 497; and Christine Stansell, *City of Women: Sex and Class in New York, 1789–1860* (New York: Knopf, 1986), 66–71, 132–33.

28. Letter of Juvenus, *Columbian Museum and Savannah Gazette,* January 25, 1817.

29. SFSS Mins., January 1839; November 1842; and *Savannah Republican,* October 27, 1856.

30. This was the most common outcome for children at the Union Society and Female Asylum. More than two thirds of boys and girls were indentured: the next most common outcome, for about 15 percent of children of either sex, was to be returned to their mother.

31. Union Society Mins., 70.

32. For example, Joseph Eppinger was first bound to merchant Petit De Villiers and later to carpenter J. H. Ash. John Trevoyer was moved from cabinet maker Dougald Ferguson to carriage-maker William Warner, and Alexander Wilson was moved from printer J. M. Cooper to blacksmith L. S. Bennett.

33. SFA Rule no. 6, *Georgia Analytical Repository,* vol. 1, no. 2, July/August 1802, 71.

34. SFA Mins., December 5, 1827. In 1857 the board gave former inmate Caroline Williams $8 while she underwent training to become a teacher. SFA Mins., February, July 1857.

35. For a discussion of white servant girls working alongside slaves, see my "Spheres of Influence: Working Black and White women in Savannah" in *Neither Lady nor Slave: Working Women of the Old South,* ed. Susannah Delfino and Michele Gillespie (Chapel Hill: University of North Carolina Press, 2002), 102–20.

36. SFA Mins., December 13, 1819; and April 24, 1818; see also October 9, 1823.

37. SFA Mins., August 3, 1815.

38. For examples of mothers intervening, see SFA Mins., August 5, 1818; and January 2, 1823; for the case of Mary Ann Flynn, see April 6, 1820; Bellows, "'My Children, Gentlemen'"; and Murray, "Fates of Orphans."

39. SFA Mins., December 1, 1825.

40. SFSS Mins., November 28, 1828.
41. Those receiving land in the lottery are listed online at http://www.rootsweb.com/~gagenweb/lottery/1827/county/byname/chatham.txt.
42. Address of Howell Cobb, 18 (paginated separately in Union Society Mins.).
43. Union Society Mins., Federal Census for Chatham County, 1860.
44. It was mainly Irish-born laborers, for example, who built the Chatham County sections of the Savannah, Ogeechee, and Altamaha Canal. *Daily Georgian,* April 20, June 26, and November 17, 1827. Savannah City Council Minutes (Georgia Historical Society), August 30, 1827.
45. For a biography of Cobb, see Horace Montgomery, "The Two Howell Cobbs: A Case of Mistaken Identity," *Journal of Southern History* 28 (1962): 348–55.
46. Union Society Mins., 68, 104.
47. Sheftall had written a letter of thanks to the directresses of the Free School in 1825. SFSS Mins., May 11, 1825.
48. See Lockley, "Spheres of Influence," 111.
49. Charity Green and Betsey McPike both had personal estates of $50 in 1860, and both were working as seamstresses.
50. Data on marriages and deaths come from *Marriages Of Chatham County, Georgia. Vol. 1, 1748–1852; Vol. 2, 1852–1877* (Savannah: Georgia Historical Society, 1993) and *Register Of Deaths In Savannah, Georgia. 6 Vols. 1803–1847* (Savannah: Georgia Historical Society, 1989). The directresses of the SFA on one occasion gave a tea set to one of the girls as a wedding present. SFA Mins., October 1831.
51. Both epidemics killed about six hundred people, though only about 10 percent were native-born Savannahians. William R. Waring, *Report to the City Council of Savannah on the Epidemic Disease of 1820* (Savannah: Henry P. Russell, 1821), 3, 62; and W. Duncan, M.D., *Tabulated Mortuary Records of the City of Savannah, from January 1, 1854 to December 31, 1869* (Savannah: Morning News Press, 1870), 9.
52. SFA Mins., September 7, 1820; SFA records, Folder 11, Admissions and Dismissions; Union Society Mins., April 23, 1855, p. 141. Only one of the girls resident at the Female Asylum in 1860 was foreign-born, Canadian-born Margaret Donnelley. Murray, "Bound to Charity," 224–25.
53. SFSS Mins., November 24, 1851.
54. SFSS Mins., November 28, 1848; *Address of the Hon Thomas U.P. Charlton, delivered before the members of the Union Society on their seventy-third anniversary AD 1823* (Savannah, 1860), 12 (paginated separately in Union Society Mins.).
55. Howell Cobb was jailed on April 18, 1815. Savannah Jail Register, 1809–1815, GHS.
56. Cases of James Fountain, William Cahill, William Simpson, William Mahew, and John Gilbert. Savannah City Council Minutes, November 2, 1818; October 18, 1819 [2]; March 10, 1823; and May 20, 1830. William Thompson was fined for retailing liquor without a licence, City Council Minutes, March 3, 1836. SFSS Mins., Annual Report 1824.
57. Timothy J. Lockley, "Trading Encounters between Non-Elite Whites and African Americans in Savannah, 1790–1860," *Journal of Southern History* 66 (2000): 25–48. More than a thousand residents were jailed between January 1860 and December 1862. City of Savannah, Jail Register, 1855–62, GHS.
58. Betty Wood, "'For Their Satisfaction or Redress'": African Americans and Church Discipline in the Early South," in *The Devil's Lane: Sex and Race in the Early South,* ed. Catherine Clinton and Michele Gillespie (New York: Oxford University Press, 1997), 109–23; and Stephanie McCurry, *Masters of Small Worlds: Yeoman Households, Gender Relations, and the Political Culture of the Antebellum South Carolina Lowcountry* (New York: Oxford University Press, 1995), 178–95. See also Jean E. Friedman, *The Enclosed Garden: Women and Community in the Evangelical South, 1830–1900* (Chapel Hill: University of North Carolina Press, 1988), 78; Janet Cornelius, "Slave Marriages in a Georgia Congregation," in *Class, Conflict, and Consensus: Antebellum Southern Community Studies,* ed. Orville Vernon Burton and Robert C. McMath (Westport, Conn.: Greenwood Press, 1985), 128; and Sylvia R. Frey and Betty Wood, *Come Shouting to Zion: African American Protestantism in the American South and British Caribbean to 1830* (Chapel Hill and London: University of North Carolina Press, 1998), 183–206.

59. *Savannah Republican,* November 18, 1856.

60. Howell Cobb, *A Scriptural Examination of the Institution of Slavery in the United States; with its Objects and Purposes* (Perry, Ga.: for the author, 1856), 8, 11.

61. Union Society Mins., 162–64. A list of those from Savannah who served with the Confederate forces can be found in F. D. Lee and J. L. Agnew, *Historical Record of the City of Savannah* (Savannah: J. H. Estill, 1868), 119–28.

62. *Address of the Hon. Thomas U. P. Charlton,* 12.

63. [Savannah] *Daily Morning News,* May 11, 1854.

64. SFSS Mins., November 1840; November 28, 1848.

65. SFSS Mins., May 11, 1825; and Address of Howell Cobb, 16.

66. *Savannah Morning News,* April 27, 1860. Kern was a thirty-three-year-old laborer, according to the 1860 census.

Chapter 10. Responsive Justices

1. Somerset County Court (Judicial Record), MSA C1774–31:216, hereafter Somerset Judicials. All manuscript sources are located at the Maryland State Archives, Annapolis, Maryland.

2. On Talbot, see Jean B. Russo, *Free Workers in a Plantation Economy: Talbot County, Maryland, 1690–1759* (New York: Garland Publishing, 1989), esp. pt. 1; and Paul G. E. Clemens, *The Atlantic Economy and Colonial Maryland's Eastern Shore: From Tobacco to Grain* (Ithaca: Cornell University Press, 1980). On Somerset, see J. Elliott Russo, "'The Interest of the County': Population, Economy, and Society in Eighteenth-Century Somerset County, Maryland" (Ph.D. dissertation, University of Minnesota, 1999); and Lois Green Carr, "Diversification in the Colonial Chesapeake: Somerset County, Maryland, in Comparative Perspective," in *Colonial Chesapeake Society,* ed. Lois Green Carr et al. (Chapel Hill: University of North Carolina Press for the Institute of Early American History and Culture, 1988), 342–88.

3. In Virginia, courts shared responsibility for children's welfare with parish vestries, but because the Church of England did not become Maryland's established church until sixty years after settlement, the vestry's secular responsibilities devolved to the county court early in the seventeenth century. In 1692 the establishment act provided for elected vestries in each parish but did not grant them the same range of authority as exercised by their Virginia counterparts. In this, as in several other areas, the treatment of orphans in Maryland differs markedly from the practice in Virginia, as described by Holly Brewer in chapter 12 of this volume. On the powers of the Virginia's vestries, see William H. Seiler, "The Anglican Church: A Basic Institution of Local Government in Colonial Virginia," in *Town and Country: Essays on the Structure of Local Government in the American Colonies,* ed. Bruce C. Daniels (Middletown, CT: Wesleyan University Press, 1978), 148, 150. On the role of Maryland vestries, see Lois Green Carr, "The Foundations of Social Order: Local Government in Colonial Maryland," in *Town and Country,* ed. Daniels, 73, 93.

4. For two useful introductions into the larger literature on patriarchy in early America, see Mary Beth Norton, *Founding Mothers and Fathers: Gendered Power and the Forming of American Society* (New York: Alfred A. Knopf, 1996), esp. ch. 2; and Kathleen M. Brown, *Nasty Wenches, Good Wives, and Anxious Patriarchs: Gender, Race, and Power in Colonial Virginia* (Chapel Hill: University of North Carolina Press for the Omohundro Institute of Early American History and Culture, 1996). Note that Mary Beth Norton explicitly avoids the use of "'patriarch' and its variants... in the interest of achieving greater precision and adhering to terminology appropriate" to the period. Norton, *Founding Mothers,* 413n5.

5. Carr, "Foundations of Social Order," 85.

6. See, in particular, Bruce C. Daniels, "Introduction," in *Town and Country,* ed. Daniels, 7–10; as well as other essays in the same volume.

7. Lois Green Carr, "The Development of the Maryland Orphans' Court, 1654–1715," in *Law, Society, and Politics in Early Maryland,* ed. Aubrey C. Land et al. (Baltimore: Johns Hopkins University Press, 1977), 41–62; Lorena S. Walsh, "Community Networks in the Early Chesapeake," in *Colonial Chesapeake Society,* ed. Carr et al., 70–115, 200–241,; and Allan Kulikoff, *Tobacco and Slaves: The Development of Southern Cultures in the Chesapeake, 1680–1800* (Chapel

Hill: University of North Carolina Press for the Institute of Early American History and Culture, 1986), 386–87.

8. Talbot County judicial records begin in 1662 but have significant gaps, while the Somerset judicial records begin in 1665, with complete coverage after 1687; all counts of children and their status thus represent lower bounds.

9. It is assumed that not all women who bore children out of wedlock were charged with a criminal offense. Court records document cases of women punished for bastardy whose children died prior to prosecution; we have not included these cases in the minimum numbers of bastard children at risk for placement by the court. We have used annual averages of extant cases as proxies for missing court proceedings to estimate the total number of bastardy cases. Again, Maryland practice contrasts sharply with Virginia, where "courts left few illegitimate children with their mothers or even with their fathers," according to Brewer's essay in chapter 12 of this volume.

10. Somerset Judicials, C1774–8: 98 and C1774–35: 98–99.

11. Talbot County Judgments, C:1875–23: 96, hereafter Talbot Judgments. Siblings frequently had different masters, particularly if the family was a large one, as few households had the resources to absorb several extra members.

12. Talbot Judgments, C1875–21: 26.

13. Somerset Judicials, C1774–17: 108; Talbot Judgments, C1875–22: 228; and Somerset Judicials, C1774–18: 269.

14. Talbot Judgments, C1875–20: 60.

15. Somerset Judicials, C1774–16: 52.

16. Carr, "Orphans' Court," 41.

17. "An Act for the Preservacon of Orphans Estates," William Hand Browne, ed., *Archives of Maryland* (Baltimore: Maryland Historical Society, 1883), vol. 1, *Proceedings and Acts of the General Assembly January 1637/8-September 1664*, 494.

18. Many children were bound at quite young ages, indicating that householders were willing to gamble on caring for very young children in the hope of eventual benefit from their labor, even when the potential workers were white girls whose service would be limited to domestic help. Thus foster care was generally a temporary expedient until a child could be matched with a master, rather than a means of providing care for children too young to earn their keep.

19. Talbot Judgments, AB 8, 1696–1698, C1875–9: 466 and 467.

20. "An Act for the better Administration of Justice in Probate of Wills granting Administrations recovery of Legacies and securing filial Portions," William Hand Browne, ed., *Archives of Maryland* (Baltimore: Maryland Historical Society, 1894), vol. 13, *Proceedings and Acts of the General Assembly, April 1684–June 1692*, 433.

21. Talbot Judgments, C1875–20: 195; and Somerset Judicials, C1774–17: 107.

22. Browne, *Archives of Maryland*, 1:494.

23. Talbot Judgments, C1875–19: n.p., 3/1705 court.

24. Neither Talbot nor Somerset contained any settlement larger than a small village during the colonial period. For a different pattern of apprenticeship, one influenced by the presence of a flourishing town, see Christine M. Daniels, "Alternative Workers in a Slave Economy, Kent County, Maryland, 1675–1810" (Ph.D. dissertation, Johns Hopkins University, 1990), esp. chs. 2, 6, and 8.

25. Orphans who did not inherit real property nonetheless frequently received a share of their father's personalty, including livestock.

26. Somerset Judicials, C1774–30: 186.

27. The group of mixed-race children bound by the Somerset court after 1740 includes seventeen boys and nine girls; four boys and one girl were bound without provisions for reading.

28. The reasons for the noticeable difference between the two counties in the treatment of mixed-race children remain unclear. Although we expected that the size of Somerset's oft-cited free black and mulatto population might be a factor, the 1755 census records a larger nonwhite free population in Talbot (71 adults) than in Somerset (48 adults). We therefore hypothesize that the different economic structure of the two counties played a more important role, with Somerset's regional and West Indian trade creating a demand for rudimentary skills that was absent

in Talbot's tobacco and wheat economy. "The Population of Maryland, 1755," from *Gentleman's Magazine* 34 (1764), reprinted in Edward C. Papenfuse and Joseph M. Coale III, *The Hammond-Harwood House Atlas of Historical Maps of Maryland, 1608–1908* (Baltimore: Johns Hopkins University Press, 1982), 37.

29. Talbot Judgments, C:1875–23: 12. Emphasis added.

Chapter 11. The Stateless and the Orphaned among Montreal's Apprentices, 1791–1842

1. For more on orphanages and adoption in Montreal, see N. C. Pearce, *A History of the Montreal Ladies' Benevolent Society, 1815–1920* (Montreal: The Society, 1920); *Historical Sketch of the Montreal Protestant Orphan Asylum* (Montreal: John Lovell, 1860); and *Constitution and By-Laws of the Montreal Protestant Orphan Asylum* (Montreal: John Lovell, 1860).

2. Peter Moogk, "Childhood in New France," in *Interpreting Canada's Past: Volume One, Pre-Confederation*, 2nd ed., ed., J. M. Bumsted (Toronto: Oxford University Press, 1993), 130.

3. Antoine Roy, *Inventaire des Greffes des Notaires du Régime Français*, vol. 19 (Quebec: Archives nationale du Québec, Ministère des affaires culturelles, 1960), 399.

4. Roy, *Inventaire*, 100.

5. J. M. Cadieux (notary), no. 189, June 7, 1812, Archives Nationale du Québec.

6. J. J. Curran, ed., *Golden Jubilee of St. Patrick's Orphan Asylum* (Montreal: Catholic Institution for Deaf Mutes, 1902), 41. See also sources cited in note 1 of this chapter. Moogk, "Childhood," 26. For more on the Grey Nuns, see Peter Gossage, "Abandoned Children in Nineteenth-Century Montreal" (M.A. thesis, McGill University, 1983).

7. Geoff Blackburn, *The Children's Friend Society: Juvenile Emigrants to Western Australia, South Africa, and Canada, 1834–1842* (Northbridge, Australia: Access Press, 1993), 239.

8. Children's Friend Society, 5th Annual Report (1835), cited in Blackburn, *Children's Friend Society*, 241. At least thirty-two apprentice contracts involving Mr. Orrok have survived (drawn up by a Montreal notary); eleven of them do not meet the sample selection criteria (for example, two are missing age information, one involved a girl, and six did not involve a craft).

9. The outcome is unknown for forty-four of the 2,385 foundlings left at the Grey Nuns Hospital between 1820 and 1840. See Gossage, "Abandoned Children," 118.

10. Gossage, "Abandoned Children," 120.

11. For an example of the different types of placements from one institution, see Gossage, "Abandoned Children."

12. Half of the domestic orphans with English names and a bit more than one-third of the domestic orphans with French names relied on a tutor instead of extended family to indent them into an apprenticeship.

13. Ordinary least squares regression analysis indicates that the signing rates for domestic orphans (tutor and family) were not significantly different than that for children with parents but that the rate for CFS orphans was significantly lower than the rate observed for parents, all else being equal. Results for logistic regressions were similar. Apart from the controls for orphan status (family, tutor, CFS), the regression includes apprentice characteristics (whether the boy had a French last name, and an age and age-squared), a dummy variable for whether the sponsor signed his name, and single-year effects for the years the contract was active.

14. Guardians might have had less incentive to try and find a high income trade for their charges for two reasons: first, they may have cared about the child's welfare less than a parent, and second, they may have been less likely to receive remittances from the child.

15. Letter from John Orrok to Mr. Scobell, November 1, 1836 (no. 3221–4). Lennox and Addington County Museum, John Benson Papers.

16. Reported for the northeastern United States. See Robert A. Margo, *Wages and Labor Markets in the United States, 1820–1860* (Chicago: University of Chicago Press, 2000), 55. These four trades were the only categories in Margo's data set, which consists of payroll records of civilians hired by the army.

17. Robert Campbell, *The London Tradesman* (1747; repr. New York: A. M. Kelley, 1969), 331–40.

18. The obvious caveat is that while masters in high-income trades could afford to pay their apprentices well, they could also pay poorly since the supply of boys willing to train in such trades

may have been relatively high. In addition, training costs were high for occupations with high masters' income.

19. Part of the explanation for the differences in average pay across trades is that the average boy entering some trades was older or more likely to have been literate, for example, traits that commanded higher pay.

20. 15 percent of tutor orphans, 8 percent of family orphans, and 10 percent of boys with parents were employed in these five trades.

21. All of this assumes that the relative setup costs for trades in London were not that different from the setup costs in Montreal.

22. The different currencies found in the contracts have been converted to a single unit of account, Halifax currency, which became increasingly common over time. The exchange rates employed are: $4 (Spanish silver) = £1 currency (Halifax) = 24 *livres* (old money; *ancien cours*) = £0.90 sterling (before 1820). To calculate real values, payments were deflated using a clothing price index. For the details on calculating apprentices' pay, see Gillian Hamilton, "The Decline of Apprenticeship in North America: Evidence from Montreal," *Journal of Economic History* 60 (2000): 627–64.

23. Blackburn, *Children's Friend Society*. Indenture between Gwenderlam Isreal and John Benson (no. 3831–2), dated November 1, 1836, Lennox and Addington County Museum, John Benson Papers.

24. See, for example, the document of notary: N. B. Doucet, no. 23004, November 20, 1835 (Archives Nationales du Québec à Montréal, or Quebec National Archives—Montreal).

25. One could question whether the 15 shillings going to the tutor was for the tutor or the apprentice. This problem arises in other contracts when payments from the master were directed to the parent instead of the child. In many cases it is clear that the money is intended specifically for the apprentice's upkeep, although the ultimate use of the money is obviously uncertain. In any case, these payments are all part of a master's cost of hiring an apprentice.

26. It is not possible to convert all the in-kind compensation to a monetary equivalent to construct a summary total cash payment. First, there is no basis for imputing a monetary value to mending and washing services. Second, many contracts did not specify the amounts or types of clothing provided, making it difficult to assign them a value. Third, the end payments in some contracts were in kind (a set of tools, or the like), which are again difficult to value. The process is further complicated by the fact that it is necessary to make comparisons across time. Therefore, it is not just a way of valuing, say, clothing that is required, but a way of valuing it at different points of time over the sample period. A single set of prices used to value the in-kind compensation throughout the sample period might mask some important changes in the orphan/non-orphan compensation ratio.

27. As noted in the table, the binary variable "cash" equals 1 if the contract specified cash payments during the term, independent from an end payment.

28. Farley Grubb reported that the absence of a father did not affect contract length for English indentured servants destined to work in America. Grubb, "Fatherless and Friendless: Factors Influencing the Flow of English Emigrant Servants," *Journal of Economic History* 52 (1992): 86. In contrast, Steve Rappaport found that a father's status was an important determinant of apprentice's situations in seventeenth century London. Rappaport, *Worlds within Worlds: Structures of Life in Sixteenth-Century London* (New York: Cambridge University Press, 1989).

29. Unfortunately, it is not possible to determine whether the choices reflected Orrok's preferences or "network" in Montreal, the boys' preferences, or the masters' interest.

30. They were more likely to receive provision for schooling, but it seems unlikely that a promise to teach the apprentice to read and write entirely accounted for the extra six months.

Chapter 12. Apprenticeship Policy in Virginia

1. "Frederick County Order Books," 3:388, February 15, 1751. These records and all other manuscript materials cited below are available at the Library of Virginia in Richmond. My thanks to Brent Tarter there for his kind help.

2. Richard Morris attributes the decline in apprenticeship to industrialization, but sees its impact mostly in terms of an increasing animosity to labor monopolies. Morris, *Government and*

Labor in Early America (New York, 1946), 363–89; see also W. J. Rorabaugh, *The Craft Apprentice: From Franklin to the Machine Age in America* (New York, 1986); and Ian Quimby, *Apprenticeship in Colonial Philadelphia* (New York, 1985). In their classic study of apprenticeship in England, O. J. Dunlop and Richard Denham argued that apprenticeship was abolished partly because of abuses of the system by factories, in which apprentices were worked very long hours without the supervision that had earlier been part of the system in the eighteenth century. Dunlop and Denham, *English Apprenticeship and Child Labour* (New York, 1912).

3. Pamela Barnhouse Walters and Carl M. Briggs summarize the recent research that has contradicted the "longheld view that industrialization reduced the need and the opportunities for children's employment." Walters and Briggs, "The Family Economy, Child Labor, and Schooling: Evidence from the Early Twentieth-Century South," *American Sociological Review* 58 (1993): 163–81.

4. John K. Nelson, *A Blessed Company: Parishes, Parsons, and Parishioners in Anglican Virginia, 1690–1776* (Chapel Hill, 2001), 75. John kindly gave me his index cards for all of these cases. Trying to figure out the relevant populations for these counties over time would be a massive undertaking given that the rates would have to be computed from tithables lists (which do not list children, only white male adults and male and female enslaved adults, not differentiated) and that the data on apprenticeships from the Minute Books and Order Books has survived so inconsistently. For the difficulties of these calculations using tithables for just one county, see note 22 below.

5. Warren Hofstra, "These Fine Prospects: Frederick County, Virginia 1738–1840" (Ph.D. dissertation, University of Virginia, 1985), 131.

6. Between 1751 and 1760, of the children apprenticed, seventy-four were "orphans" whose mothers were probably alive (the term meant only that their fathers had died); forty-six were bastards, where otherwise the mother would have had custody; and only forty-one were classed as "poor," meaning the father, but likely both parents were alive. "Frederick County Order Books," vols. 3–9.

7. See, for example, the 1751 cases of Zachariah, William, and Thomas Connell, "three children of the said parish whose parents neglect to educate them as the law directs"; in 1787, Hugh Morrison's children were apprenticed because he did not "take proper care in [their] provision and education." The court ordered that Deana Merryfield be bound because "the said father doth not provide her sufficient clothing." See "Frederick County Order Book," Connell 3:509, August 16, 1751; Morrison (Minute Book 1786–90): 107, December 4, 1787; and Merryfield 7:360, February 7, 1758.

8. Holly Brewer, "Beyond Education: Thomas Jefferson's Republican Revision of the Laws Regarding Children," in *Thomas Jefferson and the Education of a Citizen in the New Republic*, ed. James Gilreath (Washington, D.C., 1999), 48–62.

9. P. Thomas Mason, "Child Abuse and Neglect: Part 1, Historical Overview, Legal Matrix, and Social Perspectives," *North Carolina Law Review* 50 (1972): 293–349; and Walter I. Trattner, *From Poor Law to Welfare State: A History of Social Welfare in America*, 4th ed. (New York, 1989), 106.

10. Trattner, *From Poor Law to Welfare State*, 23. For a similar argument, see also Walter Fraser, "The City Elite, 'Disorder,' and the Poor Children of Pre-Revolutionary Charleston," *South Carolina Historical Magazine* 84 (1983): 167–79.

11. William Waller Hening, ed., *The Statutes at Large, being a Collection of all the Laws of Virginia, from the first session of the legislature in the year 1619* (New York, 1823), 5:452–3 (1748). It specifies that each apprentice shall be taught a trade and that each "master or mistress ... shall find and provide for him or her, diet, cloaths, lodgings, and accommodations fit and necessary, and shall teach, or cause him or her to be taught to read and write, and at the expiration of his or her apprenticeship, shall pay every such servant, the like allowance as is by law appointed for servants by indenture or custom.... And if upon complaint made to the county court, it shall appear, that any such apprentice is ill used, or not taught the trade or profession to which he or she was bound, it shall be lawful for such courts to remove and bind him or her to such other person or persons as they shall think fit."

12. Of fifteen complaints for insufficient food or clothing, "immoderate correction," "ill-usage," or "insufficient care," in the Order Books for Frederick County in the 1750s, two were

brought by the churchwardens in their oversight capacity, and one was initiated by neighbors. Dewey, March 1754 (5:337); Sarah and William Pearce, April 1758 (8:1); and Colston, February 1760 (8:33). The rest were brought by parents or by the apprentices/servants themselves. In one case the master and mistress were imprisoned for a short period for "abusing" their servant. Servant unknown, Peter and Catherine Bradford imprisoned, June 1754 (6:14). Otherwise, three apprentices/servants were transferred to new masters (Bayley, October 1752 (4:320 and 4:339); Buckley, November 1752 (4:378); Colston, see above), one was released on her own recognizance (Tapling, November 1753, 5:263 and 5:301), four reprimands were given to masters with orders that they improve (Haycroft, May 1751 (3:428); Scot, July 1752 (4:215); Ferrill, April 1755 (6:199); William Finnichan, April 1757 (7:222)), two complaints were dismissed (first complaint of Buckley and Margaret Finnichan, November 1752 (4:338) and Stewart, December 1756 (7:155)) and four the results are unknown.

13. For a fascinating discussion of why the Catholic church prohibited adoption in medieval England, see Jack Goody, *The Development of the Family and Marriage in Europe* (Cambridge, UK, 1983). Goody argues that it enabled them to acquire more land by the rules of inheritance. For a history of adoption in America, see Jamil S. Zainalden, "The Emergence of a Modern American Family Law: Child Custody, Adoption, and the Courts, 1796–1856," *Northwestern University Law Review* 73 (1979): 1038–89; and Stephen B. Presser, "The Historical Background of the American Law of Adoption," *Journal of Family Law* 11 (1971): 443–516.

14. I elaborate on the distinctions between the contracts of indentured servants and poor-apprentices in chapter 6 of my dissertation, "Constructing Consent: How Children's Status in Political Theory Shaped Public Policy in Virginia, Pennsylvania, and Massachusetts, before and after the Revolution," UCLA, 1994. Briefly, however, poor apprenticeship contracts, at least by the 1780s, did not contain the allowance for "assigns" that most indentured servants contracts contained. In other words, the contract was just between the Overseers of the Poor and the master, not between the Overseers of the Poor and the master or his assigns. The clause "assigns" allowed salability. For an example of the restrictions this placed even on simple transfers, let alone sales, see the petition of Hannah Carter, executrix of her husband's will, who asked the court to be able to reassign her dead husband's apprentice to "George Bush." The court granted this request "on the condition that he oblige himself to teach [Charles Hannagan Rook, a bastard child] the trade of a weaver." "Frederick County Order Books," 8:318, September 6, 1759.

15. For example, when the court ordered the Churchwardens of Frederick Parish to bind [Male] Wallace, on October 7, 1755, they requested that they "provide that he not be removed out of this colony." "Frederick County Order Books," 6:406.

16. See, for example, the petition of Margaret Harper and her three children for her husband to support them. "Frederick County Order Books" 7:5 December 3, 1755.

17. There were three cases during the 1750s. James Jack was "charged with begetting on the body of Sarah Vanmeter a child... to give a security so that the parish will not have to support the child." "Frederick County Order Books" 8:133, November 7, 1758; John Hagen 6:91, October 1, 1754; and Thomas Low 5:3, June 5, 1753. Because the vestry records are missing prior to 1762, it is not clear whether they had to make good on their promise. The vestry records of the 1760s record only one case where a reputed father had to reimburse the parish. In the case mentioned above, Hester Ryan was bound to her "reputed" father (her mother's master) at the age of one month, apparently in lieu of paying support. "Frederick County Order Books" 3:388, February 15, 1751. In another case, James Brown, the bastard son of Bridget Brown, was bound to Bridget's master Robert Glass at the age of a month even though Glass was not the "reputed" father. Virginia law stipulated that in cases where masters were the fathers of their servants' children, they could not have the benefit of the year's extra service that would otherwise recompense them for the loss of their servant's labor during her pregnancy and nursing. In this case, Bridget was required to serve the extra year; if Glass were the father, no mention was made of it in the courtroom. Bridget might have had some reason to deny his paternity even if true, as otherwise he would not pay her fine for bastardy and she would be publically whipped. See 4:141–2, June 2, 1752.

18. "Frederick Vestry Book," 20–28, 41. "Indemnifying the parish" seems to have been a synonym for apprenticeship in these cases, as is clear from a cross-reference of the vestry book with the Frederick County Court Minute Book for the 1780s.

19. See, for example, the petition of Jane Callahan for the return of her daughter. The daughter, in this case, was mulatto, and had apparently been bound to the age of thirty-one. "Frederick County Order Books," 4:418, March 7, 1753; and 7:274, August 3, 1757.

20. Hening, *Statutes at Large* 1:336 (1646); "Frederick County Order Books," Martin 7:191, March 1, 1757.

21. William Finnichan's story is particularly revealing of the limits of protection. William was first bound at the age of almost four to his mother's master even though his mother (Margaret Finnichan) had complained that her master had abused her. His first complaint of abuse (when he was nine) led only to a reprimand of his master. Only after a second complaint was he finally returned to his mother—even then he was first transferred, briefly, to a new master. His mother had to beg the court to regain custody (she was married and apparently comfortably off). Her plea was finally heeded in 1760, when he was twelve (see August and September 1760 (9:94 and 138)). See note 12 in this chapter, for the citations for the Finnichan case.

22. Between 1751 and 1760, the Churchwardens of Frederick Parish bound 60 girls out of an average population of 1,348 girls/year. 113 boys were bound from an average population of 1,775 boys/year. I arrived at these percentages by calculating the

$$\frac{(\# \text{ girls bound}) \times (\text{length of service})}{(\text{pool of eligible girls}) \times (\text{time})}$$

I had to estimate the number of boys and girls by comparing lists of tithables (all white males over sixteen and all slaves over sixteen) to accumulated data from various age groups in the census of 1790. Given data from 1755 on the percentage of tithables who were slaves, this gives a fairly close approximation. Average length of service for boys was 12.9 years, since boys were bound, on average, at 8.1, until they turned twenty-one, and for girls was 10.6, since they were bound on average at 7.4 until they reached eighteen. The pool of eligible girls was estimated by calculating the average number of girls and multiplying by the average length of service. Time = 10 years (1751–60). The pool of eligible boys was estimated in the same way.

I included such factors as length of service because the total number of girls bound in any given year reflects not only those bound in that year but many that were bound in previous years. Generally, however, length of service cancels out, since it appears also as a multiplier in the "pool of eligible children."

23. Pension plans in Virginia have received little attention. A general introduction to colonial pension plans is William H. Glasson, *Federal Military Pensions in the United States* (New York, 1918), which is a revised edition of his earlier book on the same subject, *History of Military Pension Legislation in the United States* (New York, 1900). The act of October 1779 in fact replaced earlier, partial pension plans. The first pension plans in Virginia included benefits only for soldiers maimed or wounded, such as that passed during the French and Indian war in 1755. Hening, *Statutes at Large* 6:527; for earlier legislation that provided pensions for wounded veterans, see 1:287 (1644) and 2:331 (1675), 347 (1676), and 440 (1679).

The 1675 law provided for "indigent families" of the slain, but the provision lasted only a year. In 1775, at the beginning of the Revolutionary War, partly to encourage more to enlist, the legislature promised that it would provide financial support for all those maimed in the war (9:14). In 1777, for the first time, temporary support was to be provided to widows whose husbands had died while soldiers in the Continental or Commonwealth Armies (9:344–45). In October 1778 that was substantially reinforced by giving pensions to all widows of soldiers for the remainder of their natural lives "equal to half the pay that her husband was entitled to when in the service" (9:566). The purpose of this law was explicitly to provide "for the family of such officers and soldiers."

In October 1779 these earlier plans were abrogated for widows who did not have financial need but provided for additional family members who could demonstrate poverty. The new plan gave county courts the power "to grant allowances to the wives, parents, and families of any soldier now in actual service, upon proof to them made, that such wives, parents, or families are so poor that they cannot maintain themselves; such allowance not to exceed one barrel of corn and fifty pounds of nett pork for each person, annually." Earlier acts that gave pensions to all widows were disallowed, but special, and broader, provisions were made for indigent families: these would have been the families most likely to fall upon poor relief, and the children in these families would have been the most likely to have been bound out (10:212). In 1782 the provisions for the families of soldiers were made easier to obtain, and in 1785 pensions for the maimed soldiers and for the families of soldiers killed in the Revolutionary War were upheld and the process simplified (11:11, 11:146 and 12:102–6).

24. Pensions were equal to half the pay of the former soldier.

25. From bill number 64, on crimes, in the revisal of the laws. Julian P. Boyd, ed., *The Papers of Thomas Jefferson* (Princeton, NJ, 1950), 2:494. A law had been in force in Virginia, as indeed it had been in Massachusetts and Pennsylvania, based on an English law that presumed that mothers who bore a bastard child in secret, where the child was found dead, were guilty of murdering their child. This law had argued that concealing by itself signified an intent to kill the child. Jefferson challenged this assumption: Indeed, the evidence I have from Frederick County, Virginia, shows that prosecution of "murders" of bastard children dropped precipitously between the 1750s and the 1810s, probably in part because this presumption of guilt was dropped.

26. The laws themselves were somewhat vague about procedure, yet they remained essentially unchanged between 1750 and the 1780s; indeed, since the statute that had framed basic policy, 18 Eliz. ca.3.

> Two justices of Peace ... in which parish any Bastard childe (begotton and borne out of lawful Matrimony) shal be borne, upon examination of the cause and circumstances, shal and may take order (by their discretion) as well for the reliefe of the parish, and keeping of the childe, (by charging the mother or reputed father, with the payment of money, or other reliefe,) As also for the punishment of the mother and reputed father. *But such a Bastard childe must bee one that is left to the charge of the Parish,* or one likely to be (or which may be) chargeable to the parish. [emphasis mine]

The English law was reprinted directly in the guides used by Virginian Justices of the Peace, who were the implementers of local policy, such as the above passage from the Elizabethan law, which is taken from Michael Dalton, *The Countrey Justice* (London, 1618; repr., Amsterdam, 1975), 31. Dalton's guide was recommended for use of Justices of the Peace in Virginia by an act of 1666 for "the better conformity of the proceedings of the courts of this country." See Hening, *Statutes at Large,* 2:246. Dalton's *Justice* was still popular in the eighteenth century, as shown by Herbert Johnson's *Imported Eighteenth-Century Law Treatises in American Libraries, 1700–1799* (Knoxville, 1978), 17; and William Hamilton Bryson's *Census of Law Books in Colonial Virginia* (Charlottesville, 1978), 46.

For Virginia guidelines that echo this policy, see Hening, *Statutes,* 1695 (3:110), 1769 (8:374–77), 1785 (12:28–29).

27. Between 1751 and 1760 twelve women were fined, five women were whipped twenty-five lashes (with one woman, Elizabeth King, whipped twice for two separate children), and seventeen women agreed to serve their masters for one year or more in exchange for his paying their fine. Not all suits were successfully prosecuted: women apparently ran for cover when they saw the sheriff delivering their bond to appear in court, since he was so unsuccessful at getting them to even acknowledge the court order to appear. In the October 1753 session, of nine cases for bastardy, only two women appeared. See "Frederick County Order Books."

There is still an occasional case in the 1780s in which a female servant had to serve her master one year more for bearing a bastard child, but this seems to be the only holdover of the older policy of punishing the mothers of bastard children. The laws themselves outlawed whipping in 1769 (Hening, *Statutes at Large,* 8:376), but the Churchwardens were still empowered to assess fines, an ability transferred to the Overseers of the Poor (along with all other tasks relating to poor apprenticeship) in 1780. This was formally confirmed in 1785 (12:29).

28. See Glasson, *Federal Military Pensions in the United States* (New York, 1918), 65–69.

29. This issue is difficult to pin down because such settlements would have left no public record. A glimpse of how they operated can be seen in the confession of a woman executed for killing her children. She claimed that their father had killed them when she tried to get him to support them, threatening that she would get a formal order of support from the court if he did not do so informally. Pennsylvania had a similar policy in the 1780s. This shows that settlement

for bastard children was normally done outside of court, with the court serving as backup enforcement. See [Elizabeth Wilson], *A Faithful Narrative of Elizabeth Wilson*, originally published in 1786 concerning events that had occurred in Chester County, Pennsylvania, in 1784. It is reprinted in Daniel E. Williams, ed., *Pillars of Salt: An Anthology of Early American Criminal Narratives* (Madison, WI, 1993), 273. Wilson, who had just had illegitimate twins, confronted their father. "When I told him I had two children [twins], he looked me in my face, saying, 'the devil! you have?['] I requested him to do something for my [sic] by fair means, assuring him, if he did not consent, I should apply to the law: He answered, I need not go to law, for he would do for me.... I then requested him to put one of the dear children to nurse, the other I proposed to keep, on condition of his giving me a supply of money."

30. For a discussion of the broad transformation of the legal status of illegitimate children in the years after the American Revolution, including how their ability to legally inherit changed after the Revolution as well as maternal custody of such children in the nineteenth century, see Michael Grossberg's *Governing the Hearth: Law and the Family in Nineteenth-Century America* (Chapel Hill, NC, 1985), 196–233.

31. Both Virginia and Pennsylvania made this punishment of the children an extension of the crime of miscegenation they found the parents, particularly the white mother, guilty of committing. See [Virginia], *Statutes at Large*, ed. Hening: 3:87, 453 (1691 and 1705). This law was repealed in 1765, 8:134–5.

32. See the case of Kesia Carey, alias Newman, the daughter of free black woman Flora Carey. She was bound at age six in January 1812. In October 1815, she complained of mistreatment for the first time. She was transferred to a new master on December 2, 1816. "Frederick County Minute Books" 3:353, 4:196, 4:372.

33. The free blacks who learned a trade in the 1810s were most likely to be males in their mid- to late teens. William Wilkinson, for example, was eighteen when he was bound to learn the trade of a blacksmith in 1817.

34. Frederick County Minute Books, 1782–86 (1) and 1786–90 (2). The six children taught to read and write included Lazurus Penton (age five) (August 1782, 1:35); Erasmus and Buel [no last names or ages] (September 1784, 1:275); Janey (age fourteen), Margaret (age five) and Cale (age nine) [no last names] (September 1790, 2:423, 427).

35. See, generally, the apprenticeship file for this period from Frederick County. While most contracts are missing for the early period, the contract collection seems fairly complete for the period after 1810. This observation is clear, as well, in the court records themselves.

36. Douglas R. Egerton, *The Virginia Slave Conspiracies of 1800 and 1802* (Chapel Hill, 1993), esp. ch. 10.

37. In 1790, Frederick County, Virginia, had a total free black population of 116, of which approximately half (58) were probably under the age of sixteen (sixteen was the average age for the U.S. population as a whole), compared to a white population of 15,315, of which approximately half (7,658) were children under sixteen. While the white population grew only slightly between 1790 and 1820, the free black population grew dramatically. In 1810, the population had grown almost sixfold, to 610, and by 1820, the population of free black children under fourteen was 349, while the population as a whole was 970. See the Federal Censuses for 1790, 1810, and 1820. For the average age in 1790, which was exactly 15.9 years, see U.S. Bureau of the Census, *Historical Statistics of the United States, Colonial Times to 1957* (Washington D.C., 1960).

38. The latter is quoted in Margaret A. Burnham, "An Impossible Marriage: Slave Law and Family Law," *Law and Inequality Journal* 5 (1987): 187.

39. Tomlins, *Law, Labor, and Ideology in the Early American Republic* (Cambridge, 1993), 244–46.

40. Lawrence William Towner, "A Good Master Well Served: A Social History of Servitude, 1620–1750," Ph.D. dissertation, Northwestern University, 1955); David Galenson, *White Servitude in Colonial America: An Economic Analysis* (Cambridge, UK, 1981).

41. The question of changing attitudes toward children's labor is somewhat problematic. Republican political theory itself, while emphasizing child development and education, did not necessarily prohibit the labor of poor children, for whom development was not an issue, since they did not need to become citizens (to vote, be on juries, and so on), an issue relevant to Virginia,

which did not revise its franchise rules after the Revolution. John Locke had recommended that the children of the poor labor to support themselves in workhouses, primarily by spinning, from the age of three, while he had written a guide for the extensive and prolonged education of other children in *Some Thoughts concerning Education* (1693). For a brief discussion of Locke's position on the children of the poor, see Edmund Morgan, *American Slavery, American Freedom: The Ordeal of Colonial Virginia* (New York, 1975), 322. It is clear that Jefferson sought to go beyond this in including provisions for the remaining poor apprentices to attend public schools, and Locke himself may only have written the pamphlet on the labor of young poor children as a compromise political position while he was on the Board of Trade in the 1690s. Thus it did not necessarily represent his ideals, but rather a compromise.

Following Carl Degler's *At Odds: Women and the Family from the Revolution to the Present,* Viviana Zelizer has argued that changing attitudes toward childhood and the ability of children to labor went hand in hand with changing attitudes toward mothers and domesticity in the nineteenth century, two changes also coinciding in this study. Zelizer, *Pricing the Priceless Child: The Changing Social Value of Children* (New York, 1985), esp. 9. I see the idealization of childhood by romantics, including Rousseau (but not John Locke, who distinguished childhood from adulthood but did not idealize it) as key to this transition.

Certainly, however, this change, while it may have begun, was not universally accepted, and would come later in the nineteenth century. Alexander Hamilton encouraged the use of very young children in factories, for example. Commenting on the success of the English economy and the fact that the new cotton mills enabled even very young children to be more productive, he recommended that the United follow England's example. "It is worthy of particular remark, that, in general, women and children are rendered more useful, and the latter more early useful, by manufacturing establishments, than they would otherwise be. Of the number of persons employed in the cotton manufactories of Great Britain, it is computed that four-sevenths, nearly, are women and children; of whom the greatest proportion are children, and many of them of a tender age." See Grace Abbott, *The Child and the State* (Chicago, 1938), 1:276–77, citing Hamilton's address to the House of Representatives while Secretary of the Treasury, dated December 5, 1792.

42. Holly Brewer, *By Birth or Consent: Children, Law, and the Anglo-American Revolution in Authority* (Chapel Hill, 2005).

43. Michael Katz has posited a "merchant-capitalist" phase to explain why public schooling began to increase before the advent of industrialization. Katz, *Reconstructing American Education* (Cambridge, MA, 1987), 13.

44. Robert P. Sutton, *Revolution to Secession: Constitution Making in the Old Dominion* (Charlottesville, 1989).

45. For a fascinating discussion of the relation between these nineteenth-century programs and the distinct nature of modern American welfare policy, see Theda Skocpol, *Protecting Soldiers and Mothers: The Political Origins of Social Policy in the United States* (Cambridge, MA, 1992).

46. Lasch, *Haven in a Heartless World: The Family Besieged* (New York, 1977), xiv; see also page 168, where he argues that "From the moment the conception of the family as refuge made its historical appearance [in the early nineteenth century], the same forces that gave rise to the new privacy began to erode it.... This so-called privatization of experience went hand in hand with an unprecedented assault on privacy."

47. Nancy F. Cott, *The Bonds of Womanhood: "Women's Sphere" in New England, 1780–1835* (New Haven, 1977); Linda K. Kerber, *Women of the Republic: Intellect and Ideology in Revolutionary America* (Chapel Hill, NC, 1980); Michael Grossberg, *Governing the Hearth: Law and the Family in Nineteenth-Century America* (Chapel Hill, NC, 1985); and Ruth H. Bloch, "American Feminine Ideals in Transition: The Rise of the Moral Mother, 1785–1815," *Feminist Studies* 4 (1978): 101–206.

48. Bill 60, Jefferson, *Papers,* 2:487. Also bill 32, "A bill for the support of the Poor," 2:420 and bill 51, "A bill concerning slaves," where it was directed that mulatto children should be bound out just as were poor orphans, 2:471 and bill 17, "A bill concerning seamen," which allowed poor boys over ten to be bound apprentices to the masters of ships, 2:383.

49. Fraser finds that many children were supported directly and not apprenticed until ten or eleven in Charleston. Fraser, "City Elite." I find almost no children beyond infants supported

directly before the pensions for the survivors of Revolutionary War veterans. The "Vestry book of Frederick Parish" contains a survey of the people in the poor house in the 1810s. It contained no children over six, and only two between three and six, one of them with a "ruptured [illegible]," p. 302–3.

Conclusion. Reflections on the Demand and Supply of Child Labor in Early America

1. Edmund S. Morgan, *The Puritan Family: Religion and Domestic Relations in Seventeenth-Century New England* (1944; repr. New York: Harper and Row, 1966), 77.

2. Ann Kussmaul, *Servants in Husbandry in Early Modern England* (Cambridge, UK: Cambridge University Press, 1981); and Hugh Cunningham, "The Employment and Unemployment of Children in England, c. 1680–1851," *Past and Present* 126 (1990): 126.

3. Besides the essays in this volume, see also Colin Heywood, *A History of Childhood: Children and Childhood in the West from Medieval to Modern Times* (Malden, MA: Blackwell, 2001); and W. J. Rorabaugh, *The Craft Apprentice: From Franklin to the Machine Age in America* (New York: Oxford University Press, 1986).

4. See chapters 5, 10, and 11 in this volume.

5. Aaron Fogelman, "From Slaves, Convicts, and Servants to Free Passengers: The Transformation of Immigration in the Era of the American Revolution," *Journal of American History* 85 (1998): 43–76; David W. Galenson, "The Rise and Fall of Indentured Servitude in the Americas: An Economic Analysis," *Journal of Economic History* 44 (1984): 1–26; and Farley Grubb, "The Disappearance of Organized Markets for European Immigrant Servants in the United States: Five Popular Explanations Reexamined," *Social Science History* 18 (1994): 1–30; see also Christopher Tomlins, "Reconsidering Indentured Servitude: European Migration and the Early American Labor Force, 1600–1775," *Labor History* 42 (2001): 5–43. On the decline of craft apprenticeship in the urban north, see Rorabaugh, *The Craft Apprentice;* on the decline of indenturing poor children in the countryside, see the chapters 3, 4, 5, and 10 in this volume.

6. Hugh Cunningham, *The Children of the Poor: Representations of Childhood since the Seventeenth Century* (Cambridge, MA: Blackwell, 1991).

7. See chapters 6, 8, and 11 in this volume.

8. See chapter 3 in this volume, in which Herndon graphs the expansion in numbers of pauper apprenticeships in New England during this period; it is unclear, however, whether the sources of that growth lie in a growing population or an increase in poverty. Data on historical mortality rates are too spotty for generalizations about the impact of war or economic recession on poor relief rolls, but Robert Fogel's genealogical sample shows life expectancy at age ten for native-born white males to be rising, not falling, during the years 1750–1790 and declining thereafter, reaching its lowest point in 1850. Robert William Fogel, "Nutrition and the Decline in Mortality since 1700," in *Long-Term Factors in American Economic Growth,* ed. Stanley L. Engerman and Robert E. Gallman, *Studies in Income and Wealth* 51 (Chicago: National Bureau of Economic Research, 1986), 511.

9. See Gloria L. Main and Jackson T. Main, "The Red Queen in New England?" *William and Mary Quarterly* 56 (1999): 121–50.

10. Robert William Fogel and Stanley L. Engerman, *Time on the Cross: the Economics of American Negro Slavery* (Boston and Toronto: Little, Brown, 1974), 74–76.

11. Richard H. Shryock, *Medicine and Society in America* (New York, New York University Press, 1960), 88. I thank Susan Klepp for pointing this out.

12. Frontier farming required an adaptable workforce capable of multitasking, needing brawn and agility rather than technical expertise. Farms that specialized in grains utilized labor more seasonally and required fewer hours of work over the course of the year but tall, well-muscled boys were in especially high demand during harvest time. Dairying and raising animals for market were more labor-intensive year-round and made comparatively good use of female help. Based on the combined and averaged income of adult men and women in Lee Craig, "The Value of Household Labor in Antebellum Northern Agriculture," *Journal of Economic History* 51 (1991): 74, table 3.

13. Andrew Shankman, "'A New Thing on Earth': Alexander Hamilton, Pro-Manufacturing Republicans, and the Democratization of American Political Economy," *Journal of the Early Republic* 23 (Fall 2003): 323–52. Alexander Hamilton's "Report on the Subject of Manufactures" was based on extensive correspondence with a wide variety of writers and may be found at "A Century of Lawmaking for a New Nation: United States Congressional Documents and Debates, 1774–1875," in *American State Papers:* Finance, I: 123–145 on the American Memory website hosted by the Library of Congress. The discussion of the division of labor and the use of women and children may be found on page 126.

14. For an extended treatment of parent-child obligations in rural New England and the contributions of children toward family production, see my *Peoples of a Spacious Land: Families and Cultures in Colonial New England* (Cambridge, MA: Harvard University Press, 2001).

15. The best introduction to craft apprenticeship in the United States is Rorabaugh, *Craft Apprentice*.

16. One mother in seventeenth-century Maryland complained to a judge that her son's master was not teaching the boy the craft skills for which he had been indentured but was working him "in th ground" instead. The master explained to the judge that the boy simply wasn't strong enough yet to wield the tools of his trade. Gloria L. Main, *Tobacco Colony: Life in Early Maryland* (Princeton: Princeton University Press, 1982), 112.

17. See chapters 3, 4, and 10 in this volume.

18. See chapters 3 and 4 in this volume.

19. Rorabaugh, *Craft Apprentice*, 32–75, but see the criticisms of these views in chapter 4 of this volume.

20. Adrienne D. Hood finds that weaving was carried out in rural Chester County, Pennsylvania, by traditional craftsmen throughout the eighteenth and early nineteenth centuries. She argues that high quality standards were sustained by a steady stream of immigrant artisans from Britain and the Continent. Hood, *The Weaver's Craft: Cloth, Commerce, and the Industry in Early Pennsylvania* (Philadelphia: University of Pennsylvania Press, 2003).

21. Daniel Vickers, "Competency and Competition: Economic Culture in Early America," *William and Mary Quarterly* 47 (1990): 9–11; Alan Dawley, *Class and Community: The Industrial Revolution in Lynn* (Cambridge, MA: Harvard University Press, 1976); Paul G. Faler, *Mechanics and Manufacturers in the Early Industrial Revolution: Lynn, Massachusetts, 1780–1860* (Albany: State University of New York Press, 1981); and Mary Blewett, *Men, Women, and Work: Class, Gender, and Protest in the New England Shoe Industry, 1780–1910* (Urbana: University of Illinois Press, 1988).

22. J. Leander Bishop, *A History of American Manufactures from 1608 to 1860*, 3d rev. ed. (1868; New York: A. M. Kelly, 1966), 2:258.

23. Edith Abbott, "Harriet Martineau and the Employment of Women in 1836," *Journal of Political Economy* 14:10 (December 1906): 620; and Thomas Dublin, "Rural Putting-Out Work in Early Nineteenth-Century New England: Women and the Transition to Capitalism in the Countryside," *New England Quarterly* 64 (1991): 531–573. Thomas Dublin, "Women and Outwork in a Nineteenth-Century New England Town: Fitzwilliam, New Hampshire, 1830–1850," in *The Countryside in the Age of Capitalist Transformation: Essays in the Social History of Rural America*, ed. Stephen Hahn and Jonathan Prude (Chapel Hill: University of North Caroline Press, 1985) uses storekeeper records to illustrate the extent of the domestic manufacture of straw hats among farm women in rural New Hampshire.

24. Hood, *Weaver's Craft*, 85–139.

25. Jan De Vries, "The Industrial Revolution and the Industrious Revolution," *Journal of Economic History* 54 (1994): 249–70; Main and Main, "Red Queen." For gendered analyses of these processes in New England see my "Gender, Work, and Wages in Colonial New England," *William and Mary Quarterly* 51 (1994): 39–66; and, more forcibly, Laurel Thatcher Ulrich, "Wheels, Looms, and the Gender Division of Labor in Eighteenth-Century New England," *William and Mary Quarterly* 55 (1998): 3–38.

26. Hood argues that handsome returns to agriculture in the mid-Atlantic states, particularly in dairying, curtailed the employment of women and children in alternative occupations, including textile manufacture. Hood, *Weaver's Craft*, 85–106. Lee A. Craig, however, found that the

contribution to farm output by children under the age of thirteen and teenage girls in northern agriculture in 1860 was worth only about 17 percent of the wages of a hired man. Even in dairying in the Northeast, the contributions of children and teenage girls were relatively small compared to those by adult women and male teenagers. Lee A. Craig, *To Sow One Acre More: Childbearing and Farm Productivity in the Antebellum North* (Baltimore: Johns Hopkins University Press, 1993), 80–85; as Craig points out, his estimates "omit the value of domestic production or housework" 81. It is, therefore, likely that the work of young girls in the home released their mothers to work in the dairy so that, indirectly, they made higher farm income possible.

27. George S. White, *Memoir of Samuel Slater: The Father of American Manufactures* [1836] (New York: Augustus M. Kelley, 1967), 29–46, 83–112; Barbara M. Tucker, *Samuel Slater and the Origins of the American Textile Industry, 1790–1860* (Ithaca and London: Cornell University Press, 1984), 71–86, quotation 80.

28. Victor S. Clark, *History of Manufactures in the United States* (1929; repr. New York, Peter Smith, 1949), 1:559.

29. Joyce Appleby provides a succinct, highly readable, and up-to-date summary in *Inheriting the Revolution: The First Generation of Americans* (Cambridge, MA, London: Belknap Press of Harvard University Press, 2000) See also Francois Weil, "Capitalism and Industrialization in New England, 1815–1845," *Journal of American History* 84 (1998): 1334–54.

30. Carolyn Tuttle, *Hard at Work in Factories and Mines: The Economics of Child Labor During the British Industrial Revolution* (Boulder, CO: Westview Press, 1999), 7.

31. [Louis McLane, Secretary of the Treasury], *Documents Relative to the Manufactures in the United States* [1833] (New York: Augustus M. Kelley, 1969), 1:340–41.

32. For the city of Baltimore, see chapter 4 of this volume.

33. George Rogers Taylor, *The Transportation Revolution, 1815–1860*, vol. 4, *The Economic History of the United States* (New York: Holt, Rinehart and Winston, 1951), 78; and Theodore Steinberg, *Nature Incorporated: Industrialization and the Waters of New England* (Cambridge, UK, and New York: Cambridge University Press, 1991).

34. Thomas Dublin, *Women at Work: The Transformation of Work and Community in Lowell, Massachusetts, 1826–1860* (New York: Columbia University Press, 1979); and Abbott, "Harriet Martineau," 614–26.

35. Claudia Goldin and Kenneth Sokoloff, "Women, Children, and Industrialization in the Early Republic: Evidence from the Manufacturing Censuses," *Journal of Economic History* 42 (1982): 741–74.

36. Henry Carey, *An Essay on the Rate of Wages* (Philadelphia, 1836), 69–70, 95.

37. *Documents Relative to the Manufactures in the United States*, vol. 1, covers the New England states, and it is this volume that I have used, but Anthony Wallace's Chester Creek, Pennsylvania mills were likewise small. Wallace, *Rockdale: The Growth of an American Village in the Early Industrial Revolution* (New York: Knopf, 1978).

38. Abbott, "Harriet Martineau," 614–626. Lucy Larcom worked as a doffer at the age of eleven in the Lawrence Mill. Larcom, *A New England Girlhood: Outlined from Memory* (Boston: Houghton Mifflin, 1889).

39. Labor statistics in Great Britain are not strictly comparable due to different boundaries of age categories. The percentage of males under the age of nineteen working in cotton manufacturing there fell from 21 percent in 1835 to 17 percent in 1845 but the drop in the proportion of females in the same age group was similar: 28 percent to 23 percent. There was little change in their proportions in British wool manufactures. Tuttle, *Hard at Work*, 95.

40. As in previously cited works on the mid-Atlantic states, Philip Scranton contrasts the size, organization, and composition of the labor force of textile firms in Philadelphia with those at Lowell and Lawrence in *Proprietary Capitalism: the Textile Manufacture at Philadelphia, 1800–1885* (Cambridge, UK, and New York: Cambridge University Press, 1983). Since most textile manufacturers in New England were also small and unincorporated, Scranton missed an opportunity to make more substantive comparisons between the two regions.

41. Hugh Cunningham, *Children and Childhood in Western Society since 1500* (London and New York: Longman, 1995), 138.

42. Maris Vinovskis, *Fertility in Massachusetts from the Revolution to the Civil War* (New York: Academic Press, 1981).

43. J. David Hacker works through these factors efficiently and systematically in "Rethinking the 'Early' Decline of Fertility in the United States: New Evidence from the Integrated Public Use Microdata Series," *Demography* 40 (November 2003): 605–20.

44. Gloria L. Main, "Rocking the Cradle: Marital Fertility in Early New England," *Journal of Interdisciplinary History* 37 (Summer 2006): 35–58.

Bibliography

"An Act for Relief of the Poor" [ca. 1741] in John D. Cushing, ed., *The Earliest Printed Laws of Delaware, 1704–1741* (Wilmington, DE: Michael D. Glazier, 1978), 221.

Bailyn, Bernard, *Education in the Forming of American Society: Needs and Opportunities for Study* (Chapel Hill: University of North Carolina Press, 1960).

Blackstone, William, *Commentaries on the Laws of England*, 4 vols. (Oxford: Clarendon Press, 1765–69).

The Book of the General Lawes and Libertyes Concerning the Inhabitants of the Massachusets [1642] (Cambridge, 1648).

Bynum Victoria E., *Unruly Women: The Politics of Social and Sexual Control in the Old South* (Chapel Hill: University of North Carolina Press, 1992).

Carr, Lois Green, "The Development of Maryland's Orphans' Court, 1654–1715," in *Law, Society, and Politics in Early Maryland*, ed. Aubrey C. Land, Lois Green Carr, and Edward C. Papenfuse (Baltimore: Johns Hopkins University Press, 1977), 41–62.

Cohen, Patricia Cline, *A Calculating People: The Spread of Numeracy in Early America* (Chicago: University of Chicago Press, 1982), esp. ch. 2.

Daniels, Christine M., "Alternative Workers in a Slave Economy: Kent County, Maryland, 1675–1810," (Ph.D. dissertation, Johns Hopkins University, 1990).

———, "From Charity to Labor: Orphan Apprenticeship in Maryland, 1675–1835," paper presented at the Fifth Annual Conference of Omohundro Institute for Early American History and Culture, Austin, Texas, June 11–13, 1999.

Demos, John, *A Little Commonwealth: Family Life in Plymouth Colony* (New York: Oxford University Press, 1970).

Farber, Bernard, *Guardians of Virtue: Salem Families in 1800* (New York: Basic Books, 1972).

Fass, Paula S., and Mary Ann Mason, *Childhood in America* (New York: New York University Press, 2000).

Fischer, Kirsten, *Suspect Relations: Sex, Race, and Resistance in Colonial North Carolina* (Ithaca: Cornell University Press, 2002).

Galenson, David W., *White Servitude in Colonial America: An Economic Analysis* (New York: Cambridge University Press, 1981).

Graff, Harvey, *The Legacies of Literacy: Continuities and Contradictions in Western Culture and Society* (Bloomington: Indiana University Press, 1987).

Greven, Philip J. and James Martens, eds., *Children in Colonial America* (New York: New York University Press, 2007).

Grubb, Farley, "The Auction of Redemptioner Servants, Philadelphia, 1771–1804: An Economic Analysis," *Journal of Economic History* 48 (1988): 583–603.

———, "The End of European Immigrant Servitude in the United States: An Economic Analysis of Market Collapse, 1772–1835," *Journal of Economic History* 54 (1994): 794–824.

Hall, David D., *Worlds of Wonder, Days of Judgment: Popular Religious Belief in Early New England* (New York: Knopf, 1989).

Hamilton Gillian, "The Market for Montreal Apprentices: Contract Length and Information," *Explorations in Economic History* 33 (1996): 496–523.

Hindle, Steve, "'Waste' Children?: Pauper Apprenticeship under the Elizabethan Poor Laws, c.1598–1697," in *Women, Work and Wages in England, c.1600–1850*, ed: Penny Lane, Neil Raven, and Keith Snell (Woodbridge, U.K.: Boydell and Brewer, 2004): 15–46.

Illick, Joseph E., *American Childhoods* (University of Pennsylvania Press, 2002).

Jabour, Anya, ed., *Major Problems in the History of American Families and Children: Documents and Essays* (Boston: Houghton Mifflin, 2005).

Kaestle, Carl E., *Pillars of the Republic: Common Schools and American Society, 1780–1860* (New York: Hill and Wang, 1983).

Kent, James, *Commentaries on American Law,* 4 vols. (New York: O. Halsted, 1832).

Knight, Edgar, *Public Education in the South* (Boston: Ginn and Company, 1922).

Lasser, Carol, "A 'Pleasingly Oppressive' Burden: The Transformation of Domestic Service and Female Charity in Salem, 1800–1840," *Essex Institute Historical Collections* 116 (1980): 156–75.

Levy, Barry, "Girls and Boys: Poor Children and the Labor Market in Colonial Massachusetts," *Pennsylvania History* 64 (Summer 1997), 287–307.

Main, Gloria L., "An Inquiry into When and Why Women Learned to Write in Colonial New England," *Journal of Social History* 24 (1991): 579–89.

McCusker, John J., and Russell R. Menard, *The Economy of British America, 1607–1789: Needs and Opportunities for Study* (Chapel Hill: University of North Carolina Press, 1985).

Millar, W. Graham, "The Poor Apprentices of Boston: Indentures of Poor Children Bound Out by the Overseers of the Poor of Boston, 1734–1776" (M.A. Thesis, College of William and Mary, 1958).

Monaghan, E. Jennifer, *Learning to Read and Write in Colonial America* (Amherst: University of Massachusetts Press, 2005).

———, "Literacy Instruction and Gender in Colonial New England," *American Quarterly* 40:1 (1988): 18–41.

Morris, Richard B., *Government and Labor in Early America* (New York: Columbia University Press, 1946).

Murray, John E., "Generation(s) of Human Capital: Literacy in American Families, 1830–1875," *Journal of Interdisciplinary History* 27:3 (Winter 1996): 413–35.

———, "Family, Literacy, and Skill Training in the Antebellum South: Historical-Longitudinal Evidence from Charleston," *Journal of Economic History* 64:3 (September 2004): 773–90.

Murray, John E., and Ruth Wallis Herndon, "Markets for Children in Early America: A Political Economy of Pauper Apprenticeship," *Journal of Economic History* 62 (2002): 356–82.

Pagan, John Ruston, *Anne Orthwood's Bastard: Sex and Law in Early Virginia* (Oxford: Oxford University Press, 2003).

Patchen, Mary, "Apprenticeship on the Frontier: Indentured Children in Antebellum Ohio" (M.A. Thesis, The University of Toledo, 2003).

Perlmann, Joel, Silvana R. Siddali, and Keith Whitescarver, "Literacy, Schooling, and Teaching among New England Women, 1730–1820," *History of Education Quarterly* 37:2 (1997): 117–39.

Reeve, Tapping, *The Law of Baron and Femme; of Parent and Child; of Guardian and Ward; of Master and Servant; and of the Powers of Courts of Chancery* (New Haven: Oliver Steele, 1816).

Rorabaugh, W. J., *The Craft Apprentice: From Franklin to the Machine Age in America* (New York: Oxford University Press, 1986).

Salinger, Sharon V., *"To Serve Well and Faithfully": Labor and Indentured Servants in Pennsylvania, 1682–1800* (New York: Cambridge University Press, 1987).

Shammas, Carole, *A History of Household Government in America* (Charlottesville: University of Virginia Press, 2002).

Soltow, Lee and Edward Stevens, *The Rise of Literacy and the Common School in the United States: A Socioeconomic Analysis to 1870* (Chicago: University of Chicago Press, 1981).

Steinfeld, Robert J., *The Invention of Free Labor: The Employment Relation in English and American Law and Culture, 1350–1870* (Chapel Hill: University of North Carolina Press, 1991).

Tomlins, Christopher, "Early British America, 1585–1830: Freedom Bound," in *Masters, Servants, and Magistrates in Britain and the Empire, 1562–1955,* ed. Douglas Hay and Paul Craven (Chapel Hill: University of North Carolina Press, 2004), 117–52.

Towner, Lawrence William, "A Good Master Well Served: A Social History of Servitude in Massachusetts, 1620–1750," (Ph.D. dissertation, Northwestern University, 1955), reprinted as *A Good Master Well Served: Masters and Servants in Colonial Massachusetts, 1620–1750* (New York: Garland Press, 1998).

———, "The Indentures of Boston's Poor Apprentices, 1734–1805," *Past Imperfect: Essays on History, Libraries, and the Humanities,* ed. Robert W. Karrow and Alfred F. Young (Chicago: University of Chicago Press, 1993), 36–55.

Wall, Helena M., *Fierce Communion: Family and Community in Early America* (Cambridge: Harvard University Press, 1990).

Walsh, Lorena S., "Child Custody in the Early Colonial Chesapeake: A Case Study," unpublished paper, 1981.

Wilson, Lisa, *Ye Heart of a Man: The Domestic Life of Men in Colonial New England* (New Haven: Yale University Press, 1999).

Zipf, Karin L., *Labor of Innocents: Forced Apprenticeship in North Carolina, 1715–1919* (Baton Rouge: Louisiana State University Press, 2005).

Contributors

MONIQUE BOURQUE is Director of Student Academic Grants and Awards at Willamette University.

HOLLY BREWER is Associate Professor of History at North Carolina State University.

GILLIAN HAMILTON is Associate Professor of Economics at the University of Toronto.

RUTH WALLIS HERNDON is Associate Professor of History at Bowling Green State University.

STEVE HINDLE is Professor of History at the University of Warwick.

PAUL LACHANCE is Professor of History at the University of Ottawa.

TIMOTHY J. LOCKLEY is Associate Professor of Comparative American Studies at the University of Warwick.

GLORIA L. MAIN is Professor Emerita of History at the University of Colorado, Boulder.

JOHN E. MURRAY is Professor of Economics at the University of Toledo.

JEAN B. RUSSO is Historian at the Historic Annapolis Foundation.

JEAN ELLIOTT RUSSO is an Independent Scholar.

ADRIANA E. VAN ZWIETEN is Research Assistant for the Biographical Dictionary of Pennsylvania Legislators.

T. STEPHEN WHITMAN is Associate Professor of History at Mount St. Mary's University.

Index

adoption, 18, 104, 166, 187, 245n13
African-Americans, 7, 15–18, 34, 40, 43, 48–50, 52–54, 56–58, 77, 79–80, 82–83, 103, 106, 108, 118, 120–21, 126–32, 134, 147, 153, 163, 187, 164, 185, 186, 189, 191, 193–95, 197, 200
Africans, 20, 37, 50, 93, 153
almshouses, 49, 61, 71–83. *See also* poorhouses
American Revolution, 41, 43–45, 184–86, 191, 193–97, 205, 212

Baltimore, 5, 9, 14, 53–64, 67, 69–70, 83, 126, 135, 206, 208
bastardy, bastards. *See* children, bastard children
begging, 25
benevolence. *See* charity
bonuses. *See* premiums
Boston, 2, 5, 17, 39–51, 56, 81, 103, 135.
Boston Almshouse, 15, 49
boys, 8, 13, 14, 16, 28, 30, 48, 59, 61–68, 80–81, 86, 92, 113, 114, 116, 120, 135, 137–44, 146–47, 158–59, 161–64, 166–82, 186, 189, 192–94, 200, 203–6, 208–10
Burn, Richard, 22

Canada, 9, 167, 169, 176
charity, 6, 8, 13, 20, 23–24, 26, 28, 32, 39, 61, 65, 72, 104, 110, 118, 138, 147, 200, 201

Charleston, South Carolina, 5, 9, 10, 14, 26, 81, 102–18, 126, 136, 139
Charleston Orphan House, 9, 15, 102–18, 122, 134, 141
Chester County, Pennsylvania, 71–83
Chester County Almshouse, 15, 71–83
children
 abandoned or deserted children, 1, 3, 7, 9–10, 14, 18, 56, 61, 74, 76, 109–11, 167
 abused or neglected children, 1, 3, 9, 11, 13–14, 18, 41, 77–79, 95, 100, 109–10, 112, 141, 155, 187
 bastard children, 1, 3, 9, 10, 56, 77, 96, 151–65, 167, 171, 183, 186–91, 194, 197
 disabled children, 31, 79, 112, 157
 maintenance of children, 1, 12, 16, 22, 51, 52–56, 59, 62–63, 65–67, 69, 80, 87, 92, 95, 116, 124, 156–58, 170, 174, 176, 180, 182, 186, 188, 190, 191, 200, 202–3, 205, 207–8
 orphaned children, 1, 3, 7, 9, 14, 18, 27–28, 31, 52–70, 90, 91, 94, 100, 102–18, 135–37, 142–43, 145–48, 151–65, 166–82, 186, 187, 190, 192, 197, 201, 203
 poor children, 1, 3–4, 10, 18, 27, 31–32, 56, 71–83, 93, 102–5, 107–9, 112–13, 118, 122, 133–48, 157, 164–65, 183–92, 196, 199, 201, 203, 204, 206
Children's Friend Society, 9, 168–69, 173, 176, 181

civil authorities, 1–4, 6–10, 12, 14, 17, 19, 22, 23–26, 28–30, 34–35, 39–41, 44–47, 50–51, 52, 58–59, 61, 64, 71–74, 77–78, 90, 95, 97–100, 104–5, 108–15, 138, 151–65, 187. *See also* overseers of the poor
civil law, 89, 95, 122, 166, 182
common law, 24, 104, 122, 201–2
community leadership. *See* civil authority
Connecticut, 5, 15, 39–51
Countryman's Lamentation, 3–4, 6, 8–13, 27
craft apprenticeship, 2, 5, 8, 20, 37, 54–55, 126, 168, 170, 171, 181, 201, 204, 205
crafts and trades
  apothecary, 114
  blacksmithing, 63, 64, 67, 116, 139, 140, 159–60, 170, 174–75, 181, 193
  brewing, 32, 89, 170
  bricklaying, 140, 144–45, 159–60, 170
  brickmaking, 54, 170
  bridle and bit making, 55
  carpentry, 54, 63, 64, 67, 91, 116, 139–40, 159–60, 170, 174
  cigarmaking, 54
  coachmaking, 54, 63, 170
  cordwaining, 31
  cotton textiles, 31, 57
  hatting, 54, 59, 160, 170, 175
  horstler, 78
  ironworking, 53, 54, 116, 144
  joining, 154, 160, 170
  mantuamaking, 58, 141, 192
  millinery, 58, 144
  millwright, 54, 91, 160, 170
  nailmaking, 54
  pianoforte making, 55
  ropemaker, 53, 54
  painting, 54, 82, 113, 143, 160, 174
  printing, 50, 140, 143, 170, 174, 175
  saddler, 140, 170, 175
  sailmaking, 53
  shipbuilding, 53, 54, 159, 160
  shoemaking, 31, 51, 54, 55, 59, 63, 64, 66, 67, 91, 96, 155, 159, 160, 164, 167, 170, 174, 175, 204, 206
  silversmithing, 63, 69, 170
  spinning, 30, 47, 48, 57, 65, 91, 142, 158, 206, 207
  sugar refining, 55
  tailoring, 55, 58, 64, 67, 78, 91, 110, 139, 159, 160, 170, 174, 204
  tanning, 32, 155, 160, 164, 170, 174–75, 193
  umbrella making, 58
  watchmaking, 69
  weaving, 32, 48, 57, 69, 155, 159, 160, 206–8

Delaware, 23, 73, 149
Dutch communities in North America, 2, 87–101, 199

England, 2, 4, 5, 19–36
  English communities in North America, 2, 20
  English laws, 1, 19, 34, 104, 186
  English precedent for pauper apprenticeship, 4, 19–20, 23, 52, 116, 186

families, 1–2, 3–4, 6–7, 10–11, 14, 18, 46–47, 74–76, 96, 102–18, 128, 134, 141, 153, 166–68, 171, 177, 180, 181, 184, 185, 187–88, 190–94, 196–97, 200–205, 207, 211
farming and husbandry, 4, 8, 31–32, 50, 53, 57, 63–66, 72, 78, 81–82, 90, 92, 96–97, 137, 141, 145, 163, 170–71, 199, 202–5, 208
fathers, 4, 7, 9, 10, 14, 64, 69, 82, 89, 97, 99, 104–6, 113, 115, 120, 123, 128, 129, 132, 136, 152–53, 163, 168, 183, 184, 186, 188–92, 202, 204. *See also* parents
foster families, 18, 123, 153, 156, 167, 187, 196, 201
France, 2, 120, 166, 199
French communities in North America, 2, 62, 119–32, 166–82
Franklin, Benjamin, 50, 66

Georgia, 5, 22, 25, 106, 132–48
girls, 8, 12, 13–14, 16, 18, 30, 47–48, 57–58, 83, 91–93, 113, 120, 135, 136, 138–42, 144–45, 155, 158, 161–64, 185, 189, 192–95, 200, 203, 206–9
Greenleaf, Joseph, 22
guardians, 7, 9, 11, 73, 88, 90, 91, 93–97, 99, 100, 104, 105, 107, 110–11, 113, 129, 137, 154, 156, 173–74, 192

Hakluyt, Richard, 22
housewifery and female domestic labor, 4, 8, 12, 16, 31–32, 48, 50, 58, 64, 81, 91–92, 107, 119, 139, 141, 144, 158, 163

illegitimate children. *See* children, bastards
immigrant indentured servitude, 2, 6, 37, 122, 201
immigration and immigrants, 20, 41, 52, 88, 103, 105, 126–31, 134, 136, 145, 161, 169, 181–82, 199, 201, 210. *See also* Children's Friend Society
indentures, 1, 5
  behavioral and vice clauses, 1, 33, 217n49
  cancellation or reassignment, 14, 43, 51, 68, 69, 75–77, 91, 116, 155, 187–89, 245n14

INDEX

consent of children or parents, 56, 73, 82, 113, 116, 117, 124, 141, 183, 188, 200
documents, 6, 13–14, 17, 19–20, 25, 29, 45, 47, 71–73, 76, 78–81, 90, 105, 119, 122–23, 137, 140, 141, 166–67, 173, 193, 200
    freedom dues clauses, 1, 13, 16, 26, 33, 48–50, 59–60, 62–63, 65, 81, 137, 151, 153, 157–58, 162–63, 175–78, 188
    literacy clauses, 1, 13, 16, 19–20, 32, 48, 60–61, 64, 81, 119–20, 128, 161, 176, 193, 200
    signing or marking, 30, 46, 76, 90–91, 115, 117, 119–32, 137, 140, 166, 168–73, 175, 178
    skill training clauses, 1, 13, 16, 19, 20, 48, 65, 81, 157–59, 161, 164
    See also crafts and trades
Industrial Revolution, 31, 43, 57–58, 102, 184, 195–96, 207–8, 210–11

Jefferson, Thomas, 186, 190, 192, 197, 207
"Jersey Man." *See Countryman's Lamentation*

literacy and literacy education, 1, 3–4, 13, 16, 32–33, 44, 45–46, 50, 61–62, 81, 93, 119–32, 139, 162, 164–71, 168–73, 204. *See also* indentures, literacy clauses; indentures, signing or marking
Locke, John, 186, 195n41
London, 29, 174, 177

magistrates. *See* civil authorities
marriage and remarriage, 4, 13, 17, 34, 51, 90, 92, 115–16, 130, 137, 144–45, 192, 194, 202, 211
Maryland, 5, 9, 10, 15, 16, 17, 34, 41, 50, 52–70, 73, 81, 88, 151–65, 201, 210
Massachusetts, 13, 23, 39–51, 187, 206, 208–9
masters, 1, 2, 5, 7, 8, 11–13, 17, 27, 29, 33, 34, 37–38, 46–47, 71–72, 74, 76–77, 79–80, 87–101, 104, 113–18, 120–26, 140, 152, 155–59, 162–64, 168, 170, 171, 173–82, 183–84, 187–89, 193, 200–206
mistresses, 75, 77, 79, 87, 97, 99, 114, 141, 142
Montreal, 5, 9, 122, 132, 166–82
mortality rates, 3, 9, 52, 88, 116, 145, 154, 199, 210–11
mothers, 4, 9, 10, 11, 14, 32, 43, 75, 87, 94, 98, 102–18, 120, 128–32, 136, 137, 142–45, 152–55, 166–67, 184, 186, 188, 190–94, 197, 201. *See also* parents

Napoleonic wars, 54, 199, 208, 210
Native Americans, 20, 34, 37, 50, 99, 210
Netherlands, 2, 15, 87, 93, 98, 100
New England, 5, 26, 33, 39–51, 83, 152, 199, 203, 206–11

New Hampshire, 23
New Haven, Connecticut, 40, 47
New Jersey, 23, 99
New London, Connecticut, 40, 43, 47, 50
New Netherland, 5, 15, 16, 87–101
New Orleans, 5, 18, 119–32, 134, 139
North Carolina, 24
notaries, 88, 122–23, 166, 167

Ohio, 9
orphanages, 1, 6, 18, 61, 91, 102–18, 134–36, 140, 167, 212
orphans. *See* children, orphaned
orphan trains, 18
overseers of the poor, 1, 6–7, 8, 25–26, 28–29, 71–72, 80, 83, 186–91, 193

Panic of 1819, 57, 68, 103, 106–7, 123
parents, 1–4, 7–11, 14, 17, 22, 23, 26–29, 30, 35, 54, 58, 59, 64, 66, 68–69, 73–76, 88–90, 93–96, 99–100, 110–13, 115–16, 119, 129–31, 137, 142, 147, 154, 164–65, 168, 170–76, 178–80, 184–86, 188–92, 194, 196–97, 199, 200, 203–4, 206, 211. *See also* mothers, fathers
parish apprenticeship (England), 19–38
Pennsylvania, 5, 23, 63, 71–83, 185
Philadelphia, 71, 72, 73, 78, 80, 103, 186, 210
poorhouses, 1, 72, 75, 82, 103–5, 108–9, 152, 197. *See also* almshouses
poor laws, 2, 6, 10, 20–25, 27–29, 34, 40–41, 44–45, 49, 73, 85, 104, 197
poor relief, 3, 6–7, 10, 19–20, 24, 26, 28, 33, 35, 72, 73, 82, 83, 104, 188, 189, 191, 194, 197, 212
poor taxes, 7, 19, 21, 23, 30, 35, 72, 79, 117, 151, 156, 201
poverty, 4, 6–7, 10, 19, 20–22, 24, 34, 41, 51, 53, 82, 105–7, 136, 144, 146–47, 186, 191, 194, 202, 203
Providence, Rhode Island, 40, 43, 47, 50
premiums, 13, 16, 26, 28, 31–32, 35, 204

religion, 10, 23, 33, 40, 61, 78, 79–80, 88, 93, 117, 118, 137, 138, 146, 167, 205
    Anglican/Episcopalian, 24–25, 135, 183, 185–88, 190–91
    Dutch Reformed, 88, 94, 96
    Jewish, 25, 103, 117
    Methodist, 53, 144
    Quaker, 25, 43, 53, 79
    Roman Catholic, 61, 103, 112, 117, 126, 135, 167, 170–71
Rhode Island, 9, 10, 15, 16, 17, 31, 34, 39–51, 81, 207, 209

runaways, 9, 29, 34, 66–69, 77–78, 95, 97, 114, 157, 177

Saint-Dominigue, 126, 127–30
Savannah, 5, 9, 17, 122, 133–48
schools and schooling, 4, 16, 32, 44, 60–62, 81, 83, 93–94, 98, 104, 115, 119–20, 122–25, 127–28, 130–32, 135, 137–39, 142–45, 147–48, 175–77, 195, 197, 204, 206–8. *See also* indentures, literacy clauses
seafaring, 10, 43, 48–49, 91, 106, 111, 202
servants, 5, 12, 14, 27, 45, 47, 50, 55, 57, 97, 107, 123, 141, 144, 163, 164, 171, 183, 195, 199, 200, 203
slavery and slaves, 2, 5, 15, 18, 20, 34, 37, 43, 53–55, 57, 58, 70, 94, 103, 118, 122–23, 125, 134, 143, 145–47, 153, 164, 185, 188, 193–95, 202, 206
South Carolina, 5, 17, 22, 23, 25, 33, 102–18, 143
stepfamilies, 70, 86, 106, 109–10, 113, 115–16, 153, 158

Thomas, Gabriel, 22
Thomas, Isaiah, 50
trustees of the poor. *See* overseers of the poor

Virginia, 5, 10, 14, 15, 16, 17, 18, 23, 24, 29, 50, 63, 93, 152, 167, 183–97

widows and widowers, 12, 14, 46, 77, 98, 106, 108, 109, 111, 115–17, 135, 153, 155, 201, 202

www.ingramcontent.com/pod-product-compliance
Lightning Source LLC
Chambersburg PA
CBHW050122020526
44112CB00035B/2249